MW01096607

THE LAST PEASANT WAR

The Last Peasant War

VIOLENCE AND REVOLUTION IN TWENTIETH-CENTURY EASTERN EUROPE

JAKUB S. BENEŠ

PRINCETON UNIVERSITY PRESS
PRINCETON & OXFORD

Published by Princeton University Press
41 William Street, Princeton, New Jersey 08540
99 Banbury Road, Oxford OX2 6JX

press.princeton.edu

ISBN 978-0-691-21253-1
ISBN (e-book) 978-0-691-26758-6

British Library Cataloging-in-Publication Data is available

Editorial: Ben Tate and Josh Drake
Production Editorial: Jenny Wolkowicki
Jacket design: Heather Hansen
Production: Danielle Amatucci
Publicity: Alyssa Sanford and Carmen Jimenez
Copyeditor: Maia Vaswani

Jacket image: Courtesy of the Museum of Independence in Warsaw

This book has been composed in Arno Pro

Printed in the United States of America

10 9 8 7 6 5 4 3 2 1

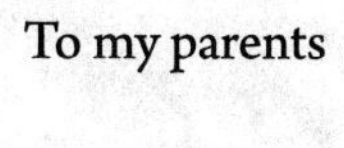

To my parents

CONTENTS

ILLUSTRATIONS

Figures

Maps

THE LAST PEASANT WAR

Introduction

"IN OPTING FOR WAR, we came to understand who we were. Only in armed conflict could we affirm ourselves and force the enemy to understand us and grant us recognition."[1] The words of dissident Yugoslav Communist Milovan Djilas about the Partisan struggle in his country during the Second World War could well describe the path taken by peasants in central and eastern Europe in the first half of the twentieth century. They opted for war most spectacularly toward the end of the First World War, when hundreds of thousands of peasant soldiers deserted from the armies of Austria-Hungary and Russia—both Tsarist and revolutionary, eventually forming their own "green" forces. From their forested and hilly redoubts, the green armies fought against vastly expanded states, which seemed to them intent on ruining their families' livelihoods and destroying the village communities from which they hailed. Rural deserters along with their confederates in countless villages from the Alps to the Urals contributed to the internal collapse of the Habsburg and Romanov Empires. In Russia, they fought the Bolsheviks to a stalemate that lasted almost a decade. In east central Europe, their actions provided a script for rural resistance through the next war.

The green forces were in fact shock troops in a much broader, multifront war waged by villagers to affirm themselves and to determine their own future. This book is about east central European peasants' decades-long campaign in its various forms, not all of them armed, but nearly all of them forgotten or pushed to the margins of historical consciousness. Yet Europe's last peasant war shaped the most calamitous era in the continent's modern history. It conditioned the outcome of the First World War, left its imprint on the strained geopolitics of the 1920s and 1930s, and influenced the course of the Second World War. It allowed peasants to understand who they were, inaugurating a golden age of agrarian political movements. It forced some of those who wished for the peasantry's disappearance to understand them, though this ultimately made it possible to neutralize the threat they posed.

The threat was real, for at the end of the First World War the actions of peasants across much of central and eastern Europe amounted to a genuine rural revolution. It was unrecognizable as such in the eyes of anxious and bemused urban observers, for whom such a revolution was a contradiction in terms. Indeed, in some places the peasant revolution of the years 1917–21 merged with simultaneous national and pacifist revolutions, rendering it difficult to distinguish in the welter of upheaval.[2] It was nevertheless distinct in its aim to recast village society, above all through the seizure and fair redistribution of large, usually noble-owned estates. In addition to breaking the power of the landed elite, peasant radicals sought to eliminate the influence of their perceived lackeys, many of whom resided in towns: officials, gendarmes, merchants, and moneylenders. Once liberated from oppressors and parasites, villagers would set about implementing democratic rule and laying the foundations of a cooperative economy. In numerous instances they did just that, establishing village republics. To the extent that peasant activists during and after the revolutionary period envisioned solutions for the state or nation as a whole—and they often did when they established their own authorities or joined political parties—they demanded decentralized government with considerable local autonomy. This was a direct challenge to the industrializing, warmongering states of the period. But the rebels did not only seek to escape from the state's expanding reach. Through military self-organization, grassroots experiments in self-government, and the parliamentary agrarianism that flourished in the 1920s, they aimed to remake states in their own image.[3] This level of ambition, and particularly the means used to realize it, marked an innovation in the long history of peasant revolts.

The revolutionaries themselves were heterogeneous, often lacking awareness of their shared purposes across boundaries of time and place. Villagers had little knowledge of events beyond their local area, let alone beyond the borders of the empire, nation-state, or ethnic-linguistic zone they inhabited. Agrarian politicians, many of whom espoused far-reaching visions of societal change, were more conscious of similar parties and movements abroad. Their wider horizons inspired them in the interwar years to build international agrarian organizations devoted to political and economic reform. But they too were constrained by the national parliamentary systems that they committed themselves to working within. Nor were various modes of action mutually intelligible—armed insurgents and elected parliamentarians dismissed each other, and still do. Nonetheless, in the first half of the twentieth century, a shared peasant program and outlook gave common direction to a strikingly diverse cast of characters in central and eastern Europe. They ranged from Polish populist tribunes to renegades from the Soviet Red Army to Slovak and Slovene enthusiasts for cooperatives to Croatian bandits. And the presence or legacy of peasant deserters ran like a slender red (or green) thread through the countries of the region.

A sense of what and whom they were against united the rural activists of the period at least as much what they were for.[4] They opposed cities as places that both exploited them and excluded them. Although a great many peasants regularly visited relatives in cities or worked seasonally in them, the First World War deepened long-standing urban-rural divides. Warring states introduced draconian new laws to secure food products in the countryside for urban consumers, especially for workers in wartime industry. At the same time, the Central Powers of Austria-Hungary and Germany failed to meet the urban population's needs, causing city dwellers to blame their privations on greedy hoarders in the countryside, whose fields they sometimes plundered. Villagers felt squeezed from two directions. Their perception of cultural and geographical distance from increasingly assertive industrial-urban centers became more acute, defining them as a social class.

As with other forms of identity, social class is perhaps best understood as something that "happens" in oppositional relationships, which themselves change in character and intensity over time, rather than as something that reliably "is."[5] The circumstances of the First World War caused a peasant class to come into sharper relief. Not that social-economic definitions of class are irrelevant. Alongside a sense of hostility toward, and distance from, urban centers, economic activity defines peasants: as small-scale agricultural producers who are engaged primarily in family-based subsistence farming on land they control, if not own outright, but who also sell as much possible on the market.[6] By 1914, European peasants found themselves surrounded by other peasants as never before. Industrialization had in many places compounded their social isolation by eliminating the occupational diversity that had characterized the premodern European countryside. Rural crafts and cottage industries were decimated by competition from cheap, machine-produced goods, rendering rural areas more homogeneously agricultural by the end of the nineteenth century.[7] Yet perceptions of difference likely gave more cohesion to the sundry peasant initiatives of the first half of the twentieth century, both within individual movements and between them. The idea of a peasant class premised on opposition to the world of cities was able to bridge substantial socioeconomic divides between various categories of villagers; for instance, between poor and wealthy peasants, between cultivators and pastoralists, between those who had acquired their own land generations ago and those who acquired it only recently, and even between landless laborers, village craftsmen, and peasant farmers. It also connected people engaged in very different forms of agriculture, depending on climate, soils, access to capital and technology, and culture. Ultimately, however, the socioeconomic and relational definitions of the peasant class were difficult to separate.[8] The experience of toil in fields, highland pastures, and forests made a sense of distance from, and opposition to, cities possible in the first place. Perceptions of exploitation of the countryside by cities imbued the facts of rural labor with meaning.

Contrary to popular wisdom and much scholarship on class struggles in history, it was not the landless poor who figured most prominently in the radical movements of the countryside. More significant were smallholding peasants who tilled their own fields but whose existence was becoming increasingly precarious. In the late 1960s, the anthropologist Eric Wolf identified such peasants as the key actors in the "peasant wars" that defined the twentieth century, since they were most vulnerable to the upheavals associated with the worldwide spread of market capitalism.[9] They had the most to lose as new market pressures led to the consolidation of small holdings into large commercial farms, to the increased indebtedness of penurious cultivators, and to the evaporation of older communal forms of solidarity and mutual aid. Crucially, though, they possessed just enough resources (land above all) to give them "tactical mobility" when they chose to rebel against the existing political and economic order.[10] Harboring fundamentally conservative instincts, smallholders made unlikely revolutionaries because they rose in defense of older understandings of community. Propertyless agricultural laborers, though hardly absent from rural insurrections, seldom have led them because of their greater dependence on landlords.

Wolf did not address Europe west of Russia in his landmark study. Nor did the experience of war itself play any appreciable role in his analysis of peasant revolutionism in Mexico, Russia, China, Vietnam, Algeria, and Cuba. The peasant war charted in the pages below erupted as a direct consequence of the strain of the Great War and featured village conscripts as its principal combatants. Its center was in east central Europe; more precisely, in the lands that made up the Habsburg Empire and its so-called "successor states": Czechoslovakia, Poland, and Yugoslavia foremost, as well as, to a lesser degree,

Hungary and Romania. These territories experienced a ferment of rural violence and activism throughout the "age of catastrophe."[11] Whereas peasant movements likely gripped the territories of the former Russian Empire more dramatically between 1917 and 1921, they were later broken by Stalin's campaign of forced collectivization in the late 1920s. In Bulgaria too, peasant power reached its vertiginous apex in the years 1919–23, but then disintegrated in the wake of a bloody coup. In the former Habsburg dominions, by contrast, agrarian activism and violent risings persisted beyond the end of the Second World War. And while large portions of post-1918 Poland and Yugoslavia included territories that lay outside the former Austro-Hungarian Empire, peasant politics were most developed within its erstwhile borders.

It was this part of the European continent that was also the most volatile. Both world wars started in east central Europe—the first with an assassination in Habsburg-ruled Bosnia-Herzegovina and the second with Hitler's invasion of Poland. The First World War did not end in the region until the early 1920s, following a period of chaotic, sometimes extreme violence that sowed the seeds of the next conflict.[12] Despite their achievements, the states that emerged after the dust had settled were riven by internal ethnic, religious, and class divisions and threatened from without by the territorial revisionism of their neighbors. The instability of the successor states heightened perceptions of their apparent malleability, especially in the completely new creations of Czechoslovakia and Yugoslavia but also in resurrected Poland. This belief would be brutally acted upon at the end of the 1930s by Hitler and Stalin.

Muscular peasant movements were both consequence and cause of the region's combustibility in the first half of the twentieth century. They emerged in part from frustration with the weaknesses of central and east European empires, later nation-states. At the same time, they further eroded the legitimacy of those states. Peasant violence in the wake of the First World War had especially serious ramifications. Efforts by new governments in multiethnic Czechoslovakia and Yugoslavia to discipline the unruly countryside of Slovakia and Croatia, respectively, produced centralizing impulses that fatally undermined both states. Peasant violence against Jews in reunited Poland played an important role in the genesis of minority treaties that the western victors imposed amid great resentment on the Habsburg successor states and other postimperial countries. The minority treaties compromised the faith of east central European governments in the nascent international order, further isolating them. But revolution in the countryside also flowed into political parties, which worked concertedly to put the new states of east central Europe on more stable footing. Energized by the apparent failings of governments during the Great War, interwar agrarianism—or "peasantism"—offered a bold vision of modernity rooted in village communities. They combined commitments to representative democracy with demands for land reform and blueprints for a cooperative society in which farmers would pool their resources to obtain credit, to cultivate their land with advanced technology, and to sell their products at fair prices.[13] This was not just an east central European phenomenon, even if it attained its greatest influence there; in the post–World War One era, agrarian parties arose across Europe and in North America.

The apparent failure of east central European agrarians to safeguard democracy and rural livelihoods during the Great Depression drove many peasants to embrace antidemocratic solutions, such as fascism or communism. Some welcomed the demise of the successor states in the fires of Nazi invasion and occupation. But many quickly found Hitler's New Order intolerable, leading them to join or support various resistance groups. Peasants' willingness to fight against occupiers and their collaborators proved decisive in Yugoslavia as well as, to a lesser degree, in Poland—two key battlefields of the Second World War. Communists were forced to make concessions to their peasant allies in the anti-Nazi resistance, particularly in the immediate aftermath of the war when they spearheaded sweeping land reform in east central Europe. Such tactical expediencies were discarded when Stalin's lieutenants had secured power in the countries that now lay behind the "Iron Curtain." In the final phase of the peasant war that this book reconstructs, villagers resisted the collectivization of agriculture, registering some notable successes, even if they could not halt the forced industrialization and urbanization campaigns that transformed eastern Europe from the 1950s onward.

Considering the monumental stakes of European peasant movements in the previous century, it is striking that they have been the subject of so little scholarship. Since the end of state socialism, pathbreaking histories have reinterpreted the cataclysmic years 1914–50 and their legacy, highlighting, for instance, the contest between ideologies of the European Enlightenment (liberalism and communism) and their opposite (fascism); the formative impact on Europe's trajectory of fascism and authoritarianism more broadly; and the rising global hegemony of the United States as a catalyst for the aggression of insurgent powers such as Nazi Germany.[14] Meanwhile, the significant part played by peasants in the epochal changes of the period has largely remained in the shadows. Peasants' demographic weight alone warrants attention to their ambitions; until the middle of the last century, half of Europe's overall population lived in rural areas, with a much greater proportion in the continent's eastern and southern reaches.[15]

The perennial problem of sources goes some way toward explaining this neglect: peasants have left little in the way of written records. Well into the modern era, most of them were still illiterate. Their actions and voices must be excavated from official records, whose authors were seldom interested in villagers' own views. The historian must often rely on conjecture, even for the history of modern Europe, where state institutions have produced reams of official records. A dearth of sources on the countryside has focused historians' attention even more on urban areas, where, especially in the modern era, intellectual life has flourished. The past of individual villages or mostly rural regions has by default become the preserve of nonhistorians—chroniclers, parish priests, and, more recently, local enthusiasts whose primary aim is to show that their places of origin are not as uninteresting as they may at first sight appear. While such research is often impressively meticulous, works of local history tend to reinforce impressions of a parochial countryside, even as global, comparative, and transnational historical approaches have flourished in the academy.

A more serious issue is the assumption—widespread in Europe since the middle of the nineteenth century among both scholars and the educated public—that history simply does not happen in the countryside. "World-history is town-history," lamented the German historian Oswald Spengler just after the First World War, expressing his pessimistic view that all civilizations reach their apex in large cities before their inevitable decline.[16] In the modern era, cities are seen as the sole drivers and sites of change. The rural world commonly figures in the historical imagination as a static realm "unchanged" or "untouched" by modernity; peasant lives are thought to have unfolded in the same way as they did for centuries. Such notions are hardwired into much Marxist and Western liberal thought, which tends to dismiss peasants as relics of the past. They also underpin ostensibly rural-friendly conservatism, which makes a virtue out of constancy. Conservatives and many nationalists cast a benevolent if paternalistic gaze at the countryside, descrying in it a deep reservoir of piety, deference, and national authenticity. That such prized attributes rarely conformed to expectations—for example, with the nineteenth-century efflorescence of unruly popular devotional practices or the persistence of indifference to national categories of identification—did little to unseat stereotypes.[17] In the much less urban Global South, suppositions about the unchanging character of the countryside have underwritten wholesale dismissal of non-Western history and justified European imperialism on the grounds that the great masses of African and Asian villagers somehow stood outside of historical time.[18]

While Marxists and conservatives tried to channel peasant energies into their own projects of proletarian revolution or nostalgic ruralism, liberals and Marxists both plotted the peasantry's eventual disappearance through means like free trade, industrialization, and urbanization. All of them viewed peasant political ambitions as confused, immature, parochial, and unmodern; cause either for alarm or celebration, depending on their outlook. Barrington Moore Jr., one of the last century's most influential political sociologists, challenged orthodox theories of development by proposing in 1966 that peasant revolutions from France to China had both inaugurated and accelerated modernization processes.[19] But he balked at the notion that peasants could do more than simply demolish premodern systems of rule: "The peasants have provided the dynamite to bring down the old building. To the subsequent work of reconstruction they have brought nothing; instead they have been . . . its first victims."[20] The notion of a peasant revolution yielding new blueprints for society was, and remains, an epistemological challenge; it is "unthinkable," just as the Caribbean slave revolution launched at the end of the eighteenth century had been.[21] For their part, villagers have embraced dominant ideologies in heterodox ways, assimilating them to their own agendas or else selectively appropriating parts of diverse, mutually opposed positions. Though far from passive, their existence on a political spectrum defined without their input has been nomadic.[22]

Twentieth-century European peasant mobilizations are among the biggest casualties of historians' implicit urban bias. In the era of world wars, peasant revolution was especially unthinkable, not only because it was not *of* the city but because it was openly or tacitly *against* the city. Even in their most moderate organizations like the Czech Agrarian Party (later the Republican Party of Farmers and Peasants), peasantists sang paeans to rural life, implying that urban society was somehow inferior. But in general, they were not implacably opposed to the existence of cities. In notable instances, rural activists sought alliances with some categories of urban dwellers. They directed their greatest hostility toward cities as seats of "high modernist" states that projected coercive, exploitative, and standardizing power onto a putatively backward and antimodern countryside.[23] In their eyes, cities had transformed into something more fearsome than merely the age-old abode of tax collectors and absentee landlords. Today, peasants have largely disappeared from Europe, as have the kind of states that prevailed a hundred years ago. Nonetheless, the early twenty-first century has witnessed a resurgence in antiurban movements, this time against metropolitan centers whose primary purpose, in the eyes of their detractors, appears to be safeguarding the flow of globalized capital. Seen in this light, the task of reconstructing Europe's last peasant war is imperative to understanding the continent's more recent history.

1

Peasant Europe Goes to War

FEW PERIODS OF UPHEAVAL have caused such profound soul-searching among artists and writers as the First World War. Looking back, the 1914–18 conflict was unique in combining cataclysmic destruction with a staggering sense of futility—and all this in an age of mass literacy and rapidly circulating information. A profusion of "war novels" wrestled with the apparent senselessness of the killing. Many lamented the self-immolation of nineteenth-century European civilization, what Austrian Jewish writer Stefan Zweig would later nostalgically dub "the world of yesterday." Others deemed it necessary to explode the self-satisfied complacency of pre-1914 life. Some even hailed the invigorating effect on European societies of industrial warfare—the "storm of steel," in Ernst Jünger's words. In the broad genre of First World War literature, there are numerous variations on the themes of an old world ending and a new world being born, but one variation endemic to east central Europe has been little remarked upon: that of mostly peasant peoples transformed by the violent crucible. For the protagonists of Croatian author Miroslav Krleža's *The Croatian God Mars* (1921–22) and Slovak writer Milo Urban's *The Living Whip* (1927), the war irreversibly discredited the authorities to whom villagers had shown obeisance for so many generations. These definitive works of war literature in their respective national canons depict the process of peasant awakening in the Habsburg army (Krleža) and the home front village (Urban).[1] Both Krleža and Urban regarded the crystallization of a rebellious peasant consciousness as one of the most important effects of the war. The inferno had produced a new rural collective subject, inured to violence and aware of its strength.

The central insight of these iconic east central European literary works flowed from the actual experience of the First World War in countless villages across the Habsburg monarchy, not just Croatian and Slovak ones. In 1914, this was a state that, despite rapid modernization in many aspects of life, remained the personal realm of the grandfatherly emperor-king Franz Joseph I. Soldiers of the imperial and royal armed forces, beholden to neither Austrian nor Hungarian parliament, swore an oath directly to him. The peasants who made up the majority of conscripts looked to Franz Joseph with particular affection; he was the embodiment of stability and tradition in the face of modernity's often hostile winds. Most peasant soldiers did not welcome the outbreak of the war, but they accepted that they had to fulfill their duty, not least to their long-suffering monarch, who, over the course of the preceding decades, had lost his brother, his son, his wife, and finally his nephew Franz Ferdinand to violent deaths. All of this changed within several years. Mass slaughter at the fronts, incompetent army leadership, and the introduction of draconian military-bureaucratic rule cast a dark shadow over the final years of Franz Joseph's reign; his successor Karl I, who ruled from 1916 to 1918, could not restore his family's credibility. Of the peasant infantrymen serving in 1916 on the Eastern Front in the Croatian Home Guard, part of Hungary's own territorial army, Krleža wrote, "Those are the royal Hungarian veterans who have seen through the imperial and royal cards and have realized that they are being cheated in this gentlemanly game of theft."[2] Worst of all, the government could not feed its people and set about extracting agricultural produce from the countryside with increasing brutality. The illusion of the peasantry's relative safety in the cocoon of dynastic loyalty and religious piety was shattered.

At the same time, villagers began to see that they were the ones upon whom the entire war effort depended. War in the trenches swiftly became a contest of endurance between the industrial capacities of the Entente and Central Powers, behind which lay the decisive factor of food supply. Agrarian output arguably decided the outcome, with Germany and Austria-Hungary starving behind the British sea blockade, while their western foes were flooded with grain shipments from the British overseas dominions and the United States.[3] But the costs, and responsibilities, borne by the countryside to sustain this conflict were immense, particularly in the Central Powers and the less advanced economies of Russia and the Ottoman Empire. Late in the war, the Slovak inhabitants of the fictional village of Ráztoky in *The Living Whip* "realized that they are the body, the basis of humanity: everything else aside from them was parasitism, an organization for exploiting their strength."[4] As this belief spread, some belligerent powers tried to ease the burden on the countryside, introducing new rewards and paying higher prices for agricultural products. Austria-Hungary and the Russian Empire did not tread this path, a decision that certainly played a role in their demise.

The experience of the years 1914–18 put the peasants of central and eastern Europe on a collision course with the massively expanded state apparatuses that also emerged in these years. Out of this clash came new and radicalized peasant efforts to regulate their own affairs. Yet the political implications of peasant campaigns were, as we will see in subsequent chapters, difficult to define, and could lead in wildly different directions. Krleža had entered the war as a convinced south Slav nationalist, resulting in his expulsion from the prestigious Ludovica officers' academy in Budapest. By the end of the war, he was a committed Marxist-Leninist, and remained a Communist for the rest of his life, even though he refused to join Josip Broz Tito's Partisan movement during the Second World War. The younger Milo Urban, by contrast, embraced the Catholic and national autonomist platform of the Slovak People's Party in interwar Czechoslovakia, eventually supporting its clerical-fascist wing. From 1940 to 1945, under the Slovak collaborationist regime of Father Jozef Tiso, he served as chief editor of *Gardista*, the principal organ of the paramilitary fascist Hlinka Guard. Decisive for both men's trajectories was the attempt to make sense of what had befallen the peasant nations of east central Europe after 1914. Peasants had always suffered, and they had often borne the brunt of war's depredations without necessarily blaming their governments. Some certainly remained loyal during the First World War, but many saw the ordeal as a betrayal without precedent.

For most villagers in Austria-Hungary, it began on the last July night of 1914. Officials dispatched by automobile from the principal district towns summoned local authorities for emergency meetings. Around midnight, car horns blared and drums sounded on village greens to announce general mobilization: all men up to thirty-eight years of age had to report to their units within twenty-four hours.[5] Although the possibility of war had been widely discussed since the assassination of the heir to the throne, Archduke Franz Ferdinand, in Sarajevo on June 28, mobilization still came as a shock. The rural population was fully occupied with the summer harvest and, as the Czech chronicler in the southern Moravian village of Hrušky noted, the announcement arrived "during the period when there is no time for reading newspapers."[6] In fact, Austria-Hungary's declaration of war on Serbia had been postponed until July 28 to allow for as much of the harvest as possible to be brought in. Peasant soldiers had been sent home on leave for fieldwork at the end of June and could not be called back so quickly. There was also the risk that recalling soldiers from leave would arouse the suspicions of rival countries, which then might begin mobilization themselves.

FIGURE 1.1 The death of a Croatian peasant soldier in an illustration by Ivo Režek for Miroslav Krleža's *The Croatian God Mars.* Varaždin City Museum

By delaying the declaration of hostilities, the dual monarchy may have fatally squandered the international sympathy that it enjoyed in the immediate wake of Franz Ferdinand's assassination.[7] By the time Franz Joseph issued his July 28 proclamation "To My Peoples," explaining that it was incumbent upon the ancient monarchy to defend its honor in the face of Serbian aggression, the Triple Entente of Britain, France, and Russia was convinced that Austria-Hungary and Germany hungered more for conquest than the maintenance of peace. Several days before, Serbia had narrowly rejected an intentionally unacceptable ultimatum crafted by hawks in the Habsburg foreign ministry; it demanded, among other things, that Serbia allow Austro-Hungarian authorities to lead the investigation into the murder of the archduke and his wife on Serbian territory, effectively forcing the Balkan kingdom to renounce its sovereignty. Indeed, those in the Habsburg government clamoring most loudly for war, above all the chief of the general staff, General Franz Conrad von Hötzendorf, believed that Austria-Hungary could restore its faltering great-power status only through a victorious show of arms, however long the odds of success might be.[8]

Already before June 28, 1914, Serbia was the obvious target of such scheming. Regarded as a dangerous rogue state for at least a decade, its involvement in the Sarajevo tragedy seemed beyond doubt, if murky. The "Black Hand" terrorist organization to which Gavrilo Princip and his fellow assassins were linked had ties to high-ranking officers in the Serbian army. Whether King Petar Karađorđević or members of the Serbian parliament had knowledge of the affair, let alone approved of such murderous provocation, remains open to debate, though many of them broadly supported national irredentist aims.[9] Specifically Bosnian dynamics, in which ethnic and social grievances were painfully fused, likely motivated the perpetrators at least as much as Great Serbian expansionism. As Princip explained to his jailors several months into the war, "I am the son of peasants and I know what is happening in the villages. That is why I wanted to take revenge, and I regret nothing."[10] Bosnia-Herzegovina had a unique position in the Habsburg monarchy: occupied in 1878 and then annexed in 1908, it belonged to neither Austria nor Hungary, instead administered directly by the joint Finance Ministry, one of the few shared governing institutions (along with the Foreign Ministry and the military) arising from the 1867 Compromise that created Austria-Hungary. To win the support of local elites, Habsburg rulers had left virtually intact an Ottoman social structure under which mostly Orthodox Christian peasants still labored as serfs on the estates of lordly Muslim *agas* and *begs*. Feudal social relations persisted in Bosnia-Herzegovina longer than anywhere else in Europe by at least two generations.

If Bosnian Serb villagers like Princip may have had comprehensible reasons for triggering a major European war, the vast majority of Austro-Hungarian peasants greeted the outbreak of hostilities with resignation, even despair. "Nothing was to be heard on all sides but weeping and lamentation," wrote Jan Słomka, the Polish village mayor of Dzików in western Galicia.[11] "Weeping and wailing" accompanied the departure of men from many villages in eastern and southern Moravia.[12] The possibility of injury or death no doubt worried relatives the most. Not far behind were concerns about what would happen to family farms after the physically strongest workers departed for an indefinite period. Although a good portion of the grain harvest was in, much remained in the fields. The rural population of Austria-Hungary was mostly smallholding peasants who tilled family-owned properties not exceeding ten hectares.[13] Unable to afford farmhands, such peasants relied heavily on family labor. Rural trepidation was a worldwide phenomenon as peasants composed a significant proportion of all the armies mobilized in 1914, except for Britain's, the only truly urban society at that time. They made up 30 percent of Germany's army, 43 percent of France's, and a staggering 75 percent of Russia's armed forces.[14]

These figures by and large reflected the peasant share of each belligerent power's population. For centuries, states had recruited heavily among the peasantry to wage wars. This was logical in view of the rural population's numerical predominance, but townsfolk also had enjoyed exemptions and privileges. What was new in the early twentieth century was the far-reaching militarization of European societies, extending to the peasantry as well. Militarization meant several things: the proliferation of paramilitary and patriotic organizations that assisted in expanding the armed forces and celebrating armed conflict; the development of ideologies that saw war as necessary for historical progress and prioritized preparedness for war over other policy areas; and the spread of military values, ideas, and practices throughout society.[15] According to this definition, the European countries that declared war on each other in late July and early August 1914 were all militarized. Austria-Hungary, Germany, Russia, and Italy (which entered the war in 1915 on the Entente side) also belonged to a category that historian Laurence Cole has dubbed "military monarchies," where the army, enjoying privileged status and removed from parliamentary oversight, functioned both as a force for maintaining internal order and as a central pillar of collective identity in a dynastic state.[16] The ability of the army to forge a common sense of identity

MAP 1. The Habsburg monarchy in 1914

MAP 2. The central regions of the Habsburg monarchy

and purpose among diverse recruits was particularly important in multiethnic, multilingual Austria-Hungary.

The biggest step toward societal militarization in the dual monarchy was taken in 1868 with the introduction of universal male military service. Austria's humiliating 1866 defeat by Prussia demonstrated that genuine reform could not wait any longer. Alongside the reorganization of command structures under a real general staff, conscription underwent fundamental change. Previously, regions or districts had supplied a quota of new recruits, the selection of whom very much depended on the whims of the local authorities.[17] This system had evolved considerably since the seventeenth century, when centrally administered standing armies first arose. Responsibility for recruitment shifted over the course of the eighteenth century from provincial estates, which received reduced tax burdens in exchange for assembling and equipping conscripts, to regiments that operated in individual conscription districts, an innovation that mimicked Prussia's "cantonal system." Yet nobles, burghers, merchants, and wealthy free peasants paid for exemption from service. This, combined with local recruiters' aim to rid their districts of surplus inhabitants, meant that armies drew their manpower overwhelmingly from the rural lower classes. The system changed little through the Napoleonic Wars, although some of the harsher forms of punishment were eliminated and efforts were made in the first half of the nineteenth century to standardize the length of service across all Habsburg territories. In 1808, the *Landwehr*, or home defense formation, was inaugurated to boost conscription numbers, though its initial size and performance were disappointing.

The law that passed on December 5, 1868, put in place recruitment by lot for all adult men between nineteen and forty-two years of age. Recipients of the lowest numbers had to serve for twelve years: three in active service, seven in the reserves, and two in one of the home defense forces—the *Landwehr* in Austria or the Hungarian *Honvéd*, established in 1867 as part of the Compromise. Holders of middle numbers completed two years of active service in the home defense forces and ten years in the reserves. Those who drew the highest numbers avoided formal training altogether; they were deployed to the "replacement reserve" (*Ersatzreserve*) or the militia (*Landsturm*) and called up only in case of war. Privileged classes could no longer buy themselves out of military duties, but young men of the nobility and bourgeoisie who had graduated from academic secondary school (*Gymnasium*), and thus qualified for university studies, still possessed the option of becoming "one-year volunteers," undergoing the relatively easy training for reserve officers. The initial recruitment target was set at 95,474 conscripts annually, with 54,541 drawn from Austria and 40,933 from Hungary; these figures were to be recalibrated every ten years on the basis of population and agreed to by deputations from the Vienna and Budapest parliaments.[18]

Millions of young men passed through the Habsburg army after 1868. Yet the proportion of those called up remained lower than in other large European states. In part because neither half of the empire had control over the common army, neither was keen to pay for it; the acrimonious decennial negotiations in Vienna and Budapest over the common budget often hinged on the question of military spending. The Hungarian parliament triggered a constitutional crisis more than once over objections to German as the language of command, refusing, in effect, to contribute to the common defense budget until the Hungarian language was accorded equal status. As a result of such disputes, less of the state budget went to the Austro-Hungarian armed forces than in rival European states: in 1910, only around 16 percent compared with 20 percent in Russia, 25 percent in Italy, and nearly 30 percent in both France and Britain.[19] In absolute terms, the monarchy's paltry expenditures on the military stood out even more, with 420 million crowns spent in 1911 versus almost 1.8 billion in Germany, 1.65 billion in Russia, and 528 million in Italy.[20] The extent of peacetime conscription was also correspondingly lower. Only around a quarter of those qualified for military service in Austria-Hungary actually served, while nearly a third of those eligible served in Italy, around half in Germany, and up to two-thirds in France. These figures caused increasing consternation among top Habsburg military men in the first decade of the twentieth century. The fear that they were falling hopelessly behind rival powers played no small part in their rushed decision for war in July 1914. War, wagered Conrad and others, would not only force a steep increase in military expenditure. It would also silence the querulous nationalist movements that seemed intent on tearing the empire apart and would restore the dominant position of the conservative aristocratic elite to which men like him belonged.

Such feverish anxieties ignored the fact that universal military service had, in spite of the state's sometimes dizzying ethnic-linguistic diversity, done much to militarize Habsburg society. Veterans' associations proliferated in the final decades of the nineteenth century, indicating a broad acceptance of the military's privileged position in society and its centralizing ethos.[21] Active service transformed young peasant men across Europe. Through the barracks, many of them experienced urban life for the first time. They often found the new context intoxicating. In *The Croatian God Mars*, Krleža described Zagorje peasant conscripts' first encounter with Zagreb after being called up:

> To the tillers and cowherds who had all their lives slept in stables and jostled with horned animals, to them being in an asphalted city (where, when it rains, pavements glisten like mirrors) seemed at first easier than that desperate and dark drudgery, so they felt as if they had surfaced from their unbearable, hard, convict-like existence—for a minute. . . . Nothing but

> shops with cured meat products! Rumps and ribs and red bacon of fat pigs . . . Hams hanging like flags! . . . [A]nd there are girls and tamboura and accordion, dancing rattles the inn, and the female breasts are warm.[22]

Whether or not they yearned for their home villages, all conscripts learned practical skills, such as washing, folding, making up their beds, and using a knife and fork.[23] But this coming-of-age experience did not always endear them to their fellow villagers. Jan Słomka recalled, "The soldier came home in his uniform, and would put it on for Sundays and holidays as long as it held together. After his military service he would speak bad Polish, and there were some who pretended not to understand their mother tongue, but muttered something of German, or Czech, etc. They would talk other tongues of the Austrian lands, but not the one they had learned to pray in and should have prized and known best."[24] Yet most soldiers in the Habsburg monarchy completed their military service in their home regions; the Habsburg regimental system, the basis of the army, was more territorialized than in some other European states. This was intended to boost morale and avoid local grievances with "foreign" troops, as well as to save costs and facilitate mobilization in case of war.[25] For all the Hungarian elite's hand-wringing over the supposed discrimination against their language, the Habsburg military proved more sensitive to the multilingual makeup of its enlisted men than neighboring Germany or Russia. While the language of command was German, the administrative languages of each regiment varied according to its ethnic-national composition. Most regiments had two or more languages (out of the ten officially recognized), and officers were required to be proficient in all of them. The officer corps, however, was disproportionately German: 76 percent, despite the fact that Germans made up 24 percent of the monarchy's population.[26]

This, then, was the army that was called up at the end of July 1914. Peasant soldiers may have greeted the mobilization orders with grim resignation and anxiety, but they accepted their duty to the emperor and fatherland. Village priests, taking their cues from the often zealously pro-Habsburg Catholic ecclesiastical hierarchy, attempted to convince parishioners of the righteousness of the conflict.[27] In light of the relatively low conscription rates in the dual monarchy, a large portion of the rural population had no inkling of life in the army. And, like most of the belligerent societies in Europe in 1914, few military-age men, whether villagers or townsfolk, had any experience of combat.

The horrifying reality of modern, industrial warfare became known to European societies within several weeks of mobilization. In a summer in which all sides entertained lethal fantasies about what armies in the field could achieve, and how quickly victory could be reached, the Habsburg Empire stood out for its astonishing delusions. As effectively commander-in-chief, Conrad bore much responsibility for Austria-Hungary's shambolic initial campaigns. His mania for offensive warfare, along with his baffling underestimation of Serbia and Russia, led to chaos in summer and autumn 1914. A poorly executed punitive expedition against Serbia faced stiff resistance from a foe composed of battle-hardened veterans from the 1912–13 Balkan Wars. Russia advanced westward more quickly than expected (although its mobilization plans were well known to the Habsburg general staff), forcing the armies deployed in the south to abandon their positions in a rush to reinforce the Eastern Front. Transportation in the dual monarchy failed utterly; in 1914, many troops had to march to the front on foot owing to railway bottlenecks.[28] Once sufficient infantry divisions had reached the eastern war zone in Galicia and Bukovina in late summer, Conrad insisted they press forward without sufficient artillery support, resulting in 100,000 deaths, 220,000 wounded, 120,000 taken prisoner, and a disorderly retreat to the Carpathian Mountains as Russian forces pressed deep into Habsburg territory.[29] In the bitter winter campaign of 1914–15, thousands of troops froze to death. In March 1915, the besieged and starving fortress city of Przemyśl in Galicia surrendered to the Russians. Over 120,000 men were taken prisoner. By the end of 1914, nearly a million of the 1.7 million troops mobilized by Austria-Hungary had been wounded, captured, or killed.[30]

The first year of the war proved most deadly for all belligerents. The Habsburg Empire's experience was especially sobering, particularly after the May 1915 entry of Italy (technically an ally since the 1882 Triple Alliance) on the side of the Entente. Its military recovery from spring 1915 was thus something of a miracle. By the end of 1916, the monarchy had mobilized five million men, formed twenty new infantry divisions, and was mass-producing the artillery that it had lacked in 1914–15. Yet it never reached the technological sophistication of Germany, France, or Britain and possessed limited flame-throwers, trench mortars, or aircraft. Moreover, its achievements in the field became increasingly dependent on its principal ally. Only in concert with German divisions could Habsburg forces win battles or occupy territory. This was patent in the summer 1915 Gorlice-Tarnów campaign that pushed Russia out of Galicia, in the late 1915 defeat of Serbia, the halting of Russia's summer 1916 Brusilov offensive, the crushing operation against Romania in late 1916, and the October 1917 rout of Italian forces at Caporetto. Conrad's relations with

German generals were frosty, and he deeply resented their ascendancy in the alliance, though his own strategic initiatives proved uniformly disastrous. In spring 1917, the new emperor Karl I replaced him with Arz von Straussenberg at the top of the general staff, removing all remaining obstacles to the Habsburg Empire's complete, and fateful, subordination to Germany.

Besides tribulations at the front, the Habsburg monarchy soon confronted an existential crisis of legitimacy, largely of its own making, behind the front lines. In a matter of days in the summer of 1914, the country familiar to generations of Austro-Hungarians transformed almost beyond recognition. On July 25, just before war began, a state of emergency was declared throughout the empire. This permitted activation of the War Performance Law of 1912, which subordinated all industry relevant to the war effort to military law, prohibiting employees from striking or seeking work elsewhere. It also provided the legal basis for commandeering agricultural produce and equipment. Joint military authorities gained direct control of large areas of the Austrian half of the empire that were adjacent to the front, including Galicia, Bukovina, and Dalmatia. Bosnia-Herzegovina was already effectively under military rule. With Italy's entry to the war, Vorarlberg, Tyrol, Salzburg, Styria, Carinthia, Carniola, and the Austrian Littoral were all added to the list of provinces adjacent to the front.[31] Hungary, jealous of its autonomy, administered the state of emergency through its own civilian administration, which to some extent curtailed the expanding competencies of the army.[32] Under military rule, many types of crimes could be tried according to martial law, which often permitted only two outcomes: acquittal or death. On July 27, a semisecret War Surveillance Office was established in the Austrian half of the monarchy to control the flow of information (primarily through censorship of newspapers and letters), to detect and suppress subversion, and to monitor internees and prisoners of war. The Austrian parliament had been prorogued already in spring 1914 because of nationalist obstruction, but civilian authorities continued to function alongside bloated military authorities. This led to considerable confusion as well as hostility between the different branches of government, with the civilian authorities trying, often in vain, to defend citizens' civil rights against what they saw as military overreach.[33]

The sudden takeover of many aspects of civilian life by the military was bad enough. Much worse was the deployment of the formidable military-bureaucratic apparatus against peoples that top military commanders regarded as inherently suspect. This category included virtually any nationality that might harbor sympathies for enemy states, particularly Serbs, Ruthenians/Ukrainians,

Italians, and Romanians, but also the pan-Slavically inclined Czechs, Slovaks, and Slovenes. Of the monarchy's Slavic peoples, only Bosniaks, Croats, and Poles were considered more or less reliable, though yearnings for independence among the latter two somewhat attenuated their trustworthiness. The Czechs possessed the most boisterous and best organized prewar nationalist movement, which the military leadership hoped to muzzle for the foreseeable future. Franz Joseph himself overruled army requests to put Bohemia under military administration. Nonetheless, by stigmatizing whole populations, the high command succeeded in instilling fear and resentment in a sizable portion of the empire's fifty million inhabitants. Czech nationalist political leaders were arrested and convicted of high treason. Slovene priests were rounded up and jailed for alleged Serbophilia. Summary executions of "Russophilic" Orthodox priests and Greek Catholic or Uniate priests became commonplace on the Eastern Front. Between twenty-five and thirty thousand Galician Ruthenes (Ukrainians) may have been killed by Habsburg authorities.[34] For the mostly peasant Slavic peoples in Austria-Hungary (all except the Czechs), persecution raised immediate questions about the legitimacy of the country they inhabited.

But the largest blow to the state's legitimacy for peasants of all nationalities was the collapse of the agricultural economy, for which wartime regimes were themselves at least partially to blame. The departure of hundreds of thousands of village men for the front, along with the commandeering of draft animals for military service, precipitated a drastic fall in agricultural output. Natural fertilizer became scarce, and the supply of artificial fertilizers based on nitrates and phosphates—before the war imported chiefly from South America—dried up because of the British naval blockade. By 1917, yields in the Habsburg monarchy had fallen to between 40 and 80 percent of prewar levels. In Bohemia, one of the most productive provinces before the war, quintals per hectare of rye (the most common cereal crop in the province) plummeted from 18.7 in 1913 to 7.1 in 1917.[35] With so much of the labor force at the front or casualties of the war, the amount of fallow land increased. In the Austrian half of the monarchy—not including the war zones of Galicia, Bukovina, the Littoral, and Tyrol—total cultivated land declined by nearly 270,000 hectares.[36] The deployment of Russian prisoners of war in hinterland agriculture could not make up for the shortfall. Only the Russian and Ottoman Empires witnessed comparably steep declines in cereal crop production, of 20 and 30 percent respectively in 1916–17.[37]

Austria-Hungary had other problems too. Galicia, the breadbasket of Austria, despite relatively low productivity per hectare, was laid waste as the front lines shifted back and forth across the province. The amount of its cultivated land dropped by nearly half.[38] Jan Słomka recorded how Habsburg troops marched in good spirits through Tarnobrzeg district in late August, only to return in headlong retreat several weeks later. Russian shelling from the other side of the Vistula River damaged his house. After a brief Russian occupation, Austro-Hungarian troops drove the Russians out in October, but then conceded the territory yet again for a longer period. Słomka noted that just three months of war had devastated the villages of his district, wiping out the gains of the rich summer 1914 harvest. Cows and horses had all been taken, few pigs or fowl remained, and cavalry horses had consumed nearly all the grain stocks. The passage of armies had left the roads filled with potholes.[39] Altogether in the first year of the war, armies swept through Słomka's village of Dzików nine times: the Russians four times and the Austrians five.

Fighting in Galicia caused immediate food shortages in Austria. At the same time, food imports from Hungary virtually ceased. Before the war, the more industrial Austrian provinces had relied on grain and meat from agrarian Hungary, giving the Magyar estate owners disproportionate power in both Budapest and Vienna. The lobby of agrarian magnates had been strong enough to dictate the empire's prewar foreign policy, forcing the state in 1906–9, for example, to wage a customs war with Serbia over livestock imports. Yet no law obliged Hungary to keep produce flowing to the west. With the outbreak of hostilities, the regime in Budapest, ever preoccupied with the possibility of social unrest owing to the restricted electoral franchise, withheld exports to ensure domestic supply. Already in 1915, grain exports from Hungary to Austria amounted to a mere 37 percent of what they had been in 1913.[40] Vienna was especially dependent on imports from Hungary, and authorities there had to introduce rationing earlier than in other European capitals.

The governments of both halves of the monarchy took steps to regulate the rural economy and safeguard domestic food production. Their aim was to shield mostly urban consumers from rising prices and looming shortages. Many belligerent states instituted comparable measures, restricting farmers' freedom to sell their produce when, where, and to whom they pleased. But the approach of the Central Powers and Russia effectively undermined morale in the countryside. State institutions were established to buy staple agricultural products, especially grain and potatoes, and eventually everything else, at fixed prices. A key innovation in the Habsburg monarchy was the central grain offices (*Getreidezentralen*).[41] Jan Bařina, the village chronicler in southern Moravian Vrbice, noted in 1915 that the grain and maize harvest could be sold only to the grain office's subcommittee in the local town of Hustopeče at fixed prices.[42] The problem was that the amount small farmers received could not keep pace with galloping inflation on the household consumer goods that they needed to buy annually. Bařina observed that the price of men's shoes—between twelve and eighteen crowns before the war—had risen to between sixty and eighty crowns one year into the war.

It was the combination of worsening shortages and increasingly arbitrary and harsh enforcement of agricultural production controls that distinguished the situation in central and eastern Europe from elsewhere. In Vrbice, the grain stores of small peasants with up to five hectares of land were checked on the fifteenth of every month by decree of the local district captaincy.[43] Production quotas were set based on these inspections, and farmers who delivered on time received a premium; latecomers were paid a reduced rate. If peasants did not deliver their produce to the centrally administered purchasing agencies, the state could requisition produce (that is, seize it in exchange for compensation at fixed, invariably low, prices) as well any other goods deemed necessary for the war effort. Across central and eastern Europe, villagers began to hide products that they feared would be requisitioned. Potatoes, grain, lard, smoked meat, and other comestibles were concealed in holes dug in the garden, in straw in barns, in trees and bushes, even in manure piles.[44] Under the cover of night, peasants took grain to mills to process for their own consumption.[45]

The list of essential resources subject to requisition lengthened uninterruptedly. At the end of August 1915, state officials arrived in Vrbice to requisition all the boilers that people had at home for distilling plum brandy (*slivovice*); the owners of the twenty-six seized boilers received only around fifteen crowns apiece.[46] Seizing villagers' *slivovice*-distilling equipment was one of the ways in which the dual monarchy tried to make up for a shortage of copper, an essential component of bullet and shell casings, which had also been primarily imported before 1914 from South America. Lead, nickel, and tin were also in short supply. Authorities required civilians in town and country to draw up inventories of metal items in their possession and subsequently began requisitioning them. Doorknobs, curtain rods, pots and pans disappeared from households.[47]

Alongside draconian regulation of the rural economy, peasants were confronted with rising resentment from the inhabitants of cities, who regarded them as hoarders and profiteers.[48] The urban press regularly featured cartoons of rustic peasant households suddenly awash in luxury items that desperate townsfolk had traded for food. Inhabitants of Vienna, Prague, and other urban centers smarted from their perceived loss of status vis-à-vis boorish peasants.[49] In the final two years of the war, city dwellers in the Central Powers journeyed into the countryside on so-called "hoarding trips" (*Hamsterfahrten*) to exchange household goods for food. The urban poor who had nothing to trade simply raided fields and orchards. Clashes sometimes resulted. In the relatively remote southern Bohemian hamlet of Sumrakov, people with backpacks arrived from the distant western Bohemian towns of Pilsen and Kladno in search of potatoes.[50] In Vrbice, city dwellers brought manufactured and luxury goods to barter for grain, eggs, milk, lard, and other items.[51] For their part, peasants felt victimized by ungrateful urban hordes who did not appreciate the sacrifices they were making or the labor that went into feeding the country.

On average, people in the countryside had more consistent access to food than those in the cities, who were dependent on rationing. In 1917, hunger riots erupted in major Austrian cities, as starvation menaced the urban poor. But regional disparities in provisioning were significant. Urban unrest rocked the Bohemian Lands in particular, where up to 50 percent of the much-reduced 1915–18 harvests was exported to feed the army and other provinces.[52] In mid-1918, the weekly personal milk ration in Bludenz, Vorarlberg, was, at a quarter of a liter, twice that of Meran/Merano in south Tyrol.[53] Hungarian cities remained better provisioned to the end, but there too hunger gnawed at wartime morale. Nor were all rural areas hit equally hard. Near-famine conditions prevailing in the Dalmatian, Istrian, and Herzegovinian hinterland prompted the relocation of peasant children to relatively well-fed Croatia-Slavonia. In 1917, better-off Slavonian peasant families took in seventeen thousand children from Herzegovina alone.[54]

Some peasants profited from the war. Owners of large farms were often exempted from front service because of their importance to the war economy. Labor shortages affected them less since they could also supplement their workforce with Russian prisoners of war. Prosperous farmers who banded together were able to influence the price indexes of the new central regulating agencies.[55] Their subsequent denials notwithstanding, many no doubt hoarded grain, selling it for exorbitant prices on the black market or using it as livestock feed despite prohibitions. Meanwhile, poor peasants suffered privations, subsisting in Vrbice, for instance, exclusively on ersatz coffee and potatoes.[56] With money increasingly devalued, successful farmers were able to pay off debts, but they had no reason to deplete their growing capital stocks with further investments since new equipment and seeds could not be had at any price. It was in their households that the Persian rugs, pianos, and silver cutlery of the urban bourgeoisie ended up.[57] The Czech rural economy actually grew overall during the war: deposits in major rural Bohemian and Moravian savings banks increased threefold, demand for arable land among farmers ready to pay cash far outstripped supply by 1917–18, and a combination of inflation and accumulated liquid capital in the countryside alleviated peasants' chronic indebtedness, though mortgage debt, a key indicator of peasants' financial health, hardly budged over the same period.[58] The advanced transportation network of the Bohemian Lands allowed a sizeable minority of Czech farmers to profit during the war. "Backpack provisioning" became ubiquitous, as city dwellers travelled to the countryside to purchase foodstuffs directly from producers. The majority of the Czech urban population, concentrated in the province of Bohemia, was at most two generations removed from a rural existence, and contacts with the countryside became a lifeline for many of them in the latter war years. Villagers preferred to sell directly to relatives and acquaintances at prices that far exceeded the officially determined rates but were still a bargain compared with black market prices in the city.

Unscrupulous middlemen, colloquially referred to as "chain traders" (*Kettenhändler*), amassed fortunes by buying produce for slightly more than official prices and selling it on to other merchants or consumers at heavily inflated prices. *Kettenhändler* were drawn from all strata of rural and urban society, though suffering Christian villagers and townsfolk increasingly associated the practice with Jews. Rising anti-Semitism also targeted village shopkeepers, many of whom were Jewish in the Habsburg monarchy outside of the mostly Alpine "hereditary lands." Jewish shopkeepers were accused of profiting from general misery, demanding unaffordable prices, and denying credit to impecunious villagers. According to the chronicler in east Moravian Hluk, "The prices of goods in the stores increased rapidly and hardly any goods could be had. Everything was sold only under the table and at night. Through this mode of trading some merchants who had larger stores and stocks of goods accumulated great riches. In Hluk, for example, [it was] Grünfeld (a Jew, who had a store on the square)."[59] More balanced in his assessment, if still prejudiced, was the Catholic priest Koch in the central Croatian village of Voloder, writing in his parish chronicle that "the Jews gained ground. Competent merchants acquired millions through various transactions [*liferacijama*] which made them almighty. . . . Not that I would gladly blame the Jews, however. They make the profits, but they at least provide for us in some degree. If they would not, it would be worse."[60]

A chasm opened in rural society between a small minority of farmers and traders who got rich on the one hand and the vast majority of smallholders who struggled to make ends meet on the other. By the later war years, social divides in the Austro-Hungarian countryside were stark.[61] Confronted with a worldwide crisis in the agrarian sector, some belligerent states tried to alleviate the burden on producers. France and Britain raised prices for agricultural produce and launched propaganda offensives to celebrate peasants' contribution to the war effort. Investment in new technology, seeds, and services in villages accompanied this remobilization effort.[62] Even in Italy, the debacle of Caporetto compelled the government to offer new incentives to peasant soldiers, promising "land to combatants"—an ultimately risky strategy as postwar political radicalization revealed. But in the Central Powers and Russia, regime policy toward peasants if anything harshened.

In Imperial Germany, peasants felt themselves to be the losers of a radical social-political reorientation ushered in by the controlled economy (*Zwangswirtschaft*). Before the war, agrarian interests in the *Kaiserreich* had enjoyed a relatively privileged position through the favorable distribution of parliamentary or Reichstag seats, which gave more weight to rural voters, and through regularly renewed protective tariffs against cheap agricultural imports, a policy zealously defended by the powerful Agrarian League (founded 1893) and its magnate leaders. Yet peasants felt deliberately excluded from the 1914 *Burgfrieden* (fortress peace) among the state, industrialists, and organized labor to prosecute the war effort.[63] As in Austria-Hungary, a haphazard system of production controls and maximum prices on agricultural products arose that was clearly skewed toward urban consumers. Peasants tried to safeguard their own survival by circumventing controls—for instance, by feeding grain to livestock instead of delivering it to the grain office at artificially low prices—or by diverting their products to the black market. Faced with worsening shortages and inflamed by the urban press, both socialist and liberal, city dwellers raged against allegedly selfish, even treasonous, peasants. Antiurban sentiment among villagers correspondingly deepened alongside tightening of controls, punitive fines for any violations, and humiliating farm and house searches. Agrarian political organizations succeeded in directing peasant ire toward urban trade unions and their socialist leaders. In summer 1918, a widely reprinted newspaper article compared what the soldier had gained from the war (honor), what the worker had earned (higher wages, respect, and attention of state officials), and what the peasant received:

> A year's prison sentence and 10,000-mark fine, expropriation and confiscation, checks, threats of punishments, house searches, mandatory levies,

> controls of acres planted, harvest checks, livestock checks, mandatory registration, mandatory deliveries, denial of the right to control one's own food supply . . . Am I a criminal, the peasant asks himself, and if so, what is my crime? . . . We protect the general welfare from the peasant with maximum prices. But who protects the peasant? . . . The German peasant will begin to get bitter if this continues.[64]

In far less urbanized Tsarist Russia, the war did not poison urban-rural relations to the same extent. Because the government's approach was even less coherent than in the Central Powers, it was less obvious whom the wartime economy benefitted or was designed to benefit.[65] The divide between city and country also remained more porous than in states to the west: in 1900 nearly a third of industrial workers in Russia still owned plots of agricultural land and returned to their villages for planting and harvesting.[66] Initially, the conscription of agricultural workers on large estates improved the market position of many small peasant households, which also received an infusion of cash from the sale of livestock to the Russian army. Between 1915 and 1917, deposits in agricultural cooperatives more than doubled. But shortages of agricultural equipment and soaring prices for manufactured goods wiped out peasants' advantage. Like elsewhere, the wartime authorities appeared to have assumed intolerably broad powers over agricultural production and distribution. And the combined burdens of controlled production, livestock and grain requisitions, and the absence of able-bodied male labor fell heaviest on smallholders. The introduction of price controls on staple crops encouraged many peasants to use potatoes and grain as animal feed or to retreat into self-sufficiency, awaiting the easing of price controls. In autumn 1916, the Ministry of Agriculture instituted compulsory grain deliveries (*razvertska*), though enforcement proved impossible, in part because of widespread peasant resistance.[67]

Peasants clashed with state authorities earlier in the Russian Empire than in either Austria-Hungary or Germany. However, these "disturbances" were often related to prewar disputes over the implementation of Pyotr Stolypin's sweeping land reform program, begun in 1906. As minister of the interior in the wake of the 1905 Russian Revolution, Stolypin had introduced legislation aimed to rationalize agriculture, particularly by consolidating scattered strips of land, and to incentivize rural entrepreneurship, allowing ambitious peasants to break away from the repartitional commune (*mir*) and to assume full legal control over their property. Most Russian and Ukrainian peasants regarded the reform as a way of forcing them to take on the unacceptable risk of crop failures or ownership of inferior land. They also saw it, correctly, as an assault on their entire communal way of life. Early in the war, crowds of peasants in the fertile Kharkov/Kharkiv province, now in eastern Ukraine, often led by mobilized soldiers' wives (*soldatki*), attacked officials working for land reorganization committees, forcing them to suspend their activities in May 1915.[68] Even in Viatka province in the northeast of European Russia, where levels of private land ownership were unusually high, village pressure on "separators" from the commune contributed to the virtual cessation of applications for independent farms.[69]

Before the war, villagers in Austria-Hungary had had few, if any, reasons to distrust the imperial government. From the summer of 1916, this picture changed dramatically. Requisitions in the Habsburg monarchy became more intrusive, even violent, in response to what was perceived as rural tightfistedness or even attempted sabotage of the war effort. State officials and gendarmes were responsible for carrying out the seizures, but from late 1917 army units were called up to assist. In the last year of the war, parliamentary deputies from Ukrainian and Polish districts in Galicia as well as from mostly Slovene Lower Styria brought official complaints before the assembly about the conduct of requisitioning soldiers in their home districts. Soldiers, by this time themselves suffering from insufficient provisioning, allegedly proceeded as though they were on enemy territory, breaking down doors and seizing goods at bayonet-point.[70]

For many villages, a turning point was reached when the state began to seize church bells. From summer 1916, the military demanded that the bronze bells be melted down to extract precious copper and tin. These traumatic requisitions perhaps did most to delegitimize the Habsburg monarchy in rural communities. Although bells were taken in cities too, there were hardly any competing noises in villages, and, as Claire Morelon has written, the requisitions appeared as an attack on local identities.[71] Solemn funereal ceremonies were held for people to part with their beloved bells. In early October 1916 in Slavonian Petrijevci, villagers decorated the confiscated bells with flowers and formed a somber cortege accompanying them to the train station.[72] A year later, Petrijevci's two smaller bells were removed, and in summer 1918 the organ was dismantled and the metal pipes carted away. In Moravian Hluk in 1917, "when the bells rang for the last time, many had tears in their eyes."[73] The only bell left in the Hluk belfry, as in many parishes, was the smallest one, which appropriately sounded the death knell. In Milo Urban's *Living Whip*, the departure of the church bells is one of the more poignant episodes of the book.[74]

Deacon Mrva dissuades three youths from hiding the large bell, nicknamed Ondrej (Andrew), before the scheduled removal, though he admires their "peasant combativeness." In a scene laden with symbolism, Ondrej is heartlessly cast from the belfry by requisitioning officials and breaks apart before the assembled inhabitants of Ráztoky. Their illusions about the war are shattered once and for all. In some cases, though, church bells were successfully hidden, as in Moravian Sobůlky where the parish priest led the rescue operation.[75] Such recalcitrance among lower clergymen only underscored the widening rift between the village world and the military-bureaucratic regime supported by the ecclesiastical hierarchy.

Those responsible for enforcing requisitions at the local level accumulated immense power. The gendarmerie, or rural police force, became objects of particular fear and hatred. In Hluk, "gendarmes were the terror of everyone and the unchallenged lords in the municipality. People brought them sustenance, meat, eggs to win their favor. They eventually got so used to this that they regarded it as a matter of course and paid a few *kreutzers* or crowns for such gifts—they could not take anything for free, since that could be judged as bribery."[76] In the Kingdom of Hungary, notaries headed civil administration at the village level and, along with the gendarmes, had ample opportunity to abuse their power. Some became famous for their heartlessness: in Subotište, Slovakia, the notary allegedly told a local woman and mother of fourteen children pleading for a larger flour ration to "roast one of your children and eat your fill."[77] Though likely exaggerated by prurient gossip, it was not unheard of for notaries to demand sexual favors from young women whose husbands were at the front in exchange for performing routine services.[78] The tyrant of fictional Ráztoky, the notary Okolický, impregnates the penurious village beauty Eva Hlavajová after deceiving her with promises of an imminent furlough for her husband Adam. Disowned by Okolický and ostracized by other villagers for having a child in Adam's absence, Eva eventually drowns herself in a frigid stream. Okolický also enforces the strict registration of livestock in the highland Slovak village of Urban's imagination. Corruption in fact tempted all officials responsible for dispensing scarce resources in wartime. In the far western Slovak village of Kúty, teachers were authorized to ration sugar, salt, and petroleum and allegedly issued them only in exchange for bribes.[79]

In areas near the Eastern Front, the Habsburg army itself menaced lives and property on home soil. A Polish peasant memoirist from the village of Lutcza in Rzeszów district recalled the appalling conduct of soldiers from eastern Galicia billeted in his family's house one night in autumn 1914. He and his family awoke to find their supplies of grain gone as well as much of the straw from the roof of the barn; the unmilled grain had been poured out on the floor of the barn to make a more comfortable sleeping surface. This, he recalled, contrasted markedly with the well-behaved Russian soldiers who later occupied the area.[80] Likewise, Jan Słomka complained bitterly about the Hungarian troops quartered in and around Dzików, of which there were around fifteen thousand at one point: "In a few days there wasn't a straw of fodder left, for what the animals didn't eat they trampled underfoot: and the rest was carried off for the baggage teams that stood outside. None of my requests was of avail, no cries of the women that now during winter there would be nothing to keep the cows alive."[81] The aged Słomka, then seventy-two-years old with four decades of service as village mayor behind him, was taken hostage after a local barn burned down and army officials suspected peasant subversiveness. The Honvéd, the Hungarian territorial army, became notorious for their callous and brutal behavior toward local non-Hungarian people in Austria-Hungary. Speaking a language that remains an outlier in the central European region, Honvéd soldiers regarded other peoples of the monarchy with suspicion, particularly Slavs, whom they had been taught were inferior.[82]

Pressed from all sides, the peasants of central and eastern Europe began to turn against the governments that ruled them. Much of this rebellion was silent. Peasants challenged state power by concealing produce, dissimulating or feigning ignorance, deserting, and all of the other ways that social scientist James Scott dubbed the "weapons of the weak."[83] Only exceptionally did they openly express their grievances, and if they did, they tended to use the cover of anonymity. In early 1918, authorities in Carniola received a threatening letter from a semiliterate Slovene peasant who called himself Janez Kral (figure 1.2). Investigations into the sender's identity remained fruitless, but the rambling text gives eloquent testimony to the anger seething under the mostly placid surface of Habsburg rural society:

> Our robber government wants to take from us everything that the poor peasant martyr prepares with toil. The robber government is stealing from us peasants and in this way wants to starve us, but the peasant will only supply what he needs for himself. What mischief has the Robber government been up to with our potatoes? . . . How many peasants still have not planted potatoes for themselves, because the Robber government stole everything in the autumn so that they had nothing to plant. . . . Today the

Robber government creates such conditions for the peasant that there will be a general collapse in the whole state, you will soon see, you High lords. You have taken from the peasant all his happiness for work and for his farm [*gospodarstvo*]. Who produces bread for you? Who produces wine? Who raises [*zredi*] the oxen? Who raises the pigs? Who produces potatoes, though this year you will not cart off as many from the land as you did last year, because the peasant could not plant them. This year the general collapse will start. . . .

Now the Robber government wants to have everything that the peasant produces, so that the hungry peasant will labor for you devil's frock-coat wearers [*frakarji*]. . . . You wrote in the papers that our enemies want the war to last as long as possible and that they will thus starve us. Who are these enemies of ours? These enemies are the Priests [*farji*] and the Robber government. Before the war they had made a plan for how to squeeze the people and now when the peasant is in complete despair the priests would like it if he would constantly stand in church. Where can he find the time, if he needs to work 18 hours per day and walks in wooden clogs all day? A person is so tired that on Sunday he does not feel like going to church and if he does, he falls asleep in the pew.

THE FAMOUS LORDS WILL SOON SEE, WHAT the consequences will be of taking from the peasant all his liberty, in the coming year 3 parts of the people will die of hunger, that is just about guaranteed. . . . How can one such priest hope to be received in God's hands, when he is guilty of spilling so much innocent blood. Do you have any compassion for those close by? You are murderers and you dare to step before the altar! . . . I survived 16 whole months in the trenches and have seen hundreds die in terrible suffering, and I thought how if our priests would experience what we have to, they certainly would not go to ask the Robber Government to prolong the war. In the newspapers one constantly reads that our enemies do not want to conclude peace, that is a bare lie. ALL THE STATES ARE FRIENDLY AMONG THEMSELVES AND JUST WANT TO STARVE THE PEOPLE, but tough consequences will be born of that in 1918.[84]

"Janez Kral" directed most of his fury against state elites, whom he was convinced had hatched a plot to squeeze peasants for their own profit. In his imagination, the conspiracy extended across the borders of Austria-Hungary to include the ruling circles of all other belligerent powers. Barely less guilty for the slaughter, in his view, were the pro-dynasty Catholic clergy, who

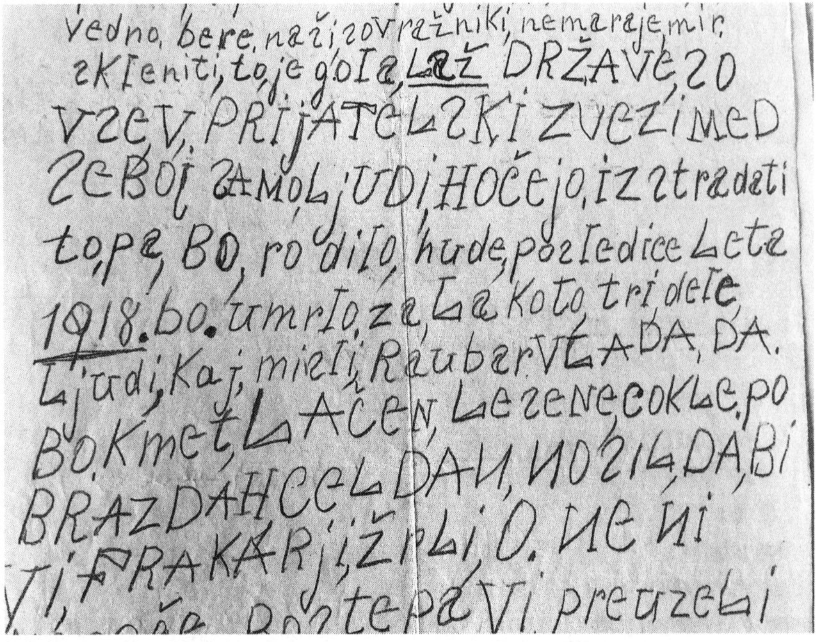

vedno, bere, naši zovražniki, nemarajemir,
zkleniti, to je gola LAŽ DRŽAVE, zo
vzev, PRIJATELZKI ZVEZI MED
ZeBoj ZAMOL, LJUDI HOČejo, iz ztradati
to pa, BO, rodilo hude posledice Leta
1918. bo. umrlo za lakoto tri dele
Ljudi, Kaj mieli, Rauber VLADA, DA.
Bo Kmet LAČEN, Lezene coKle, po
BRAZDAH CeL DAN, NOZIL DA BI
TI FRAKARJI ŽRLI, O. NE NI
V ... pa vi prevzeli

FIGURE 1.2 An anonymous 1917 letter from a Slovene peasant threatening the "robber government". Archive of the Republic of Slovenia

preached the righteousness of the war and the need for further sacrifices. Such vitriol against men of the cloth was hardly representative of the pious Slovenian peasantry, though it was certainly becoming more common, particularly among those who had served at the front.

Villagers perceived a widening rift between "our" priests, who sympathized with peasant tribulations and even defended them against the state, and "their" priests, who saw themselves as executors of orders from above. Milo Urban devised two characters to embody this contrast in the Slovak village where *The Living Whip* is set: the agreeable deacon Mrva and the authoritarian chaplain Létay, who envisions God as an urban gentleman wearing a bowler hat, a stiff collar, cufflinks, and clenching a cigar between his teeth: "With his ironed trousers, he [God] did not visit villages where it would be necessary to jump over ditches, nor did he go into houses. Peasant houses have high thresholds and low doors: if you do not watch out, you immediately have a bump on your head like a fist. Létay entertained these fantasies since childhood, and although grown man now, he could not rid himself of them."[85] While Mrva preaches forbearance, Létay scolds parishioners for their stubbornness during the livestock registration, later threatening them with hellfire after a disturbance outside the notary's house. Few readers would fail to notice, moreover, that Mrva is a Slavic name while Létay is of Hungarian origin.

The Slovene peasant Kral predicted that the "robber government" would face a "general collapse" later in 1918, primarily due to requisitions. His anonymous letter was in some ways prophetic. Incidents began to multiply of peasants openly resisting state representatives who had come for agricultural products, including in the relatively peaceful Slovenian lands. The weapons of the weak were being cast aside in favor of more dangerous implements. In January 1918, a tax official assisting with requisitions in the Slovene village of Formin near Pettau/Ptuj in Lower Styria was beaten to death.[86] Crowds of mostly women attacked requisitioners in the Czech Bohemian villages Chrast, Křenice, and Parník.[87] In late April 1918, Jurij Ačko, the Slovene village mayor of tiny Ošelj in Lower Styria, led an assault on requisitioning officials billeted in his own house. On April 23, a Grain Requisition Committee composed of six soldiers and one civilian official arrived in the villages on the southern slopes of the Pohorje massif from Maribor, the principal town of Lower Styria. According to testimonies of local peasants, they not only commandeered all the grain and potatoes they could find, but also helped themselves to eggs and dried fruit, disregarding villagers' pleas to leave them some supplies to live on. The desperate inhabitants of Ošelj and neighboring hamlets appealed to their mayor, a wealthy farmer and tavern owner with over twenty thousand crowns' worth of property. Ačko later told interrogators that the requisition committee "took everything, even the potatoes for planting, so that people complained to me, as mayor of the municipality, and asked for help. Women were screaming and weeping in order to convey they will have nothing to eat. . . . The uproar in the municipality was indescribable."[88] On April 25, Ačko tried to intercede on behalf of peasants in Zgornja Nova Vas, at which point one of the soldiers pressed a revolver to his chest and told him to leave. Infuriated, Ačko took refuge in the tavern where he drank two liters of cider followed by several liters of wine and fruit brandy. That night, he compelled the shepherd Ferdinand Borko and the army deserter Jožef Janžič to accompany him into the lodgings of the committee with the words: "Let's go, we're going kill those soldiers who want to rob us; I'll shoot, you beat them." Ačko's revolver misfired, but the four members of the committee sustained injuries from pickaxes wielded by Borko and Janžič. The fifty-year-old village mayor claimed to have no knowledge of what transpired that night, having awoken drunk in the forest the next morning. In June 1918, he was sentenced to eight months in prison, but successfully postponed the punishment several times because his large farm was deemed necessary to the local economy.

Peasants began to resist any state intrusion into the rural economy. A severe dearth of tobacco available through the Hungarian state monopoly compelled peasants in Croatia-Slavonia to cultivate their own, in direct violation of the law. Enforcement of the ban on private cultivation led to clashes in the summer of 1918. Customs officials who arrived in the central Croatian village of Donje Orešje on June 19 to uproot tobacco plants were attacked by a crowd including many women and children.[89] Pelted with stones, the officials opened fire, mortally wounding a young soldier on leave who had recently been a prisoner of war in Russia. The incident prompted an interpellation a week later by deputy Ivan Kovačević on the floor of the Croatian diet, the Sabor, calling on the government to soften its stance toward illegal tobacco planting. There is little evidence that Kovačević succeeded, yet peasants' resolve hardened. On the morning of August 27, eight customs officials arrived in central Croatian Ruševac to assess the extent of tobacco planting. As they entered the village, church bells began ringing and 120 armed inhabitants assembled to hound the intruders out; reports alleged that they possessed a machine gun.[90] Gendarmes searching for deserters had received a similar welcome in Ruševac a week before: church bells rang and a large armed crowd of peasants gathered before the church shouting "hurrah," forcing the gendarmes to flee.

Rural deserters were pivotal in the "general collapse" foreseen by Janez Kral, as we will see in the next chapter. It was often their mothers, fathers, sisters, and wives who influenced their decision not to enlist or return to the front. When questioned, civilian accomplices invariably feigned ignorance, or justified their support for the deserters by pointing to fallow fields and unharvested crops at home. Marija Mlakar, a fifty-two-year-old Slovene widow and proprietor of a farm in the Drava River floodplain southeast of Maribor, pleaded innocence against charges that she helped her son Janez Mlakar avoid front service between November 1917 and March 1918.[91] "I don't know how much leave he had at that time since I can't read," she told investigators in May 1918. Moreover, she claimed to have been ill for much of the winter and needed help tending livestock. For this reason, she had in February filed a dictated request to extend her son's leave, casting doubt on her claim not to have known how much leave he had in the first place. But she insisted that she "didn't know that he wasn't supposed to wait at home for the request to be answered." Nor was she to blame that Janez had fled from gendarmes when they came to arrest him in March. Marija's prevaricating defense typified peasant reactions when confronted with the disciplinary apparatus of the state.

While some peasant attitudes toward authorities remained constant through the war, others underwent a profound transformation, particularly among peasant soldiers mobilized to the fronts in faraway places. Venturing for the first time beyond their home region, or sometimes their home village, they saw unfamiliar ways of life and observed contrasts between town and country. Above all, they learned how to kill and became accustomed to it. By the last two war years, conscripted peasants were showing far more assertiveness than their relatively docile pre-1914 selves.[92] Tsarist conscripts from the villages of the Kharkiv province, in eastern Ukraine today, even promised in letters home that they would set about seizing large estate land upon their return.[93]

Adam Hlavaj, the chief protagonist of Milo Urban's *The Living Whip*, exemplified the rising self-confidence of peasants after several cataclysmic years of war. After deserting from his unit on the Eastern Front, Hlavaj makes his way southwest to Ráztoky in the Slovak Carpathian Mountains. Repeatedly evading capture by gendarmes in the snowbound forests, he is instrumental in turning his covillagers against the wartime authorities. At one point he asks them: "Do you think we fought for ourselves or for all of you here? Far from it! What do you or your land mean to anyone? There is enough land. We fought for the fatherland, for that enormous yoke, to which a clutch of idlers bound us so that they could live carefree from our callouses."[94] The author thus captured villagers' sense of unjust exploitation by a cabal of mostly urban outsiders. Such themes found expression in literary works less exalted than Urban's and Krleža's. The 1928 war novel *Revolt of the Cottages* by Moravian Czech author Vojtěch Rozner, a native of the small village of Hýsly, who experienced the wartime home front as a young boy, lyricized the populist anger welling up in the countryside by 1918:

> The cottages rose up. It was only too clear and understandable. They straightened their unkempt hair, lifted up their heads, defiant like bandits. They did not recoil any more from the fact that they are such puny, deformed, and dilapidated runts, for they recognized that there is strength in numbers. They recognized that the power and size of those mighty palaces that command half the world is very problematic; indeed it is questionable, hanging on a weak thread. . . . Those small warped cottages recognized that they are in fact that half of the world that does not need to let itself be ordered around by the ones they feed.[95]

As the peasantry became more conscious of itself and its antagonism with "parasitic" outsiders, some enlisted men became aware of their essential affinity with peasants from beyond their native region or national territory. Enthusiasm for an inchoate peasant internationalism came naturally to the communist Krleža. Deployed to the east to face the Tsarist enemy, his home guard conscripts from the hilly Zagorje region feel pangs of an "instinctive Slavism," an inchoate peasant class consciousness stretching from the northwest Croatian town of Zabok to Vladivostok. For "peasants, soldiers without rank, are often closer to each other, whatever nationality they might be of, than are officers and soldiers of the same nationality."[96] The Slovak nationalist Urban also envisioned natural solidarity between the Slovak *sedliak* and Russian *muzhik* sent to kill each other. Given the chance, these "half-brothers" would fraternize with each other and surely lament that they cannot scythe their fields in the beautiful summer weather instead of allowing their wives and children to go hungry.[97]

Such sentiments helped undermine the legitimacy of dynastic empires in central and eastern Europe. By 1917, they were spreading fast in the Habsburg monarchy, even as the new emperor Karl made efforts to reverse some of the damage done to civil society during the first two war years: he amnestied political prisoners, abolished the feared War Surveillance Office (though its competencies were simply shifted to another department), allowed the revival of parliament in the Austrian half of the empire, and dismissed Conrad as chief of the general staff. Salutary though they were, the reforms could not stem the rising tide of rural disaffection. Peasants saw little alleviation of the severe wartime economy that dictated which crops they grew, which animals they raised, and the prices at which they could sell their products. Requisitioning officials confiscated property with increasing ruthlessness, extending their rapacity to church bells—inanimate, though cherished members of village communities. While city dwellers imagined peasants feasting and prospering while they queued for scarce goods, villagers themselves felt victimized by regimes that put the interests of ungrateful urban consumers above their own livelihoods. Although narrow segments of agrarian society did indeed thrive, most rural households suffered privations, even if few ever starved.

The startling expansion of the state during the First World War would prove a major turning point in twentieth-century history. After the inconclusive and lethal campaigns of 1914, belligerent powers dug in for a long war, casting aside the liberal economic norms of peacetime that were based, at least domestically, on

FIGURE 1.3 A village in the Záhorie region of western Slovakia around 1920. Záhorie Museum in Skalica

free-market ideas. The exigencies of wartime armaments production and provisioning of immense, often immobile armies in the field led, among other things, to the establishment of new government offices to oversee the production and distribution of critical agricultural products. The free market ceased to exist with the implementation of price controls and mandatory grain deliveries. Imperial Germany went the furthest in asserting state control over agriculture and industry, providing a model for the Bolsheviks' "war communism" during the Russian Civil War as well as for the Soviet state's command economy during the entirety of its sixty-nine-year existence. Austria-Hungary emulated its senior alliance partner as best it could, though the dual monarchy's structural weaknesses, above all Hungary's virtual independence in key areas, hampered its efforts.

In all warring states, industrial labor found its position strengthened by its pivotal role in munitions production. Aside from Russia, socialist party leaders acquiesced in the war effort, pledging loyalty in exchange for the possibility of concrete rewards. Incipient forms of social partnership arose in wartime as new regulatory agencies allowed socialists to help manage them. This, along with the menace of resurgent labor militancy in the final war years, hastened most governments' postwar legislation of the eight-hour day, expanded insurance provisions, voting rights for women, and compulsory collective bargaining.

Peasants reaped no such benefits. Although the protracted war of endurance heightened the importance of the agricultural sector, smallholding peasants in central and eastern Europe saw themselves as the controlled economy's victims. Much had to do with the arbitrary and chaotic manner in which wartime states incrementally expanded their authority over villagers' livelihoods. Rural piety and traditional dynastic loyalty, pillars of order in the countryside, cracked under the strain of relentless, intensifying intrusion into the agrarian economy. Such betrayal could not be easily rectified. Political elites who survived the years 1914–18 realized that twentieth-century warfare required the swift, complete, and uncompromising mobilization of resources; the quicker prewar norms were abandoned, the better. By contrast, the main lesson that peasants drew from the conflict was that they could not rely on governments for their survival—they would have to go it alone. In the last two years of the war, the European peasantry was far more self-aware and dangerous than it had been in 1914. Milo Urban described this epochal transformation as a moment of heroism, but also of ruthless violence:

> Here, in the blood was born a new era, full of bold words and courageous talk, full of confrontations between people, here in the blood was born a new person, who found his hands, bold, strong hands that cannot be so easily bound anymore, and which do not shake so easily anymore. In the bloody contradictions, laws were broken, societal forms unraveled, and the masks were torn from the faces of this world's untouchable authorities. The new man did not want medieval armor or mysteries: he did not want to be a conjuror or a pharisee, but just that what he is, a bold, rebellious, predatory being, a person without ornament.[98]

2

Secret Armies

IN THE SPRING OF 1918, a Slovene peasant soldier named Andrej Zlobec decided he would fight no longer for Austria-Hungary. Seriously wounded in the high mountains of the Italian Front, he was sent to a field hospital in Meran, South Tyrol. It was here, in his own telling, that he resolved "to flee to the Green Cadre, where freedom reigned."[1] His determination only grew when he was moved to a hinterland hospital in Ljubljana to make room for recent casualties from the front. Zlobec and a handful of other convalescing Slovene soldiers conspired to join the so-called Green Cadres, thereby committing "the greatest sin of the Austro-Hungarian army at the time."[2] Everyone knew of the existence of these shadowy groups of armed deserters, but how could one enlist? The conspirators made contact with a certain sergeant Kovačič, who was facilitating passage to the Green Cadres in the Trnovo Forest, today in northwest Slovenia, not far from Zlobec's home village of Ponikve in the coastal Karst region. Posing as a patrol with rifles furnished by Kovačič, the deserters met another confederate before dawn in a tavern on the western outskirts of Ljubljana. They exchanged the password *Grünwald* (green forest, in German), toasted the success of the operation with plum brandy, and headed west across country, taking their lunch at the house of a sympathetic peasant. By nightfall they had reached the Trnovo Forest.

Zlobec and his companions found themselves in the middle of an astonishingly multinational armed organization. Croats, Czechs, Germans, Magyars, Romanians, Serbs, Slovaks, and many Slovenes were assigned to units (comfortingly called *čete* in Slovene), which controlled sections of territory. Zlobec's unit, under the command of a Czech corporal, guarded the southern edge of the forest overlooking the Vipava Valley. He knew that the commanders of the Trnovo Forest Green Cadres were in the village of Lokve, but he had little contact with them. The discipline that the deserters had learned in the

Habsburg army was now repurposed to subvert the old monarchy itself. As Zlobec recalled, "Here in the Green Cadre we all found our refuge. We were united by the desire to fight for the smaller homeland and not for sprawling old Austria."[3] While the anticipated assault on their lair by still-loyal troops never came, fresh arrivals swelled their numbers. Not only more Austro-Hungarian deserters joined them, but also Italian and Russian prisoners of war, Reich German soldiers, and a handful of French and British infantrymen. Heavily armed and savoring their freedom, they awaited the end of the war in tense expectation.

In 1918, Habsburg military and civilian authorities feared precisely the kind of Green Cadres that Zlobec described: organized, disciplined, and devoted to liberating their smaller, presumably national, homelands. But even as alarming reports of armed deserters reached them from rural areas across the empire, their investigations could not confirm whether the Green Cadres existed beyond myriad local contexts. Officials doubted whether they constituted an organization at all. They appeared to have no clear program, no political representation, and there was no evidence of broader military coordination. While anti-Habsburg nationalist leaders set great hopes on the clandestine armies of deserters that coalesced in 1918, the Green Cadres played at most a peripheral role in the "national revolutions" that established new Czechoslovak and Yugoslav states and resurrected Poland as Austria-Hungary disintegrated. In the eyes of new state elites in Prague, Warsaw, Zagreb, and Belgrade, the deserters and their concerns were ultimately too rural and too parochial to be of much use. These factors have conspired to keep the Green Cadres in historiographical oblivion for much of the century since the First World War ended. But although urban politicians and urban-focused historians struggled to make sense of them, the peasant deserters who in 1918 seized control of large swaths of rural Austria-Hungary deeply imprinted east central Europe for decades to come.

For the Green Cadres were both less and more than the forces looming in the troubled imagination of Habsburg authorities. The multinational, militarily disciplined, and politically mature *čete* described by Zlobec were exceptional, though they did exist in some places. More typical were countless small groups spread over forested and mountainous areas distant from the actual fronts—unlike the Trnovo Forest, located in the rear of the Isonzo Front—and only loosely affiliated with one another. Most deserters camped in the immediate vicinity of their villages, returning home as often as possible for food, fresh clothes, and a warm bed. Survival was their main goal. Yet they embodied a groundswell of peasant anger and revolutionary ambition that the rulers of Austria-Hungary fatally underestimated. Backed by millions of villagers, scores of thousands of Green Cadres helped bring down the ancient empire from within. Farther east, the peasant green armies that emerged in the Russian Civil War across immense territories from western Ukraine to the Urals posed perhaps the most serious threat to the fledgling Bolshevik regime before their final subjugation in 1921. In both places, the appearance of green peasant forces marked the culmination of rural resistance to the states waging the Great War.

Rural desertion plagued all belligerent powers, even the United States of America, though Tsarist Russia and Austria-Hungary were most afflicted by it.[4] After the hungry winter of 1916–17, desertion posed an existential threat to both states. Russia's war effort could not recover from the February Revolution's eruption in Petrograd. Despite strenuous efforts by the Provisional Government to rally troops to honor Russia's alliance with the Entente, and maybe even to conquer the coveted Black Sea straits, peasant soldiers "voted with their feet," as Lenin is reported to have said, returning to their home villages amid revolutionary enthusiasm. They refused to go back to the front, instead establishing local councils (soviets), dispossessing large estate owners, and thus hastening the Bolshevik seizure of power in autumn 1917. The Central Powers did not face collapse in 1917. They had weathered Russia's mighty summer 1916 offensive led by General Brusilov and had, in a stunningly swift campaign, inflicted on Romania a humiliating defeat that culminated with German troops' entry into Bucharest in December. Britain's 1916 Somme offensive on the Western Front had proved colossally wasteful, and Italy was held at bay in the Alps. But despite a positive military balance sheet, the Austria-Hungarian and German home fronts began to unravel. The "remobilization" of belligerent societies in 1917–18, partially successful in Germany under the ruthless regime of Generals Paul von Hindenburg and Erich Ludendorff, failed in the dual monarchy. Alongside grievous food shortages and a resurgence of political discontent after the young emperor Karl I reconvened parliament, desertion accelerated at an unnerving rate.

Desertion took many forms. Recruits called up for the first time sometimes refused to report to their units. Others absconded while on active duty, particularly while they were in transit. Busy train stations provided opportunities to disappear from one's unit but were also closely monitored for this reason.[5] Some men daringly jumped from trains proceeding through wooded terrain.

By contrast, instances of soldiers deserting to the enemy across the front lines were rare. While the Habsburg army made much of such cases, eventually blaming the empire's defeat on the alleged disloyalty of the subject nationalities, most soldiers of all ethnic backgrounds fought well when deployed to the front. Instead, soldiers most often deserted by refusing to return to active duty after periods of leave.

The Habsburg military's criminal code addressed different types of desertion and their varying degrees of severity. Deserting to the enemy was considered treason, punishable by death, but the penalties for overstaying periods of leave in one's home district were relatively mild. These, too, varied according to how long, and under what circumstances, one remained unaccounted for. Relatively innocent cases of overstaying leave (*Urlaubsüberschreiten*) contrasted with deliberate "self-removal" (*eigenmächtige Entfernung*), which, aggravated by time, was considered open desertion (*Desertion*). According to the Habsburg military's 1855 criminal code, a key criterion in defining desertion was the intention to permanently evade one's duty, but how such intent could be proven was not specified.[6] Although length of absence from one's unit hardly demonstrated intent—someone who wanted to permanently abandon the army might be caught immediately, for instance—it was military prosecutors' only tool. In this respect, Habsburg military justice was relatively lenient; in Italy, by contrast, just twenty-four hours' absence from one's unit sufficed to accuse a soldier of desertion.[7] Not surprisingly, most cases in Austria-Hungary were dismissed for lack of evidence. Those that advanced beyond pretrial rarely resulted in conviction, and even when a soldier was found guilty, punishment was usually deferred until after the war so that the offender could be redeployed to the front.

The circumstances of the final two war years, along with a lack of effective deterrence, led to a surge of desertion in the hinterland and rear areas (*Etappengebiete*) of Austria-Hungary. The extent of the increase is difficult to quantify. In August 1918, the head of military intelligence, Maximilian Ronge, conservatively estimated the number of deserters in the hinterland at 100,000.[8] Two months later, on the eve of the monarchy's collapse, the deputy commander of military railways put the figure at 250,000, or 5 percent of the entire armed forces. Likely the most accurate numbers could be extrapolated from how many deserters were caught. These painted a distressing picture for military authorities. In June 1918, the inspector general of the Royal Hungarian Gendarmerie reported that in 1917, 81,605 deserters had been apprehended in the Hungarian half of the empire—over double the number that had been captured in 1916 (38,866), and over ten times the figure from 1914 (6,689). Just in the first three months of 1918, 46,111 had been brought in, leading the inspector to estimate that 150,000 would be arrested by the year's end. And these numbers, he surmised, were only a fraction of those that remained at large.[9]

Of all the lands of the Hungarian crown, Croatia-Slavonia appeared to be the worst affected. Fully a quarter of the deserters caught in 1917 were in this semiautonomous province, even though it made up only 12 percent of Hungary's population.[10] When the Croatian viceroy, or *ban*, requested that county prefects investigate the situation at the start of 1918, he received alarming reports. Forest-based deserters threatened to overwhelm the gendarmerie in many districts, and their numbers were sure to increase with the arrival of spring.[11] Although the situation was direst in the south of the empire, rural desertion plagued a number of provinces, such as Galicia, where in the first half of 1918 the authorities apprehended almost thirteen thousand deserters, along with eight thousand soldiers overstaying furlough and sixteen thousand vagabond prisoners of war.[12] With the front lines shifting frequently across Galician territory, there were ample opportunities to abscond. Nonetheless, the core problem faced by authorities in the monarchy's northeast mirrored those elsewhere: the gendarmerie simply did not have the resources to stem the rising tide of desertion. And an increasing proportion of deserters possessed military rifles and ammunition that they had taken with them on leave, despite strict orders to the contrary.[13] Armed clashes between gendarmes and deserters in the Kingdom of Hungary increased by a factor of three between 1916 and 1917 and would again, according to projections, between 1917 and 1918.[14]

The Habsburg military resolved to take sterner measures. In June 1918, army command centers across the empire ordered raids of rural areas where large numbers of deserters were known to be hiding. Tens of thousands of men were mobilized for these operations, but the results were disappointing. In mid-July, for instance, the military command center in Przemyśl, Galicia, deployed twenty-eight companies amounting to 3,350 men and 76 officers for a raid that brought in only 194 deserters.[15] Superficially more successful was a June operation organized by the military command in Budapest that deployed 4,200 soldiers and brought in over 11,000 men for various offenses; around half were deserters and over 2,000 were vagabond prisoners of war.[16] But hardly any of them possessed weapons or had strayed from their home villages. Armed deserters camping in the forests repeatedly eluded the authorities, while soldiers staying at home who had only recently failed to return to their units easily fell prey to raiding companies. This pattern repeated itself in the jurisdictions of army command centers in Cracow, Graz, Lemberg, Leitmeritz, Poszony, Sarajevo, Vienna, and Zagreb.[17] Military raids continued through the summer and autumn, bringing in thousands of deserters, but they could not discourage many thousands more from refusing to fight for Austria-Hungary.

The civilian population's complicity posed the single biggest obstacle to military authorities combating desertion. Complaints were legion that villagers closed ranks to protect their own sons, fathers, and husbands. Deserters received ample warning that gendarme or army patrols were approaching. In one north Bohemian village, residents loudly shut their doors to signal the arrival of a patrol.[18] Such warning systems indicated high levels of coordination among local peasants. In some places, civilian authorities themselves aided and abetted the deserters. Dismayed commanders of raids reported on the uncooperativeness of village mayors in locales across the empire.[19] The Sarajevo-based commanders of Dalmatia and Bosnia-Herzegovina demanded the dissolution of civilian authorities on the southern Adriatic island of Korčula, along with removal of the gendarme officer Popović, whose peasant wife had allegedly turned him into an ally of the deserters.[20] When gendarmes or soldiers managed to arrest deserters, they faced open hostility from the local population. In the southwest Moravian district of Třebíč, crowds gathered on multiple occasions to jeer patrols escorting captured deserters, sometimes showering them with stones.[21] Occasionally, such local vigilantism turned deadly. On the night of June 10, 1918, "soldiers and civilians" attacked the gendarme station in the Galician village of Grodzisko Dolne to liberate recently arrested deserters, killing the commanding officer. A note hammered to the building read: "If you give us peace, we will leave you in peace, otherwise you will forfeit your lives."[22]

In some instances, the "assistance units" sent to hunt miscreants only drove rural civilians and deserters closer together with their callous behavior. Magyar soldiers made an especially bad name for themselves in Slavic territories, where they tended to have no knowledge of the local language. During a June 1918 dawn raid in one central Croatian village, they violently stormed houses, killing one innocent man and seriously wounding another. The incident prompted official complaints by deputies on the floor of the Croatian Sabor.[23] An August 1918 petition against Magyar soldiers in Zagreb County accused them of treating the local intelligentsia just as roughly as the peasants, who presumably deserved little better.[24] More commonly, the demoralized and often poorly coordinated assistance units had little motivation to persecute deserters or their families. Vojtěch Berger, a Viennese Czech carpenter originally from the south Bohemian hamlet of Todně, served as a sapper on several fronts starting in 1914 before his assignment to an assistance battalion in June 1918. While never openly insubordinate, the staunchly socialist Berger detested the war from the start and expressed admiration for the deserters he was sent to catch in his detailed diaries. His unit was deployed in the Galician countryside near Przemyśl in July 1918, then in Moravia in August and early September, and finally in Croatia-Slavonia in late September and October. In many places, Berger and his comrades spent more time picking fruit than looking for fugitives.[25] Villagers regularly complained about thefts committed by assistance units deployed in their districts, with petitions sometimes reaching the Viennese parliament.[26] Yet soldiers also fraternized with local people of the same ethnicity, with whom they could easily communicate. While stationed in the south Moravian village of Bořetice at the end of August 1918, Berger's unit attended an all-night village dance party along with many local deserters, whom they left unmolested because, as they archly informed the innkeeper, the gendarmerie had not yet provided a list of those to arrest.[27]

For their part, the deserters proved adept at using the rural terrain to their advantage. Commenting on the summer 1918 raids, military authorities ruefully noted that fugitives had easily found refuge in the extraordinarily high grain in the fields that year. As a solution, they recommended organizing raids immediately after the harvest was finished.[28] Where desertion threatened to completely undermine public safety, such as in the region of Syrmia in eastern Croatia-Slavonia, civilian authorities ordered the grain to be cut as soon as possible to deny the deserters their hiding places.[29] Less penetrable forested areas, by contrast, were increasingly regarded as off limits by the authorities. Scores of armed deserters near south Moravian Kobylí forced a twenty-man army patrol to retreat, causing a stir among the soldiers of Vojtěch Berger's battalion.[30]

Not only was desertion surging from the spring of 1918, but its character was changing with the return of hundreds of thousands of Austro-Hungarian prisoners of war from Russia. Between the start of the war and the end of 1917, Russia captured over 2,000,000 soldiers and 56,000 officers from the Central Powers. Of these men, only 167,000 prisoners of war were from Imperial Germany; the rest were from Austria-Hungary.[31] Following the 1917 October Revolution, the Bolsheviks could no longer administer the vast internment camps they had inherited from the Tsarist regime and Provisional Government. Hundreds of thousands began the westward journey home by any means possible, often on foot. By the end of June 1918, when the terms of prisoner exchanges were finally agreed upon by the governments in Vienna and Moscow, 517,000 Austro-Hungarian soldiers had already returned.[32] Another 150,000 made it back before the end of the war. These "returnees" contributed to accelerating desertion rates in the last year of the war and were responsible for radicalizing and politicizing all forms of insubordination in the Habsburg armed forces.

Of greatest concern to the regime was the returnees' potential for spreading the Russian revolutionary contagion. The Austrian Jewish novelist Joseph Roth evoked anxieties surrounding the returning soldiers in his 1932 novella *Hotel Savoy*: "They came out of Russia and brought with them the breath of the great revolution. It was as if the revolution, like some active crater, were spitting them out like lava into the West."[33] Lenin himself set great hopes on former prisoners of war as carriers of the "bacillus of Bolshevism."[34] Although relatively few of the returnees harbored revolutionary designs, those that did included some prominent future Communists, such as Béla Kun, founder of the 1919 Hungarian Soviet Republic; Josip Broz "Tito," future dictator of Yugoslavia; and the Czech interwar activist Alois Muna. To Habsburg rulers already shaken to their core by news of violent antimonarchical upheaval in Russia, the menace posed by their own returning soldiers was not to be underestimated. Reports indicated that many Austro-Hungarian prisoners of war in the former Tsarist dominions were attending revolutionary assemblies and voluntarily joining Red Guard units, some with overtly subversive intentions; one cell of Hungarian Bolsheviks allegedly devised a plot to assassinate a member of the imperial family.[35] According to later estimates, as many forty thousand of the two hundred thousand south Slavs interned in Russia may have joined the Red Army or the new Soviet administration.[36] Confronted with a deluge of soldiers reentering Habsburg territory, some of whom "were strongly incited to Bolshevism," the dual monarchy's high command urged extreme vigilance as the repatriated soldiers arrived home.[37] At the same time, it appeared that revolutionary ideas had taken root among some Russian prisoners of war interned in Austria-Hungary, whose "ultimate goal was the creation of a situation similar to that which is prevailing in Russia."[38]

In fact, Habsburg authorities' inflated fear of revolutionism among the returnees created the very situation that they tried at all costs to avoid. Suspicion and harsh treatment awaited those crossing into Austria-Hungary from the east, which often led directly to insubordination. Upon reentry, these men had to pass through receiving stations for returnees (*Heimkehrerübernahmestationen*), then quarantine stations (*Quarantänestationen*), and finally army

FIGURE 2.1 Soldiers discussing Lenin in an illustration by Ivo Režek for Miroslav Krleža's *The Croatian God Mars*. Varaždin City Museum

education groups (*Armeeausbildungsgruppen*) for "disciplinary reeducation," before being deployed to "replacement regiments," where it was determined whether they were eligible for a period of leave at home.[39] From early 1918, the sheer numbers of returnees forced the army to dump responsibility for reeducation on the understaffed quarantine stations located in present-day Poland and Ukraine. Men wasted away in these camps for weeks, enduring constant medical examinations, drilling, filthy lodgings, and insultingly small food rations. Staff sometimes extorted money for issuing blankets.[40] Redeployment in replacement units meant further humiliating investigations into their conduct while in Russia; armed escorts accompanied them whenever they marched from place to place. Although few of the returnees were punished for their behavior while on enemy territory—of the 41,784 men redeployed in replacement units in the first three months of 1918, only 708 were deemed ineligible for leave and 165 labeled politically "dubious"—the experience was deeply dispiriting.[41]

Nearly all Austro-Hungarian prisoners of war yearned to return home as soon as possible. But the cruel realities of rejoining the Habsburg armed forces convinced many that they had made a mistake by leaving Russia in the first place. In the military command center at Kassa (today Košice, Slovakia), the men who had recently returned from the east allegedly avoided the company of those who had not, spoke excitedly about their experiences, and sang Russian songs.[42] In May 1918, Hubert Jindra, a spy for the military intelligence division, reported on the dejected mood among replacement soldiers of the mostly Slovak Seventy-First Infantry Regiment stationed in Kragujevac in occupied Serbia.[43] They complained bitterly about the miserable provisioning in Galician quarantine stations. Noncommissioned officers (NCOs) Juraj Brna and Ján Bača regretted having left Russia at all, claiming they received bread only six times during an entire month spent at one makeshift quarantine camp. They and others agreed that life as a prisoner was bad under the Tsar, but everything changed when the Bolsheviks came to power: everyone was thenceforth treated as equal and received generous food rations. They also had the freedom to travel around the country and made a good living doing various jobs. Upon their return, they found themselves persecuted, while the officers—mostly Jews, they alleged—enjoyed themselves in the brothels.

The misconception that Jews had somehow escaped front duty and wheedled their way into comfortable posts behind the front lines was ubiquitous by the last year of the war. The Polish village mayor of Dzików, Jan Słomka, wrote, "Friends of Austria though [the Jews] were, they squirmed out of every sort of military service. In the general mobilization very few of them joined the colors, a great contrast to the situation in Christian circles. In addition those who did get into the army were soon reporting on sick-list at the hospitals; or found doing duty behind the lines, or in the storehouses, where there was no danger. Mighty few ever saw front line service."[44] According to a district official in Brzesko, Galica, soldiers on leave grumbled that only Jews were to be found in the rear areas and the ambulance corps. Some Jewish officers, they alleged, "treated peasants arrogantly," and extorted a fee of hundred crowns for each furlough.[45] Although anti-Semitism had a long history among the Christian popular classes of central and eastern Europe, it appears to have intensified in the apocalyptic conditions of the world war, which, among other things, transferred tens of thousands of Galician Jewish refugees to the western provinces of Austria-Hungary, where they were an unfamiliar and unwelcome presence. A specifically peasant strain of such thinking identified Jews—already seen as alien outsiders for centuries—with the apparent wartime exploitation of villages by towns and cities.

Disillusionment and anger led to revolt. In the spring of 1918, mutinies erupted in garrisons throughout the empire where returnees predominated.[46] In mid-May, Slovene soldiers revolted in the Styrian garrisons of Judenburg and Murau. A week later, insubordination broke out among Slovene, Croat, and Italian soldiers in Radkersburg, Styria; among Czech soldiers in Rumburg, northern Bohemia; and among south Slav, German, Hungarian, and Slovak soldiers in Pécs, Hungary. The Slovak soldiers of the Seventy-First Infantry, about whom Hubert Jindra had reported, revolted on June 2, seizing control of the garrison in Kragujevac. Smaller disturbances by Slovak returnees occurred in late May in Nagybecskerek (today Zrenjanin, Serbia), Trenčín, Veľka Kubra, and Lučenec, as well as on June 6 in Poszony (Bratislava). Altogether there were twenty-five mutinies across the empire in the spring and early summer of 1918.[47] Everywhere, the army managed to reassert control within forty-eight hours. The mutineers lacked planning and coordination, often responding spontaneously to worsening food rations. Ringleaders were located as quickly as possible and executed. These events nonetheless further rattled the military establishment, underscoring the danger posed by the men coming home from Russia.

Rumors of subversive plots coursed through the armed forces in the summer of 1918. In one widely reported-on scheme, returnees aimed to bring the Habsburg war effort to an immediate end by setting alight grain fields across the empire.[48] Homecoming Slovene soldiers in Lower Carniola supposedly planned to cleanse the "Slavic soil" of German intruders, following the example of what they had witnessed in Ukraine.[49] While never carried out, these chilling designs reflected a broader mood of pessimism and fear that regime censors detected in letters sent at this time, especially those sent by peasants.[50] Industrial workers seem to have been more prone to the revolutionary optimism sweeping Europe in the wake of the Bolshevik takeover. They drew a direct connection between events in Russia and socialistic mass actions in early 1918 in Austria-Hungary, particularly the January strike, in which hundreds of thousands of workers in Lower Austria, then Budapest and Bohemia, downed tools. Initially a protest against a further diminution in the flour ration, the strike quickly adopted overtly political aims, demanding an immediate end to the war and peace without annexations or indemnities. The Social Democratic Party leadership, fearing reprisals and uncontrollable radicalism among their followers, convinced strikers to return to work after only minor concessions in rations and workplace conditions.[51]

Yet of all the types of mischief involving returnees, none preoccupied the military authorities as much as the so-called Green Cadres of deserters. From the spring of 1918, the army's high command feared that a vast "green" conspiracy was taking shape on the rural home front, fueled by the return of former prisoners of war from Russia. Talk about the green forces sped along the monarchy's rail network. On the westward train journey from Russian captivity, a Hungarian infantryman learned from several soldiers that the strongholds of well-armed Green Cadres were in Galicia, Lower Austria, eastern Slavonia, and Croatia between Zagreb and Rijeka. He promptly informed his brother-in-law, a military inspector in Szeged district.[52] An officer returning from the east via the quarantine station at Volodymyr-Volyns'kyj heard from a Silesian Czech on the train that the "green guard" was ready to "pull something off."[53] Another Czech returnee told his interrogators that the organization of Green Cadres in Bohemia followed the model of Red Guards in Russia. These forces, already six thousand strong, were preparing for an autumn revolution in Austria-Hungary in coordination with similar forces throughout the state.[54] Such reports seemed to indicate that the Green Cadres originated among soldiers in Russian internment, or perhaps among native Russians who then inspired the prisoners of war. But talk of the Green Cadres had been noted before the bulk of returnees had arrived. Already in February 1918, the "Green Cadre" was a familiar "catchphrase" among Bosnian and Herzegovinian soldiers stationed in Budapest, evoking their desire to escape from the poorly provisioned, louse-ridden barracks as soon as the weather improved.[55]

Around the same time, enlisted men under the military command center Temesvár were found to be in possession of poems urging desertion to the Green Cadres.[56] Still, it remains possible that the Russian Revolution of 1917 inspired the formation of Green Cadres, as news about events in the east circulated widely before the bulk of former prisoners of war arrived home.

Along with suspicions persons on military transports, officials noted strange slogans among the enlisted men, some implicating secret organizations of deserters. From Bohemia and Moravia to the south Slav territories, there was concern that an antistate terrorist conspiracy lurked behind the phrase "fourteen days' vacation."[57] Pronouncements by the subversive Slovak returnees in Kragujevac lent credence to this fear. Several of them told the spy Jindra that everything would fall into place once they were granted leave.[58] Slovak soldiers who mutinied in Poszony and joined the Green Cadres used the slogan "Shave him!" (*Ohol ho!*), which in the context of the war meant "Cut off his head," and had its origins in the western Slovak peasantry's mocking of Hungarian gendarmes.[59] Mostly unbeknown to their higher-ups, Czech soldiers communicated their intention to desert, or their belonging to the Green Cadres, with the phrase "Army, ease up, heave ho!" (*Vojno povol, hej rup!*).[60] And there were yet other ways in which deserters signaled their belonging to a clandestine movement. The military command center in Sarajevo claimed that Green Cadre members in Dalmatia and Bosnia-Herzegovina had the letters "Ž. S." tattooed on their left arm, meaning *živila sloboda*, or "long live freedom."[61] Some of the same deserters apparently used an argot among themselves with special terms for "rich folks," "poor folks," "rifle," "railway," and more.[62]

In early summer 1918, as the army conducted extensive raids on deserter lairs, the Austro-Hungarian regime decided that it needed to get to the bottom of the Green Cadre rumors. Were the deserters in fact plotting the demise of the monarchy? If so, what kind of revolution were they planning and who were their leaders? The investigations conducted across the empire could give no definitive answers to these questions. In the middle of June, the military command center in Zagreb reported that among soldiers, the phrase "Green Cadre" simply denoted a free life of poaching game and camping in the forest without any political aims.[63] A replacement battalion of the Third Infantry operating in Moravia substantiated such impressions. The conclusion from their early June investigations was that the pervasive stories about "Green Cadres" or "Green Brigades" were seriously overblown. Many soldiers talked about the Green Cadres in affectionate, even humorous, terms—referring, for instance, to their intention to "spend the night with the green bed lady"—but there was no movement as such.[64] The threat posed by the deserters to public safety in eastern Moravia, while serious, not least because of the support of the civilian population, did not correspond to any larger organization. In July, the Moravian governor reiterated that the "alleged Bolshevik subversion" by deserters in the forests near Buchlovice was pure fantasy, though he admitted that many deserters hid from gendarmes by "camping with the Green Cadre" during good weather.[65]

Doubts still gnawed at military leaders. The Green Cadres were close to the top of the agenda at a July 18 meeting in Vienna convened by the head of military intelligence, Maximilian Ronge, to discuss the movement for Czechoslovak independence. Numerous letters intercepted by military censors testified to the existence of some sort of Green Cadre organization, and coordination between it and antimilitarist circles in Prague could not be ruled out.[66] Yet the source for the alleged link between anti-Habsburg nationalist leaders and rural deserters soon proved unreliable. Despite reports from Moravia denying any political program among the Green Cadres, fear of revolutionary conspiracy led the Vienna police prefecture to accept the testimony of Bohuslav Čech, a one-year army volunteer and petty fraudster who before 1914 had unsuccessfully tried to become a police informant.[67] Čech claimed to possess inside information about the Moravian Green Cadres, having supposedly befriended their commander, Ensign František Pokorný. The Viennese police learned from him that the Moravian Green Cadres comprised two corps, each with over a dozen units: one in the vicinity of Břeclav and the other in the Zlín area. According to Čech, they enjoyed the support of Czech nationalists as well as a certain influential industrialist named Štěpánek in Zlín. To verify the story, the authorities arranged for Čech to return to eastern Moravia under police escort and reestablish contact with Pokorný, which he supposedly did through a tavern-keeper in the small town of Luhačovice. On July 25, gendarmes surrounded the area of an anticipated dawn meeting between Čech and Pokorný on the forest edge. When neither party showed up, police agents burst into Čech's room at the inn, rousing him from sleep. Confused and weary, he admitted that he had fabricated the entire story, including Pokorný. The Austrian Interior Ministry tersely summed up the affair: "Bohuslav Čech is a notorious liar and has been exposed again."

In early September, civilian and military officials across Austria-Hungary were notified that "the numerous reports from all parts of the monarchy" about the existence of a Green Cadre organization could not be verified.[68] Instead, it appeared that deserters frequently used the phrase "Green Cadre" as shorthand for "a free life, poaching game, hanging around in the forests, etc." Among the civilian population, meanwhile, "fantastical exaggerations" about the extent of the purported organization were widespread. Even in the south Slav territories, where desertion threatened public order the most, no politically motivated Green Cadre organization could be said to exist. An officer sent by the army high command to investigate the situation in Bosnia-Herzegovina reported that "any proof that the [deserter] gangs are spreading Bolshevik or Yugoslav propaganda is lacking."[69] The deserters were more concerned with harassing local landowners than with undermining the authorities; further evidence, the officer concluded, of their fundamentally apolitical nature.

Criminal syndicates were the only kind of Green Cadre organization whose existence the authorities could confirm with any confidence. Sulejman Ćuran, a Bosniak deserter apprehended in July 1918, admitted that the deserter organization to which he belonged was involved in forging documents and selling them to soldiers on trains and in military hospitals.[70] According to another deserter arrested by gendarmes in September near Daruvar in central Croatia, his Green Cadre group comprised forty to fifty men from various regiments who had built up a criminal network across the monarchy, involved mostly in extortion and robbery.[71] They had stolen over a million crowns to date, with most of the loot going to an evidently interfaith leadership—he gave the names Petar Zdelar, Ibrahim Perković, and Franz Löwy. To avoid detection, they used their own argot and signaled to each other, the arrested man improbably claimed, with frog-like croaking. South Slavic deserters involved in criminal activities apparently found it easier to move around civilian-ruled Croatia-Slavonia than in Bosnia-Herzegovina, which was under stricter military control. The authorities noted an abundance of Bosnian deserters in regions along the southern borders of Croatia-Slavonia.[72] Armed deserter gangs involved in smuggling also flourished in the eastern border regions of the monarchy in Galicia and Bukovina.[73]

Even after numerous reports had allayed their worst fears, officials still worried that rumors about revolutionary Green Cadres could become reality. Not only could such dangerous prattle act as a catalyst for further desertion, but some deserters, investigators pointed out, might undertake to organize the very movement that they had heard so much about.[74] Soldiers on leave in eastern Moravia were said to have inquired as to the whereabouts of the Green Cadres with the intent of joining them.[75] "Terrifying rumors" had fed "vivid imaginations" about the scale of the deserter organization in the nearby Buchlov Forest, according to one officially sanctioned Czech newspaper article.[76]

Meanwhile, press outlets in Entente and neutral countries ran occasional articles, some hyperbolic, about the green threat faced by Austria-Hungary within its borders.[77] A Hungarian Communist periodical in Russia hailed the "Green Cadre revolutionaries" at work behind the front lines.[78] The Interior Ministry in Vienna feared the effect that such news might have on the Austro-Hungarian populace. In late September, civilian authorities across Austria received orders to suppress all mentions in the press of "Green Cadres" or "Green Guards."[79]

The extent and nature of the Green Cadres eluded the government in Vienna to the end. The deserters did in fact represent a mortal danger to the old empire, but not in the shape of its familiar bugbears that the authorities searched for and failed to find. Despite the surge of returnees from Russia into their ranks, and despite their hostility to an army dominated by German and Hungarian speakers, the Green Cadres were neither unambiguously Bolshevik nor conventionally nationalist. Although they varied widely in their ethnic composition and their locally oriented activities, the secret armies sought more than anything else to protect the peasantry from the depredations of the world war.

The origins of their name remain mysterious. The most prosaic explanation for their color coding is likely the most convincing: green referred to the forests and fields where they found refuge.[80] If the inspiration for deserters to form armed antistate paramilitary groups originally came from Russia, they may have deliberately chosen a color other than red in order to both distinguish themselves from, and invite comparison with, Red Guards—the voluntary paramilitary groups that formed in 1917 to safeguard Soviet power. In Austria-Hungary, green forces most often referred to themselves as "cadres," suggesting that they were highly trained in their craft, though "Green Guards," "Green Brigades," and "Green Reserves" were also common labels. The designation "cadre" may have originated with NCOs and veteran enlisted men who fled from mostly south Slavic troop formations; one informant reporting to Serbian commanders in Italian exile identified the Seventy-Ninth and Ninety-Sixth Infantry Regiments as well as the Twenty-Sixth Croatian Home Guard Regiment as their wellspring.[81]

Whatever their origins, they were strongest in the Slavic territories of the Habsburg monarchy, and especially among south Slavs. Among the first of their bastions that the authorities identified was the wooded Fruška Gora massif, today in northwest Serbia, then in far eastern Croatia-Slavonia. Already a hideout of deserters since 1915, by mid-1918 Fruška Gora provided cover for up to six thousand men of various regiments and ethnicities.[82] During the May 20,

1918, mutiny in the Pécs garrison, as many as two thousand mostly Serb troops of the Sixth Infantry Regiment succeeded in breaking through a cordon of men dispatched from Osijek, Novi Sad, and the Petrovaradin to contain the rebellion and joined the Fruška Gora *zeleni kadar*.[83] It was likely these deserters who made the surrounding region of Syrmia (Srem/Srijem) into one of the most lawless parts of the empire in the last months of the war.

To the west of Fruška Gora, the broad Slavonian flatlands enclosed by the Drava, Danube, and Sava Rivers also harbored large numbers of deserters, many of whom stayed in woodlands close to their villages, sleeping at home whenever possible.[84] The key strongholds for the *zeleni kadar* in central and western Slavonia were Krndija and Papuk, twin summits in a range of low, forested mountains running east to west and rising southward from the wide floodplain of the Drava River. Deserters from surrounding villages found ample hideouts in the dense forests on their flanks.[85] Green Cadres formed in many areas of central Croatia as well, particularly in the hilly Moslavina region, located between Zagreb in the west and Slavonia in the east, and the uplands of the Banovina, south of the town of Sisak.[86] The Petrova Gora mountains, straddling the Banovina and Kordun regions, probably sheltered the most formidable Green Cadres in the entire monarchy. Under control of deserters from 1917, contemporaries estimated the strength of the green forces there between eight and fourteen thousand men organized militarily into eight battalions, possessing machine guns and even three artillery pieces.[87] While mostly made up of Croats and Serbs from the regiments based in Karlovac, Otočac, and Sisak, numerous Czech and Italian deserters found their way into the Petrova Gora force.

The sparsely populated mountains of Bosnia-Herzegovina supported some organized deserters—one source estimated that there were ten thousand between Sarajevo and Mostar—but general privation in the province along with draconian military rule spurred many of them to cross into neighboring Croatia-Slavonia and Dalmatia.[88] In spite of severe food shortages in Dalmatia, Green Cadres roamed in parts of the hilly inland region (Dalmatinska zagora) as well as on some of the islands, from Betina in the north of the province to sun-baked Korčula and Šćedro in the south.[89] However, these were much smaller groups than those that assembled in Croatia proper and Slavonia. Istria, just south along the coast from the fighting of the Italian Front and devastated by food shortages, witnessed even less desertion.[90]

Among the traditionally conservative and relatively prosperous peasants of the mostly Alpine "Hereditary Lands" of the Habsburg monarchy, desertion rates were lower, and deserters had fewer opportunities to band together. The wealth of these provinces was evident in the fact that farmsteads over ten hectares in size were more numerous in the crownlands of Carinthia, Salzburg, Styria, and Upper Austria than anywhere else in the monarchy.[91] Yet there is some evidence that a *Grüne Kader* existed in the vicinity of the Wechsel Mountains in German-speaking upper Styria.[92] In mostly Slovenian lower Styria, Carniola, and parts of the Littoral, the *zeleni kader* remained a well-kept secret long after the war ended. It was not until after the Second World War that historians began to question statements by interwar Slovene politicians that Green Cadres had been a solely Serbo-Croatian phenomenon.[93] Besides the Trnovo Forest group that Andrej Zlobec joined, small bands operated in Styria on the Pohorje plateau above Maribor and on the slopes of Boč Mountain.[94]

Southeast Moravia was also a center of *zelený kádr* activity, notwithstanding inconclusive probes by the authorities. The largest groups of armed deserters were in the Ždánice Forest and the Chřiby, a hilly wooded area just west of Buchlov Castle, where, in September 1908, the Austro-Hungarian foreign minister Aehrenthal claimed his Russian counterpart Izvolsky had consented to Habsburg plans to annex Bosnia-Herzegovina. Czech village men, primarily from the subregion of Slovácko, absconded to these forests to avoid being caught by gendarmes. Relatively well organized, they had guard and provisioning units, and some of them actively recruited on trains passing through Hodonín and Uherské Hradiště.[95] Reports about their trenches and machine guns may have been exaggerated, but they evidently had commanding officers and maintained at least a semblance of discipline. The numbers of organized deserters in this region can be surmised rather more accurately than elsewhere: the Czechoslovak army's volunteer Slovácko Brigade, which formed in Hodonín in early November 1918 (and is the subject of chapter 5), was composed overwhelmingly of former Green Cadres; at its peak in January 1919, it counted 5,262 enlisted men.[96] To the west, deserters in the districts of Třebíč and Jindřichův Hradec also banded together, as did scattered groups in southwest and northern Bohemia. To the east of Moravia, Slovak Green Cadres mustered in several areas of what is today western Slovakia, particularly in the Váh River valley between Nové Mesto nad Váhom and Hlohovec and in the Malé Karpaty range (Little Carpathians) north of Poszony (Bratislava).[97] The latter group likely received reinforcements from soldiers who escaped the Poszony garrison after the June 1918 mutiny.[98] The Slovak *zelený káder* possibly numbered four thousand by the autumn of 1918.

North of the Tatra Mountains lay the strongholds of Polish *zielona kadra* in Galicia. Although desertion impacted the south Slavic lands the most, talk of

FIGURE 2.2 Buchlov Forest in Moravia, Czech Republic—a stronghold of Green Cadres. Author's photo

the "Polish vacation" (*polski urlop*) spread far and wide in the Austro-Hungarian army.[99] Many of those who opted for the Polish vacation banded together for mutual support. Formidable deserter gangs controlled forested areas in the western regions of this sprawling province between Cracow and Przemyśl, concentrating especially in districts north of Rzeszów—Łańcut, Tarnobrzeg, Nisko, Mielec, and Kolbuszowa—as well as in the foothills of the Carpathians, from the Podhale region in the west, home to the Polish subethnic group of "highlanders" (*górale*), to the Jasło and Sanok districts.[100] The protagonist in the popular 1927 novella *Zielona kadra* introduces himself laconically as "a peasant. A highlander. A deserter from the Twentieth Infantry Regiment."[101] Perhaps up to forty thousand deserters (not all in organized groups) were at large in the province by the summer of 1918.[102]

Throughout the empire, the deserters organized themselves into groups of between five and twenty armed men, which, often in coordination with other groups of similar size, controlled certain wooded or highland areas. By spring of 1918, the band led by Slovene Alfonz Šarh on the Pohorje massif above his home village of Ruše numbered sixteen men, mostly peasants from the southern slopes of the plateau. They established their headquarters in a cavern on the flank of Pesek Mountain, where they kept supplies, weapons, and ammunition. They lived off woodland game and trout caught in local streams and were, Šarh recalled warmly, "prepared to last to the end [of the war]."[103] Nonetheless, danger was never far away. The local villagers, from whose ranks Šarh and his companions hailed, by and large assisted the deserters, warning them of approaching gendarmes by laying green spruce twigs across paths or planting them in the ground in front of houses. When the weather was bad, the Pohorje Green Cadres bedded down in various friendly peasant houses and barns, including the Šarh family homestead, changing locations on short notice to avoid capture. Such peregrinations within a small region were quite common. The Slovak group founded by Augustín Nuhál and Jozef Ferančík in the Váh River valley was constantly on the move in the foothills of the Malé Karpaty between Nové Mesto and Trnava, visiting their home village of Veselé as often as possible.

Deserters in densely populated provinces such as Bohemia sometimes ranged even more widely. As early as 1915, there were itinerant Czech- and German-speaking deserters in the western Bohemian region of Pilsen, some of whom hailed from the local Roma community. Among these was the teenage Josef Serinek, who decided to join his friends and older brother in the forests before having actually served in the army—and who left behind detailed recollections of his experiences in the Green Cadres (though it is likely

FIGURE 2.3 Green Cadres, as imagined for Josef Pavel's 1927 novel *Zelený kádr*

the label came into use only late in the war).[104] By 1916, they found refuge in the long chain of forested hills that made up the Bohemian Forest (Český les/ Böhmerwald) and Šumava, now in the southwestern Czech Republic. Gendarmes arrested Serinek in spring 1916, forcing him into military service despite his protestations that he was still underage. Sent to a Honvéd regiment in Hungary, he went through weeks of training in preparation for deployment to the Italian Front, but then fell ill and received a generous furlough from a collusive Czech doctor. Back in Bohemia in late summer 1916, he rejoined a small group of mostly Roma deserters west of Pilsen who were traversing a wide expanse of country between Šumava in the south and the small town of Teplá in the north.

It was in the northern sector that Serinek's group joined forces with a well-organized Czech-German contingent under the command of Sergeant Franz Lefner, a German socialist from the town of Mies/Stříbro. The group, now twenty-five strong, returned to the Šumava forests, where in late 1916 they merged with a similarly sized band, some of whom had come all the way from the Buchlov Forest in Moravia. Now with over fifty men and possessing a machine gun, Lefner decided in the interest of safety to divide his force into smaller groups of six to eight, which would rendezvous nocturnally once a week in predetermined locations. Group commanders were to meet more frequently. Whichever group arrived first at a meeting point was responsible for preparing food for the rest of the Šumava deserters. In March 1917, on a pre-meeting provisioning expedition in the vicinity of Domažlice, Serinek's small group encountered hostile villagers who sent for the gendarmes; a firefight ensued, in which his brother-in-law was killed and the rest scattered. Serinek was arrested soon after and spent the remainder of the war in jail. His testimony reveals that before 1918, deserters faced much incomprehension and antipathy from civilians, even among the rural population. Despite his Czech patriotism, Serinek's Roma ethnicity no doubt awakened prejudices among some potential village allies. Stereotypes about idle gypsies fused with resentment that some felt toward "shirkers" (*flákači*), while their own sons suffered at the front.

Political goals no doubt motivated some soldiers to desert. As a fifteen-year-old boy, Serinek certainly had no lofty ideals when he first joined his brother and brothers-in-law in the forests near Pilsen. But the leaders of his Green Cadre detachment did espouse revolutionary ideas, which Serinek quickly imbibed. His brother, an NCO, and Sergeant Lefner held counsels deep in the Šumava forests on how best to undermine the Austro-Hungarian war effort, settling on a strategy (never executed) of detonating viaducts and railroad tracks. Just before capture, Serinek and his brother had agreed that they would escape to Russia to join the great revolution, about which word was just starting to spread. In June 1918, the Slovak Ferančík also despaired of the seemingly interminable war, leaving Nuhál and the rest of the Váh River

Green Cadres behind for Bolshevik Russia—a society congenial to his inchoate socialist sensibilities. Nuhál and Josef Ferančík's brother Alexander remained in western Slovakia to lead a local national revolution in November 1918, disarming gendarmes in Borovce, raising the first Slovak flags in the valley, and forcing Magyar troops to withdraw. Alfonz Šarh, a committed Yugoslavist, basked in the Slovene nationalist euphoria of November 1918 when he and his companions emerged from Pohorje sporting Yugoslav blue-white-red cockades to cheers of "Long live the Pohorje deserters! Long live the Green Cadre!" For Andrej Zlobec, the deserter forces in the Trnovo Forest away to the west were soldiers of national liberation as they constituted "the beginnings of new, independent armies."[105]

All these men underscored the patriotism of the green deserters in the recollections they recorded years, sometimes decades, later, when sovereign nation-states appeared to be the irreversible outcome of east central European history. Nonetheless, in 1917 and 1918, Slavic Austro-Hungarian soldiers appeared increasingly committed to vague notions of national autonomy or independence and to the dream of completely reordering society, which many of them had witnessed in Russia. The more politically minded among the deserters gravitated toward a hazy amalgam of socialism and liberation from the German- and Magyar-dominated military regime. The Czech anarchist writer Michal Mareš captured this position in his semiautobiographical novel *The Green Guard* (1927) about southwest Moravia. A one point in the story, local deserters from the villages of Bolíkov and Sumrakov welcome into their midst a transplant from the Buchlov Forest, Josef Přibyslavský, described as "a bit of a Bolshevik and man of letters," who brings with him a radical ditty that the group sings:

> This Green Cadre of ours
> Like stags they hunt us,
> But when we come from the wood into the fray
> The red banner will wave.[106]

In Mareš's telling, social radicalism and emancipatory nationalism were indistinguishable for the deserters: "Amidst the great sea of military discipline and bloody violence those groups were tiny islands, unsettling the authorities and armed power in the hinterland, tireless and nameless heroes of the national revolution and vanguard of the coming social revolution: the Green Guard!"[107] Přibyslavský, a real person, became as a martyr for this noble cause when he was shot dead by gendarmes in mid-October 1918 (a grisly photograph of his bloodied corpse adorns the frontispiece of Mareš's novel).[108] As elsewhere, the return of prisoners of war from Russia swelled the number of deserters in Sumrakov and Bolikov. The returnees injected desertion with radical ideas, a more aggressive stance toward the authorities, and expectations of sweeping societal change when the war was over.[109] Authorities in southeast Moravia identified returnees spurning reenlistment as the main culprits behind a flood of minatory letters from the "Green Guard" sent to gendarme posts.[110] One received by gendarmes in the village of Moravská Nová Ves thundered, "You lackeys of militarism! Payback time is coming for your destructive and rotten behavior. That's right, soon we will be doing the accounting and woe to you! . . . And you claim to be Czechs? Traitors, hyenas, and bloodsuckers of our nation!"[111]

Other Green Cadre recruits, including many of those recently repatriated from the east, simply wanted to escape the war. František Sedláček, a peasant from Kobylí in the Břeclav district of Moravia, found little to admire in Bolshevism or in its leaders Lenin and Trotsky, "both converted Jews" in his erroneous estimation.[112] Taken prisoner in the initial days of the summer 1916 Brusilov offensive, he worked until early 1918 on the estate of a Russian baroness, where "Bolshevism" first manifested itself in 1917 when a barn went up in flames and several *muzhiks* drowned in the manorial pond trying to fish for the first time. In early March 1918, Sedláček, with two other Austro-Hungarian prisoners of war, reached the quarantine station in Volodymyr-Volyns'kyj and, after seventeen days of miserable treatment and reeducation, returned home on leave before his deployment to an NCO training school in Bruck an der Leitha. He secured leave again for summer threshing work, but this was delayed when he caught influenza. When his request for an extension of his leave was denied, he resolved not to return to the army: "How could I? So much work at home, the whole family in the hospital. Then and there I decided not to go anywhere. I joined the Green Cadre."[113] Working by day in the fields and sleeping in nearby forests, Sedláček was among the deserters hunted without success by Vojtěch Berger's replacement battalion of the Ninety-First Infantry Regiment, which arrived in Kobylí in August.

Villagers protected Sedláček, whose surname means "little farmer" in Czech, as they protected tens of thousands of other Green Cadres across Austria-Hungary. For Anna Francová, a wartime chronicler in the neighboring village of Vrbice, the deserters were "our poor lads," suffering persecution from heartless gendarmes like a certain Captain Dřímal, who became a notorious figure in local recollections.[114] But some gendarmes abetted the deserters, either out of ethnic solidarity (much celebrated in interwar Czechoslovakia) or, more commonly, to preserve good relationships with local communities. The Moravian peasant Marcel Bimka avoided redeployment twice thanks to timely warning from the gendarme Metelka in his home village of Šardice.[115] Commander Barek of the Železný Brod gendarmerie station in northern Bohemia became the "guardian angel" of the local deserters, earning himself the affectionate nickname "green daddy."[116] In Moravia, a handful of nationalist Czech gendarmes along with confederates in the postal service devised a system to warn deserters of impending raids.[117] Elsewhere in the monarchy, notaries and priests were suspected of being on the side of the miscreants.[118]

The most important allies of Green Cadres were peasants themselves. Village children brought them supplies and acted as sentries, warning them of approaching gendarmes and military patrols.[119] In the Vojvodina region, today in northern Serbia, deserters relied on the support of so-called *perjanci*, children sporting green caps with long white feathers who signaled danger by whistling and other means.[120] Women played a crucial role in supporting the fugitives, providing their sons, brothers, and husbands with food and shelter. A clear gender divide between armed male soldiers-cum-deserters and unarmed women tending the home fires mostly held up, but there were exceptions. Deserters sometimes avoided capture by dressing as women, as in the Bačka region of northern Serbia, where they worked the fields in drag.[121] There were also instances in Moravia when a surprise house search by gendarmes forced deserters to take to bed in women's nightclothes, pretending to be an elderly, infirm mother or grandmother.[122] And in at least a couple Croatian locales, women joined the Green Cadres. Officials reporting on deserter bands in the Petrova Gora region remarked disappointedly that "local women dressed in military clothes" were among them.[123] Ljubica Lalić, described by authorities as a tall, dark woman carrying a pistol, accompanied her deserter husband Stevo Lalić and several others dressed in military uniforms in the summer of 1918 as they carried out armed robberies in western Slavonia.[124]

Smallholders who found their livelihoods devastated by the war made up the most important social stratum of support and recruits for the Green Cadres. Struggling and embittered, peasants possessing just a few hectares of land still had enough food and land to support relatives and friends who deserted.[125] By contrast, the Hungarian plains—dominated by large latifundia and cultivated by a numerous agricultural proletariat—produced very few Green Cadres. In fertile eastern Slavonia, meanwhile, large-estate production had not yet eliminated villages of smallholders with traditional strip plots. The dense forests and hilly terrain of non-Magyar Hungary (including Croatia-Slavonia and Slovakia) provided much better cover for deserters than the wide expanses of the Pannonian Plain. Incomes varied significantly within the category of smallholding peasants—for instance, between impoverished Galicia and relatively prosperous Moravia—but Green Cadres seldom formed among the prosperous, market-oriented farmers of the Alpine lands and parts of Bohemia. Too much privation also mitigated against the formation of armed deserter bands: relatively few appeared in arid and hungry Dalmatia.

The desperate situation that smallholders felt themselves to be in by the last year of the war accelerated desertion and the formation of Green Cadres. Like František Sedláček, peasant deserters felt compelled to stay home and help their wives, children, and elderly relatives instead of returning to the front. Augustín Nuhál in the Váh River valley and Alfonz Šarh in the Pohorje highlands both took regular breaks from leading their respective deserter squads to help with fieldwork at home, particularly during harvest time. "Our lads" from the Green Cadres, wrote the village chronicler in Moravian Malá Vrbka, cut grass in the meadows, prepared hay for drying, and helped with all manner of other work, going out of their way to help women whose menfolk were still at the front or in internment.[126] Authorities in Croatia-Slavonia tried to draw an impossible distinction between the bulk of deserters, who, happy to have escaped the war, tilled their fields peacefully, "living their former peasant lives," and the *zeleni kader*, or "militarily armed deserters [who] hold up in forests and ready themselves for all manner of mischief, threatening lives and property, committing crimes, and in no way distinguishing themselves from mere bandits."[127] In reality, the tranquil peasant deserters helping their families on their home fields often doubled as armed, forest-based fugitives. Nonetheless, the dichotomy that existed in the authorities' minds sometimes proved useful when captured deserters had to defend their actions. Accused of theft, Obrad Panić of the Twenty-Sixth Croatian Home Guard Regiment alleged that he had absconded from a military hospital with the sole intent of helping his wife and child plow their meager three hectares of land in eastern Slavonia.[128] Murder suspects Dimitar Čavić and Mihajlo Repak insisted that they were at home in the southern Banovina working on their fields for the entirety of their absence from the Ninety-Sixth Infantry Regiment, never venturing into the forests or participating in any skullduggery there.[129] They were acquitted for lack of evidence.

If rural deserters were often motivated to help their struggling families, this does not mean that there were not opportunities to live the "free life" that military authorities dismissively concluded was the essence of the "so-called

Green Cadre." Poaching game, drinking, and sleeping under the stars were pleasant ways to while away the rest of the war. Jozef Ferančík recalled the thrill of camping with his companion Nuhál and copious amounts of wine in an abandoned shepherd's hut: "A fire burned about two meters high, from which thick sparks flew to the roof, but didn't catch. We cavorted around the fire, we ate, drank, washed, baked, cooked, and there was a real feast."[130] Ferančík, a self-taught poet, wrote no fewer than nineteen poems while living as a deserter in the vicinity of his home village.[131] Most of his unsophisticated verses celebrated his and his comrades' pluck for spurning the war and embracing the liberty of Slovakia's wide-open spaces. The concluding stanzas of his "In the Green Cadre" taunted the hapless authorities from his group's highland lair and offered a nationalist rhapsody about his native land:

> Well, they're not coming for us, they wouldn't dare,
> They're afraid! They won't come! They lack courage!
> And if they would, we'll shorten their way
> We'll prepare for them here—a fanged bride.
>
> Mountains, our mountains! Your strength embraces us!
> You are our hope, you our great power,
> The enemy runs in vain, hither and thither,
> Never will he conquer these Slovak mountains![132]

The remarkable density of taverns in the Czech countryside proved too great a temptation for some deserters. In late summer 1918, they emerged from the forests to attend village dance parties, taking care to return to their sylvan hideouts by dawn.[133] Such hijinks eluded the authorities, though the innkeeper in the village of Hartvíkovice near Třebíč reported that at one point during a September fête, the musicians suspiciously played a "solo for the greens."[134] Around the same time, armed Polish deserters threw a house party in the small Galician village of Smolarzyny, located in Łańcut district, boisterously firing their rifles in the air to provoke the authorities. The gendarmes turned up around midnight, just as the revelers had run out of ammunition, forcing them to beat a hasty retreat to the forests.[135]

The mischievousness of the green deserters reflected peasants' traditionally schizophrenic attitude toward higher authority, admiring and deferential on the one hand, mocking and disrespectful on the other. They playfully invoked King-Emperor Karl I and Queen-Empress Zita of Bourbon-Parma as their protectors, even coconspirators, knowing full well that they had violated their personal oath to the sovereign as supreme commander of the Habsburg armed forces. In Syrmia, the local cadres, or *komitas* (rebels) as they were frequently called, sang "Long live our queen Zita, who doesn't allow anyone to shoot the *komitas*."[136] Deserters in the southern Slavonian village of Vrbanja had a somewhat more detailed version:

Emperor Karl and empress Zita,
You make war, and you have no grain [*žita*].
God protect this queen Zita,
She will not kill the *komitas*.
Oh, *komitas*, do not fear Zita,
Even Karl has become a *komita*.[137]

Such songs riffed on the age-old myth of the benevolent sovereign, or the monarch who would surely stand up for his oppressed peasant subjects if only he were aware of the abuses perpetrated in his name by local grandees, recruiting him for the peasant movement itself. Not all deserter ditties treated the imperial house so gently. On the Dalmatian island of Korčula, a popular couplet ran: "Emperor Karl, I fuck your sweetheart / You made me to enlist."[138] Zita was a popular subject in illicit verse in part because, by 1918, rumors had spread far and wide that she was trying to undermine the monarchy.[139] This was a rather uncharitable reading of her role in the so-called Sixtus Affair, when Karl tried to negotiate a separate peace with the French through his brother-in-law, Prince Sixtus of Bourbon-Parma, an officer in the Belgian army. The 1917 negotiations with Zita's brother led nowhere, not least because France's Italian ally considered any peace with Austria-Hungary without major territorial revisions a nonstarter. But they landed Karl and the monarchy in an awkward position when the French press published details of the talks in spring 1918, including Karl's allegedly accommodating stance toward French designs on Alsace-Lorraine. These revelations forced the Habsburg monarch to mollify his principal ally. On May 12 in Spa, Belgium, he humiliatingly agreed to the complete subordination of Austria-Hungary's war effort to Germany.

More sinister invocations of Karl and Zita appeared in threatening and extortionate letters sent by Green Cadres to local officials as well as to Jewish shopkeepers, wealthy farmers, or anyone who did not appear to stand on the side of smallholding peasants. "There are a million of us . . . , we have more munitions than Karl and military materiel," read one shrilly anti-Semitic letter sent to shopkeeper Albert Weiss in Virje, a village in central Croatia.[140] In nearby Đurđevac, Doctor Lichtenberger received a letter that began in an ironically warm tone: "Greetings from the Green Cadre with a salutation from your good friends."[141] The addressee was exhorted "in the first instance" to bring two hundred thousand forints, fifty kilograms of bacon, and a hundred loaves of bread to a specified location between Virje and Novigrad on July 14, on pains of having his house and family destroyed. The letter went on to blame Jews for people's suffering and put the strength of the green forces (somewhat more realistically) at one hundred thousand. A couple of weeks later, in early August 1918, shots were fired at night through the sleeping Weiss's windows while Albert Pollak, another Jewish shopkeeper in Virje, had his windows smashed with rocks. At the end of the month, in the nearby hamlet of Donji Mosti, a placard signed by the Green Cadre of (distant) Petrova Gora was affixed to the wall of a tavern, severely warning anyone who would molest the "Zita Army."[142] Enemies of the Zita Army would be crucified upside down in front of their houses, which would be torched, and suffer the complete annihilation of their families. The Zita Army would dispense such punishment monthly until the approaching Green Cadre army reached the district. Offenders might save themselves with protection payments of a thousand crowns. "Peasants," on the other hand, "have nothing to fear from this army because it is working for their benefit." The extreme violence threatened in the placard, recalling the martyrdom of Saint Peter, evoked the mental universe of popular Christianity inhabited by rural rebels, along with its tropes of suffering, martyrdom, and redemption. Imagining their ability to mete out biblical punishment, peasant deserters likely affirmed their own sense of righteousness.

With the end of the war approaching, the desire to punish those guilty of oppressing the peasantry was sometimes acted upon. In early October 1918, six heavily armed deserters forced their way into the home of Tanasije Predojević, one of the largest landowners in the vicinity of Novska in western Slavonia, demanding food and drink. After consuming ten liters of wine and two liters of spirits (*rakija*), they robbed Predojević of four thousand crowns and attempted, in the early hours of the morning, to plunder the treasury of the Serb Agricultural Cooperative, whose operations had ceased in 1914. The deserters found their way to the house of Predojević's friend, the estate-owning local administrator Dragutin Agić, who was allegedly in possession of the Cooperative cash box keys. Having hauled Agić out of hiding, the attackers robbed and beat him, abusing him with shouts that he had "swindled the poor, and withheld support [for them]." They also demanded to know why he was not at the front. The deserters piled up everything of value they could find, informing him grandiosely that they were "komitas," or armed rebels, with between four and five thousand confederates among the "Serbs, *Šokci* [Croats from Slavonia, Baranja, Syrmia, and western Bačka], and Turks [Bosniaks]." Then, "their commander" shot Agić dead.[143]

As the Green Cadres grew in strength, it became clear that they saw themselves as guardians of the peasantry, not just of their families. In the south Slav lands, they attempted to stop state requisitions of produce and livestock from smallholders. In May 1918, leaflets found in the barracks in Osijek, the Slavonian capital, called on soldiers to tolerate no further requisitions, urging them to fight for the redistribution of land.[144] In early June, deserters in the forests between Bjelovar and Đurđevac agitated among villagers against a scheduled upcoming requisition of cattle. Peasants proved receptive because, in the words of the Đurđevac district captain, livestock is the peasant's "most sensitive point," with which he is less likely to part than money or even his blood on the battlefield.[145] Around the same time it was reported in Zemun district that an armed deserter had strolled nonchalantly into the village of Pećinci and accosted the notary with the words: "Don't be like some other notaries because we'll kill you if you bother with requisitions"; after issuing a similar warning in Sibač, he walked back toward the forest softly singing a "rebel song."[146] By autumn, forest-based deserters had halted requisitions in a number of places by intimidating authorities and any peasants who may have been willing to comply. In mid-October, the Bjelovar-Križevci county prefect alleged that Green Cadres had made any further requisitions of grain or cattle impossible by threatening the authorities and compliant peasants with arson and murder.[147] Soon after the killing of Agić in Novska, three armed deserters intercepted villagers driving their cattle into town as ordered by the local military commission and forced them to return home. Local authorities complained, "the Green Cadre is little by little becoming the top authority in all matters."[148]

Elsewhere, the deserter movement lacked the strength to confront state officials so brazenly. But peasant livelihoods could be defended with smaller-scale action as well. In western Slovakia, Jozef Ferančík's contingent seized an entire cartload of vegetables from the local landowner's garden to help a poor woman who had nothing to feed her child or her cow. A Green Cadre group in the Buchlov Forest in Moravia resolved to punish a strict head forester named Pelikán, who had become the scourge of village women visiting the woods to gather firewood illegally. Disguised in wide skirts and short coats, the deserters set about collecting firewood until Pelikán arrived and began verbally abusing them. They fell upon him, stripped him naked, and tied him to a tree beside a large anthill; eventually freed by his own dog, who chewed through the bonds, the chastened Pelikán thenceforth turned a blind eye to all firewood infractions.[149] With similar dangers facings its own employees on a daily basis, the forestry department in Croatia-Slavonia decided to suspend its work in early autumn 1918.[150]

In mid-1918, anti-Habsburg nationalist leaders had high hopes that the Green Cadres might help liberate their peoples from Habsburg tyranny. Moravian Czech officers in the conspiratorial Brno-based Zádruha society, for instance, saw much subversive potential in the movement of former Austro-Hungarian soldiers. From spring 1918, they issued furloughs indiscriminately to their men, aiming to thus encourage further desertions.[151] One of the Zádruha officers, Richard Sicha, coordinated an operation to arm the *zelený kádr*: two machine guns were hurled from a moving train at a designated spot near the Ždánice Forest. The Maffie organization in Prague, the secret domestic arm of Tomáš Masaryk and Edvard Beneš's émigré movement for Czechoslovak independence, also tried to win the green deserters for their cause. In August 1918, they entrusted military preparations for a national revolution against Habsburg rule to Major Jaroslav Rošický, who drew up a seven-point action program. Point four was "to organize the so-called 'Green cadres', at that time forming in Moravian Slovácko and in southern Bohemia, which were composed of military deserters from replacement regiments and from the field. These soldiers, armed and partially organized among themselves, would need leadership and financial support. Both [of these tasks] would be our responsibility."[152] Point four was never fulfilled, however. Rošický himself was intensely interested in the Green Cadres and wanted to see to the task himself. Some men from his regiment, whom he knew personally and valued as reliable and nationally conscious Czech soldiers, had deserted to the Cadres. But other tasks distracted him in the final months of the war, and the travel limitations imposed on military personnel kept him from making his planned journey to southeast Moravia.[153]

Attempts by Yugoslav activists to coopt the deserters in the south Slav territories likewise came to naught. In spring and summer 1918, south Slav prisoners of war in Italy, along with officers who had deserted to the enemy, gave stirring accounts to nationalist leaders in exile about the extent of the deserter movement.[154] In July, the famous Slovenian turncoat Ljudevit Pivko, who deserted to the Italians to fight against the Habsburg army, dispatched a Croatian infantryman to bring a message to Green Cadres in Croatia. He was to cross the front lines by pretending to be an escapee from Italian internment, while carrying a coded message hidden in a prayer book.[155] There is no evidence of the success of the mission. In August 1918, two Dalmatian Serb activists representing a clandestine Yugoslav Revolutionary Committee in Zagreb crossed the southern frontier, reaching the Serbian government-in-exile's interior ministry in Korçë, Albania. Among other things, they requested arms and munitions for the "green guard" in the hinterland, which the committee regarded as a "popular reserve army," though the Serbian government remained skeptical.[156] The following month, the Croatian exile leader Ante Trumbić drew up plans for an Entente maritime strike against Austria-Hungary from the Adriatic, in which the 150,000-strong Green Cadres would attack in the rear.[157] Shortly before Habsburg authority collapsed, Trumbić received a report from a confidante in Croatia-Slavonia about preparations then underway for the transition to a new south Slav government, along with the assurance that the *zeleni kader* would submit to its authority.[158] Events of the following weeks would expose the naiveté of such plans.

The green deserters had, by and large, organized themselves with specifically peasant grievances and goals in mind. Like anti-Habsburg nationalist leaders, they often yearned for the liberation of their national homelands from dynastic rule, and especially from wartime administration, but, as we will see, they imagined a distinctly rural process of emancipation and more radical outcomes than those countenanced by men like Sicha and Trumbić. This prevented the Green Cadres from playing a more central role in the national revolutions of 1918 in east central Europe and consigned them to the margins of official national memory cultures. Liberal nationalists and monarchist conservatives were not the only ones who misread the revolutionary ferment of the central and east European countryside late in the First World War. So too did the Bolsheviks in the former Russian Empire, even if it was commonly assumed that they inspired, or even steered, the deserter bands in Austria-Hungary.

Peasant support for the Bolshevik regime was initially extensive. Lenin's Decree on Land, issued at the Congress of Soviets on October 26, 1917, convinced villagers that the new regime was on their side: local land committees and soviets established over the preceding months were ordered to take control of "the landed estates, as also all crown, monastery and church lands, with all their livestock, implements, buildings and everything pertaining thereto." The second part of the decree, the Peasant Mandate on Land, proclaimed that "private ownership of land shall be abolished forever; land shall not be purchased, sold, leased, mortgaged or otherwise alienated," and furthermore that all land would "become property of the whole people, and shall pass into the use of those who cultivate it."[159] For Russian peasants accustomed to communal land ownership, and who in the months since February had on their own initiative seized much estate land, parceling it up among themselves, this was a ringing endorsement of their actions. When Lenin and the Bolsheviks decided at the start of 1918 to dissolve the newly elected Constituent Assembly, which was to decide how to administer the land now under villagers' control, peasants shrugged it off, convinced that the government had their best interests in mind.

Yet resistance to the Bolsheviks grew over the course of 1918 as conscription, production quotas, and requisitions were all reintroduced. Peasants began to desert in droves from the Red Army. To consolidate state power in the countryside, Lenin's government invested Village Committees of the Poor—often comprising outsiders and nonpeasants—with dictatorial powers, including the right to requisition, further alienating the smallholding majority. In spring 1919, at the height of the civil war between Reds and Whites, "green" deserters mustered in forested areas across European Russia and the Ukraine. The peripatetic revolutionary Victor Serge recalled about that year that:

> a most mischievous movement had grown up inside the armies engaged in the Civil War, White, Red, and the rest: that of the Greens. These borrowed their title from the forests in which they took refuge, uniting deserters from all the armies that were now unwilling to fight for anyone, whether Generals or Commissars: these would fight now only for themselves, simply to stay out of the civil war. The movement existed over the whole of Russia. We knew that in the forests of the Pskov region, the Greens' effective forces were on the increase, numbering several tens of thousands. Well organized, complete with their own general staff, and supported by the peasants, they were eating the Red Army away.[160]

Fantasies about green general staffs followed the patterns of hyperbolic rumor in central Europe. As in the lands to the west, the Russian greens had no central leadership or obvious program besides defense against encroachments on peasant livelihoods. To "go to the greens" (*uiti v zelenye*) was a form of rebellion focused on peasant soldiers' home districts, outwardly devoid of any broader political commitment.[161] In June 1919, one Cheka patrol reported: "The character of the uprising is still unclear. There is evidence of some organization among the insurgents, who are well-armed with rifles and even possess a machine gun."[162] Because of the general breakdown of state power in much of Russia outside its cities in summer 1919, the green movement briefly reached immense proportions; official Communist sources estimated there were fifty thousand of them in Tver province alone. But by the autumn of 1919, in the face of fresh Red Army offensives, the self-proclaimed greens had all but disappeared.

Nonetheless, the grievances that fueled the 1919 uprising in the Russian countryside did not go away. They sustained the peasant armies that supported individual warlords (atamans) in the Ukraine. Here, in a context of complete state collapse, the convergence of dire food shortages, ethnic-nationalist autonomism, and peasant social revolutionism created a particularly lethal brew, as discussed in the next chapter. The charismatic peasant anarchist Nestor Makhno commanded the most effective force, based in the villages of left-bank Ukraine. Initially allied with the Reds against the White invasion of the Ukraine, Makhno's fighters then opposed the Communist disciplining of the countryside. Although often labelled "green" by his opponents, Makhno evidently did not use it himself. Nor did the rebellion in Tambov province in 1920–21, which nonetheless bore all the hallmarks of the "green" uprisings. Under the command of the seasoned revolutionary Alexandr Antonov, a peasant force assembled from Red Army deserters that, at its height, numbered over twenty thousand men in sixteen regiments. The insurgency relied on the support of hundreds of village-based peasant unions. In addition to providing food and intelligence to the rebel army, these had clear demands: removal of the Communist Party from power and the return of the Constituent Assembly as the basis of state authority.[163] As elsewhere, the memberships of these anti-Communist village organizations were nearly identical with the revolutionary soviets of 1917. Perhaps because peasant forces drew support from so many former enthusiasts for the revolution (unlike the Whites), and because their fighters could move so seamlessly between the Red Army and deserter detachments, Lenin remarked in March 1921 that they were "more dangerous than [White generals] Denikin, Iudenich, and Kolchak combined."[164] In response to the danger, the Soviet regime abolished forced requisitions and centrally defined production targets, opening the road to the New Economic Policy (NEP) that would define its relationship with the countryside for much of the remainder of the decade. With peasants' primary objections ostensibly addressed, Antonov's partisan army lost much of its support, and Antonov himself was murdered by undercover Soviet agents in summer 1921.

The peasant forces that arose during the Russian Civil War were stronger than anything in Austria-Hungary in 1918. Their relative might was a function of the enormity of Russian and Ukrainian territories, the relatively low density of transportation and communication networks in the lands of the former Tsarist Empire, and the much more spectacular collapse of state authority outside of the major cities there. In neither context could the green forces coordinate themselves beyond individual regions, however. Although the Tambov rebellion was remarkably well organized within the province itself, Antonov had no meaningful contact with other similar insurgent forces. In late spring 1921, his dwindling followers believed fantastical rumors that Makhno was coming to relieve them. It is telling that the Soviet agents who killed Antonov posed as envoys from a spurious pan-Russian rebel conference. Rooted in local village communities, peasant deserters across central and eastern Europe struggled to form a broader front. But despite their limitations, they succeeded in bringing down several belligerent powers from within. In 1917, Russian peasants' departure from the front in the hundreds of thousands sealed the fate of the Provisional Government. In Bulgaria in September 1918, a mutiny of peasant soldiers at Radomir forced the abdication of King Ferdinand and prepared the ground for the peasant leader Aleksandar Stamboliiski to form a government in early 1919. And in Austria-Hungary in autumn 1918, the Green Cadres undermined imperial authorities across large areas of the hinterland.

At the end of the First World War, curtains closed on over six centuries of Habsburg rule in central Europe. The western Allies issued the death sentence on the ancient monarchy after Austria-Hungary prostrated itself before its German ally; ideas about a separate peace that might preserve the Danubian state lost all validity. Wilson's fourteen points in January 1918 had demanded only an independent Polish state, but by the summer of that year France, Britain, and the United States granted official recognition to the émigré government of "Czechoslovaks" and dangled similar support to the "Yugoslavs." With no traditions of political unity, these aspiring composite nations still existed on paper only. Emperor Karl's October 16 last-ditch proposal to federalize the empire into autonomous units held together by a personal union came much too late. The emperor's manifesto was unacceptable to the fledgling national governments largely because it left the Kingdom of Hungary intact, effectively stranding most of the Habsburg south Slavs and the Slovaks. The empire's disintegration began shortly thereafter.

The role of the Green Cadres in the next act was, for the moment, uncertain. What was clear was the extent to which armed and organized peasant deserters were getting the upper hand in large portions of the rural hinterland. They were robbing trains in Syrmia, near Rzeszów in Polish Galicia, and in southeast

Moravia.[165] Special precautions had to be taken for Emperor Karl's rail journey in May 1918 through south Slavic territories to visit allied sovereigns in Sofia and Istanbul.[166] In the Syrmian districts of Ruma, Zemun, and Mitrovica near their stronghold in Fruška Gora, the Green Cadres had created "a state of affairs resembling that of Russia when the state government began to quake," according to one local official, who had conversed with returnees about conditions in the east.[167] Deserters there were responsible for numerous cases of theft, armed robbery, and extortion, along with murder and rape. Starting in February 1918, the authorities declared martial law in many south Slavic districts, but with little effect. In the central Croatian district of Daruvar, Green Cadres felt confident enough to issue written orders to soldiers stationed in the area to leave their units and enlist in the deserters' ranks.[168] Seven entire infantry divisions amounting to forty-one thousand troops had been deployed in the hinterland to stanch the flow of deserters from the army.[169] They were simply not up the task and, it seems, sometimes joined the rebels instead of arresting them.

Armed and increasingly well organized, the green forces readied themselves—but for what? Some, like Andrej Zlobec in the Trnovo Forest, regarded them as the armies-in-waiting of newly liberated nation-states. "The Green Cadres of all lands, which had for long centuries survived under the wings of that [Habsburg] eagle, were preparing the ground for a new era," he wrote.[170] For others, the deserter units could only midwife a new epoch through violent revolution. At the end of September 1918 in the central Croatian village of Gračenica, a woman named Kata Gnilšek asked her friend Anka Sokol, servant of the local district captain, "How can you serve here? If you knew what I know you wouldn't want to, for a revolution is coming and it will slaughter all the gentlemen."[171] Subsequently detained and interrogated, Gnilšek related how eight days prior, deserters had come to her house to recruit her husband, then still serving in the army, for a general uprising led by the Petrova Gora Green Cadres. Kata, though fearing for her friend, took heart from their assurance that "peasants have nothing to fear because the revolution will be raised against the gentlemen." As a new era beckoned, the secret armies of peasant deserters were poised to emerge from the forests where they lay hidden. The diverse impulses incubating among them, from heterodox nationalism to local self-determination to thirst for retribution against rural oppressors, would fuse in various ways and lead them in a number of directions in the months and years that followed.

3

Revenge

IN AUTUMN 1918, groups of nationalist leaders established new, or reborn, independent nation-states atop of the rubble of Austria-Hungary. On October 28, the Czechoslovak Republic was founded amid jubilant scenes in Prague. The following day in Zagreb, south Slav representatives from various Habsburg territories proclaimed the State of Slovenes, Croats, and Serbs; a country that would last just over one month before its incorporation into the Kingdom of Serbs, Croats, and Slovenes—known colloquially as Yugoslavia. Already on October 7, a Polish Regency Council had declared Polish independence, although the settling of resurrected Poland's boundaries after 123 years of partition took much longer. On October 30, Polish forces assumed control of Cracow, the principal city of western Galicia, and on November 11, Marshal Józef Piłsudski entered Warsaw in triumph. Three years of war with neighboring countries ensued. On October 31, open revolution erupted in Budapest after a week of street protests, leading the next day to the establishment of independent Hungary; it officially became a republic on November 16. German parliamentary deputies in Vienna had already on October 21 declared themselves to be the government of all Germans in Austria. Following the last Habsburg emperor Karl's abdication on November 9, the Republic of German Austria was proclaimed on November 12.

As these urban "national revolutions" unfolded, much of the rural hinterland of the former empire descended into bloody anarchy. Peasants turned on their putative oppressors throughout the erstwhile Kingdom of Hungary, where the limited franchise had excluded them from electoral politics, and from nonviolent forms of conflict resolution. The bloodshed did not spare the Austrian half of the empire either, in particular impoverished and war-ravaged Galicia. In explaining these rural convulsions, the evaporation of state authority was a necessary though not a sufficient condition. Without a doubt, prolonged periods of statelessness and continuing warfare, or the looming threat of war, intensified rural violence, as was evident in parts of reborn Poland, and even more so in the lands of the former Romanov Empire during the Russian Civil War. Yet the upheavals had a clear and vengeful logic of their own.

In many villages and towns, the end of Habsburg rule ushered in a frightful time for their nonpeasant inhabitants. The experience of Károly Erdélyi, a Hungarian Catholic priest in the small Slavonian market town of Donji Miholjac, exemplified the trauma of those who became targets of peasant fury. In early October, rumors began to spread that the Green Cadres would soon leave the forests and go on the attack, though the exact date was not known. "The peasants were not afraid," Erdélyi recorded in the parish chronicle, "because it naturally did not concern them, but rather the gentlemen and the Jews. The people responded with mockery to the district captain's call to form a citizen militia for defense [of Donji Miholjac]: 'Let the gentlemen defend themselves as well as they can, we will not defend them.'"[1] On Sunday October 27, news reached Donji Miholjac, located on the Drava floodplain, that the deserters were laying waste to Orahovica, some twenty-five miles to the south in the foothills of the Papuk and Krndija Mountains. Any day now they would be in Donji Miholjac. Crowds of people milled around in anticipation, while local notables stayed behind locked doors. The count and countess, recently arrived from Budapest, were jeered as they returned home by carriage from the train station. As their confessor, Erdélyi advised them to leave Miholjac as soon as possible. Despite the countess's valiant resolve not to flee, they departed for Hungary with their most valuable possessions the next morning.

It was a gloomy and misty late afternoon on Tuesday, October 29, when the chaplain brought news that the Green Cadres had arrived and begun looting. Erdélyi held evening mass for a few parishioners. As he made his way back to the presbytery, he saw one of the armed deserters calling on villagers to join in the plunder. Local Jewish families had already fled across the Drava River to Siklós in Hungary. After dinner, the priest's household staff abandoned him; the cook and maid took refuge with acquaintances, while the sexton and coachman joined the looters. Alone and filled with trepidation, Erdélyi listened to the growing din outside. At one point a rampaging soldier smashed some of the presbytery windows and shouted threats inside, prompting the clergyman to hide in the storehouse. From there he could watch the infernal scene, well lit by the high flames consuming a shop owned by a Jewish family named Reich. Toward dawn he heard more of his windows breaking as a hoarse voice bellowed, "Now we're going to haul out that Magyar priest!"[2] The mob proceeded to rob and destroy his quarters. All his shoes and garments were taken, even his priestly garb; most everything else was damaged beyond repair. Erdélyi found sanctuary with friends for ten days until the attacks had subsided and his lodgings were repaired.

In his view, the people had disgraced themselves most when they sacked the manor house. "Even the most respectable citizens" had participated in plundering livestock, grain, carts, and the manor's extensive stores of wine and spirits. Some later regretted their actions and sought atonement, "but at that time, under the influence of the masses, they did not think about God or their honor."[3] Many at the time would concur with Erdélyi's verdict on the suggestibility of the masses, even if they did not share his religious framing of events. Dangerous agitators had capitalized on a situation in which the old laws and their enforcers no longer held sway. Even respectable citizens were swept up in irrational mob attacks on Jews, manor houses, officials, and priests. Evidence for this view was not limited to rural spaces; urban pogroms sharing many of the same characteristics as the unrest in Donji Miholjac proliferated, for instance in Galicia in autumn 1918 and spring 1919.[4]

But many, if not most, spasms of popular violence at this time possessed a distinctly peasant character. They overlapped with anti-Jewish aggression and other forms of ethnic antagonism where these things fused with, and amplified, social grievances against the manorial economy or seemingly exploitative towns and cities. Peasant violence was rarely about just anti-Semitism or nationalism, however. The desire to avenge wrongs inflicted on peasant villagers was often at the forefront of perpetrators' minds, though violence that started with social motives could assume primarily ethnic coloring and vice versa. Nor could material privation account for the theatrical, vindictive, and often wasteful course of attacks. Flush with the confidence of returning soldiers and deserters, embittered after four years of hardship and humiliation, entire villages rose in anger across east central Europe. The Slovak novelist Milo Urban described in *The Living Whip* how his humble protagonists make sense of the violent plundering they commit in November 1918: "Perhaps the strongest feeling that reigned that day in Ráztoky was pride, a consciousness of strength, that they had not shrunk away before the army, before the nobility, before whom they had trembled for so many years. And they came alive mightily, they stood up after so many years of cowering. . . . 'We are not so weak as it had seemed, after all,' they thought to themselves, 'look, we can even kill.'"[5]

The causes of the violence were both old and new. Peasants nursed centuries-old grievances against the grandees of the manorial economy: noble landlords along with their deputies who, down to 1918, enforced their privileges and extracted rents in cash and kind from the peasantry. Serfdom had been abolished in the Habsburg domains during the 1848 revolutions and somewhat later in Russia (1861) and Romania (1864). In Habsburg central Europe, emancipated peasants assumed legal title of the land they cultivated, allowing them to buy and sell land as they pleased. Most importantly, the end of serfdom marked the end of compulsory labor services on estate land, the so-called *robot* (derived from *robota,* a Slavic word for "work," used in contemporary Polish and Slovak). Yet the lot of the peasantry did not everywhere improve. Lacking capital and expertise and now obliged to pay taxes, many peasants fell quickly into crippling debt. They mortgaged their shrinking properties to obtain new loans, but often fell behind on payments; distraints and foreclosures soared.

Population increases in the second half of the nineteenth century, along with the division of farms into ever-smaller plots among multiple inheriting children, exacerbated rural poverty and indebtedness. In 1850, the average farm size in Galicia was around 8 hectares, but by the turn of the twentieth century over 80 percent of farms were less than 2 hectares in size.[6] Similarly, in central Croatia, the land survey of 1895 revealed that the proportion of holdings under 2.8 hectares in size had increased from two-thirds of the total at mid-century to 85 percent, while those possessing a meager 1.5 hectares or less had risen from just over a third of holdings to 56 percent.[7] Many peasants were forced to sell their unviable holdings and return to the local estate to earn a living as wage laborers. Added to this humiliation were the considerable privileges that landlords retained, such as the sole right to own weapons and hunt in the forests. In Galicia, they maintained a monopoly on alcohol distillation down to 1910. In both Galicia and the Kingdom of Hungary, the state compensated landowners for land that after 1848 passed into the possession of former serfs. Elsewhere in the Habsburg dominions, peasants shouldered this burden themselves, though compensation payments were generally manageable, and certainly less oppressive than in the Russian Empire.[8] The end of feudalism also meant the end of common forests and pastureland, which either passed to landlords as recompense for lost arable land or were divided between the estate and local villages in ratios that the peasantry viewed as deeply unfair.[9] Among the most common infractions reported in the post-emancipation countryside were illegal firewood collection and poaching.

The end of feudalism and the subsequent halting spread of capitalism in rural east central Europe generated resentments, decades-old by 1918, against the perceived beneficiaries and enforcers of the new order. Public administration had grown during the eighteenth-century era of "enlightened despotism," but its expansion accelerated after the revolutions of 1848.[10] The post-emancipation officialdom oversaw universal male conscription, compulsory schooling, tax collection based on land surveys, the orderly purchase and sale of property, and more besides. Such officials wielded considerable new power at the local level, and their salaries were largely financed by onerous taxes on the peasantry.[11] To many villagers, the most visible beneficiaries of the uncertain post-feudal world were shopkeepers and merchants, of whom a significant number doubled as money lenders, and who were often Jewish. In Galicia, an important region of continuous Jewish settlement for centuries, deeply rooted folk prejudices, some attributing supernatural and malevolent powers to Jews, aggravated popular resentment of those who appeared to profit from peasant suffering in the wake of emancipation.[12] In the Kingdom of Hungary, the Jewish presence in rural areas dated from the eighteenth century in places like Slovakia, but was rather more recent elsewhere. In 1918, Jewish families in Croatia-Slavonia had resided in places like Donji Miholjac for no more than a couple generations.[13] Nonetheless, peasants everywhere reproached Jewish tavern keepers and merchants for usurious moneylending and congenital miserliness. For their part, Jews in small towns and villages practiced the trades to which they had been confined prior to their emancipation. Premodern bans on Jewish ownership of farmland (beyond what was necessary for keeping a garden or raising livestock) meant that there were very few Jewish cultivators, further heightening their foreignness in Christian peasant eyes.

The First World War, as we have seen, sharpened such resentments. Loss of faith in the Habsburg dynasty harshened preexisting animosities toward officials, who now assumed dictatorial powers over requisitions and furloughs. In many places, the gendarmerie appeared as the scourge of humble peasants. Shopkeepers and merchants dealing in scarce essential goods gained reputations as merciless profiteers. A flourishing wartime black market tempted more than a few of them to sell their wares only at exorbitant prices, while an entire stratum of unscrupulous "chain traders" emerged to meet mostly urban demand for foodstuffs, fuel, and household items. Jews were widely thought to have gained the most from these unhappy circumstances, just as it was commonly believed that they had somehow been exempted from serving at the fronts. As a corollary of this misperception, many peasants were convinced that the towns, where most Jews lived, had suffered less during the war, while the villages had to quarter troops and surrender their produce to officials.

Towns, with their conspicuous population of merchants and officials, became objects not just of peasant suspicion but of their hatred.

The searing pain of injustice, inflicted by wounds both long-festering and fresh, ignited peasant rage in 1918. As villagers took their revenge, they often enacted ritualized scripts familiar from previous explosions of peasant anger stretching back to the Middle Ages. What distinguished the 1918 violence from earlier conflagrations was the prominence, if not always direct leadership, of paramilitary "green" forces. The movement of Austro-Hungarian army deserters led, encouraged, inspired, and provided vague legitimation for countless acts of peasant violence in the centers of rural unrest: Croatia-Slavonia, western Slovakia, and western Galicia. The role of armed deserters in the violence in these regions showed the extent to which the central and east European countryside had been militarized since the introduction of universal conscription, but particularly over the preceding four years of total war. Soldiers who had not deserted and were just returning from the fronts to their home villages, or leaving their hinterland garrisons, initiated most of the remainder of the disturbances. While they sometimes acted in concert with the green forces, in many places they proceeded alone, and they were usually the sole perpetrators in the non-Slavic rural areas of empire that experienced upheavals: the Magyar heartland of Hungary and Transylvania with its mostly Romanian peasantry.[14] Similar patterns can be detected in the peasant unrest that shook parts of the former Russian Empire. As likely never before, ordinary people across the territories of the former dynastic empires put their faith in armed, uniformed solutions to pressing social and political problems.[15]

The fledgling governments of east central Europe recognized that the Green Cadres could pose a serious threat to public order if they were not swiftly brought to heel. In Moravia, Czechoslovak authorities wagered that an encouraging call in a progovernmental newspaper might suffice. "Czech soldiers, deserters of the Green Cadres," one published announcement read, "report immediately to your respective supplementary commands. Give your strength willingly to serve the national army. Every individual is needed for the holy national cause. Do not tarry! To work!"[16] As we will see, such patriotic appeals persuaded many Czechs, but the deserter movement in the south Slav lands was far more menacing. On October 28, the day before the Croatian Sabor in Zagreb severed all ties with the Kingdom of Hungary, in effect dissolving itself, the National Council of Slovenes, Croats, and Serbs issued a pronouncement to "all soldiers of the so-called green cadre on the territory of Croatia [who] are absolved from their military oath and are summoned to honor their human and national duties and return immediately home, or to their regular business, so they too with their honorable work will assist in first putting in order our free Croatian state, and then the unified independent state of all Croats, Serbs, and Slovenes."[17] The public statement, which appeared in local variations (figure 3.1 shows an example from Varaždin), also called upon deserters to voluntarily join units of national defense organized by local National Council committees. Military and civilian authorities were warned against disturbing the Green Cadres in their return to a dignified and peaceful life. Such a benevolent approach did not sit well with all members of the council. The assembly president, Bogdan Medaković, protested on October 29 that "these are not just thieves and arsonists, bandits and murderers, they are already enemies of their own people. We therefore need to eradicate this plague."[18] A sterner declaration issued that same day, and signed by the National Council's executive, urged men in uniform "not to destroy, not to burn, not to kill, because you will destroy and burn property that belongs to you, soldiers!"[19]

These exhortations came too late or fell largely on deaf ears. Green Cadres led a wave of violence in the post-Habsburg countryside as they emerged from the forests. Small towns closest to their wooded lairs bore the brunt of the initial attacks. Officials in Slunj in the Kordun region of southern Croatia fled before the green forces as they debouched from the Petrova Gora mountains, announcing their arrival with machine gun fire.[20] Plunder and arson ensued, as in numerous other places in Croatia-Slavonia. Violence and destruction were reported in the small towns of Delnice, Garešnica, Križpolje, Martijanec, Našice, and in Klanjec, where defenders exceptionally managed to repulse the insurgents.[21] The Zagreb-based National Council of the State of Slovenes, Croats, and Serbs was flooded with urgent pleas for military assistance. The gendarmerie in the larger town of Vukovar sought reinforcements to retake outlying stations of Vuka, Podgorač, and Đakovo that had fallen to the green forces.[22] Authorities in central Croatian Daruvar implored Zagreb for six hundred men and machine guns as soon as possible, because "the entire area is threatened by the Green Cadres."[23] The National Council committee in the southern Slavonian town of Brod (now Slavonski Brod) requested urgent dispatch of a battalion to restore rail transport between them and Zagreb; insurgents had forced the return of an armed train heading toward the capital halfway along the track at Okučani.[24]

VOJNICI!

Postali ste gradjani slobodne države Slovenaca, Hrvata i Srba.

Ne trebate se više boriti za tudje gospodstvo već samo za domovinu.

Vi, koji ste odbjegli od svojih četa u zelene kadre vratite se svojim kućama. Naša vrhovna vlast — Narodno Vijeće — sve Vam je oprostila.

Vojnici!

Prijavite se odmah zatim kod najbližih svojih vojnih zapovjedništava, da zajedno s nama branite slobodu svog naroda i podržavate red i mir, da se može na čvrstim i sigurnim temeljima izgraditi slobodna, svima jednako, pravedna država svih Slovenaca, Hrvata i Srba.

Domovina Vas zove! Ona treba svakog čovjeka!

Svaki onaj, koji od sad počinja izgrede i ne vrši svoju dužnost, izdajica je svog naroda.

U Varaždinu, dne 28. listopada 1918.

Pukovnik Ivan Kolak
zapovjednik narodne vojske u Varaždinu.

Tiskara Stifler, Varaždin.

FIGURE 3.1 An October 28, 1918, circular ordering soldiers of the Green Cadre in Croatia to return home. Varaždin City Museum

To the north, in western Slovakia, deserter bands descended from the Little Carpathians to the west and the east, invading small towns as they proceeded. The Green Cadre group led by Augustín Nuhál swept into his native village of Veselé, "distributed requisitioned goods to the poor and chased the Jews and lords to hell."[25] The avengers supposedly shouted, "Shave him!" (*Ohol ho!*), the wartime the slogan of rebellious Slovak soldiers.[26] On the western slopes of the Little Carpathians, haystacks between Sološnica and Rohožník were set ablaze to signal the arrival of the deserters, who then continued south and west into the lowlands of the Záhorie region.[27] Even the relatively orderly Czech and Slovenian lands witnessed scattered, smaller-scale retributive attacks by the forest-based rebels. In eastern Moravian Hluk, deserters hurled a hand grenade through the window of the local gendarme commander, forcing him and his family to flee the village.[28] The southern Bohemian Green Cadre group that counted author Michal Mareš among its members stormed into the small town of Studená seeking revenge for the murder of their comrade, but the gendarmes had already absconded themselves.[29] Slovene deserters and their peasants allies attacked gendarme stations in and around the Lower Styrian town of Krško polje.[30]

Larger towns in the most-affected areas attempted to defend themselves. In eastern Slavonian Vinkovci, where "the sky around was red from arson," the local committee of the National Council reported to Zagreb that measures were being taken to prevent incursions from the surrounding countryside: "The city will be enclosed like a fortress to save itself."[31] Such preparations often proved futile. Already on October 24 in Slavonian Požega, a mutiny of barracked soldiers due to poor clothing prompted an invasion of the town by forest-based deserters and their peasant followers.[32] The mayor reported that several hours after the soldiers had defied their officers, the commander of a company of deserters rode forebodingly into town "on a black horse" and held counsel with the mutineers before returning to the woods. Later in the evening he rode in again leading his men with "many peasant wagons behind him." The dam was breached, the post office telephone demolished, and telegraph wires cut. The deserters broke the iron shutters of shops, allowing the "mob" to commence looting; Jewish shops were especially hard hit, but three owned by Catholics were also pillaged. Women were conspicuous in the plunder. "Terrible shooting" lasted through the night. Only the following morning did news of an approaching unit of hussars succeed in dispersing the "rabble," after which students and officers formed a town self-defense brigade.

On October 29, green forces sacked Osijek, Slavonia's largest town. Officials sent the following telegram message: "Agitated peasants from surrounding villages attacked the town as well as estates in the vicinity. Three dead and many wounded."[33] The next day, it was reported that "large masses of people" were marching toward Osijek. As the county prefect later explained, "the population of the outlying parishes, believing that clothes, shoes and food were being freely distributed in the Osijek army warehouses and storehouses, rushed into Osijek with a hundred wagons and with the armed support of the green cadre forces and discharged troops."[34] Captain Krešimir Košak assumed command of the disintegrating Austro-Hungarian Seventy-Eighth Infantry Regiment garrisoned in town and met the invaders with machine gun fire, killing at least five and earning the sobriquet "savior of Osijek from the green cadre."[35]

In early November, towns across Polish western Galicia succumbed to invasion from the rural hinterland. Often led by deserters, peasants stormed Brzesko, Brzozów, Kolbuszowa, and Rozwadów, targeting Jewish shops and taverns.[36] Units loyal to Major Jerzy Dobrodzicki kept marauders out of Bochnia, to which large numbers of Jews from the surrounding countryside had fled. The nearby smaller towns of Niepołomice, Łapanów, Wiśnicz, and Nieprześnia were not so fortunate. Niepomołice's two Christian shopkeepers, along with two Jewish merchants, managed to save their property by paying off the invaders.[37] Oświęcim with its population of over fifty thousand narrowly avoided wholesale plunder by compelling Jewish shopkeepers to sell their goods at heavily discounted prices.[38] Abortive attacks maybe outnumbered those that occurred. The town of Tarnobrzeg, for instance, was the objective of peasants from Jeziórko and Żupava, but after marching halfway there, they lost their nerve and returned home.[39] Army units dispersed villagers from Wieprz and Rzyki as they proceeded toward the town of Wadowice.[40] Authorities reported how "bandits" (by which forest deserters were usually meant) planned a second attack on Brzesko just days after a lethal pogrom there, but they quarreled violently among themselves, thus sparing the town a second onslaught.[41]

An investigation into the attacks in the vicinity of Bochnia, which left several Jews and at least one notorious "bandit" dead, attributed the violence to "hatred toward gendarmes for hunting deserters and requisitions as well as against Jewish exploitation that was supported by the Austrian government."[42] With the Austrian authorities departed, the mostly unarmed Jewish population of Galicia served as vulnerable proxy targets of peasant retribution. As the Polish commander in Brzesko reported at the end of November, "in this predominantly peasant district, villagers fanatically hate everything that would even ostensibly resemble Austrian rule."[43] Two weeks later, the chief justice of the Brzesko county court admitted that local peasants, led by deserters, had wanted for some time to "settle scores with Jews," especially alleged wartime profiteers.[44] But he regarded the victims themselves as culpable for having provocatively established an armed Jewish guard unit, and for their supposedly half-hearted Polish patriotism.

Social and ethnic antagonisms also combined potently in Bosnia-Herzegovina, where the landlord class was over 90 percent Muslim, while 95 percent of their estate tenants and laborers were Orthodox or Catholic.[45] Peasant violence erupted in November 1918 in the impoverished former Habsburg territory, lasting intermittently until 1921. Orthodox villagers, who increasingly saw themselves as Serbs, took violent revenge on the "Turks" for centuries of oppression. Led by Green Cadres, or simply invoking the name, they laid waste to manor houses, occupied estate land, and murdered their owners, particularly in the northern Bosnian districts of Bosanska Dubica, Derventa, Tešanj, Odžak, Bijeljina, Gračanica, Banja Luka, and Brčko.[46] The insurgents also targeted free Muslim peasants, showing that ethnic animosity sometimes eclipsed other divisions. As many as several thousand may have perished.[47]

In some places, villagers took their revenge without the clear presence of deserter bands or demobilizing soldiers. In the remote central Slovak village of Čierny Balog, situated in densely forested hills east of Banská Bystrica, local woodsmen exacted terrible retribution for the "old crimes" of the authorities and their perceived accomplices, turning their axes on foresters, gendarmes, and the local notary; several were butchered to death.[48] The woodsmen proceeded to ransack Jewish properties. They then cut Čierny Balog off from the outside world, severing telegraph and telephone cables. In Slovene Carinthia, over three hundred peasants sacked the Pugelnik estate near Libeliče, while Slovene villagers in Styria and Carniola attacked shopkeepers and pro-Habsburg clergy in several places.[49] Although many of the more dramatic town invasions were led by deserters, in other instances peasants simply turned their weekly market excursions into something more menacing. Across east central Europe, villagers habitually journeyed to town to sell their produce and livestock, often lingering long after in taverns and squandering at least a portion of their earnings on drink. The potential for violent disturbances and riots, always present on such occasions, increased exponentially during times of social-political turmoil.[50] On two successive autumn 1918 market days in the eastern Moravian town of Uherský Brod, peasants rioted against Jews. The local chronicler described the incidents as violent deviations from familiar practice:

> On Thursday, November 14 and then on the 21st of the same month very threatening conditions took shape here with an influx of country folk. The

town's Jews were afraid, had no confidence, and pleaded for rescue. . . . Country folk were arriving by road from [the villages of] Bánov, Nivnice, and Vlčnov and it was immediately apparent what their purpose was in going to the marketplace: their axes, cudgels, truncheons, and empty bundles gave them away. Asked where they were going, they proclaimed completely shamelessly that they are going to loot.[51]

The invaders emptied several Jewish shops of their wares and smashed the windows on their proprietors' homes. In Vrbovce, western Slovakia, the notary blamed the riot there in early November on market days that drew in turbulent people from outlying villages; the inhabitants of Vrbovce itself were too docile to take the initiative themselves, he claimed.[52] Besides markets and fairs, church services also assembled villagers, many of whom repaired to taverns afterward, heightening the risk of collective violence. Numerous instances of plunder occurred on Sunday, November 3, 1918, just after mass had finished.[53]

Attacks led by Green Cadres revealed more revolutionary ambition than those where they were absent. In Slavonia, for instance, the deserter bands seemed intent not only on punishing individual landlords and merchants but on dismantling the entire manorial economy. Among their first targets as they issued northward from the Papuk-Krndija highlands into the Drava floodplain were the vast holdings of the Gutmann family, the largest landowner in the region. Since 1884 when the family first established a forestry operation to exploit Slavonia's then-vast oak forests, the Gutmanns had gradually diversified their business interests to include field agriculture, horse breeding, and mineral water production.[54] At the turn of the twentieth century, their company was the largest producer of milled oak and beechwood in Europe and owned 35,023 hectares of Slavonian land. Originally Jews from Nagykanizsa in Hungary, in 1904 Franz Joseph elevated them to hereditary Barons de Gelse et Belišće—the second part of the appellation referring to the company settlement they founded near the small town of Valpovo. The Gutmanns acquired estates in Voćin, Orahovica, Suha Mlaka, and elsewhere, many of which included imposing manor houses and castles, inspiring scions of the family to cultivate the lifestyle of country squires.

On October 26, peasants around Orahovica joined deserter bands and mutinous soldiers in setting fire to the local Gutmann Company offices and plundering their extensive wine cellars.[55] Talk of this episode reached the priest Erdélyi in Donji Miholjac. Two days later, having ravaged the small town of Našice, Green Cadres reached the Gutmann estate at Krivaja, located between

Slatina and Donji Miholjac.[56] According to fieldworker Ivan Bendek, the "komitas" (a synonym for Green Cadres) demanded the key to the Krivaja storehouse from its overseer, István Bogner. Having opened the building, "the soldiers told us employees and peasants, who were arriving from all sides, that each can take as much food as he needs." Bendek helped himself to eight sacks of wheat, while his mother and sister drove a cow from the estate herd to their family stall. Estate tenants and smallholding peasants from the surrounding villages took all they could carry; the komitas themselves abstained from the plunder, apart from relieving Bogner of some of his personal effects. With the estate storehouse and barns emptied, Bendek, along with several other field-hands, joined the soldiers for plum brandy at the expense of Jewish tavern keeper Bernard Kohn in the village of Suha Mlaka. Soon after the sack of Krivaja, a deserter band descended on the village of Voćin, bursting into the lodgings of Gutmann's local clerk, Emanuel Engelman, where the sister of their leader, Marko Tkalčić, worked as a maid. Tkalčić commanded her to leave Engelman's house immediately, since "freedom is here, and she cannot serve any more."[57] The rebels left a trail of destruction in Voćin. They set fire to the local manor house, built in the eighteenth century during the reign of Maria Theresa, and slaughtered the animals in the deer park belonging to Vilim Gutmann.[58]

Similarly, the three soldiers who arrived shooting in the air on the afternoon of October 30 at Rogovac estate, near the town of Virovitica, refused proprietor Vinko Augustin's attempt to buy them off, explaining that "there are no estates anymore."[59] They demanded horses and carriages, claiming implausibly that they sought transportation for an eighteen-thousand-strong Green Cadre army to besiege Zagreb. Having commandeered the estate's parade horses, they departed. The next evening at around ten o'clock, shooting was again heard outside of the manor house, as a large crowd of peasants from the villages of Bušetina, Lozan, and Stari Gradac advanced on the grounds. Augustin hid with his wife and small child in the undergrowth fifty paces from the building. They managed to furtively harness horses to a carriage and fled through the forest to Virovitica and thence to Zagreb. Rogovac was plundered and devastated.

Yet, as the destruction of Rogovac reveals, the actual responsibility of the deserter movement was sometimes difficult to pin down. Vinko Augustin's estate was just one of a series of properties targeted by villagers from Bušetina, whose connection with the Green Cadres was uncertain. Here, as elsewhere, peasants invoked the Green Cadres to legitimize their actions, or to intimidate

FIGURE 3.2 The Šaulovec manor house in Varaždin county, Croatia, after its plunder by Green Cadres. Varaždin City Museum

their declared enemies. They retrospectively tried to excuse their deeds, saying that they had simply followed the orders of armed deserters. Some known deserters later insisted that they were merely obeying shadowy comrades-in-arms from outside the area.

The authorities investigating the crimes committed in and around Bušetina were faced with a confusing sequence of events: on October 28, an eighteen-year-old peasant named Nikola Gjureš delivered a printed note to the estate owner Ivan Leon, ordering him to immediately deliver ten thousand crowns to the forest, having supposedly been instructed to do so by unfamiliar soldiers.[60] Leon said he would only parley with the soldiers' commander, and Gjureš fled when Leon's gamekeeper arrived armed with a rifle. Meanwhile, Jakob Lutak, another young peasant who claimed to be the Green Cadres' quartermaster, bade a wealthy, middle-aged farmer named Stjepan Franck to prepare dinner for a group of komitas, who then failed to turn up. The next day, the twenty-year-old peasant Stevan Brlas arrived at the Okrugljača estate, demanding carriages in the name of Green Cadres who had recently arrived in Bušetina. Karlo Tikas, the estate postman, and apparently a confederate, readied a carriage and two carts,

FIGURE 3.3 The Šaulovec manor house in Varaždin county, Croatia, after its plunder by Green Cadres. Varaždin City Museum

returning with Brlas, Brlas's brother, and another accomplice to the village. As they drove, they called on bystanders to loot the nearby town of Virovitica, shouting "Long live freedom!" They pillaged shops along the way, subsequently joining a large crowd that had gathered to carouse at a tavern belonging to Adolf Bing, a Jew. Bing's establishment soon fell to the revelers' destructive urges. Later that day, dozens of people made their way on foot or in stolen carts to Leon's estate and looted it. On November 1, the villagers attacked the larger Okrugljača estate, smashing windows and plundering the storehouse and the estate manager's lodgings. They shattered the windows of lodgings occupied by Antun Horvat, the forty-five-year-old foreman at Okrugljača, who was also struck in the head with an axe. A farmhand alleged that the Green Cadres were the perpetrators, but the category was clearly fluid and evolving; Horvat, after being assaulted, himself joined the plunder and stole nine sacks of wheat.

It was impossible to determine whether Green Cadres from outside the area had been involved in the violent pantomime around Virovitica. A handful of local army deserters in their mid-twenties—identified by Gjureš as "our Bušetina komitas"—appear to have recruited men a few years younger such as Gjureš, Lutak, and Brlas to act as their emissaries as they coordinated the plunder of surrounding estates and Jewish-owned shops. But the task of assembling criminal cases against them ultimately overwhelmed prosecutors. None of the Bušetina komitas had a history of criminality before the war, and during interrogation several alleged that they were too drunk at the time to remember any of their actions. Lack of a criminal past and alcohol intoxication (at the time a mitigating circumstance) were common obstacles for authorities across east central Europe who attempted to punish the perpetrators of collective violence in late 1918.[61] The villagers from Bušetina who fell under the suspicion of Osijek investigators otherwise matched the profile of the majority of those held responsible for the tumult of the post-Habsburg countryside: young, often unmarried men in uniform with little property of their own.[62]

Whether led by armed deserters, returning soldiers, both, or neither, the patterns of popular violence in autumn 1918 were, as William W. Hagen has written, "expressive of unreflected-on, if not altogether unconscious, social and cultural beliefs, fears, and wishes."[63] Such folk mentalities were perhaps most evident among peasants but were certainly not limited to them. Rituals and beliefs drawn from popular Christianity endowed brutal acts with meaning for perpetrators of collective violence, urban and rural alike, even if such meanings were not clearly articulated, or even consciously grasped. The leitmotif of the disturbances may have been revenge, but their micro-level dynamics reveal a rich and sometimes sinister repertoire of values, practices, and folk memory that had been rehearsed for generations. By providing a stage on which to perform communal meanings, the rural unrest at the end of the First World War reinforced peasants' own sense of themselves as a social class.[64] The violence, to use Max Bergholz's phrase, was "a generative force" that forged identity, or refashioned it, as much as it reflected the interests of a preexisting social group.[65]

One important way in which peasants reasserted their collective identity was by forcefully attempting to restore a "moral economy" that had been undermined by the war. As opposed to the material economy of goods and services, the moral economy refers to a complex of expectations and cultural norms, above all that the common folk have a right to a modicum of subsistence.[66] The moral economy also demands that individuals observe unwritten rules of mutualism and reciprocity in their dealings with others. It has likely had outsized significance in peasant societies, with their high levels of informal economic activity and reliance on kinship networks. In the years 1914–18, shortages, requisitions, and skyrocketing prices, along with the caprices and abuses of the black market, all contributed to the moral economy's collapse. As the war ended, villagers tried to restore it by force, punishing those deemed responsible for its abeyance.

In some instances, plunderers of shops and manor houses believed they were simply laying claim to property that was rightfully theirs. Max Schlesinger, the Jewish proprietor of a store in Budakovac near Virovitica that was sacked on October 31, remarked with some astonishment that "the looters at our place did not use any violence nor did they attack us or threaten us, rather they merely laid out the goods in our presence, which we naturally did not resist since they told us that they have no business with us and [that] they will only take the goods, since freedom has come and it is their right."[67] In the small western Slovak town of Šaštín-Stráže, those who robbed Jewish stores and wealthy houses insisted that they were carrying out their own righteous "voluntary requisitioning" in lieu of a government that no longer existed.[68] Jozef Ferančík, a Green Cadre fighter and autodidact poet, excused the perpetrators of the western Slovak disturbances in homespun verses entitled "Revolution and Plundering [*rabovky*] in 1918" on the grounds that the property of the rich did not really belong to them:

Don't blame my people
That they stood up to a murderer!
That they won justice
And buried wrongdoing.

Don't say that the people,
Plundered the rich,
Ask instead from where
Did the rich man take his property??[69]

Ferančík's exculpatory poem hinted at injustices that predated the war. Indeed, in some of the attacks, peasants sought to redress long-standing affronts to the moral economy that had been committed before the war. For instance, a fifty-six-year-old Slavonian peasant named Antun Schön and his son Martin, with the armed support of fifteen komitas, violently evicted the new occupant of a tenant farm on the Donji Miholjac estate that they had last occupied in 1903.[70] The victim, an estate forester named Stjepan Živić, fled with his family, later bringing criminal charges against the Schöns. Martin justified his actions with reference to a court case that the local nobleman had used fifteen years prior to drive his father from the land he cultivated. A peasant assembly held on October 29 in the nearby village of Breznica had galvanized the Schöns to action. Martin explained, "after the assembly I came to Živić and told him very calmly that he must leave the house within three weeks, because it is our house, and I thought I have the right to do so since people at the assembly said that freedom has come and that anyone who used to have something at the count's [i.e., on estate land], and now doesn't, can take it."

The act of laying claim to ill-gotten wealth could assume theatrical guise. On October 30 in Kutina, the principal town of the hilly central Croatian Moslavina region, Green Cadres staged a public drama of retribution and Christian charity. Already on the previous evening, local notables gathered in a tavern overheard a group of ten deserters conspiring to "make order in Kutina."[71] Surmising what this meant, the eavesdroppers tried to befriend the men and dissuade them from any rash action. But the following day, two soldiers who appeared to be Green Cadres on reconnaissance arrived in town, telling members of the provisional local National Council committee that they "wanted the head of the [district] captain," since he had ruined one of the deserter's families during the war. In the meantime, five more deserters arrived in Kutina and ordered the miller Ljudevit Hafner to ready supper for ten people. According to their own account, the provisional committee members pleaded with the intruders to rethink their plans, inviting them to the tavern for a drink. The deserters declined, explaining that they first needed to settle scores with the merchant Imbro Berger, who had led wartime provisioning; the shopkeeper Ledetzki, who got rich during the war; the district captain Mato Vrkljan (then in hiding); and a local physician named Nathan Politzer for unstated reasons (perhaps his Jewishness was reason enough). The main force of deserters now surged into town, shooting in the air as townsfolk assembled. The crowd forced its way into the district offices, taking what weapons and ammunition they could find. Unable to locate the odious Vrkljan, they returned to the square with cries of "Long live the Green Cadre!" They watched as the cadres' leader, a certain Vinko Gradinac-Mataija from the village of Zbjegovača, sporting a white feather in his army cap, made his way to Berger's shop, leading a "a half-naked and barefoot Bosnian [and] shouting that he is going to clothe the nakedness." The Bosnian received trousers at Berger's and the rest of his outfit at Katarina Skočić's shop; general plundering was restrained while the ritual of charity unfolded. Only after its conclusion were the onlookers turned loose on Kutina's retailers. Throughout the "horrible night" that followed, little could be heard except the "bestial bellowing of the drunken mob," shooting, and "smashing of axes." On October 31, the provisional committee succeeded in organizing some local people for defense of the town and dispersing the looters. They also repulsed a mass of "peasants" intent on sharing in the spoils.

The disturbances in Kutina proved rather more contentious than elsewhere. The local National Council committee laid the blame squarely on Vrkljan's alleged misrule as district captain, reporting to Zagreb that wartime profiteering and requisitioning abuses were rife during his tenure. Likewise, the Catholic priest in nearby Voloder attributed the popular thirst for revenge to poor decisions made by local administrators, and especially the provisioning office, which had needlessly slashed support to war widows and orphans.[72] While disapproving of looting and violence, the local National Council committee empathized with the squeezed lower classes, praising their patriotic spirit at a November 3 national assembly where hymns were sung, flags unfurled, and a public oath taken to the State of Slovenes, Croats, and Serbs. Vrkljan's office disputed this version of events in early December, describing the November 3 assembly as an invitation to radicalism. From a balcony on the main square, committee members had allegedly told the largely peasant crowd, "there are no more district authorities, nor district officials, there is no more provisioning or requisitions or firewood vouchers, the forests are free to fell."[73] Some of Vrkljan's allies at the local level even accused the unitarist intelligentsia—those who advocated a unitary and internally undifferentiated Yugoslav state—of inciting the October 30 plunder.

The theater of the violence in such episodes recalled, in a sinister way, the antics of carnival season, when ordinary people indulged in rough music, feasting, excessive drinking, and sexual license. Carnival was a time when social roles were reversed; the poor dressed as nobles and bishops while the rich were clad as paupers. Such public status inversions were often intended to provide release for pent-up social tensions. In the extensive territories of the former Polish-Lithuanian Commonwealth, Christian villagers commonly dressed up as Jews at carnival and Easter, or beat and drowned a Jewish effigy during the annual pre-Easter "Judas Fest" in Galicia.[74] But as in those annual interludes of "institutionalized disorder," rituals of transgression could not always contain the popular energies that were unleashed.[75] Open rebellion had in the early modern era sometimes burst forth around carnival season, or during similarly exuberant festivals, such as Corpus Christi and Midsummer. The boundaries between jollity and fury then blurred rapidly, the carnival script of playful mockery and sexual permissiveness giving way to humiliation, rape, and murder. By ostensibly following the festival rites, perpetrators of violence insulated themselves from full knowledge of, and responsibility for, what they were doing.[76]

Wartime shortages, which persisted for months, even years, after the end of the Habsburg monarchy, did not preclude carnivalesque orgies of food and drink in autumn 1918. In Malacky, located in the Záhorie region of western Slovakia, a group of youths initiated the postwar revels when they laid waste to the bakery and house of a Jewish baker who had allegedly sold inferior bread during the war. Then:

> They took the manorial horses and carriage, loaded a barrel of liquor mixed with water on it, and rode to the other end of the village, singing, shouting, and cursing all Jews. From there they went to granary, which they broke into and distributed the grain to the people. From there they set off to the distillery, where they emptied out all the barrels filled with liquor. Half-drunk they went to the notary and ordered him to prepare roast goose for them, threatening to kill him.[77]

As elsewhere, the banqueting in Malacky was inseparable from violence and threats against those who were forced to provide for the revelers. To supply their tables, villagers in the southern Záhorie region rustled livestock from rich farms, including the Pálffy estate, property of an ancient Hungarian magnate family, and slaughtered the animals indiscriminately.[78] In Plavecký Štvrtok, "the aroma from roasting meat and innards wafted through the entire municipality for a week."[79]

With the categories of perpetrators and merrymakers indistinguishable, music often accompanied the violence. During the plunder of Jewish shops in the northwestern corner of Slovakia, a witness observed that "the people were constantly singing."[80] In the Záhorie village of Kuchyňa, a former teacher playing the accordion led a throng of looters to Jewish retailers.[81] The Polish soldiers (not all peasants) and townsfolk who participated in the murderous mid-November pogrom in the eastern Galician city of Lwów sang, danced, and played music as they avenged themselves, so they claimed, for Jews' allegedly perfidiously neutral conduct during the occupation of the city by Ukrainian forces weeks before.[82] In the eastern Slavonian village of Cerna on the night of October 31, the Jewish Hirschfeld family awoke to the sound of singing approaching their house from across the fields.[83] The next thing they heard was a powerful blow to the metal shutters of their ground-floor shop and the shattering of all street-level windows. Serena Hirschfeld was at home at the time along with her four children, her brother Benjamin Zilzer, and her brother-in-law Adolf with his wife Johanna. Her husband Abraham, proprietor of the shop, was still on his homeward journey after three and a half years on the Italian Front. Earlier that evening, Adolf and Johanna had fled their own shop and home in Cerna, finding refuge with their sister-in-law after Adolf had received verbal death threats from two peasants. The attackers doubtlessly wanted the goods in Abraham and Serena's store, but the hunt for Adolf had not abated. One of the vandals shouted, "For God's sake, Šarko [Adolf's nickname in the village], where are you?!" The Hirschfelds then fled across the field at the rear of the house, finding safe haven with neighbors. From her neighbor's window, Serena watched the plunder of her shop for several hours before she fell asleep. At around five in the morning, shouts of "fire" awoke her: their store was in flames. Her shop assistant, a Russian prisoner of war, harnessed horses to a cart and the family escaped to the town of Vinkovci. Serena estimated that their losses totaled 370,000 crowns from the half-destroyed house, the store emptied of goods, and their personal effects and furniture stolen or destroyed. Numerous villagers confirmed that song had echoed through Cerna that night. In the view of some, however, revenge had to be taken. One of the ringleaders, a twenty-three-year-old peasant and army deserter named Mato Grgić, alleged that "the whole village hated" Šarko because he reported deserters to the gendarmerie and denounced peasants who illegally planted tobacco or distilled their own *rakija* (plum brandy).

One particularly chilling episode combining the topsy-turvy world of carnival with other scripts of peasant revenge occurred in 1920 during the central Croatian revolt against state-mandated livestock branding (discussed in the next chapter), which was in many ways a reprise of autumn 1918. In Sveti Ivan Zelina on September 6, 1920, peasants who had seized control of the town that morning apprehended the district captain, Oton Špiller, as he returned in the afternoon from Konjščina, where he had telephoned to Zagreb for reinforcements against the insurgents. According to charges brought in December 1920 against 240 defendants of Zelina district, the peasant crowd marched Špiller to the tavern, shouting that "he is the one who issued the decree to take people's livestock and that he is a traitor to the people."[84] He was then led to a joiner's shop where he was forced to shoulder a coffin for the deceased peasant Josip Šuliček, killed in the morning's firefight with gendarmes. Under duress, Špiller agreed and with the coffin on his back and a cross thrust into his hand, he was driven through town to the graveyard. A peasant named Stjepan Gjurenec rode behind the procession on Špiller's carriage, calling jocularly to onlookers, "Now I am the [district] captain."[85] Špiller collapsed under the weight before reaching the graveyard, at which point peasants mercilessly interrogated him, demanding he account for his conduct and asking how he would like to die. Overcome by emotion and unable to answer any more questions, the district captain was clubbed on the head and then shot. The violent ritual of forced penitence that claimed Špiller's life redressed, in peasant perpetrators' eyes, a grievous affront to the rural moral economy.

The dynamics of rural violence in the former Austro-Hungarian territories extended far beyond the defunct monarchy's former boundaries, engulfing much of the former Russian Empire as well. Peasant aggression in the two former imperial spaces differed more in degree than in kind. Unrest in the post-Tsarist lands proved far more lethal owing to persistent lawlessness and a years-long absence of clear state authority.[86] Peasant violence exploded in Ukraine and much of the Russian rural hinterland following the February Revolution of 1917. With the collapse of Tsarist rule, peasants seized estate land, hesitantly at first, then in a torrent of occupations: 17 estates were taken over in March 1917, 204 in April, 259 in May, 577 in June, and 1,122 in July.[87] From late summer, they sacked manor houses amid carousing and music, hounded officials and landowners out of numerous districts, sometimes murdering them, and destroyed written records.[88] But with the civil war that broke out after the Bolshevik takeover, violence spiraled out of control, particularly in Ukraine, site of the bloodiest postwar disturbances.

Ukraine experienced a succession of Kiev-based governments in the years 1917–21, none of which was able to wield consistent power over the country's rural expanses. In early 1918, a socialist-leaning Ukrainian People's Republic had been proclaimed by Ukrainian nationalists, breaking away from Bolshevik control. Then, with the conclusion of the Brest-Litovsk Treaty in March 1918 between the Central Powers and the Bolsheviks, Ukraine became a conservative German client state under the leadership of "hetman" Pavlo Skoropadsky. By the end of the year, a group of nationalist leaders had succeeded in deposing the hetmanate, installing themselves as the Directorate of the Ukrainian People's Republic. But the directorate could not withstand Red Army advances on Kiev in 1919 and was forced to withdraw westward to Podolia, from where it tried in vain to recapture the capital. Meanwhile, formidable "green" warlords, or atamans, among them the anarchist Nestor Makhno, seized control of vast rural areas with the support of sometimes immense, but ephemeral, peasant armies. During the peak of the bloodshed in 1919, Reds, Whites, People's Republic forces, and around one hundred atamans commanding motley peasant forces of up to twenty thousand men apiece contested Ukrainian territory. All sides were responsible for pogroms, but the atamans committed the most, and often bloodiest, anti-Jewish atrocities; they carried out 307 documented pogroms, versus 167 attributed to the Ukrainian People's Republic and 213 to the White armies.[89] And they were almost impossible to subdue so long as conditions of stateless anarchy persisted. Soviet author Isaac Babel summed up the advantages of their, especially Makhno's, guerilla-style warfare in his account of the 1920 Polish-Soviet War, *Red Cavalry*:

> Hay carts, lined up in battle formations, seize towns. A wedding procession approaches the local district's executive committee, opens concentrated fire, and a puny priest, brandishing the black flag of anarchy over his head, demands that the authorities hand over the bourgeoisie, hand over the proletariat, the wine, the music, . . . It's hard to cut such an army down, and capture is unthinkable. The machine gun is buried under a hayrick, the *tachanka* [machine gun cart] drawn off into a peasant's threshing barn—they cease to be military units. These hidden emplacements, these implied but intangible items, add up to the Ukrainian village of recent days—fierce, rebellious, self-interested. Makhno can whip such an army, with its ammunition scattered all over, into fighting condition in an hour; he needs even less time to demobilize it.[90]

Like the Green Cadres in the post-Habsburg countryside, Ukrainian warlords and their "green" forces saw themselves as defenders of the peasantry against the rapacity of towns populated by requisitioning officials, conscription officers, and unscrupulous merchants. Danilyo Terpylo, known as Ataman Zelenyi (the green ataman), darkly proclaimed, "We should annihilate the cities of the Ukraine because they are foreign to us and they hate us."[91] Makhno too steered peasant rage against urban centers as the headquarters of peasant exploitation and sinks of vice, luxury, and corruption.[92] Spatial, ethnic-national, and social antagonisms overlapped here too: toiling Ukrainian peasant people were enjoined to cast off the yoke of town-based Communist and Jewish oppressors, who became indistinguishable in an increasingly potent Judeo-Bolshevik myth.[93] Unlike the "Bolsheviks" of 1917, who had benevolently issued the Decree on Land, the "Communist" authorities from 1918 were blamed for seizing peasants' plots, conscripting their sons for endless military campaigning, and defiling Christian churches. Resisting the Communists required eliminating their supposed agents and beneficiaries at the local level, above all Ukraine's sizable and vulnerable Jewish population.[94] The hammer blows of peasant fury fell heaviest on them. While Makhno held aloft the banner of his peasant anarchist crusade against urban tyranny, many atamans focused their attacks solely on Jews. Jewish deaths in 1918–20 were in the tens of thousands, with figures of fifty to two hundred thousand commonly cited for Ukraine alone.[95] Only after the Red Army's decisive 1920 victories over the Whites were the Ukrainian warlords forced to retreat. By 1921, the peasant armies of two years prior had been reduced by ascendant Soviet forces to isolated gangs in peripheral areas. Makhno fled into exile in Paris, where he died in 1934.

Casualties of the post-Habsburg rural violence were far fewer, though still difficult to quantify. While deaths of officials and notables tended to be amply documented, those of peasant insurrectionists or Jewish victims remain in the realm of conjecture. The confirmed death toll of anti-Jewish violence in post-imperial Poland was between 400 and 532, but hundreds more probably perished.[96] Authorities in Croatia-Slavonia conservatively estimated that they had killed between 50 and 100 people in suppressing the disturbances there.[97] These numbers were certainly too low. In Našice alone, Captain Branko Kralj, commander of a company dispatched from Osijek, summarily executed in the cemetery thirty people who had been involved—or were suspected of involvement—in the plunder and destruction of local estates.[98] Magyar gendarmes and soldiers were responsible for killing over 100 villagers as they restored order in the overwhelmingly Croatian region of Međimurje (Hungarian: Muraköz), then part of Hungary proper and only incorporated in 1919 into Yugoslavia.[99] Likely dozens of people died during the "plundering" in Slovakia, particularly during its suppression, though reliable figures are lacking. In all these places, peasant unrest was extinguished, or at least contained, relatively quickly.

The Habsburg successor states enjoyed some decisive advantages over their beleaguered counterparts in the east as they undertook to discipline the countryside. First, they were able to take over and deploy the more robust state structures left over from the imperial and royal governments of Vienna and Budapest. Poland faced larger obstacles, as swaths of its rural hinterland had to be abandoned while it waged eastern border wars against Ukraine, Lithuania, and the Soviet Union. But here too, the need to prove the state's legitimacy to its western allies reined in rural collective violence somewhat. Second, apart from eastern Galicia (today in Ukraine), none of these lands witnessed sustained combat between conventional armies as in the Russian Civil War. Third, most people outside regions inhabited by Germans and Magyars welcomed "liberation" from rule by Vienna and Budapest, as well as some form of new order based on nation-states.

Yet the ways in which the new states of Czechoslovakia, Yugoslavia, and Poland asserted control over their rural hinterlands would have fateful consequences. In the former two states, the new governments succeeded in alienating much of countryside where, respectively, Slovaks and Croats lived—each a core element of the state's composite titular nationality. In Poland, the hesitant and ineffectual halting of anti-Jewish violence, some of which, as we have seen, possessed a distinctly peasant character, led to the imposition of much-resented minority treaties across east central Europe by the victors of the First World War. In all three countries, a rift opened between the new political elites, who insisted that rebellious country folk had completely misunderstood the meaning of "freedom," and peasants themselves, who believed they had the freedom to carry out their revolution as they saw fit. While misunderstanding could, from the perspective of authorities and nationalist leaders, exculpate villagers who had committed violent acts, it was further evidence to them that the business of political transformation could not be entrusted to everyone.

That "the people" had misinterpreted their newly won freedom was a refrain among contributors to a multivolume series called *The Slovak Revolution* (1930–31), compiled by Karol A. Medvecký, a leader of the Slovak People's Party, who intended to shed light on how the "national revolution" was experienced at the local level across Slovakia. "Everybody in Turá Lúka understood the slogan 'freedom' as vandalism," wrote one eyewitness.[100] In Trnava, soldiers returning from the fronts "proclaimed freedom, which found expression in them plundering shops, stealing, and looting."[101] An observer of events in Malacky concluded that "when [the people] found out about freedom, they thought they could do whatever they want."[102] For some Slovak patriots, the excesses were excusable in light of long years of suffering under the Magyar yoke and the proximate trauma of the world war. A contributor from rural northwest Slovakia described the violence as a natural reaction to apocalyptic conditions at the end of the war: "Freedom to the hungry means eating one's fill. The people were starved, exhausted, worn out. They were cooking grass and collecting mushrooms. I myself saw a scruffy group of youths walking through the mountains, searching for some kind of sustenance. Everywhere the Spanish flu, erysipelas, and epidemic typhus were raging. The soldier who made it back from the front died at home of hunger. Thus did the Magyar lords take care of our people."[103] Medvecký himself concurred in his lengthy introduction to the first volume of *The Slovak Revolution*.[104]

Others, like the priest Erdélyi in Donji Miholjac, lamented that the people had irredeemably debased themselves as they exercised their newfound freedom. The state school administrator in Šaštín-Stráže, western Slovakia, where Jewish shops and notables' houses were plundered, remarked, "It was unfortunate that so many people, intoxicated by the slogan of freedom, allowed themselves to be part of such deeds that will eternally remain a dark stain on the history of our little town."[105] Conditions in western Slovakia might have rapidly improved after the initial early November anarchy, according to some local observers, had freshly arrived Czech officials not fanned the flames of popular discontent with indiscreet public statements. Assemblies on several occasions heard that the gendarmerie and taxes would be abolished, along with manorial estates and forests.[106] The stubborn misinterpretation of freedom after the immediate euphoria of national revolutions had passed caused special consternation. Gendarmes in Lanžhot, southern Moravia, noted reprovingly that "after October 28, 1918 had finished, the consequences of incorrect thinking and understanding about the acquisition of freedom reached such a degree that armed bands of former soldiers and local inhabitants formed, threatening public security, particularly the safety of other people's property."[107] The gendarmerie in Nový Bydžov in central Bohemia agreed, after vigilantes tried to force the removal of the station commander, František Novotný: a "poor understanding of the situation" led people to think that it was "possible to eliminate individual functionaries, authorities, etc. and for each to behave according to his wish."[108]

For many peasants, the spectacular collapse of centuries-old monarchies, the sudden possibility of "self-determination" for peoples who had no memory of political independence, and ubiquitous talk of revolution all gave credence to the popular notion that the social order could be radically remade. Alongside the inebriated cries of "Long live freedom" resonating through the post-Habsburg countryside were serious efforts to transform society from the bottom up. On the same day that the National Council of Slovenes, Croats, and Serbs was proclaimed in Zagreb, several leading men in Peščenica, today an outlying suburb of the city, attempted to explain to a village assembly the concept of freedom, which included respect for the property of others.[109] A deserter named Franjo Klobučar interrupted the schoolmaster and mayor, insisting "that the newly created freedom should be understood in the sense that there is no need for gentlemen anymore and all property should already be distributed among the people." Two days of looting followed, in which a shop owned by the (Jewish) Schwarzenberg family, responsible for "swindling" people "inhumanly" during the war, became the primary target. In far eastern Slavonia, eighty-eight peasants from the eastern Slavonian village of Negoslavci, along with some agricultural laborers, stormed the Eltz family estates on November 1.[110] They subsequently claimed that the local notary Vojin Čorić had incited them to plunder, saying things like: "People, what are you waiting for, freedom is here, so go to the estates and take what you want." The people of Negoslavci, compelled to return the stolen goods later in November, may have found a ready scapegoat in the educated Čorić, who denied all involvement; many of them stressed their confusion at hearing his words. Yet it seems likely that they believed firmly that their interpretation of freedom was correct: on January 1, 1919, they returned to the Eltz estate at Gornjak and repossessed many of the items they had previously returned. "Even in Moravian Slovácko," wrote the village chronicler and schoolmaster in the Czech-speaking village of Hrušky, "they imagined freedom in their own manner, that is 'to take from the rich and give to poor people.' Many people looked forward to the 'division' of the large estate in Hrušky."[111]

The hard-pressed National Council in Zagreb hoped that guarantees of sweeping reform would placate the rebellious countryside of Croatia-Slavonia. A November 14 communique to the peasantry promised that "every family will be able, today and for a long time, to get enough fertile land for every enterprise, without causing anyone violence, injustice, or harm."[112] Peasants were admonished to embrace unity, harmony, and order instead of revenge, hatred, and humiliation. Twelve days later, the council decided to accelerate agrarian reform. All remaining feudal relations were to be abolished, particularly in Bosnia-Herzegovina, where they had remained in force, and preparations would be immediately undertaken for the parcellization of large estates.[113] But the National Council had the strength neither to carry out these measures nor to tame the countryside. A member of the council's local committee in the Slavonian town of Slatina reported despairingly on November 6 to the capital: "The people are in revolt. Total disorganization prevails. Only the army, moreover only the Serbian army, can restore order. The people are burning and destroying. I do not know how we shall feed Dalmatia and Bosnia. The mob is now pillaging the merchants, since all the landed estates have already been destroyed. Private fortunes are destroyed. The Serbian army is the only salvation."[114] The executive of the National Committee followed his advice, dispatching three representatives to Belgrade to begin negotiating terms of unification with the Serbian government.[115] With Dalmatia and Istria menaced by Italian expeditionary forces and conflict looming with Austria and Hungary in the north, Zagreb also appealed to the Entente for military assistance.[116] This was not forthcoming, in part because Italy was an Entente ally whose eastern Adriatic territorial ambitions had not yet been dashed by the Paris peace conference. By the middle of November, the Serbian army had advanced deep into Slavonia, restoring order in principal towns before turning its attention to the countryside. On the morning of November 12, a jubilant crowd in Požega greeted the entry of a Serbian cavalry squadron even as violence continued to roil the rural hinterland; four days later an infantry battalion arrived.[117] From their garrisons in the towns, Serbian forces organized policing operations in the countryside. They escorted gendarmes, notaries, estate overseers, and other officials around villages to identify stolen goods in peasant households and force their return.

The Serbian army's westward advance into the territories nominally controlled by Zagreb hastened the unification of the State of Slovenes, Croats, and Serbs (SHS) with the Kingdom of Serbia and Montenegro ruled by the Karađorđević dynasty. In principle, this outcome had the support of most of the post-Habsburg south Slav political elite; the major exception being the hard core of Croatian anti-Serb sentiment clustered around the followers of Josip Frank and his Party of Pure Right. The terms of unification proved bitterly contentious, though. Long-time Serbian prime minister and leader of the Radical Party Nikola Pašić remained adamant that Belgrade retain centralized control over any enlarged postwar south Slavic state. Despite wartime setbacks, Pašić won over influential leaders of the SHS state to his view, notably Svetozar Pribićević of the unitarist Democratic Party. They faced opposition from the Slovene People's Party leader Anton Korošec, president of the National Council, and particularly from the Croatian Peasant Party leader Stjepan Radić, who doggedly insisted on federal, if not confederal, terms of unification. Faced with continuing disorder in the rural hinterland, consensus in the Zagreb National Council shifted decisively away from Radić's position. During an all-night session on November 24, 1918, the council decided for immediate incorporation into Serbia and Montenegro. It dispatched a twenty-eight-member delegation, which arrived in Belgrade on November 30 to finalize unification, though its bargaining power was close to nil. The following day, the regent Aleksandar Karađorđević, having received pronouncements of virtually unconditional loyalty from the delegation, proclaimed the Kingdom of Serbs, Croats, and Slovenes.

The circumstances under which Yugoslav unification unfolded prompted some revolutionary and peasantist intellectuals to rue the violence of autumn 1918 and the unfulfilled promise of the Green Cadres. In 1923, Miroslav Krleža, doyen of twentieth-century Croatian letters, wrote:

> The Green Cadre, the only legitimate [*punomoćni*] representative of our people (of its political will and consciousness) during the time of the war, smashed its head at this time (when there had formed in the entire area of central Europe an objective revolutionary situation in the Marxist sense of the word) in vain. Our complete lack of politically intelligent forces was felt as never before. The Green Cadre put itself outside of Habsburg laws without a definite direction, without leadership and without the intelligentsia.[118]

For the Communist Krleža, the myopia of Croatia's political-intellectual elite condemned the disturbances of autumn 1918 to remain just that: leaderless, purposeless flailing against perennial objects of peasant rage. In his view, a south Slav Lenin, had he existed at the time, might have channeled the fury of the rural masses into a revolutionary movement.

With different political overtones, the Slovene author Ivan Zorec finished his adventure novel *The Green Cadre: A Tale from the Stormy Days of Our National Liberation*, also published in 1923, with a similar lamentation. After months of discipline and noble resistance to Austro-Hungarian tyranny, the rank-and-file peasant deserters besmirch themselves and their newly won freedom: "Yes, in that time, when the sky opened wide above us, and magnificent freedom all of a sudden found us and was dislodged from the numb limbs of the solid, old bonds, we madly and drunkenly burst onto the light, broad plain—we bellowed and smashed like a crude drunk, we senselessly destroyed and wantonly and wickedly spread devastation."[119] In Zorec's telling, the Green Cadres thus tragically abjured any possible role in the making of Yugoslavia. Among the significant casualties of postwar anarchy is the rhapsodic vision of peasant democracy espoused by the most intellectual member of the novel's Bosnia-based group, a failed writer named Josip Zidarić, who at one point proclaims: "The peasant is the greatest force on earth—he is lord of the land. If the peasants would realize their immense strength, they would transform the entire world."[120]

The desperate prostration of the post-Habsburg south Slavic lands before an expansionist Serbian kingdom was likely the most serious geopolitical ramification of the autumn 1918 rural upheavals. As historian Ivo Banac argued, the flawed unification of Yugoslavia and subsequent consolidation of Belgrade's centralist power in the 1921 constitution sowed the seeds of the rest of twentieth century's murderous ethnic-national animosities on south Slav territory.[121] But interwar Czechoslovakia also bore the marks of its campaign to discipline the Slovak countryside, which created early tensions within the new republic's ruling "Czechoslovak" people. In both cases, nationalist conceits accompanied the consolidation of state power. As with the influx of Serbs from Serbia in Croatia-Slavonia, the newly arrived Czech military men and administrators believed that they needed to school their stunted brethren, inured to life under a foreign (Hungarian) regime. The Czechs had led the formation of the wartime Czechoslovak Legions, apparently qualifying them for military leadership. Serbs from Serbia, meanwhile, regarded themselves as the martial race among south Slavs, having prevailed in three consecutive wars (two Balkan Wars during 1912–13 and the First World War), and chose to ignore the deserved prominence that Croats had enjoyed in the Habsburg armed forces. Yet while Habsburg Croatian and Slovenian territories were in general more economically developed and educated than the prewar Serbian Kingdom, the Slovaks seemed to many Czechs to lag behind them in every respect.

Following the October 30 declaration of intent by leading Slovak politicians gathered at Turčiansky Svätý Martin (today Martin in northern Slovakia) to join the Czechs in a unified state, local national council committees established themselves spontaneously in municipalities throughout Slovak territory. At least 350 committees emerged, the most influential of which were clustered in the northern central regions of Turiec and Liptov.[122] The notables behind these initiatives aimed to uncouple Slovak political life from the Kingdom of Hungary, as well to discourage attacks on private property; to this end, the national councils often oversaw the formation of volunteer national guard formations. In practice, however, the local national councils faced insurmountable obstacles. For starters, many municipalities had too few educated, "conscious" Slovaks to staff them or to command local authority. Budapest's Magyarization policies had incentivized assimilation to Hungarian language and culture among those who progressed beyond primary school, leaving a paucity of Slovak elites, particularly in the south and east of the country. In December 1918, it was estimated that of six hundred judges and notaries in Slovakia, only five could write competently in Slovak.[123] In many towns, ethnic Magyar or pro-Magyar ("Magyarone") lawyers, doctors, industrialists, and professors formed their own Hungarian national councils, which had readier access to arms and money. The local Slovak National Council committees were virtually powerless against the irregular troop formations that their Hungarian rivals mustered to maintain Budapest's hold on power.[124] Some of these evidently saw themselves as instruments of revenge against Slovak insurrectionists, carrying out violent reprisals in villages across Slovakia. In Nové Mesto nad Váhom, influential Magyar and Jewish burghers paid a company of Magyar soldiers returning from Prague to Hungary to remain in the town as security forces. On November 3, they used lethal force against Slovak villagers preparing to invade the town.[125]

Jews in many places formed their own self-defense units or, according to disapproving Czech and Slovak observers, hired deracinated soldiers to avenge the preceding plunder of Jewish shops. Bloodthirsty "Jewish guards" or "Jewish Magyar guards" allegedly caused mayhem in many towns.[126] In Žilina, they joined forces with a Magyar company to halt the eastward progress of Czechoslovak volunteers.[127] Jewish activists in Budapest had in fact dispatched armed volunteers to Slovak territories to safeguard their coreligionists' lives and property. For many Slovaks, this "Jewish revenge" wiped away any guilt they or their conationals might have previously borne.[128] In Jablonica, the retreat of Hungarian Jewish units under pressure from Czechoslovak volunteers called forth another round of attacks on the Jewish community, in which the synagogue was demolished.[129] In isolated instances, the Slovak national guards organized by local National Council committees themselves proved unreliable, joining attacks on Jewish shops and manorial estates.[130]

Order could be restored only by Czech units arriving from the Bohemian Lands. Those who chronicled the revolutionary period in western Slovakia expressed palpable relief when their western "brothers" came to halt the violence and force the withdrawal of Magyar irregulars.[131] So too did many villagers, who feared the retribution of Magyar and Jewish units for the *rabovky*. In the western Slovak village of Zohor, the arrival of a car on November 5 elicited panicked shouts that "the Hungarians are coming with machine guns!"[132] It turned out to be Ferdiš Juriga, an immensely popular Slovak nationalist activist, a leading figure in the Slovak People's Party until the early 1930s and a native of nearby Gbely. Greeted with jubilation, Juriga announced the imminent union of Czechs and Slovaks and told the Zohor peasants, who had robbed local Jewish houses the night before, "A new life has arrived, for that reason let us not rob, but rather rejoice." Although he later described the Green Cadres as elemental Slovak revolutionaries, a "true expression of the people," Juriga tried to quell the violence they had incited.[133] The next day, after Juriga had singlehandedly dissuaded a Jewish unit from entering Zohor, Czech soldiers arrived in the village and were plied with food and drink. By the last week of November, the Czechoslovak units in Slovakia, of whom most were of Czech ethnicity along with a minority of Slovaks, numbered 3,800 men.[134] But the advance of the inchoate Czechoslovak army did not always proceed smoothly, disappointing some enthusiasts of Czech-Slovak fraternity. In mid-November, official Hungarian army units assembled on Slovak territory, as well as units dispatched from Budapest, compelled the "liberators" to beat a humiliating retreat at Žilina and Trnava.[135] Not until January did Czechoslovak forces establish firm control over western Slovakia.

To administer Slovakia, the new government in Prague installed the Slovak political activist Vavro Šrobár as "minister with full power for the administration of Slovakia," a position created in mid-November 1918 with nearly dictatorial authority. Šrobár, a native of north-central Ružomberok district, was an ardent believer in Czechoslovak unity. His ministry presided over the integration of Slovakia into the new republic on unequal terms, although in late 1918 most of the Slovak political elite agreed that this was necessary given the failure of the Martin-based National Council and its local committees to control the hinterland. As Pavel Blaho, a patriotic physician and agrarian cooperative organizer in western Slovakia, wrote to Šrobár at the end of November, "Vavro, only an iron centralism can save us."[136] Šrobár evidently concurred. Facing a shortage of qualified Slovaks, Bohemian Czechs came to dominate the officer corps of the new army and occupied most positions in the new administrative organs on Slovak territory. While most Czech soldiers likely regarded Slovaks as their brothers, army officials received numerous complaints about uniformed men stealing, poaching, intimidating Slovaks, and degrading local Catholic practices.[137] And despite Catholicism's status as the majority religion in the Bohemian Lands, many Czechs were swept up in Masaryk and Beneš's Protestant-inflected Czech nationalism and its fierce opposition to perceived bastions of pro-Habsburg, antirepublican sentiment, like the Catholic Church. In the first postwar years, some Czech ex-legionnaires stationed in Slovakia and Subcarpathian Ruthenia became notorious for their brutal, sometimes murderous, behavior toward the native population.[138] Czechs controlled the new civilian authorities as well, regularly brushing aside requests to employ more Slovaks. In August 1919, the Bratislava county prefect Samuel Zoch reported that anti-Slovak sentiment was rife in the upper echelons of the postal service, financial administration, state railways, and social welfare office.[139] As both an evangelical preacher and a committed Czechoslovakist, Zoch particularly rued the recent dismissal of teachers from Slovak Lutheran schools—an unnecessary and potentially illegal act that he said would only embolden those who wanted to drive a wedge between Czechs and Slovaks.

Resentment of Czechs spread through the Slovak countryside as a prelude to the more principled, Catholic-hued autonomism of the Slovak People's Party, which was reconstituted after a wartime hiatus on December 19, 1918. Reports reached Šrobár's office of widespread popular mistrust of the Czechoslovak state. Peasants feared that the Czechs had come not as liberator-brothers but, like the Hungarians before them, as recruiters for the army and requisitioners of produce and livestock.[140] Even in the small town of Skalica, located just across the Morava River from the Bohemian Lands, where Pavel Blaho had swiftly put local administration on reliable footing after the national revolution, plundering and anti-Czech rioting erupted on January 14, 1919. The crowd shouted, "We don't want Czechs, we don't want the army, we will not enlist."[141] Vavro Černý, a priest in the central Slovak town of Šimonovany (Partizánske since 1949), encouraged peasants at a series of 1920 village meetings to resist requisitions, with violence if necessary, and reject the "government of Pepíks [a derogatory term for Czechs]," which, he contended, was worse than the Hungarians.[142] In Banská Štiavnica, Černý claimed, Czech soldiers had defiled a statue of the Virgin and stabled their horses in the church. The incremental dismantling of Šrobár's ministry and its replacement with central Prague-based institutions did little to defuse such tensions. In January 1922, the Slovak People's Party submitted its first proposal for legislative autonomy of Slovakia, setting the party on a collision course with Czechoslovak unitarists that would culminate in the 1939 establishment of a Slovak clerical-fascist German client state.

Anti-Jewish violence in Poland not only shaped the character of the interwar Polish state but to some degree influenced the global international order headed by the new League of Nations. On June 28, 1919, shortly after German representative Matthias Erzberger signed the peace treaty with the western Allies in the Hall of Mirrors at Versailles, Polish representatives Roman Dmowski and Ignacy Paderewski signed the "Little Versailles" agreement, guaranteeing the rights of minorities on Polish territory.[143] The world's first minority treaty ended months of wrangling among various parties gathered in Paris. During the first half of 1919, rival Polish factions embodied by the National Democrat Dmowski, chairman of the émigré Polish National Committee that had formed during the war, and Piłsudski's deputy Paderewski vied for western favor, pressing their own visions of reborn Poland. Britain, France, and the United States were themselves divided over the shape of the Polish state: whether it needed access to the sea, how much former German territory it should annex, and how large it should be to provide a bulwark against Bolshevism. Pogroms on Polish-controlled territory further complicated the situation, raising questions about Poland's ability to safeguard the lives and property of all its inhabitants. Worrisome was not only Warsaw's feeble suppression of peasant-led disturbances, such as the Galician town invasions discussed above, but the fact that Polish armed forces were responsible for two murderous episodes of anti-Jewish violence: the pogrom at Lwów in November 1918 and a mass shooting at Pinsk in April 1919.[144] The shock of these deadly events reverberated far beyond east central Europe. British and American Jewish communities were horrified; Zionists and non-Zionists proffered discordant long-term solutions, though both insisted on mechanisms to protect their coreligionists on Polish territory in the short term.[145] Paderewski labored to reassure Poland's would-be sponsors of his compatriots' essentially good intentions. The unrepentantly anti-Semitic Dmowski, alarmed by Britain's coldness to Polish demands and its apparent sympathy for Germany and Russia, called Prime Minister David Lloyd George an "agent of the Jews."[146]

Poland's accession to the Little Versailles treaty became a condition for its recognition by the western allies. Poles themselves regarded it, with some justification, as a breach of their sovereignty, and therefore repugnant. Article 2 stipulated that Poland must protect the life and liberty of all inhabitants of its territory regardless of "nationality, language, race or religion" and that it ensure "the free exercise, whether public or private, of any creed, religion or belief whose practices are not inconsistent with public order or public morals."[147] Article 12 proved most controversial because it made the Council of the League of Nations responsible for investigating any violations of the treaty's clauses.[148] Later in the year, the other new states of east central Europe were compelled to sign similar minority treaties, something that the western powers, though they contained abundant minorities, never imposed on themselves. Edvard Beneš of Czechoslovakia sanguinely declared that his country, the population of which was only two-thirds "Czechoslovak" (itself a dubious category), would become a "Little Switzerland."[149] Most east central European signatories, on the other hand, deeply resented what they saw as an unnecessary, even malevolent, infringement on their independence. After 1919, it would become clear that the minority treaties reflected in early and attenuated form the controversial core mission of the League of Nations, later fully expressed in the Mandates System, which put former Ottoman provinces and German colonial possessions under the tutelage of Britain and France: peoples not ready to govern themselves required the guidance of the world's most powerful liberal democracies.[150] In September 1934, Poland unilaterally decided it would no longer cooperate with the League or any other body enforcing the terms of the treaty.[151]

Peasant class violence in the aftermath of the First World War shaped east central Europe in important ways. It contributed in no small measure to the ultimately destructive centralism of interwar Yugoslavia and Czechoslovakia, ironically frustrating the revolutionary federalist ambitions harbored by many of its peasant perpetrators. By helping to generate minority treaties, starting with Poland, the violence undermined regional faith in the western-led international order. In Russia and Ukraine, it confirmed Bolshevik prejudices against the countryside, hardening their resolve but also forcing them to temporarily compromise with peasants in the form of the New Economic Policy. At the local level in east central Europe, the violence went largely unpunished. Given the immense numbers of people involved, both actively and passively, the judiciaries of the new states were quickly overwhelmed. Moreover, peasants formed the demographic majority across the region, except for Bohemia, and antagonizing large numbers of them might have had grave political ramifications. Army units assisted with the return of stolen goods in Croatia-Slavonia, Slovakia, and southern Poland, but only exceptionally did peasants have to compensate victims for destroyed or missing property.

Criminal investigations usually led nowhere unless serious physical injury or death had resulted. Official policy sanctioned this approach. Two postwar amnesty laws in Poland, one in February 1919 and another in May 1921, excused many of those involved in disturbances from culpability, while those who were tried and convicted generally received light sentences.[152] In 1919, Šrobár's ministry issued a decree disallowing legal proceedings against ordinary Slovaks who, owing to their "cultural backwardness," stole and destroyed property in the first weeks after the state revolution; the moratorium was extended in 1920 to cover the period of "anarchy" during the Hungarian Soviet invasion.[153] Czechoslovak president Masaryk himself took a lenient stance on violence committed during the national revolution, seeing forceful resistance as an integral part of Czech national history.[154] In Yugoslavia on November 28, 1920, the same day as the first statewide elections, Regent Aleksandar amnestied all suspects of political unrest from the previous two years, simultaneously releasing Croatian Peasant Party leader Stjepan Radić from prison, in a bid to drum up support for the regime. Like many peasants, the Slavonian Schön family mentioned above were eligible for forgiveness, since their actions "were part of the plunderers' movement [*pljačkaški pokret*]."[155] And investigators demurred from prosecuting otherwise upstanding members of the community, like the "well-situated" and "until now innocent and well-to-do people" who were among the looters arrested in and around the eastern Slavonian town of Đakovo, or the prosperous farmers who joined town invasions from Kutina in central Croatia to Polish western Galicia.[156]

This was small comfort to the region's Jews, many of whom forsook the villages and small towns they had inhabited for generations in the aftermath of the violence. In Ukraine, where they suffered most, the percentage of Jews living outside of cities dropped precipitously from 20 percent in 1897 to just 9 percent in 1920.[157] Elsewhere too, Jews sought the protections of urban life. In June 1919, the newly formed People's Federation of Jews for Slovakia lobbied Šrobár's ministry to fund a proletarian Jewish home in Bratislava for those of humbler means displaced by the November 1918 disturbances.[158] While some Jewish victims of the plundering attacks received at least partial compensation for their losses and returned to their homes, many did not, often because of continued local hostility. The tavern keeper Áron Tomaschoff and his family did not feel safe enough to go back to their home village of Párnica, located in the northern Slovak region of Orava, after they had been robbed and chased out after five generations.[159] The authorities proved unsympathetic to their plight, pointing to the Tomaschoffs' selfish behavior in denying the request of an agricultural cooperative to rent one of their buildings. The Tomaschoffs and other Jewish families languished in towns throughout Slovakia, and across east central Europe, unwilling to return to the countryside that shunned them.

4

Peasant Republics

PEASANTS DID NOT JUST SEEK REVENGE during the imperial collapse in central and eastern Europe. As state officials and gendarmes fled rural areas, villagers experimented with new forms of self-government, above all by proclaiming local autonomous republics with the immediate aim of breaking up and equitably redistributing large estate land. These short-lived polities, which sprouted up in numerous places in 1918 and 1919, ran parallel to the efforts of nationalist leaders, who at this time strove to install representative, republican government amid the wreckage of the Habsburg, Hohenzollern, and Romanov Empires. Emigré and domestic political elites who seized power in Prague and Warsaw were convinced that postwar Czechoslovakia and Poland should take republican form. Republicanism animated the leaders of the Ukrainian People's Republic, steered fitfully from Kiev, as well as a significant proportion of the Zagreb-based government of the ephemeral State of Slovenes, Croats, and Serbs; in both places, supporters of a republican solution were devastated by the more or less brutal swallowing of their homelands by mightier neighbors based in Moscow and Belgrade. Liberal and leftist politicians in both Budapest and Vienna welcomed the opportunity to replace the Habsburg monarchy with republican government, though with considerable trepidation about the extent of their territories after the peace settlement. Leaders of the Hungarian "Aster Revolution" hoped to maintain the integrity of the Kingdom of the Crown of Saint Stephen, while German Austrians across the political spectrum insisted on unification, or *Anschluss*, with Germany.

The wave of republican enthusiasm sweeping postwar central and eastern Europe reached into the most remote rural areas. But attempts by peasants to implement nonmonarchical government ended in repression. Their political autonomism thus met with the same fate as other experiments in regional separatism and socialist workers' self-rule, which rose and fell with precipitous speed at this time. For instance, the movement of newly christened "Sudeten" Germans in Bohemia and Moravia to unify with German Austria capitulated soon after clashes with Czechoslovak volunteers. The plebiscite-backed decision of Vorarlbergers in Austria's far west to join Switzerland led nowhere, particularly after the Swiss snubbed their overtures.[1] Kurt Eisner's socialist Bavarian Free State, proclaimed in Munich in November 1918, lasted no more than three months before its prime minister was murdered by a reactionary nobleman; the subsequent Bavarian Soviet Republic lasted a mere three weeks, perishing in bloody political violence, from which radical right-wing paramilitaries (the Freikorps) emerged triumphant.[2] In the territory of the Kingdom of Hungary, a multiethnic Banat Republic centered in Timişoara/Temesvár and a coal miners' "Black Diamond Republic" in Transylvania's Jiu Valley existed from the end of October 1918 into early 1919.[3]

By comparison, many of the peasant republics were even more fleeting. Their champions used the term "republic" flexibly, sometimes imprecisely, and in some cases only in retrospect to describe brief stints running their own affairs. Like the term "freedom" discussed above, political elites accused riled peasants of grievously misunderstanding the meaning of the term "republic." They could point, for example, to the violent looters in the western Slovak village of Plavecký Peter, who supposedly lamented the restoration of order in the municipality with the words: "Pity that the republic only lasted two days."[4] Yet peasant attempts at self-government during the remaking of central and eastern Europe were in many places the culmination of their revolution as they sought to enact their understandings of self-determination—perhaps the most consequential political slogan of the twentieth century. Originally an Enlightenment-era affirmation of individual autonomy associated with the philosophy of Immanuel Kant, "self-determination" had, over the course of the long nineteenth century, morphed into a collectivist creed legitimizing the liberation movements of entire peoples.[5] This was the sense in which Vladimir Lenin invoked the term in 1917 to justify the Bolshevik Revolution.

American president Woodrow Wilson also had collective self-determination in mind during his momentous February 11, 1918, speech before Congress, declaring it to be the guiding principle of international relations thenceforth. Wilson's intervention, substituting his previous catchphrase "consent of the governed" for a much more nebulous formulation, set the stage for his global celebrity status in 1918–19, with movements for autonomy and independence around the world vying to associate their aims with the American president's prestige.[6] In east central Europe, Wilson's portrait replaced that of the

Habsburg emperor in public buildings, while public facilities, like Prague's main train station, formerly Franz Joseph Station, were renamed after him. The mostly German and Magyar city of Pressburg/Poszony/Prešporok enjoyed a brief career at the very end of 1918 and beginning of 1919 as Wilsonov, or Wilsonovo mesto (Wilson's city), before Czech and Slovak leaders settled on the comfortingly Slavic name of Bratislava, Slovakia's present capital.[7] The risks inherent in trumpeting self-determination were not lost on statesmen at the time. In December 1918, on the eve of the Paris peace conference, Wilson's own secretary of state, Robert Lansing, jotted down his anxious thoughts: "When the President talks of 'self-determination' what unit has he in mind? Does he mean a race, a territorial area, or a community? Without a definite unit which is practical, application of this principle is dangerous to peace and stability."[8]

Peasants inhabiting the territories of now-defunct empires in central and eastern Europe appear to have had a clear understanding of self-determination in their own minds. In numerous locales, not only those where "republics" arose, they ejected former officials and officeholders—gendarmes, notaries, customs officials, mayors—often by force. They held popular assemblies at which they elected their own governing bodies, sometimes called "councils" to denote their provisional character. They formed committees to address what they regarded as the most pressing issue confronting village society: insufficient farmland owned by peasants and an excess of arable land, along with previously common forests, pastureland, and streams, in the possession of large landowners. They began to seize neighboring large estates without compensation. And they recruited rudimentary armed forces—often volunteer "village guards"—to protect their gains and prevent interference from outside; to this end, they sometimes cut telegraph and telephone cables. The many peasant republics that were established in Croatia-Slavonia, Slovenia, Poland, Russia, and Ukraine generally combined all these actions and went a step further, declaring sovereignty in their territory. In many instances, they pursued complete self-sufficiency (a centuries-old peasant dream) equipped with the slogans, institutional forms, and weapons of the modern era. In other cases, they attempted to form alliances and establish mutually supportive relations with the incipient urban-ruled successor states, preparing the ground for eventual and equitable unification on terms that would preserve villagers' autonomy. The successor states' suppression of the rural republics surprised no one, not even some of their founders, but these grassroots initiatives amply showcased peasant determination to governments struggling for legitimacy. Urban governments in what had been Austria-Hungary decided that agrarian reform to benefit smallholding and landless peasants could not be staved off any longer, even if they wondered whether small farms had any future in modern Europe.

Although peasant republics had existed before the end of the First World War, their sheer abundance in the years 1918 and 1919 had no precedent. Nor is it clear that the peasants who set up their statelets in the former Habsburg and Romanov domains looked to past models. Russian and Ukrainian peasants may have drawn inspiration from the efflorescence of village politics during the 1905 Russian Revolution, which yielded at least a couple of localized republics. One was established in Markovo, in the northwest of Moscow province, where at the end of October 1905 a peasant assembly repudiated all external authority and refused to pay further taxes and rents or provide conscripts until their list of progressive political demands was fulfilled.[9] In the period before the village's occupation by troops seven months later, the Markovo Republic's leadership organized the distribution of estate resources, particularly timber, and involved itself in national political issues, demanding, for instance, a peasant majority in the local Zemstvo board. In remote western Georgia, several years of strikes and boycotts against landlords culminated in the so-called Gurian Republic, which lasted over a year between late 1904 and early 1906, when it was brutally suppressed.[10] With the support of Georgian Menshevik Social Democrats, who took a much more accommodating stance toward peasant demands for land than their Great Russian counterparts, Gurian peasants confiscated large holdings, organized the fair redistribution of land, and protected grazing rights. They introduced general suffrage for men and women and established "people's courts" in each village to oversee administrative and judicial affairs. Alongside the ambitious Markovo and Gurian Republics, the Russian Empire in 1905–6 witnessed countless smaller-scale instances of peasants rejecting state authorities and administering their own affairs.[11]

Russia and Ukraine in 1917–18 provided a more plausible model for would-be rural republicans in Habsburg and east central Europe. The dramatic evaporation of state authority over the course of 1917 nurtured the soil for flourishing experiments in peasant self-rule. Especially in the wake of the Bolshevik takeover, Russian and Ukrainian peasants seized and divided up large estate land, along with mills and orchards. Encouraged initially by the provisional government, later in stronger terms by the Bolsheviks, village councils and peasant committees multiplied. The new peasant-led authorities, often loyal only to their home villages, sometimes quarreled with each other over the spoils.[12] Peasants established district-sized republics in the regions of Pokrovsk, Kazan', Tver', Viatka, Altai, Kursk, and Kaluga.[13] Countless villages became completely autonomous and refused to recognize outside authorities. In early 1918, nearly all villages in Kaniv district south of Kiev declared themselves republics, many digging trenches around their micro-territories to repulse outsiders. Peasants of one village in Mohyliv district, located in southwest Ukraine, murdered the local "propertied people," and then set up machine guns at all entrances to thwart interference from without.[14]

In Ukraine during the civil war, various urban-based claimants to power—Bolsheviks, White armies, and Ukrainian nationalist leaders—struggled to match the legitimacy that peasants saw in their own institutions. In his memoirs, Vsevolod Petriv, a high-ranking officer in the directorate, admiringly recalled a peasant republic that formed in late 1917 from a number of villages in the south Ukrainian district of Ekaterinoslav (Dnipro since 1926): all matters were discussed openly and solutions reached by consensus; private property was allowed to exist up to a certain limit, beyond which it was socialized and redistributed to landless or land-hungry villagers; and peasants raised a conscript defense force that was mobilized both against Red Army requisitioners and in support of the Red Army against Austro-German troops who occupied the Ukraine in 1918.[15] Pressed from all sides, Ukrainian peasants sought the armed neutrality of their home village or local region, often violently cleansed of nonpeasant "outsiders," while at the same time laying the foundations of an imagined postwar future. Starting in autumn 1917, many Austro-Hungarian peasants were eyewitnesses, as returning prisoners of war, of conditions in the former Tsarist Empire. A year later, these men often led republican initiatives in the east central European countryside.

The first of them appeared in the south Slav lands. Isolated from one another, most were suppressed within a few weeks, some within a matter of days, and none left behind much in the way of documentation. Nonetheless, they open a brief window onto what villagers expected from their revolution. The Slavonian Petrijevci Republic was launched at the end of October when assembled peasants rejected the Valpovo county clerk's proposal to parcel out the local baronial estate at discounted prices. "Why should we pay?" asked one recent returnee from Russian internment, "Give us the land for free!"[16] In the following commotion, a revolutionary republican committee was formed under the leadership of another returnee, named Đuro Kormanuš.

Villagers assembled before the church, unanimously backing the old tailor Ivan Bogdanović's laconic pronouncement that "the land must be shared among us."[17] Before its suppression on November 14, the Petrijevci Republic prepared plans for land redistribution, disarmed local gendarmes, formed a militia, and posted sentries around its jurisdiction.[18] In nearby Donji Miholjac, a national guard composed of insurgent peasants (the "biggest pillagers," according the official report) proclaimed a republic after relieving the local officialdom and "eminent" citizens of their responsibilities.[19] They set about parceling out the surrounding latifundia and introduced censorship of post and telegraph. Self-designated "republican authorities" in Našice forcibly taxed the rich and organized a defense force.[20] As mentioned in the preceding chapter, a company dispatched from Osijek crushed the Našice experiment, summarily executing thirty "looters, gypsies and riffraff" in the churchyard. Among the victims were, unusually, two revolutionary young Jewish men recently returned from Russian imprisonment.

The region of Slavonia, with its highly unequal distribution of arable land, was the center of this deluge of do-it-yourself republicanism. But republican fervor gripped much of the Croatian countryside. On November 3 in the village of Goričan, located in the Croat-majority Međimurje region of (then) Hungary, peasants established a "commune," propagating agrarian reform and Croatian national liberation.[21] The commune's national guards could not prevent its bloody disbanding by Magyar troops two weeks later. Local elites throughout the former Habsburg south Slav lands remarked with alarm on the depth of republican conviction. In December, the district administrator in Donja Stubica, in the hilly northwest Croatian Zagorje region, recommended liquidation of the local national guard, since "the entire population is with momentary exceptions for a republic."[22]

For many, President Wilson was the guiding spirit of the moment. On October 28 in the Slavonian town of Valpovo, eighty peasants, Green Cadres among them, boisterously rejected the local National Council committee chosen by local elites. After a committee of technocrats was appointed to mollify the opposing factions, the deserters bayoneted a portrait of Emperor Karl in the assembly chamber and demonstratively hoisted a picture of Wilson and a Yugoslav flag in its place. They proceeded to loot the town warehouses and manorial properties.[23] On November 24, seventy-four inhabitants of the central Croatian village of Tomašica signed a resolution calling for the annulment of price controls, the removal of undesirable officials, elections to the constituent assembly, and a republican state, preferably "on the American model."[24]

Reflecting on these events in the 1930s, the prominent Croatian journalist and historian Josip Horvat wrote:

> Among all the peoples of the Austro-Hungarian Monarchy, Wilson's message, his ideology, surely had the strongest influence on the Croats. They immediately received his political philosophy with all the fervor of feeling. . . . Like Christ, Wilson brings good tidings primarily to the small and weak, to the humiliated and insulted he brings the idea of equality. . . . Wilsonianism suits the bourgeois element in the first instance with its refined, emphatic sense of political rights, but it fits the broadest popular classes with its pacifistic slogans, because for the person of the Croatian village the victory of pacifism is a very concrete, practical goal: it promises abolition of the army, and this brings with it tax reductions; the words about freedom and self-determination have for the man of the village primarily economic content; the eternal hunger for land will acquire demonic revolutionary strength.[25]

Horvat captured the autonomist impulses that underpinned Croatian villagers' new political consciousness, but he underestimated the extent to which peasants of other nationalities, including other south Slavs, embraced the republican model. In early November 1918 in the Loška Valley of southern Slovenia, for instance, peasants formed a "republican" commission to oversee the redistribution of manorial land and forests. A detachment of a thousand troops overwhelmed the local self-defense units on November 24.[26] At the end of December, near the southern Slovene town of Novo Mesto, former Russian prisoner of war Tone Pirnar, a deserter from the Habsburg army called Ivan Florjančič, and the socialist army veteran Jože Pirnar initiated events that would lead to the establishment of a short-lived republic. Having led a protest march of five hundred peasants to the village mayor's house in Kandija, they forced the resignation of the mayor and existing village councils, forming a republican government that lasted four days before its suppression.[27] Horvat also disregarded peasants' expanded political horizons, characteristically locating the appeal of Wilson's message in their narrow economic concerns. In fact, genuine political ambitions often accompanied the establishment of peasant republics in the former Habsburg-ruled lands. These sometimes extended to the larger state frameworks that were just coming into existence. While instituting local autonomy and taking measures to safeguard their gains, peasant republicans tried to cooperate with, and shape, incipient postimperial states.

The best example of such ambitions was in Galicia, where Polish peasants elected a republican government centered on the market town of Tarnobrzeg, located in the northernmost tip of the old Austrian province on the banks of the Vistula River. One of the founders of the Tarnobrzeg Republic was Tomasz Dąbal, a man whose turbulent political career embodied the ferment of the post-Habsburg countryside.[28] Born in 1890 to a relatively prosperous peasant family in the village of Sobów (now part of Tarnobrzeg), Dąbal's parents possessed too little land to guarantee a sufficient inheritance to each of their five children and decided to send Tomasz to academic secondary school (gymnasium). After completing eight years of gymnasium in Dębica, a town some forty-five miles south of Tarnobrzeg, Dąbal enrolled in 1911 on a course of medicine at the University of Vienna, transferring just a few months later to the Jagiellonian University in Cracow. It was around this time that he became involved in the Galicia-based Polish People's Party (Polskie Stronnictwo Ludowe), penning articles for the Cracow party organ, *Przyjaciel ludu* (Friend of the people). During the war, he underwent training as a reserve officer in Lower Austria and then served as the commander of a machine gunners' company on the Russian, Italian, and Albanian fronts. Despite his valorous conduct in the Habsburg army, for which he was decorated multiple times, at some point around the beginning of 1917 he joined the Polish Legions under the command of Józef Piłsudski. Initially a volunteer-based Habsburg auxiliary force, by the last years of the war, Piłsudski's legions were fighting for complete Polish independence. Dąbal appears to have maintained a toehold in both organizations; it was as an Austro-Hungarian officer that he was in 1918 discharged from front service for injuries sustained. Convalescing in his home district and mourning the sudden death of his young wife from a blood infection, he came into contact with a socially radical priest named Eugeniusz Okoń, a native of the nearby village of Radomyśl nad Sanem.

The officer and the priest headed the Tarnobrzeg Republic for the approximately three months of its existence, after which, despite persecution, they both entered the reconstituted Polish parliament, or *sejm*, as deputies of the radical Wyzwolenie (Liberation) wing of the Polish People's Party based in the former Russian partition. For the next two years, Dąbal changed his parliamentary allegiance no fewer than five times—a record for the period—settling in summer 1921 on the semi-illicit Communist Party. Arrested shortly thereafter and sentenced in mid-1922 to six years' imprisonment, he won release less than a year later by agreeing to be part of a prisoner exchange between Poland and the Soviet Union. More than anything else, the Tarnobrzeg Republic shaped Dąbal's career and political identity. The circumstances of its origins, its unsuccessful attempts to win durable recognition from the fledgling Polish state, and its incremental radicalization all left an indelible imprint on its leaders, as well as on the peasants of the region.[29]

On October 28, as Austrian rule evaporated, Polish leaders in Cracow established a temporary Galician administration called the Polish Liquidation Commission (Polska Komisja Likwidacyjna), headed by Wincenty Witos, leader of the conservative "Piast" wing of the People's Party. A couple of days later, news of the empire's disintegration reached Tarnobrzeg, where Polish officers under Major Karol Pawlas formed a District Command of Polish Armed Forces (Powiatowa Komenda Wojsk Polskich), which over the following days disarmed all remaining Austrian troops and disbanded the Austrian gendarmerie. Pawlas appointed Dąbal to head the new gendarmerie force. New civilian authorities replaced the Austrian district captaincy when, on November 2, at the initiative of local noble magnate Count Zdzisław Tarnowski and members of the intelligentsia, a District Committee of Self-Defense (Powiatowy Komitet Samoobrony) was called into existence. Headed by the engineer Jan Bochniak, the eight-man committee included local notables, along with two prominent peasant leaders: Jan Słomka, the mayor of Dzików, and Wojciech Wiącek, a former deputy to the Austrian parliament from Machów. Yet it shortsightedly excluded representatives of the peasant political movement. Unperturbed, the District Committee contacted the Liquidation Commission in Cracow and received the latter's blessing to act in its name in Tarnobrzeg district. On November 6, Bochniak was elevated to the position of district commissioner.

Meanwhile, Dąbal began to reorganize the gendarmerie according to the principles of peasant justice. He arrested his predecessor, the German-speaking commander Friedl, and evicted the family of an Austrian gendarme who had killed a deserter during wartime, transferring ownership of the house to the deserter's widow. Having called upon former Austrian soldiers to volunteer for gendarmerie service, he was able to set up new posts in Grębów, Razwadów, Radomyśl, and Baranów. The character of the new recruits raised concerns. The parish priest in Grębów alleged that Dąbal enlisted "only bandits and criminals."[30] Former Green Cadres appear to have been heavily represented among them, as well as others who had chased out gendarmes in the first days of the revolution. Beside his controversial actions as gendarmerie chief, Dąbal started to involve himself in politics, organizing and attending meetings of peasant activists who wanted to change the composition of the District Committee, which was widely seen as a conservative clique.

Matters came to a head on November 6, market day in Tarnobrzeg, when the District Committee planned an assembly to rally support. While they and their allies attended mass in the town's Dominican church, peasants from outlying villages converged on the headquarters of the district gendarmerie for a rival event. As mass finished, the peasant crowd marched demonstratively to the main square, assembling by the monument of Bartosz Głowacki, a late eighteenth-century peasant leader and a hero of the 1794 Kościuszko uprising against partitioning powers. The Głowacki statue had been erected in 1904 thanks to peasant donations. It now served as the focal point of a mass gathering of three to five thousand peasants. Okoń addressed the crowd first, allegedly telling them: "You have defended this land against the enemy, and since you defended it, you have the right to the land."[31] It was likely he who devised the slogan of the assembly: "Government for the people, land for the peasants."[32] Two days prior, he had led a throng of villagers to a pillar in Tarnobrzeg county that marked the border between Austrian and Russian Poland and ceremoniously toppled it (figure 4.1). In so many of the actions of Okoń, Dąbal, and their followers, one can discern a combustible blend of social radicalism and patriotic devotion to a reunified Poland.

Dąbal was among the five speakers who followed Okoń, proposing to raise a volunteer peasant regiment to recapture Lwów (Lemberg/Lviv) from the Ukrainian forces then occupying the eastern Galician seat. Rejecting the authority of the District Committee, the assembly appointed a seventeen-member District Peasant Committee (Powiatowy Komitet Chłopski), steered by Dąbal and Okoń, to take over local administration until elections in all municipalities could be held. Here were the origins of the Tarnobrzeg Republic. Along with electing new authorities in the district, the assembly passed a series of radical resolutions. One hailed the end of Austrian rule and demanded "the end of noble influences in all government and administration."[33] Another called for the removal of all former village mayors, the dissolution of the district council as well as all municipal councils, and elections to fill these positions with new personnel. Reproving officials saw the elimination of former village elites as the peasant radicals' primary aim.[34] On November 16, younger villagers rowdily ejected Jan Słomka from office after four decades as mayor of Dzików.[35] Likely the most significant resolution confirmed the expropriation of large estates without compensation and the redistribution of manorial land among peasants.

The November 6 assembly intended to provoke a confrontation with the District Committee, which peasants widely regarded as illegitimate. A peasant

FIGURE 4.1 Eugeniusz Okoń, with shovel in hand, leading a crowd on November 4, 1918 to topple the boundary marker between Galicia and Russian Poland near Tarnobrzeg. Museum of Independence in Warsaw.

poet and journalist named Stanisław Gąsiorowski treated the crowd gathered by the Głowacki monument to his sardonic verses entitled "You Don't Intimidate Us," which also took aim at the more conservative wing of the Peasant Party:

Don't you intimidate us with court or bullet,
Your lordships from that PKL [Polish Liquidation Commission] of yours,
Because under our coarse peasant shirts
Are the chests that we put in the line of fire
As we went into battle—as shock troops—
For you and your Berlins and Viennas.

The Cracovian philistine, black marketeer and bumpkin squire,
And that swindler "count" Lasocki,
None of them will fool us threshing folk
[Into thinking] that we'll get land as a charitable reward
[Telling us] Just not now, later, after the Sejm [is elected],
When Witos takes power in Poland.[36]

Despite the boisterous mood of the assembly, the District Peasant Committee intended to take power peacefully. Shortly after the mass gathering, the "republic" sent a delegation to the District Committee, presenting them with the assembly's resolutions and demanding their resignation; this, however, was refused. On November 7, a delegation journeyed to Cracow to lobby the Liquidation Commission directly for recognition of the decisions taken the previous day in the Tarnobrzeg main square. They received a frosty welcome from the Administrative Department head, Count Zygmunt Lasocki, who informed them, over their protests, that their efforts in self-government were futile since Bochniak had just been appointed district commissioner. General Bolesław Roja, military commander of Galicia since November 1, was even more brusque toward the peasant envoys, who requested that Dąbal be elevated to the rank of major. "Since when is it a custom to promote officers on the main square in Tarnobrzeg?" Roja asked disdainfully.[37] Turned away by the Liquidation Commission, the delegation tried to drum up favorable publicity in the press. But the editor of *Piast*, the organ of the People's Party conservative wing, counseled them to wait for the consolidation of state power before making demands for radical reform. Only *Naprzód* (Forward), Polish Social Democracy's newspaper in Galicia, agreed to publish a brief account of events by the Głowacki monument.

Stymied in Cracow, the Tarnobrzeg republicans dispatched another three-man delegation, including Dąbal, to the city of Lublin in the former Russian partition, where a provisional Polish government under the Galician socialist leader Ignacy Daszyński had just been proclaimed. The Tarnobrzeg contingent received a cordial welcome from war minister Edward Rydz-Śmigły and minister of the interior Stanisław Thugutt. Daszyński's cabinet agreed with the Tarnobrzeg leaders on the need for radical reform, but their authority was limited; within a week, Daszyński had resigned after failing to form a government that would include parties of both left and right. General Piłsudski, recently arrived in Warsaw from German captivity, appointed the moderate socialist Jędrzej Moraczewski to lead a new Warsaw-based government until elections could be held. During his Lublin visit, Dąbal nonetheless persuaded Rydz-Śmigły to order military authorities in west Galicia to furnish him with one thousand rifles, ammunition, and uniforms for a volunteer regiment named after Our Lady of Dzików. The regiment was never raised, but many of the weapons found their way into the hands of the Tarnobrzeg Republic's supporters.

A delicate truce now prevailed in Tarnobrzeg district. Commissioner Bochniak, Major Pawlas, and Count Lasocki all sought reinforcements for the local garrison. On Wednesday, November 13, another peasant assembly was held at the Głowacki monument, to coincide with market day. Dąbal reported on his deputation's activities in Cracow and Lublin, while Okoń supposedly declared to the crowd: "It's all yours," with a sweeping gesture toward the shops lining the square—or toward the fields beyond town limits; no one was quite sure. Whatever the intent of his words, riled peasants proceeded to violently plunder Tarnobrzeg's mostly Jewish-owned stores, while Dąbal and other leaders tried in vain to rein them in. Pawlas balked at armed intervention to halt the disorder, leading to his resignation shortly thereafter. General Roja replaced him with Dąbal, whom he promoted to captain after Pawlas admitted that, of all military men in the district, Dąbal enjoyed the broadest popular support. By taking up the position, Dąbal relinquished his command of the gendarmerie, which now passed to Stanisław Borowiec, a disciplinarian who set about reinstating some former Habsburg gendarmes. Angry villagers again overwhelmed and disarmed several gendarmerie posts. Dąbal's tenure as district military commander was brief. He initiated recruitment for his planned patriotic volunteer regiment, but there were few takers among the peasantry. He gave the Liquidation Commission assurances that he would not engage in political campaigning, but these were likely insincere; on November 20 and 27 he again strode the rostrum at peasant assemblies on Tarnobrzeg's main square. At the end of the month, facing denunciation by a group of local officers, Dąbal resigned his command to fully serve the "republic."

Dąbal's final break with Cracow coincided with the November 28 announcement throughout Polish territories that elections to the sejm would occur on January 26, 1919. The leadership of the Tarnobrzeg Republic now reoriented its activities to electioneering and to actively undermining the Liquidation Commission's authority. At the December 4 assembly by the Głowacki monument, in the presence of 250 soldiers in serried ranks, Dąbal thundered to the crowd: "Look, peasants, at that noble . . . army, it isn't going to relieve Lwów, but rather keeps watch over us, so that we don't do any harm to their lordships! Disarm them!"[38] Peasants began to advance on the soldiers, hurling bricks. The soldiers dispersed the crowd with rifle butts. Okoń and Dąbal extended their agitation to the surrounding areas. In a written appeal to the peasants of Nisko district, urging them to register to vote and attend a mass assembly in town on New Year's Day, they vehemently attacked Count Lasocki: "Where was your deputy count Lasocki and what did he do for you? When the gendarme organized hunts for peasant-deserters who didn't want to serve the scoundrel enemy, the German, like for wild animals; when the gendarme shot and killed peasants, beat defenseless women. Lasocki, the greatest enemy of the peasants, passed budgets and [war] loans for the Austrian government, so that the war would last longer, so that even more peasants would perish and die."[39] The flier's authors identified strongly with peasant deserters, fanning the flames of popular resistance to conscription. Although Dąbal had previously hoped to raise a volunteer regiment himself, he now decried any initiative from the Liquidation Commission, which on December 10 had reintroduced compulsory military service—handiwork of the "Jewish count" Lasocki, according to the flier.

The Liquidation Commission introduced repressive measures in the countryside. Soldiers forced their way into peasant homes to confiscate illegal firearms. Whole villages were punished for high levels of desertion or for the town invasions and riots during November; public beatings took place, often of innocent people. The authorities disallowed assemblies by the Głowacki monument, while seeking pretexts to arrest Okoń and Dąbal. Multiple reports bemoaned Okoń's evil influence over villagers, who were "blindly devoted" to him and who "[did] not recognize any military or civilian authorities."[40] Yet the campaign appears to have only further radicalized peasants, boosting the District Peasant Committee's popularity. Public order deteriorated in the western Galician districts of Tarnobrzeg, Nisko, Kolbuszowa, and Mielec. Instances of desertion, theft, and banditry multiplied, particularly around the Sandomierz Forest and the village of Grębow, areas traditionally inhabited by the fiercely independent Lasowian people. A primarily forest-dwelling subethnic group of the Poles, the Lasowians were outraged at the renewed intrusion by Polish authorities. When the bulk of troops departed from the Tarnobrzeg garrison for the Christmas holiday, the Lasowians rearmed themselves.

By late December, open conflict could no longer be averted. An illegal December 18 assembly in the Tarnobrzeg market square selected five candidates, including Okoń and Dąbal, for a People's Party–Left ballot in the upcoming elections. Just before the end of the year, the new gendarmerie commander in Tarnobrzeg obtained warrants to arrest leaders of the "republic." Okoń was detained on January 6 at an assembly in the village of Baranów, Mielec district. Dąbal went into hiding, fleeing at some point across the frozen Vistula into Sandomierz district. Their enraged supporters petitioned for Okoń's release and complained that People's Party–Piast was using the Liquidation Commission as an instrument of terror against the peasant party's left wing. The complaints reached Moraczewski's government in Warsaw, which reacted sympathetically, but Minister of the Interior Thugutt could not persuade

Lasocki to intervene in what the latter claimed was a strictly judicial affair. Despite persecution, the Tarnobrzeg Republic's leaders managed in January to publish the first issue of *Jednośċ Chłopska* (Peasant unity), a newspaper intended to be the organ of a new postelection party, never realized, called the Progressive Peasant Party.

Meanwhile, unrest roiled the surrounding countryside. On January 8, Lasowian villagers came to Tarnobrzeg to plunder Jewish and Catholic shops, beating up some Jews in the process.[41] That day and the next, armed peasants stormed an estate owned by Count Tarnowski in Tarnobrzeg district, plundering grain and potatoes. Drunken soldiers had already intimidated Tarnowski on New Year's Eve, loudly caroling outside his residence and shooting in the air.[42] On January 9 and 10, villagers from Jeziórko and Żupawa attacked the estate owned by Seweryn Dolański in Grębów. Army units suppressed the disturbances, killing 3 peasants and arresting 350. Some prosperous villagers descried Bolshevism lurking behind the disturbances. The elderly Jan Słomka observed that "one could see on all sides signs of Bolshevik influence. Agitators would point to the manor, and say: 'Everything belongs to the peasant. One should go and take it!' They urged that the farmers plough the fields of the manors in the spring for their own use. They roused folk not to fear the troops, not to join the colors, telling of the Red Guards."[43] A contemporary report on Tarnobrzeg district agreed: "In the pre-election period it was difficult to distinguish political agitation from Bolshevik and bandit agitation."[44] While "Bolshevism" could be equated with Lenin's October 1917 decree on land and giving villagers a free hand to divide up estates, many commentators at the time simply used it as shorthand for criminal activity and anarchy. In Słomka's view, order returned to the district because "the masses at heart still had faith in God and His commandments."[45]

The degree of popular support for the republic was obvious when the January 26 election results came in. Despite the harsh repression that had landed two of its leading figures in jail or hiding, the republic's candidates won parliamentary mandates on the backs of overwhelming majorities. With over 80 percent turnout, the People's Party–Left candidates won 75,673 of 96,420 total votes cast, or 78.5 percent, in Tarnobrzeg, Nisko, Kolbuszowa, and Mielec districts. This stunning vindication of the Tarnobrzeg Republic sent peasant radicals Okoń, Dąbal, Franciszek Krempa, Wojciech Marchut, and Jan Sudoł to the sejm in Warsaw. Yet the results split dramatically along urban-rural lines. Tarnobrzeg and Rozwadów towns, for instance, both around three-quarters Jewish, gave only between 2 and 8 percent of their votes to the People's Party–Left candidates, whereas over a dozen villages in Tarnobrzeg district voted exclusively and without exception for the leaders of the republic.

Victory in the sejm elections also marked the end of the Tarnobrzeg Republic, as its leaders accepted the new Polish state's legitimacy and renounced claims to local independence. Agrarian populist agitation still continued in north-central Galicia for many months after. In spring 1919, Dąbal and Okoń held numerous peasant assemblies in the region, agitating for radical land reform and fulminating against the aristocratic sejm majority that stood in their way. These gatherings coincided with another surge of deadly pogrom violence against west Galician Jews, in which instigation by the leaders of the "republic" was suspected but could not be proven since their speeches rarely contained openly anti-Semitic statements.[46] Nonetheless, their continuing support for extraparliamentary action seemed beyond doubt. On May 2 in the village of Grębów, Dąbal gave a two-hour address at an event conspicuously attended by the notorious bandit-deserter Józek Gądek, afterward proceeding to fraternize with the crowd over drinks in the local tavern.[47] Okoń and Dąbal continued to organize mass gatherings into the summer of 1920, when their paths finally diverged over the latter's growing Communist sympathies.[48]

While the Tarnobrzeg Republic sought cooperation with independent Poland—a state whose prospects were relatively good—the republics proclaimed by Ruthene villagers in the eastern Carpathian Mountains cultivated relations with much more tenuous polities in the east.[49] The mountainous northeast of the Hungarian Kingdom, inhabited mostly by Ruthenes (today considered Ukrainians), drifted away from Budapest's control in the weeks following the October 31 Aster Revolution. On November 8, former Austro-Hungarian soldiers formed a Hutsul National Council in the small town of Yasinya/Kőrösmező, a remote border outpost twenty-two hours by train from the Hungarian capital that had become an important reentry station for troops in the final months of the war. The name of the council referred to the local subethnic group of Ruthenes, populating seventeen villages on the southern slopes of the Carpathian Mountains.[50] The leader of the Hutsul council was Stepan Klochurak, the twenty-three-year-old son of a prosperous local peasant family, who had attended academic high school as well as law school in Sighetu Marmației/Máramarosszizet (today in Romania). Having served as a reserve officer on the Russian and Romanian fronts, he was appalled by the Austro-Hungarian execution of alleged Russophiles in his hometown after the 1915 Russian retreat. Klochurak and the other Habsburg army veterans who made up the Hutsul National Council established contact with leaders of the recently proclaimed West Ukrainian People's Republic, then based in L'viv. They also maintained contact with Budapest, journeying there in early December to participate in discussions led by liberal statesman Oszkár Jászi on autonomy for national minorities in the new Hungarian Republic. On December 21, the Károlyi government instituted the autonomous Ruthene province of Rus'ka Kraina in the northeast of the country.

The province's autonomy was put in doubt when Hungarian troops remanned local garrisons, prompting Klochurak to secede from Hungary once and for all. Apparently backed by the West Ukrainian People's Republic—then based in Stanyslaviv (today Ivano-Frankivsk) after the Poles recaptured L'viv—Hutsul leaders staged an uprising on the evening of January 7, 1919, Christmas Eve in the Orthodox rite. Under the guise of *koliadky*, the Ukrainian door-to-door caroling tradition, a large crowd of armed men gathered and seized control of Yasinya early on Christmas Day. The Hutsul Republic set to work organizing governmental departments for foreign relations, domestic order, provisioning, education, and the economy. New village mayors and notaries were installed, and friendly overtures were made to the local German and Jewish populations. For self-defense, Klochurak organized a Hutsul Guard, which occupied the upper reaches of the Tisza River valley and at one point attempted to seize Sighetu Marmației but was rebuffed by Romanian troops. Having cut railway and communication connections with Magyar Hungary, the Hutsul Republic's leaders intended it to be a transitional polity on the path to unification with independent Ukraine, a plan that received official sanction at the January 21 Ukrainian congress in the town of Khust. But as the Ukrainian movement's fortunes declined under Polish and Red Army pressure, the Hutsuls found themselves isolated. Their geographical remoteness allowed the republic's survival for some months more, before the Romanian army finally disbanded it in June 1919.

Integration with the West Ukrainian People's Republic was also the goal of a republican experiment among the Lemkos, another Ruthenian subgroup, which inhabited the northern slopes of the Carpathians in the former province of Galicia. In early November, eastern Lemkos representing thirty villages gathered at the instigation of a Greek Catholic priest in the village of Komańcza to proclaim what became known as the Komańcza Republic; it lasted until its suppression by Polish troops on January 23, 1919.[51] Lemkos to the west, by contrast, rejected the Western Ukrainian People's Republic because of their leaders' Russophile orientation, seeking, rather fancifully, eventual incorporation into a democratic, non-Bolshevik Russian state—the reconstituted Rus' of romantic eastern Slavophile imaginations.[52] On November 28, 1918, two thousand of them met in the village of Gładyszów, agreeing on the need for Wilsonian national self-determination. This was a precursor of a Lemko congress, which was held in the nearby village of Florynka a week later and attended by over five hundred representatives from around 130 Lemko villages and towns. The resulting Lemko Rusyn Republic featured an Executive Council and a Central National Council, both of which were able to meet in the town hall of Grzybów thanks to the permission of a local Polish official, who naively presumed the Lemkos' unshakable loyalty to Poland. Over the following months, the lawyer Iaroslav Karchmarchyk, head of the Central National Council and the republic's undisputed leader, nurtured relations with Ruthene leaders in Slovakia, viewing Czechoslovakia as a temporary haven for Lemkos until conditions in Russia stabilized enough for union with their eastern brethren. Karchmarchyk lobbied for the Czechoslovak solution by means of a delegation dispatched to the Paris peace conference and an April 20, 1919 memorandum sent jointly with Ruthenes in Slovakia. Other influential Ruthene activists, especially those in the United States, feared that coordination with Lemkos would aggravate Czech-Polish border disputes, thereby endangering Subcarpathia's incorporation into Czechoslovakia. A further blow to Karchmarchyk's designs came in June 1919, when the Paris peacemakers authorized Poland to occupy all Galician territory. Nonetheless, the republic persisted for another eight months in its highland fastness as a wild card in the tense border standoff between Czechoslovakia and Poland. As the attention of the two states was diverted to other areas, the Lemkos' potential geopolitical relevance faded. Polish authorities arrested Karchmarchyk and other leaders of the Lemko Rusyn Republic in late March 1920.

Though populated overwhelmingly by peasants, the republics established in 1918–19 by Carpathian Ruthenes lacked clear peasant-oriented agendas. They were republics *by* peasants but not clearly *for* peasants. Their primary aims were nationalistic. Above all, they pursued unification with their perceived ethnic-national brethren, whether Ukrainian or Russian. Given the wartime persecution of Ruthenes in Austria-Hungary for alleged Russophilism, as well as their long-standing awareness of being an ethnic minority in provinces ruled by Poles and Magyars, this is hardly surprising. Composed almost exclusively of villagers, the Ruthenian population also had less familiarity with the intranational class antagonisms that divided Poles, for example, and might have heightened a peasant class agenda. At the same time, the Ukrainian national movement adorned its programs with promises of peasant emancipation, as did, with rather less sincerity, the Bolsheviks. Ruthenes could embrace eastern-facing irredentism with confidence of social deliverance. Nor did the dominance of a national agenda preclude the earnest support of peasants, for whom political separatism might appear as the prerequisite for the breakup and parceling out of large estate land.

National self-determination and a radical agrarian agenda converged in the Mura Republic, a short-lived statelet established at the end of May 1919 in the far west of what was then the Hungarian Soviet Republic and is today Prekmurje, the easternmost region of Slovenia. Local peasants supported regional secession orchestrated by a high-ranking civil servant and man of dubious motives, Vilmoš Tkalec (or Vilmos Tkálecz, by Hungarian orthography).[53] Tkalec promised the Slovene-speaking villagers of Prekmurje complete autonomy as well as redistributive land reform, which two successive post-Habsburg governments in Budapest had failed to deliver. While he may have been more interested in safeguarding his lucrative smuggling operation on the Austrian-Hungarian border than fulfilling peasant dreams or Slovene nationalism, he received the benefit of the doubt when he and other members of the district soviet proclaimed the Mura Republic on May 29, 1919. It encompassed contemporary Slovenian territory beyond the Mura River (the meaning of the regional name Prekmurje) along with areas of Hungary's Vas County inhabited by Slovene speakers. With an armed force of 1,194 men commanded by 36 officers, the republic prepared to defend its territory against attempts by Budapest to recapture it. But when Hungarian Red Army forces attacked on June 2—unexpectedly from the northeast instead of from the southeast as Tkalec had anticipated—they broke through the republic's defenses and prompted its leaders to flee across the border into Austria. Scattered resistance continued until June 6, by which time the Mura Republic's fate was sealed.

Slovene villagers' willingness to go along with Tkalec's breakaway scheme was the culmination of their growing disillusionment with postimperial governments in Budapest. In November 1918, as elsewhere, they had participated in violent retribution against symbols of the old order and perceived wartime profiteers. On November 4–5, villagers in Beltinci looted the Jewish Kaufmann family's stores as well as the manor house of Countess Zichy.[54] Unrest spread to surrounding villages and engulfed the mostly Croat-inhabited Međimurje region to the south. Vilmoš Tkalec entered the scene as a commander of national guards that had formed under the authority of Hungarian national councils in Murska Sobota and Lendava, the principal towns of Prekmurje. Born in 1894 to a Slovene-speaking innkeeper in Turnišče and his German-speaking wife, Tkalec had graduated from the teacher's training academy in Čakovec, Međimurje, after which he enlisted in 1914 as a volunteer.[55] Promoted to first lieutenant, he was wounded and captured on the Eastern Front before his 1917 return to Hungary and subsequent decommissioning. As an officer serving Hungarian national councils, Tkalec showed no more clemency than others who suppressed peasant unrest in the south Slav-populated regions of western Hungary. Leading a detachment of thirty Magyar soldiers, he was responsible for the summary hanging of at least one peasant and beating of many others in the district. He then co-led the bloody repression in Međimurje.

This unlikely champion of peasant rights nonetheless supported Slovene national ambitions, though his own personal loyalties are difficult to fathom. In December 1918, the Hungarian minister of nationalities Jászi presided over the creation of a Slovene autonomous region, the Slovenska krajina. In early 1919, Jászi's emissary Béla Obál drew up plans for a Slovene assembly and, importantly, began referring in official documents to *Slovenes* instead of *Wends*, the preferred term of Hungarian officialdom until then. Since 1848, the term *Slovenes* had connoted potential political subversion and ethnic autonomism, while the reassuringly archaic moniker *Wends* (derived from the old Germanic word for Slavs) seemed to imply feudal deference and stasis. This semantic shift did not satisfy all Prekmurje's Slovenes, the more educated of which hankered for union with the newly established Yugoslav kingdom. In any case, the Slovene assembly was never established, as events in Budapest outpaced Jászi's well-intentioned schemes for ethnic autonomy. With radical Communists gaining control of the capital's streets and key factories while Romanian and Czechoslovak forces advanced into Hungarian territory with French backing, the position of Károlyi's government became untenable. The final straw came with a March 1919 French memorandum (the Vix Note), informing Budapest of the Allies' intention to force Hungary to evacuate more territory than had been stipulated under the terms of the Belgrade Armistice. Károlyi's democratic republic fell, replaced on March 21 by the Hungarian Soviet Republic. Nominally the creation of a leftist alliance of Communists and Social Democrats, the new republic's true masters were the Communists and their charismatic leader, Béla Kun, a journalist and former Russian prisoner of war who had returned to Hungary in autumn 1918. Kun's Communists discomfited many Hungarians with their internationalism and revolutionary program. But in spring 1919, they paradoxically seemed the most reliable defenders of Hungarian national territory.

As the Hungarian Red Army prepared to mobilize against Czechoslovakia in the north and Romania in the south, Soviet rule was introduced throughout Hungary, often incorporating, rather than replacing, existing administrative personnel. Obál headed a three-man directory in charge of Vas County, while Tkalec took over the Department for Slovene Affairs. For villagers throughout Hungary, the new regime's most significant initial move was its announcement of elections in April based on universal male and female suffrage to decide the composition of local and county councils, as well as, indirectly via the county assemblies, the state parliament. All citizens over the age of eighteen were eligible to vote, provided they belonged to the productive classes of society; "parasites" such as large landowners, merchants, and priests were excluded. Barred from electoral politics in late Habsburg period, Hungarians of the lower classes enthusiastically anticipated their first opportunity to vote in statewide elections, even if in practice they could only give imprimatur to preselected lists of Communist and Social Democratic candidates. Election fliers flooded the countryside in the first days of April 1919, and Communists held well-attended meetings in virtually every village to explain voting procedures and the significance of the elections. Peasants invariably raised the question of latifundia and church lands at such meetings, demanding that the authorities take immediate steps toward their redistribution. Eligible voters turned out in high numbers for the April 8–14 elections held in Vas County, overseen by Tkalec. As planned by the regime, previously vetted small peasants, landless workers, craftsmen, and teachers took their places in the newly elected village soviets, along with many established local elites, who nominally accepted new political identities. Among the latter was Tkalec himself, who was elected chair of the Slovenska krajina Soviet. Against the regime's wishes, however, many village soviets immediately established committees that began carving up local estates. Authorities in Murska Sobota ordered a halt to grassroots redistribution activities, citing an April 3 governmental decree that socialized all medium and large holdings.[56]

This was a bitter blow to peasant villagers, many of whom had nurtured cautious optimism about Kun's republic. Throughout the Hungarian lands still controlled by Budapest, the Communists' decision to preserve the integrity of large estates in the interest of provisioning Budapest and the army alienated an already-skeptical peasantry. The Károlyi government had been the first of the Habsburg successor states to make concrete promises regarding land reform. Already on November 7, 1918, the new Agriculture Ministry decreed the establishment of county-level land-redistribution committees, in the first instance to benefit war veterans. Tens of thousands of peasants registered to receive land, but progress was exceedingly slow. In the meantime, rural magnates appeared to have suffered no demotion in their position. A fresh glimmer of hope came in mid-February 1919, when the government mandated the redistribution of all estates over five hundred hectares in size, or over two hundred hectares in the case of ecclesiastical land, with the important caveat that landowners would be compensated by new peasant owners. A National Land Distribution Committee was set up and employed over 1,500 agronomists, engineers, and lawyers. It laid plans for 500 local committees, of which 188 began work before Kun's takeover. On February 23, Károlyi, himself scion of one of Hungary's richest landowning families, ostentatiously divided up and distributed his own immense estate at Kápolna, trying to set an example for others of his class. His public-relations stunt did not have the desired effect, in large part because his Social Democratic coalition partners vehemently disputed the need for parcellization. Long of the belief that such schemes would only expand a reactionary rural petty bourgeoisie, Social Democrats launched a competing bid to establish collective, or cooperative, farms.

When the Communists abandoned land redistribution, smallholding peasants saw themselves as the victims of yet another betrayal, this time perpetrated by Kun's overwhelmingly urban followers. They joined large farmers in the ranks of a still-silent opposition. As intrusions into the agrarian economy multiplied, the city's relations with the countryside worsened. On April 19, rationing was reintroduced, accompanied by compulsory sale of agricultural products at fixed prices in the new currency, which many deemed worthless. To circumvent popular suspicion of "white money," often contrasted with the old Austro-Hungarian "blue money," the government set up stores for manufactured goods where peasants could exchange their products directly for tobacco, petrol, leather, and other items. But the stores commonly lacked the items that peasants needed most, although they were expected to deliver their own products. Smuggling flourished in Prekmurje as Hungarian livestock and grain were bartered for Austrian manufactured goods—an illicit revival of internal Austro-Hungarian trade and wartime smuggling between more-urban Cisleithania and more-agrarian Transleithania. The Murska Sobota–based soviet under Tkalec's leadership assumed control of all smuggling, in part to cap prices on all incoming goods.

By the middle of May, Tkalec was hatching plans for secession from Hungary. At popular assemblies, he and his allies propagated the idea of an independent republic in Prekmurje, promising land to peasant soldiers who were prepared to defend it. He dispatched envoys to Yugoslavia, winning assurances of neutrality should Budapest decide to invade Prekmurje, but obtaining none of the arms that he had hoped the south Slav state would donate to his cause. At 11:30 in the morning on May 29, Tkalec and other members of the Slovenska krajina Soviet proclaimed the socialist Mura Republic from the balcony of the elegant Hotel Dobrai in Murska Sobota. Two days later, the republic's leaders sent a telegram to Budapest, explaining that the decision for secession had been taken in accordance with the wishes of the local population and the principle of national self-determination. The Mura Republic committed itself to the tenets of international socialism, thus hoping for cordial relations with Kun's government. The Hungarian Soviets were not convinced, as their decisive suppression of Tkalec's experiment soon after demonstrated. Nonetheless, they bowed to peasant demands to the extent that soviets in a number of Prekmurje villages were permitted to immediately redistribute baronial land. Facing military setbacks and eventually collapse in early August 1919, the Hungarian Soviet Republic once again saw Prekmurje slip from its grasp. Yugoslav soldiers marched in and occupied it permanently. Tkalec's subsequent career was predictably idiosyncratic: he moved to a village in central Hungary near Budapest to take up the position of teacher and cantor, Magyarized his surname to Tarcsay, and later became an author of Slovene textbooks and composer of popular Hungarian folk songs.

By the summer of 1919, villagers' scope for enacting self-determination at the local or regional level had narrowed considerably across east central Europe. Although adherents of peasant republics often saw them as the apex of their revolutionary activities, the isolated microstates could not hold out for long. Governments in Belgrade, Budapest, and Warsaw had already suppressed numerous breakaway attempts, while only those in remote or contested areas persisted, such as the western Lemkos' republic. Yet insurgent republicanism continued to unsettle large portions of the post-Habsburg countryside, particularly in the Kingdom of Serbs, Croats, and Slovenes, the only new monarchy in the region. Of all the states claiming lands previously ruled by Vienna and Budapest, Italy and Romania were also kingdoms, but these were merely expanded versions of prewar states that had borne the same names. In an eccentric way, Hungary from 1920 retained monarchical government in its truncated territory, though technically as a regency led by Admiral Miklós Horthy, which refused to restore its former sovereign, Karl, despite the latter's efforts to return and reclaim the crown of Saint Stephen. Yugoslavia, by contrast, was an entirely new creation on the map of Europe, fostering radical expectations among many of its inhabitants.

Within several months of its establishment, antimonarchical and republican aspirations crystallized around support for the Croatian Peasant Party led by Stjepan Radić. Soon to become the primary vehicle of cross-class Croatian nationalism, and, as discussed in chapter 7, a paragon of the post-1918 upsurge in agrarian parliamentary politics, Radić's party also won adherents among Slovene peasants, who gravitated toward its program of sweeping rural reform. At the end of February 1919, the Croatian peasant leader had brazenly refused to participate in the Temporary National Representation, the precursor of a planned constituent assembly, and on March 9 his party countered King Petar Karađorđević's claim to Croatia with official demands for a "Neutral Croat Peasant Republic." He was arrested on March 25, beginning a 339-day detention that only solidified his support in the countryside.[57] If large segments of the south Slav peasantry found republicanism ideologically attractive, the immediate economic woes faced by the Karađorđević dynasty's new subjects contributed to Radić's rising stock. Amid continuing shortages, Belgrade introduced a transitional monetary policy that fixed conversion between Austro-Hungarian crowns (now required to bear "Yugoslav" stamps) and Serbian dinars at a rate of four to one, which many in the former Habsburg territories regarded as grievously unfair. To prevent more crowns entering circulation, a deadline of January 31, 1919, was set for the stamping process, although the finance ministry predicted that another stamping period would be necessary at the end of the year.[58]

In the southern Slovene village of Vinica, rumors began to spread in February that clandestine stamping was continuing in the houses of local notables, who were also allegedly accepting bribes from Croatian villagers just across the Kolpa River to validate their private stockpiles of crowns. With Radić's arrest, agitated peasants began to openly speak of the need to free him and establish a republic. Not only was the Croatian peasant leader popular in Vinica, located as it is directly on the Croatian border, but events in the village following the collapse of the Habsburg monarchy had converted many inhabitants to republicanism. On the evening of November 1, 1918, the schoolmaster Franjo Lovšin had organized a solemn ceremony in front of the church; from behind a table decorated with lit candles and a crucifix, he declared: "Now freedom has prevailed in our country. Now we will have neither kings nor emperors, but only a republic like America and France have. The gendarmes will not chase our lads to the army anymore, gendarmes will only be municipal policemen. Only volunteers will go to the army. Nobody will be allowed to force anyone."[59] Although Lovšin later denied promising anything to the assembled people, multiple accounts agreed that he publicly heralded a republican future and underscored the voluntary character of the new army. He also oversaw an oath taken by villagers to the new south Slav state—at this point the Zagreb-based State of Slovenes, Croats, and Serbs—which was administered by the oldest parishioner present: eighty-seven-year-old Jure Pavlešič from the hamlet of Perudina.

The peasants of Vinica saw the oath they took in November 1918 as justification for the republican uprising they staged at Easter 1919. During the night before Easter Sunday, village youths menacingly fired rifles in front of the houses of local "Serbs"; that is, notables who were conspicuous in their support for the new Belgrade government and who had, according to circulating rumors, amassed fortunes during the currency reform. Then, on the morning of Easter Monday, a hastily called meeting by local elites to win popular assent for the construction of a railway line through Vinica triggered open insurrection. Villagers, enraged by the suggestion that they sell their land to facilitate transport links to Serbia, now demanded that the municipal seal used for stamping crowns be handed over. Starting at Franc Mihelič's tavern, where the meeting was held, the furious crowd ransacked all the houses suspected to contain the seal—Peter Malič's tavern, schoolmaster Lovšin's home, the merchant Jurij Šterk's store—but without success. In Malič's living quarters, invaders smashed a portrait of the early nineteenth-century philologist Valentin Vodnik, a key figure in the Slovene national awakening, thinking that it depicted the Karađorđević regent Aleksandar. The crowd abandoned the search only when the postmaster read a forged telegram from district authorities in Črnomelj, claiming that the seal was there.

Smallholder Ivan Kobe, a known Radić supporter, now addressed the assembled villagers, rejecting the "Serbian" railway, the "Serbian" kingdom, and demanding a republic. That afternoon, a meeting of three hundred people in the schoolhouse elected a new municipal government, featuring Kobe and four other peasants, as well as the educated Malič as secretary (no one else wanted the job, apparently). News of the "republic" spread to the town of Črnomelj and to nearby Slovene and Croatian villages, where peasants took heart, some vowing to come to Vinica and show their solidarity. On Tuesday, April 22, a group of Vinica liberals including Lovšin and Šterk beseeched the provincial government to immediately dispatch "sufficiently strong guard units of reliable people or a contingent of soldiers to protect our lives and our property. In case this is not done, we will be forced to leave our homes in the SHS kingdom and flee, to save our lives."[60] The next day, district authorities in Črnomelj rebuffed emissaries from Vinica who sought official sanction for their actions. On Friday, April 25, a force of gendarmes and soldiers arrived in Vinica and soon after began arresting the republic's "ringleaders." Their trial took place a year later in Ljubljana, rather than in Novo Mesto, the principal town of Lower Carniola (Dolenjska), because of concerns about the restive surrounding countryside. Peter Balkovec, a peasant member of the republic's government, received the harshest sentence: three years imprisonment. Among other unpardonable utterances, he had remarked that accepting the new king after Habsburg rule would be like going "from a swine to a pig."[61]

Around the time of the events in Vinica, officials in the central Croatian town of Sisak worried that Radić's arrest had prompted prisoners of war returning from Russia to embrace his campaign, with the goal of making "the peasant unconditional lord in a Croatian republic."[62] On April 16, a strike broke out among Sisak railway workers to protest a call-up for two months of military exercises. It quickly spread to other industries and urged unity with the republican peasantry. Many strikers established a stronghold in the forests around the villages of Odra and Žabno, forming a "railway workers' Green Cadre" and attending joint assemblies with local peasants.[63] Two of the organizers, Communists Antun Sabljak and Božo Erceg, were outspoken in demanding an end to dynastic rule and the establishment of a revolutionary republic. Sabljak, a native of the western Slavonian village of Vrbova, attempted to foster unity between workers and peasants, emphasizing their shared origins in the countryside: "I greeted the peasant brothers," he later told investigators, "and explained to them that all of us workers are peasant sons who come from poor peasant houses, which do not have enough land to support their children, forcing our parents to send us to the towns for work and in this way we became factory workers, but in essence we are all equal."[64] Whatever solidarity local peasants may have felt, the arrival of the army on April 20 caused them to retreat into passivity, while most of the strikers returned to work.

The strike in Sisak was a mere prelude to the detonation of the Croatian countryside in late summer 1920 when the government announced plans to brand livestock as a means of registering animals that might be needed in case of war. This Serbian practice was completely unknown in the former Habsburg lands, and it immediately stoked peasant fears that their coveted livestock would be confiscated without compensation. Signs of a coming conflagration were evident from late August 1920. In the district of Sveti Ivan Zelina, peasants made it known they would not render their animals to the authorities, but instead would verbally describe them for registration purposes.[65] Some villagers in Hrastovica submitted a flier for publication in the newspaper *Jedinstvo* (Unity), invoking "the holiest name of Jesus" and exhorting peasants to resist the transport of their livestock to Serbia.[66] The flier promised the assistance of the Green Cadre in killing gendarmes. On September 2, assembled peasants from four villages in Grubišno Polje district declared they would not allow their horses to be branded, prompting the interior ministry to send reinforcements to the area.[67]

Open rebellion then erupted across central Croatia. What began as a violent reaction against the livestock registration scheme swiftly developed into a coordinated movement to establish a Croatian peasant republic.[68] The first recorded violence occurred on September 3, when peasants in Garešnica district fell upon a commission branding horses; gendarmes opened fire, killing two of the attackers. The following day, villagers overwhelmed the gendarmerie station in Veliki Grđjevac after a pitched battle, which resulted in one insurgent dead and many wounded. Numerous other gendarmerie stations subsequently fell to peasant crowds, who disarmed officers and confiscated stockpiled arms for their own purposes. The insurgents often occupied the headquarters of municipal administration and post offices. Between September 4 and 7, peasant villagers violently seized control of dozens of municipalities, as well as the market towns of Čazma, Dugo Selo, Kloštar Ivanić, and Popovača. The patterns of retributive violence rehearsed two years earlier surfaced again. Nikola Čabrajec, the notary in Kloštar Ivanić, first became aware of an imminent attack on the state officials in town when he heard singing on the road leading northward to the villages of Predavec and Križci. Among the hundreds-strong crowd marching in from the countryside, he recognized a number of armed deserters with whom he had previously had "official business." Čabrajec was physically assaulted as they forced their way into his office. He managed to escape to the local Franciscan monastery, from where he could watch the insurgents taking over the customs office and gendarmerie station.

The rebels in 1920 showed more coordination than was seen in 1918. On the night of September 5–6, a throng of peasants captured the Novoselec-Križ railway station. Around midnight, the better trained and armed among them, calling themselves a "national guard," halted a military train traveling from Zagreb and disarmed the approximately one hundred soldiers aboard. Another train that arrived on the morning of the 6th to reclaim the station had to retreat under heavy fire. The "national guard" cut telegraph and telephone lines, openly proclaiming its intention to establish a Croatian peasant republic. Two days later, a detachment of troops managed to retake the Novoselec-Križ station, scattering the rebels (of whom an unknown number fell) into the surrounding forests. But on the next evening, September 9, insurgents dismantled a section of track between Lekenik and Sisak, disrupting travel on the main line between Zagreb and Belgrade, and downing telegraph poles in the vicinity. Relentless gunfire from the adjacent forest compelled workers sent the following day for repairs to flee, along with their armed escort of fifty soldiers. For several days, the town of Sisak had no communication with the outside world. The governor of Croatia-Slavonia warned the Interior Ministry in Belgrade of the "extraordinarily critical situation" and requested reinforcements of ten thousand troops for the pacification of a revolt that threatened to engulf Croatia. In several villages, rebel messengers had been apprehended as they broadcast news of their victories and called on peasants to join the uprising. Stronger army detachments arrived on September 11, allowing the repair works to proceed. The forest-based rebels were dispersed amid heavy, if indeterminate, losses. They remained a threat in the area for several days, forcing a freight train from Sisak to return and again cutting telegraph and telephone lines.

The insurgency aimed not only to remove existing authorities but also to create a defensible perimeter within which new republican administration could be introduced. By September 6, communication lines to at least a dozen central Croatian districts had been severed. In Križ and Popovača, peasants convened a joint "national council" to serve as the transitional local government, mimicking the bodies that arose in autumn 1918, though now under exclusively peasant leadership. Influential functionaries of the Croatian Peasant Party were prominent in the council. Filip Lakuš, native of nearby Širinec and a member of the party's executive, assured a crowd on September 7 that the declaration of a republic was imminent, but that its success would depend on a preemptive military strike against Zagreb. During the storming of the gendarmerie station in Križ, Lakuš allegedly told its commander, Ivan Kirigin, that officials like him who had sworn an oath to the Karađorđević king would be regarded as traitors in the new republic. Once Zagreb had been neutralized, Lakuš told Kirigin, Radić would be installed as president of the state. Indeed, a key objective of the planned attack on the Croatian capital was to liberate Radić from jail, where, at the time of the rebellion, he was languishing for yet another offense. Rebels in numerous places called publicly for his release. Preparations for an expeditionary force were reported to have begun in multiple districts.

A striking feature of the 1920 rebellion was its militarized character. Although peasants resisted mandatory service in the kingdom's army, leaders of the revolt resorted to draconian techniques familiar from both before and after 1918 to conscript their own army. On September 7 near Martinska Ves on the Sava River (very close to Radić's home village of Desno Trebarjevo), peasants were ordered to register for service in the rebel forces within two hours under the threat of beatings. In another village, near Kloštar Ivanić, a peasant recruiter arrived on horseback, warning that those who refused to join the insurgent army then assembling in Čazma would be shot. Moreover, alongside Croatian Peasant Party functionaries, leaders of the revolt were military men, such as Ivan Novosel, a former Austro-Hungarian reserve officer who went about Križ in uniform during the unrest. There was also a self-proclaimed "first lieutenant of the Green Cadre," who appeared at assemblies alongside Lakuš, claiming that the rebels possessed a cache of machine guns and artillery pieces in the Bregovica forest just south of Zagreb.

Whatever the truth of such claims, authorities correctly surmised that the campaign against livestock branding had become a pretext for pursuing much more expansive goals. By September 4, the Croatian governor had resolved to suspend the branding exercise, and word began to reach rural districts on the following day. Yet news of the suspension did little to assuage peasant anger, which now coalesced around a revolutionary program for regime change in Croatian territory. Meanwhile, the authorities mistakenly, if predictably, attributed the unrest to agitators outside of the peasantry. As a report from Čazma district stated, "the main leadership of the revolt without a doubt lay outside peasant hands, because anyone who knows peasant primitiveness must come to the conclusion that some more competent party must have led everything and that the ringleaders in question [e.g., Lakuš] were simply weapons in their hands."[69] The identity of these puppet masters remained in the realm of conjecture. Some speculated that irredentist Hungarian or Italian agents provocateurs were behind the rebellion. Apparently lending credence to such a scenario, the Italian nationalist adventurer Gabriele D'Annunzio, then in control of the port city of Rijeka/Fiume, openly wondered whether the peasant movement might not be an ally in his bid to seize more of the Adriatic coastline. Fanciful theories about foreign instigation withered under closer inspection. While homegrown Bolsheviks seemed likelier culprits, reports noted that local Communists stayed aloof from the rebellion, even if they were suspected to provide "moral" support.[70] Some authorities fell back on vague assertions of manipulation by Radić's more educated followers or "unknown Green Cadres."

Clear-headed investigators blamed the rebellion at least partially on callous administration in much of Croatia. Before its suppression, the prefect of Bjelovar-Križevci county reported that agitation among the peasantry had reached dangerous levels because of their mistreatment at the hands of gendarmes and army officials. Peasants' reluctance to enlist in the new state's army regularly elicited beatings and hostage-taking.[71] There were instances of villagers dying as a result of injuries sustained.[72] In September 1920 in the Slavonian village of Sladojevci, gendarmes opened fire on a crowd that allegedly contained several deserters whom they were trying to arrest, killing three civilians, including one woman.[73] The official postmortem on the rebellion against livestock branding underscored peasants' legitimate grievances against the state due to monetary reform, punitive regulation of the rural economy, and callous army recruitment. Radić and his followers had merely tapped into a deep reservoir of dissatisfaction in the countryside.[74]

By September 14, the revolt had ended. A week before, the gendarmerie had, with army support, begun to turn the tide against the rebels. Gendarme commanders Zvonimir Tadejević and Dragutin Kovačić led crack units that restored state control in districts southeast of Zagreb. Officials calculated that ten people in state employ had perished during the unrest (three soldiers, three civil servants, two gendarmes, and two customs officials), along with fifteen peasants, though this was surely a low estimate.[75] Hundreds of villagers were arrested. The regent's amnesty on November 28 halted many criminal proceedings, but those involving murder continued; for example, the prosecution of 240 peasants from Sveti Ivan Zelina who were held responsible for the killing of the district captain, Oton Špiller—an event discussed in the previous chapter.[76] The man whom investigators found primarily to blame for Špiller's death, Blaž Tupek, received over twenty years in prison.

Although the insurgency of September 1920 was not repeated, open republican-hued resistance to the Yugoslav kingdom surfaced intermittently in the Croatian countryside for several years afterward. Just over a year after the lethal events in Sveti Ivan Zelina, peasants there again refused to take part in six-week compulsory military exercises. On the morning of November 6, 1921, over a hundred young men accosted the district captain Franjo Domjanić and notary Franjo Kos after a placard announcing the drilling had been read aloud.[77] News of the announcement had circulated already the day before and many had arrived in Sveti Ivan Zelina from farther afield to rekindle rebellion. With memories of 1920 fresh in his mind, Domjanić explained that "all came here only because they hoped that some disturbances would begin again and that here would be their epicenter. . . . It is clear that everything was supposed to go according to some existing plan."[78] The crowd insisted that army officials be telephoned and informed of their resolve not to enlist. One of its leaders, Pavao Dragija, ordered Kos with the words: "Mister notary, call the city commander of Zagreb on the telephone and report that we will not submit to the army's summons and that we do not want to fight wars for anyone anymore."[79] Under duress, Domjanić made the call and received the unsurprising answer that the men in question had to join up unless they wanted to be punished. Peasants protested noisily, but then dispersed. Dragija and other "ringleaders" were arrested soon after.

Conscription was the flashpoint issue for many peasant republicans. In Slovenia, it motivated several militant demonstrations in May 1919.[80] From early 1921, renewed desertion, often to the "Green Cadre," surged in the Croatian countryside.[81] While some Green Cadre groups were no doubt holdovers from the First World War, the new deserter movement was primarily an expression of discontent with the new regime.[82] Deserters attended pro-republican assemblies of the Croatian Peasant Party without fear of capture. Crowds even celebrated them with shouts of "long live the deserters," as at one large May 1921 manifestation in the northern town of Koprivnica.[83] According to authorities, desertion in that county had spiraled out of control, particularly following the late April murder near Đelekovec of two gendarmes who were escorting several deserters to jail. One middle-aged man present at the Koprovnica assembly wrote a letter to the commander of the Bjelovar garrison, Colonel Marković, explaining that he had become a republican after the event; not so much out of conviction as out of astonishment at the sight of deserters everywhere enjoying themselves while he had not seen his own enlisted son in years, nor heard from him in five months.[84] Previously a supporter of the unitarist Democratic Party, the man worried his son had fallen somewhere in the south of the country—Macedonia he guessed—and wished he would join the republican deserters who go about "freely as at home."

The perception that the new Yugoslav army was no more humane, and perhaps worse, than the old Habsburg army stoked peasant republicanism. Many villagers also continued to nurture dreams of the utopian society that had seemed within grasp in late 1918, and again in September 1920. In February 1923, peasants in the vicinity of the north Croatian city of Varaždin were reported to be planning a revolt to break away from the Yugoslav kingdom and "[to proclaim] a republic in the spirit of Stjepan Radić's program."[85] According to officials, the Croatian Peasant Party's promises of a future republic had encouraged delusions among the peasantry of northern Croatia: that in the future there would be no taxes and no compulsory military service, the rich would be expropriated, and there would be "a general plunder just like after the revolution in 1918." At the beginning of 1924 in Kostajnica, located on the southern Croatian border with Bosnia, the annual Three Kings procession turned into a militant demonstration at which the crowd of hundreds shouted: "Down with the government, down with [Nikola] Pašić [leader of the Serbian Radical Party, the monarchy's chief parliamentary ally], long live the republic, long live Radić."[86]

Radić himself encouraged such boundless enthusiasm. In December 1920, his Croatian People's Peasant Party officially changed its name to the Croatian Republican Peasant Party (HRSS). The previous month's elections had given the HRSS an unassailable majority among the kingdom's Croat population. Yet, as in the case of Tarnobrzeg, there was a striking differential between votes cast in urban areas and those cast in the countryside. Less than 7 percent of Zagreb voted for the HRSS, while support for the party in the rural Zagorje region just to the north reached 90 percent.[87] Despite his electoral mandate, Radić insisted that the party continue its abstention from the representative institutions of a state whose legitimacy he strenuously denied. Instead, in 1921 the HRSS set about drafting a constitution for the Neutral Peasant Republic of Croatia, which it issued on June 26, just two days before the *skupština* (parliament) in Belgrade promulgated the stridently centralist Vidovdan Constitution.[88]

Facing militant grassroots republicanism in the east central European countryside and a concomitant crisis of legitimacy, successor state governments reached for agrarian reform as a solution. Peasant parties themselves applied pressure in the immediate postwar years, accelerating land reform, as we will see, but they generally lacked the parliamentary strength to implement it alone. The mighty and mostly urban bourgeois nationalist parties of the successor states viewed redistribution of land as a palliative against various forms of peasant revolutionism (which they often misinterpreted as "Bolshevism"). The reforms that were eventually introduced bore the imprint of compromises struck with them and, in some countries, with conservative landed elites who retained their power even after the "national revolutions." With peasant radicalism menacing large tracts of territory, governments in 1918–20 committed themselves to a rearrangement of property relations in the countryside, though the reforms were often designed, above all, to satisfy the ethnic nationalist agendas of urban middle-class parties. Wealthy landowners from the new states' titular nationalities were to be shielded as much as possible in a bid to protect native capital, while land in the possession of "foreigners"—that is, of peoples who now found themselves in the position of minorities, even if they had been there for centuries—was targeted for confiscation. In some cases, the autochthonous peasantry reaped real benefits, dampening their revolutionism. But smallholding or landless peasants wanted agrarian reform to be swift and ambitious, irrespective of landlords' ethnic identity. In practice, it was often neither.

The most radical reforms were passed in countries where large estates were exclusively in "foreign" hands. In the three newly established Baltic states—all former provinces of the Russian Empire, where Baltic German barons or Polish lords had held the lion's share of arable land—governments redistributed over three-quarters of estate property in the early 1920s: 97 percent of large holdings in Estonia, 84 percent in Latvia, and 77 percent in Lithuania.[89] At the other end of the spectrum were Hungary and Poland, both countries where native nobilities owned most of the large estates. In Hungary, landlords benefited from the conservative restoration ushered in by the counterrevolutionary Horthy regime, the successor of Béla Kun's Soviet Republic. A very modest 1920 agrarian reform carried out in partnership with the neutered peasant party essentially preserved the position of Hungary's landed oligarchy. Affecting a mere 8.5 percent of the country's arable land, it reduced the size of estates over 1,000 cadastral yokes (approximately 580 hectares, or 1,400 acres) by 14 percent and those measuring 500–1,000 yokes by 5.5 percent. Around two hundred thousand landless rural laborers and a hundred thousand smallholding peasants—many of them "dwarfholders" with less than 2 hectares—were recipients of approximately 1.2 million confiscated yokes (700,000 hectares, or 1.7 million acres), but this did little to alleviate pressure on the land.[90]

In Poland, a different constellation of forces conspired against the more radical demands of the peasant majority. The main obstacle to sweeping agrarian reform was the perceived need to preserve Polish ethnic dominance in the eastern border regions, or *kresy*. Here the redistribution of estate land would have benefitted Belarusian, Lithuanian, and Ukrainian villagers rather than estate-owning Poles. Although a generous reform law had passed in the sejm on July 15, 1920, as an incentive for peasant soldiers to defend the fatherland against looming Red Army invasion, the ruling parties balked at implementing it after the war with the Soviets had been won.[91] Among the reluctant reformers was the Piast wing of the Polish People's Party, a member of the governing coalition and a peasant party, albeit primarily of prosperous west Galician farmers who regarded far-reaching land reform as a threat to their position, and who admired the nationally conscious Polish nobility. The law that finally passed at the end of 1925 aimed to create a viable stratum of medium-sized farms by taking excess land from the largest estates to establish new farmsteads and enlarge smallholdings. It set the maximum allowable estate size at 180 hectares (445 acres) for most of Poland, but 300 hectares (740 acres) for the kresy, including eastern Galicia with its large Ukrainian peasantry. It likewise stipulated an ideal farm size of 15 hectares (37 acres), while a target of 25 hectares (62 acres) prevailed in the kresy and Poznania, the latter dominated by German landowners until 1918 and now the site of an intensive Polish colonization campaign. Moreover, estate owners themselves chose which land to donate to the state land fund, the volume of which was set annually, along with each district's quota of hectares to supply. Restrictions on the sale and use of redistributed land as well as uncertainty around which plots would be taken in any given year depressed land prices and discouraged agricultural improvement. By the onset of the Great Depression, when the program was effectively halted, a paltry 16 percent of arable land had changed hands in Poland.

The scope of reforms in Czechoslovakia, Romania, and Yugoslavia fell somewhere between the complete reorganization of property relations in the Baltics and the cautious adjustments undertaken in Hungary and Poland. In all three cases, "foreigners" controlled some of the biggest estates, but native landowners existed too, and property relations varied considerably across territories inherited from different prewar states. Administrative practices in the formerly Habsburg Austrian provinces of Bohemia, Moravia, and Silesia diverged markedly from those of the Slovak-speaking territories that had previously constituted Upper Hungary. But the rift was far wider between Habsburg Transylvania and the Regat, the prewar Romanian kingdom, or between the Habsburg South Slav territories and the Kingdom of Serbia and Montenegro.

Yugoslavia and Romania adopted a flexible approach to land reform, applying it most assiduously to the large, mostly agrarian provinces of Vojvodina and Transylvania annexed from Hungary. Minorities made up over 40 percent of the population in both territories, and ethnic Hungarians or Germans owned over 80 percent of large estate land.[92] Between December 1918 and July 1921, Romania passed a series of reforms designed to increase the size of peasant farmsteads at the expense of large landlords. The laws also encouraged more efficient farming techniques, promoting the consolidation of scattered plots and prohibiting the subdivision of holdings below a certain threshold.[93] Overall, the government confiscated six million hectares (15 million acres), distributing land to 1.4 million peasants. The 1919 reform in Transylvania was likely the most ambitious, confiscating all estates owned by "foreigners," some types of institutions, and property in excess of 500 yokes (290 hectares, or 717 acres), most of which was in Hungarian hands. It also, unlike reform legislation elsewhere in Romania, expropriated forests to create common lands for peasant villagers. Yet despite their achievements, the reforms did not deliver land to 2.3 million eligible peasants, who came resent their neglect. Scarcity of common lands continued to plague most Romanian villages, while schemes to improve agricultural efficiency went either unenforced or unheeded. Romanian peasants remained among the poorest in east central Europe throughout the interwar period.

Belgrade's Interim Decree on the land question, issued on February 25, 1919, announced the confiscation of all estates exceeding the maximum permissible size of between 100 and 500 cadastral yokes (58–290 hectares, 143–717 acres), leaving authorities much leeway to adapt the law to local ethnic-national circumstances.[94] The decree stipulated that landowners would be compensated for their losses, unless they were members of the Habsburg family or "foreigners" who had received their land from the Habsburgs. It also started the process of dissolving feudal and semifeudal land tenure systems in Bosnia-Herzegovina and Macedonia. Strikingly, the decree did not apply to the territory of pre-1912 Serbia, although large estates had been virtually eliminated there over the course of the nineteenth century. The process of the reform's implementation dragged on for over a decade, in some places two decades, breeding peasant discontent and perceptions of administrative inefficiency. Nonetheless, by the end of 1935, half a million hectares (1.2 million acres) in the Slovene lands, Croatia-Slavonia, and Vojvodina had been redistributed to around a quarter of a million peasants, most of them native to the areas where they received land. In the state as a whole, half a million peasants benefited from the reforms, though as elsewhere, their new holdings often remained pitifully small. By the mid-1930s, only 9.6 percent of land in Yugoslavia belonged to estates over fifty hectares (124 acres) in size—the most egalitarian outcome in the post-Habsburg successor states.

On April 16, 1919, Czechoslovakia's national assembly passed the Land Control Act, authorizing the government to confiscate estate land exceeding 150 hectares (370 acres) of contiguous arable land or 250 hectares (618 acres) of land of any type.[95] Owners were to be compensated at prewar prices. The reform was a compromise between moderate members of the Agrarian and Social Democratic parties—the two largest parliamentary groupings in the assembly—who found common ground against conservative agrarians, keen to avoid expropriation altogether, and more radical socialists who aimed to socialize estate land and introduce collective farming. The agrarian-controlled State Land Office administered the reform, which, over the course of the 1920s, redistributed 750,000 hectares (1.9 million acres) in the western, mostly Czech-speaking part of the country alone. Yet many of the beneficiaries of the reform remained in possession of land too small to be economically viable. While dwarf holdings of less than one hectare largely disappeared, the new norm of one to five hectares (2.5–12 acres) provided few economic opportunities. And the pace of the reform's implementation, intended to be gradual, was painfully slow for many peasants; estate owners continued to profit from their properties until the Land Office finalized the expropriation. The Land Office kept some estates for itself, selling them off at discounted prices to supporters of the Agrarian Party (renamed the Republican Party of Farmers and Peasants in 1922). Sudeten Germans vociferously protested the reform, which they regarded, with some justice, as a veiled attempt to transfer their property into Czech hands. The influential Czech journalist Ferdinand Peroutka referred to it approvingly as an act of "national reparation."[96]

Governments in Czechoslovakia, Poland, Romania, and Yugoslavia all introduced colonization schemes in ethnically mixed rural regions to tip the demographic scales in favor of their titular nations. In Czechoslovakia, the State Land Office virtually barred non-Czechs and non-Slovaks from receiving farmsteads in the mostly German Sudetenland, mostly Hungarian southern Slovakia, and Subcarpathian Ruthenia.[97] Although the law did not prescribe the ethnicity of potential applicants, it specified that, alongside veterans and invalids in general, preference would be given to former Czechoslovak legionaries, who were invariably Czech or Slovak. Similarly, land in the newly acquired Yugoslav provinces of Kosovo, Macedonia, and Vojvodina was offered on a preferential basis to "war invalids, widows and orphans of soldiers killed in action, and former soldiers and volunteers who have fought for the liberation and unification of the Serbs, Croats, and Slovenes."[98] At the end of 1920, the Polish government set up a land fund in the kresy made up of confiscated former Russian state properties and holdings of the Orthodox Church, along with some large estates. Deserving veterans and soldiers of the Polish army were eligible to receive parcels of up to forty-five hectares (111 acres), while those who "had expressed their antagonistic position towards the Polish state" were excluded from the scheme.[99] Romania's colonization program targeted the immense new territories it annexed after the Paris peace treaties: formerly Russian Bessarabia, historically Habsburg

Bukovina and Transylvania, but above all the previously Bulgarian province of southern Dobruja, where the state incentivized the emigration of Muslims and Bulgarians.[100] In none of these countries did the results of agrarian colonization schemes come close to reaching the goals governments set for them. Despite generous subsidies available to colonists, relatively few were interested in moving to distant, often impoverished regions inhabited by potentially hostile people of a different ethnicity.

Meanwhile, peasants resented the sluggish pace of land redistribution in their home districts. Those who received land often found it insufficient to improve the profitability of their farms. Given the population density of the east central European countryside, even far more radical land reform likely would have struggled to significantly raise peasants' standard of living without accompanying investment in machinery, fertilizers, and education in new farming techniques, none of which was forthcoming on an adequate scale from the postimperial governments.[101] In the monarchies of the region, particularly Yugoslavia, many peasants convinced themselves that a republican system would alleviate their woes. In the Czechoslovak and Polish republics, villagers increasingly doubted the intentions of ruling elites in Warsaw and Prague. They would come to share the cynicism of Jozef Ferančík, Slovak populist poet and apologist for the revolutionary violence in the western Slovak countryside, who in 1919 composed bitter verses about the "great" republic, entitled "Parcellization":

They take from the lords, and they make lords,
It titillates both sides,
But only a nobility
Will come of these new rascals.
Both will prosper,
Both will be lords,
It's a great republic,
This will take care of them,
And the poor will be just
What they were before.[102]

5

The Slovácko Brigade

IN JUNE 1930, Major Cyril Hluchý tried to set the record straight about his service to the Czechoslovak Republic in the first years of its existence. "During the revolution," he wrote to a potential supporter, "I organized out of the Green Cadre the Slovácko Brigade to confront Austrian military units, which [then] controlled the Germanized territories of southern Moravia. Through my intervention, the territory from Lanžhot to Břeclav, Lednice, Mikulov, and all the way to Drnholec by Znojmo, was definitively joined to the Czechoslovak state."[1] In spite of his achievements, which earned him praise from generals, professors, and local administrators, the new republic's officialdom blackballed him: "I sacrificed my civilian life for the state's interest in the conviction that some place in the new state would be found for me. At that time, I bore in mind only the state interest. However, I was deceived. My more than fifty requests for various positions were rejected or remained unanswered." Hluchý blamed "nationally unreliable" Moravian officers who envied his leadership of the Slovácko Brigade and denounced him, baselessly, to the Prague Ministry of National Defense. He was "the victim of intrigues," as he claimed to have later discovered through private contacts.

The Slovácko Brigade was uniquely successful in integrating peasant deserters from the Austro-Hungarian military into the armed forces of a postimperial state. At its height in January 1919, it counted 274 officers and 5,262 enlisted men, making it the largest volunteer unit in the new Czechoslovak army.[2] Nearly all its recruits were villagers from the southeast Moravian region of Slovácko, which straddles the border between Czech and Slovak cultural-linguistic zones. The vast majority of them had deserted in the final year of the Great War. Nowhere else did the deserter bands submit so readily and in such high numbers to new military authorities. The only comparable situation arose in the Slovene lands, where former Green Cadres like Alfonz Šarh and Andrej

Zlobec joined the volunteer force led by General Rudolf Maister to secure the entire former Habsburg crownland of Carinthia and its sizable Slovene population for the new south Slav state.[3] Yet while Maister's "fighters" drew recruits from various social backgrounds, Hluchý's brigade had an almost exclusively rural character, along with a specific regional identity. It thus embodied a solution to the problem that faced all postimperial states in east central Europe: how to win the loyalty of disaffected, militarized peasant soldiers. Their mostly agrarian societies awash in arms and radical ideas, the governments established in late 1918 struggled to integrate villagers into fledgling armies and at the same time transform them into reliable defenders of the new order.

Czechoslovakia's accomplishments in this regard were ultimately relative. The Slovácko Brigade lasted less than two years from its establishment in early November 1918, through a name change to the "Slovácko Regiment" in summer 1919, to its final dissolution in August 1920. While the makers of Czechoslovakia tried to extend the new state's democratizing, egalitarian ethos to the armed forces, the exigencies of a centralized command structure and the multiethnic profile of its conscripts militated against granting too much autonomy to regional units.[4] Soldiers organized according to their home territory might defend it heroically, but how would deployment to distant corners of the republic affect their morale? Moreover, a regionally divided army could become a serious liability if the inhabitants of certain provinces, namely the German-majority "Sudetenland," opposed the republic itself. And despite Hluchý's vehement protestations to the contrary, disciplinary problems surfaced in the Slovácko Brigade, suggesting that his recruits' "green" background had not been left entirely behind. In his 1930 letter, Hluchý referred to the Czechoslovak "national revolution" of 1918, but many suspected that his peasant volunteers had a different sort of revolution in mind. The process of assimilating rural deserters to the new state structures in east central Europe ran up against formidable obstacles, even in the most promising of circumstances.

The legacy of the Slovácko Brigade, and the Green Cadres that preceded it, divided opinion in interwar Czechoslovakia. Local community leaders could not agree on whether the deserters had benefited their areas or harmed them. Nor was there any consensus on the accomplishments of Hluchý's brigade. By the late 1920s, such debates found expression in literary works by a handful of Czech authors, who tried to locate usable pasts for the new state in village recalcitrance and in peasants' unusual path to the Czechoslovak army. In doing so, they aimed to reaffirm peasants' contribution to, and place within, the republic. But other factors threatened to undermine the project of cultural, political, and social integration, not least campaigns by radicalized Moravian smallholders, particularly in the Slovácko region, to seize and redistribute large estate land. The embittered Hluchý's involvement in this and other forms of subversion in the interwar years raised further questions about the merits of his activities immediately after the revolution.

Soon after the Czechoslovak Republic was established on October 28, 1918, the Moravian Green Cadres emerged from their sylvan hideouts in triumph. In the Slovácko districts of Kyjov and Hodonín, where they were especially numerous, the deserters left the forests and jubilantly returned to their home villages. In Kyjov itself, reported the local chronicler, the "Green Guard" was responsible for "lots of merriment and humor and even appeared with its own flag." After speeches were delivered from the church steps on the main square, "a procession proceeded through town bearing comical effigies of the Austrian regime; the eagles, badges of our centuries-long servitude, were carried at the head of the parade and then thrown into the creek."[5] The euphoric celebrations that greeted the news of the republic generally followed the same pattern across southeast Moravia: Czech citizens gathered on village greens and in small town squares to sing patriotic songs such as "Kde domov můj" (Where is my home?—the current Czech national anthem), "Hej, Slované" (Hey Slavs—a pan-Slavic staple), and "Nad Tatrou se blýska" (Lightning over the Tatras—the current Slovak national anthem).[6] Local notables organized lantern processions that culminated in the ceremonious removal of the Habsburg double-eagle insignia from post offices and other public buildings, and the hoisting of "national" red-white flags.

On October 30, a National Committee convened in Brno, the Moravian capital, to provide temporary government for the province, while subordinate bodies took shape in district towns. The next day, the National Committee in the town of Hodonín, on the southeast edge of today's Czech Republic, reported that it had assumed control of local military facilities, the train station, and municipal police.[7] In the town of Břeclav/Lundenburg, an important railway junction some twenty-five kilometers (16 miles) to the southwest, matters were complicated by the presence of a large German-speaking population that had no desire to be incorporated into the Czechoslovak state.[8] After a patriotic lantern-lit procession by Czech townsfolk, leading German burghers met at the Grand Hotel to plot the recovery of Lundenburg from the upstart Slavic population. German soldiers formed a cordon around the train station, while their commanders telephoned to Vienna for military assistance. Engineer

Rudolf Zaoral, the station chief, thwarted the "putsch" attempt by annulling the request for troops from Lower Austria, furloughing all German servicemen in town, and calling up Czech volunteers from the surrounding countryside. Břeclav's strategic importance set it apart, but local German resistance threatened to sunder much of southern Moravia, as well as other border regions, from the new republic.

Into this situation entered Cyril Hluchý, a pensioned thirty-five-year-old Austro-Hungarian army captain from the village of Moravská Nová Ves, located halfway between Břeclav and Hodonín. Hluchý made contact with the Brno National Committee, receiving permission from its military division to recruit a volunteer force in his home region, which would, in the first instance, secure the Břeclav junction and prevent anarchy among soldiers returning from the front.[9] As a first step, he and several other Czech officers set up a facility at the Břeclav station to register Czech servicemen arriving by train from the southern battlefields. Then he summoned all Czech officers in the region to attend a meeting on the morning of November 5 at the "Discussion house" (*Besední dům*) in Hodonín. With German municipalities in Moravia contemplating secession and distressing reports of rural violence arriving from Slovakia, the military men who assembled at Hluchý's bidding supported his proposal to raise a "Slovácko Brigade" from demobilized local men and Green Cadres.

Initially composed of three field battalions, the brigade would target the recruitment districts of Hodonín, Kyjov, Uherské Hradiště, and Uherský Brod (subsequently the area was extended to the environs of Hustopeče and Mikulov). On November 8, the brigade was officially established, one day before the Moravian Provincial Military Command in Brno. A proclamation signed by Hluchý and Vladimir Úlehla, chief of the Hodonín rail station, proudly stated:

> We are free, the administration of our own affairs has been passed to our hands. And it is incumbent on us to show the world that we are worthy of our freedom. We are honored and glad that the first brigade of the Czechoslovak army was established today in Slovácko. This brigade will be part of a new independent Czechoslovak army, which is being built in the first days of freedom to guarantee internal order, the security of property, and the outward defense of our young state against all enemies.[10]

The document enumerated the brigade's main tasks as securing the northern line—the old monarchy's Nordbahn between Vienna, Brno, and Cracow—and preventing plunder in Slovácko by nonlocal soldiers.

FIGURE 5.1 Cyril Hluchý, commander of the Slovácko Brigade. Regional Museum in Mikulov

The officers who had convened in Hodonín now fanned out into the countryside. They sought volunteers, but also possessed the authority to press-gang young men into state service. The Brno National Committee authorized them to conscript all men born in 1896–98 for immediate training and deployment in Hodonín; those born before 1882 were exempt, while men born 1882–95 and 1899–1900 had the option of being assigned to duties in their home municipalities. František Gavenda, a small farmer in Ždánice, recalled how First Lieutenant Felix Jelínek arrived in his village on November 7 and obtained thirty-eight volunteers, including Gavenda himself, after a fiery patriotic speech.[11] The content of recruiters' appeals likely matched printed fliers that circulated in Slovácko's towns, inviting young men to prove their mettle after the example set by the Czechoslovak legions: "The blood which our legionaries spilled for the freedom of the whole nation, indeed of the whole world, cannot have been spilled for naught. The spirit of the legions will be cultivated and kept alive in our Slovácko Brigade. We wish to defend only freedom and justice."[12]

Most of the men who marched off to Hodonín in November 1918 had recently returned from the forests as Green Cadres. Soon after October 28, František Sedláček (whom we encountered chapter 2), was informed along with his fellow deserters that they would be needed again soon. He served in the Slovácko Brigade until the end of February 1919, when his age cohort was demobilized.[13] Like Sedláček, the bulk of volunteers hailed from the smallholding peasantry. Even after the brigade's drastic diminution and renaming as the Slovácko Regiment—by which time many men engaged in farm work had been demobilized, or tried to be—the enlisted men and NCOs belonging to the category of "peasant" (*rolník*) outnumbered all other listed professions by a factor of at least two.[14] The second most common profession, "worker," also included many wage-earning agriculturalists, while a large proportion of the regiment's tradesmen (cobblers, tailors, joiners, blacksmiths, saddlers) were villagers. The flood of volunteers from rural Slovácko overwhelmed even Hluchý, who reported rapturously less than two months later that "a whole brigade [has been] built from nothing; it was stamped directly out of the earth by the work of a number of individuals, who, gathering around themselves 'Green Cadres' of Austrian deserters, assumed the most urgent work and created the framework and foundation, healthy and natural, corresponding fully to the spirit of our people, soldiers, and population: they created the Slovácko brigade on a tribal [*kmenovém*] basis."[15]

On November 17, around a thousand volunteers ceremoniously took their oath to the republic on the main square in Hodonín (figure 5.2). A month later, the brigade numbered 3,747 men and 134 officers; by mid-January 1919, the tally of soldiers had increased by another 30 percent and the officer corps had doubled in size.[16] The brigade now comprised six field battalions, an assistance battalion, and a replacement battalion, along with special units for artillery, sappers, dragoons, and telegraph communications. The Provincial Military Command in Brno supplied materiel in the form of five thousand Werndl rifles (admittedly an antiquated, nonrepeating type, accompanied by only 2,156 straps), a hundred thousand ammunition rounds, sixteen field kitchens, and two field bakeries.[17] At the Břeclav station, officers later managed to confiscate a large number of Mannlicher repeating rifles and some artillery pieces from German general August von Mackensen's retreating army, partially compensating for the dearth of adequate firepower.[18]

Alongside its growth into a serious fighting force, Hluchý's brigade could boast some strategic achievements in the first months of its existence.[19] By late

FIGURE 5.2 November 1918 oath taken by Slovácko Brigade recruits in Hodonín, Czech Republic. Masaryk Museum in Hodonín

November, it had occupied much of southern Moravia and was performing guard duty at the Břeclav station. In December 1918 and January 1919, it overcame the resistance of German militiamen (*Volkswehr*) to extend its control over the last German-speaking municipalities in the region, securing the demarcation line that today forms sections of the Czech-Austrian border. In Hustopeče, where German townsfolk had demonstratively rejected the republic, it arrived to reinforce the position of the Czech administration. The brigade was increasingly involved in operations outside of its home region too. Between mid-December and mid-January, three field battalions were deployed to the Czech-Polish borderlands in the north to secure the area around Opava/Troppau in Silesia, the area of Moravská Ostrava (today simply Ostrava), and the contested Teschen region (Těšín/Cieszyn). In the spring of 1919, two battalions of the Slovácko Brigade went to Slovakia to assist with requisitions of foodstuffs and as a supplementary labor force.

The brigade's commanding officers attributed its accomplishments to its "tribal" identity, anchored in the character and customs of the Slovácko region.

Its structure was a deliberate departure from the centralized, regimental system that prevailed in the armed forces of Austria-Hungary. In late 1918, Hluchý claimed that "only this healthy, tribal basis on which our intelligentsia and our Slovácko lads have worked together with delight and enthusiasm, detesting everything that recalled Austria and its military organization . . . only this basis and work is to be thanked for our results today."[20] His subordinate officers evidently agreed, meeting in his absence on December 8 to compose a letter to the Ministry of National Defense in Prague in which they expressed "unconditional confidence" in their commander.[21] They urged the ministry to preserve the brigade's "tribal character" (*kmenový raz*), which reflected salutary "efforts at decentralization" and could provide an effective model for the rest of the military. The Provincial Military Command, meanwhile, appeared to hinder them. "We cannot suppress the feeling," wrote the officers who signed the letter, "that our high command and provincial command are in the hands of people imbued with the old Austrian system who have only outwardly accepted a new coat of paint." Hluchý's adjutant, First Lieutenant Ladislav Jandásek, even undertook a special mission to Josef Scheiner, general inspector of Czechoslovakia's armies, to convince him of the brigade's indispensable role as a bridge between Czech and Slovak cultures.[22]

The upper echelons of the Czechoslovak army had initially tolerated the recruitment of Moravian Czech troops according to their home regions (Slovácko, Haná, Valašsko, and so on), seemingly validating Hluchý's idea for volunteer brigades. But by the end of November, it ordered a return to Austro-Hungarian organizational models and the dissolution of newly established volunteer brigades in Brno, Hodonín, Jihlava, and Kroměříž.[23] Because of its size, the Slovácko Brigade enjoyed temporary exemption, but at the start of January 1919, it was enjoined to submit plans for its disbanding and integration into regular army structures.[24] Several months later, brigade officers were still trying to delay the inevitable. First Lieutenant Julius Grosz, commander of the Third Battalion's Third Company, petitioned against the dissolution of his unit, pointing to exemplary discipline and solidarity among his men. That these former Green Cadres "were unable to escape abroad and join the legions does not diminish their merits," Grosz contended.[25]

As the Czechoslovak army took halting steps toward a revival of the old Austrian military organizational structure, Hluchý spared no effort in playing up his brigade's regional and rural character. Following his example, enlisted men stitched the letters S. B. onto their caps, and on festive occasions—of which there were not a few—they adorned their headgear with rosemary sprigs in the style of Slovácko swains. Folk songs found their way into parade protocols, while brigade celebrations revolved around village folk customs, such as feats of strength (*zatahování*), usually reserved for bridegrooms at country weddings.[26] The 1919 carnival festivities in Hodonín featured volunteers and their guests in colorful Slovácko folk costume.[27] Around the same time, brigade soldiers welcomed Minister of Defense Václav Klofáč during his stop in Břeclav with bread, salt, and red wine, in keeping with old Slovácko (and Slavic) tradition.[28] Klofáč reciprocated by promoting Hluchý to the rank of major. With the help of local artist Joža Uprka, Hluchý even designed a new parade uniform after the model of local folk costume: red embroidered breeches (figure 5.3), a purple topcoat decorated with folk motifs, and a cylindrical woolen cap. He wore the single prototype made. Among his other unrealized plans was a makeover of the brigade barracks in the decorative style of Slovácko farmhouses.[29]

Despite Hluchý's best efforts, or perhaps because of them, disciplinary problems bedeviled his volunteer force from the start. Upon his arrival in Hodonín as a fresh recruit from the village of Ždánice, František Gavenda was disappointed to see that "many soldiers had come to profit from, and to not serve, the interests of the republic."[30] Everyone showed up to receive their meals and pay, but many shirked cleanup and guard duties, having decamped to the local taverns for successive days of carousing. "There was no discipline at all," Gavenda concluded. Czech gendarmes in Břeclav attributed the brigade's woes to its near exclusive reliance on "former Austrian deserters demoralized by the war."[31] Assigning them to secure the station, the town of Břeclav, and the southern border was risky because "there was no discipline among these soldiers, and it took a long time before their military superiors were able to at least partially make of them supporters of the state." Some initial recruits may have even joined Green Cadre–led violence in western Slovakia. Brigade lieutenant Lev Ecker, a member of the brigade's general staff, knew that in the first November days some "militarily unorganized 'soldiers'" dispatched in response to pleas for help from Slovakia had "disappeared beyond the road to Holíč" (the Slovak town just across the Morava River from Hodonín) and joined robber bands.[32] It was perhaps these men who caused havoc in the Slovak village of Trstín (then called Nadáš), according to one appalled eyewitness:

> Looting started especially when the so-called "green cadre" appeared. They arrived from Moravia and were mostly tramps. The robbed not only Jews, but also the former estate mistress, Lady Pálffy, wife of Móric Pálffy,

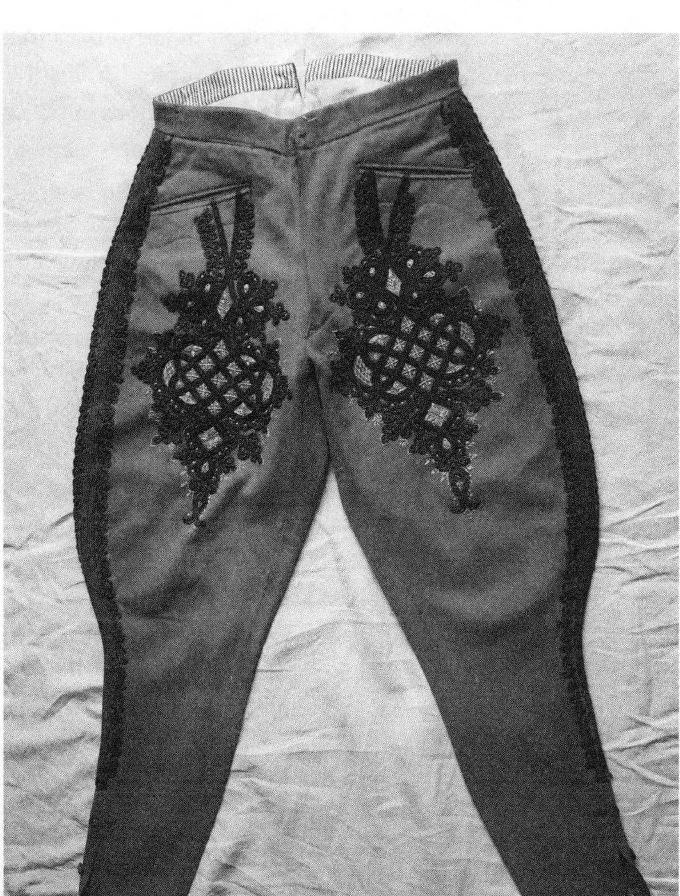

FIGURE 5.3 Trousers from Cyril Hluchý's parade uniform. Regional Museum in Mikulov

Austro-Hungarian envoy to the Vatican. They did not even spare the local large landowner Ferdinand Kriescher, whose refuge at "Bojkov" they ransacked. The "green cadre" also burst in on the local notary Gejza Čederla, whom they wanted to hang, but the people of Nadáš, for his many years of dutiful service, seized him from the hands of the cadres and saved his life.[33]

In early December, Czechoslovak army intelligence stationed in western Slovakia noted "an abundance of so-called Green Cadres," but worries about the persistence of deserter bands extended to Czech territory as well, especially in Slovácko and the area of southwest Moravia around Třebíč.[34] Reliable officers reported on "abnormal" and "unhealthy" conditions in the countryside around Uherské Hradiště, where soldiers had returned home from the front fully armed and showed little willingness to submit to new authorities.[35] While most of Hluchý's volunteers did not want to continue living as forest-based outlaws, the Moravian military command feared that indiscipline would corrode the Slovácko Brigade from within. Dispatched to Břeclav at the end of 1918 to investigate the brigade, Lieutenant Colonel Karel Korejs speculated that without vigorous action to address "inconsolable conditions [due to] weak discipline and obedience," Green Cadres might again form in the unit.[36] This, agreed commanders in Brno, would constitute a "danger to the whole empire," by which Czechoslovakia was presumably meant (fairly clear evidence of the persistent "Austrian" mentalities lamented by Hluchý's officers).[37] The brigade commander compounded his superiors' unfavorable view of his activities by insisting that "he would not listen to any Austrian generals."

In fact, Hluchý harbored few initial illusions about the reliability of his men. Just a week after the brigade's official establishment, he reported to Brno that the genuine threat of "Bolshevism" and armed revolution had forced him to take immediate steps toward the democratization of the Czechoslovak army: he had abolished the officer's mess and the practice of officers keeping servants (batmen).[38] These reforms were necessary, he maintained, in view of the fact that he and his deputy officers were "surrounded by rural areas" and knew full well the extent of the looming danger. He also requested endorsement of his decision to raise daily pay from two crowns to the five crowns normally paid to troops at the front in an effort to boost morale.[39] The Provincial Military Command, however, regarded such an increase acceptable only for men serving in Slovakia.[40] In early December, Hluchý decided to reassign men returning late from leave to a special company that would be deployed far from home in western Bohemia.[41]

He was hardly alone in calling for emergency measures to tackle problems in the new republic's armed forces. Reports about lax to nonexistent discipline among recruits piled up on military commanders' desks in the first months of Czechoslovakia's existence. Of the regions populated by the state's titular "Czecho-Slovak" nationality, rural eastern Moravia and Slovakia caused special concern.[42] In spring 1919, the army introduced training for NCOs, viewed as ideally situated in the military hierarchy to set a good example among the enlisted men. The army inspectorate in Brno prescribed that NCOs be instructed in how to concisely define key terms, such as monarchism, absolutism, republic, democracy, socialism, and Bolshevism, along with how to critically read inherently biased press articles. Heavy emphasis was to be laid on the Czechoslovak nation's unique and historic "moral idealism."[43] Federalism and decentralization, concepts implicit in the Slovácko Brigade's existence and other contemporaneous peasant initiatives, appear not to have been broached.

While the Slovácko volunteers could not be inoculated against general demoralization and undiscipline, high-ranking officers in Moravia came to believe that the headstrong Hluchý was only making matters worse. Already in mid-November, complaints surfaced about his behavior: that he declined to come to Uherské Hradiště and meet with General Štika, the first commander of Czechoslovak forces in Slovakia; that he ignored an order to send more troops to Slovakia and showed great irritability when disturbed during dinner.[44] Several weeks later, the Provincial Military Command submitted a report to the Prague Defense Ministry entitled "unreliable captain Hluchý." It addressed his unsatisfactory conduct, his unreasonable demands (particularly regarding soldiers' pay) in light of his brigade's modest achievements to date, and suspicions of poor discipline among his recruits.[45] Further undermining confidence, he categorically refused to dissolve two of his six field battalions to supplement Infantry Regiment Four and Artillery Regiment Twenty-Five, as commanded by the Provincial Military Command.[46] Not even Minister Klofáč's intervention could persuade Hluchý to accept the brigade's diminution, which he claimed was impossible given the volunteers' responsibilities in various sectors as well as an affront to his unit's tribal character, and, indeed, to the entire "Slovak nation."[47] The Brno inspectorate reiterated the order, underscoring that the army everywhere needed restructuring, and set an ultimatum of April 26 for Hluchý to submit a plan for the elimination of the Slovácko Brigade's "redundant units."[48] With the Hungarian Red Army invasion of Slovakia in late May 1919, the Czechoslovak army shifted its strength into front-line and rear formations, reducing the number of hinterland units. This provided the ideal pretext to do away with the offending brigade altogether. On June 6, it was replaced with the three-battalion Slovácko Regiment (Slovácký pluk) and in September put under the command of French Major Cayrol.[49] Although Hluchý was to stay on as Cayrol's deputy, he showed little interest in the role and applied for repeated periods of leave. In January 1920, he decided not to return after his leave and accepted retirement the following month. The remaining battalions of the Slovácko Regiment were then broken up and fed into other units, a process that was complete at the end of August 1920.

The liquidation of Hluchý's regionalist experiment did not only reflect the malice of his rivals in the Provincial Military Command. Many were keen to use an egalitarian militia system as the basis of Czechoslovakia's army, but anxieties about the loyalty of ethnic minorities along with the pressures of borderlands wars condemned locally raised units to extinction. The French military mission that took over leadership of the army in Slovakia after a near rout by Hungarian forces also insisted on centralization. Even Minister Klofáč, a nationalist socialist and enthusiast for the militia system, had to abandon his dream of a people's army. He wrote: "An emergent state of which more than a quarter is composed of foreign elements cannot entrust its security to a system of local militias. The non-Slav elements live mostly in the borderlands, and we certainly cannot trust them to defend our frontiers. The constitution of a militia system whereby solders are recruited and trained in their own local areas would reinforce separatist tendencies even in peacetime."[50] Although the rationale for a restoration of the "cadre system" was couched in concerns about Germans and Hungarians, regionalist units of Czechs and Slovaks also fell casualty to the reorientation.

To Hluchý, the repeated and ultimately successful assaults on his authority was incontrovertible proof that "Austrians" dominated the new state's commanding heights. Many others shared his conviction, not least in the villages where he levied his volunteers. Former deserter and brigade infantryman František Sedláček of Kobylí ended his terse war recollections in a disillusioned key:

> When I was on the front and in Russian internment, I always imagined that when peace finally comes, those whom fate allows to return home will live with their fellow citizens in love and harmony. But unfortunately, parties arose that divided the people. The worst divisions were during local elections. And in the second instance mammon for money, of which some had amassed heaps and others returned from the war and had nothing to eat or to wear. There's enough that needs to be cleaned up in the Republic, but it seems to me that the biggest former Austria-supporters have been promoted.[51]

Perhaps Sedláček's commander in the Slovácko Brigade had fostered unrealistic expectations among the enlisted men. As Hluchý remarked in his 1930 self-defense, "I was described as a windbag who with his orders and exaggerated promises to subordinate officers and enlisted men promised unfulfillable things."[52] But the disappointment extended far beyond army volunteers in southeast Moravia. Many Czechoslovak citizens, not just ethnic minorities, doubted the sincerity of their government's official paeans to democracy and "moral humanism." Michal Mareš, the anarchist author and former Green Cadre member introduced in chapter 2, contemptuously described a Czechoslovak officer to whom deserters submit in his lightly fictionalized *Green Guard* (1927) as "just such a democrat—a dog in a reformed coat with re-sewn buttons and a national rosette instead of his former imperial badge."[53]

Popular tropes of an incomplete or betrayed revolution have tended to accompany all major social-political upheavals. Peasants in the first Czechoslovak Republic had tangible grievances as well. The continuing of wartime requisitions of agricultural products, often enforced by military units, ranked high among them. Villagers in Vrbice, Břeclav district, expected that the 1918 state revolution would bring the confiscations to an end, but a decree published soon after in all newspapers reestablished quotas for compulsory grain deliveries, disabusing them of their naivety.[54] The village was ordered to supply 140 quintals of hay and 600 of straw—impossible amounts, according to mayor and local chronicler Jan Bařina. While the first day of requisitions unfolded without incident, peasants began to resist on the second day, prompting the terrified military commissioner to flee. In the central Moravian Haná region, an incredulous peasant greeted municipal authorities registering livestock in December 1918 with the words: "The republic orders this? Just so you know, I shit on you and the whole republic! And whoever dares to cross my doorstep will get a pickaxe in his paunch!"[55] Requisitioning officials increasingly appeared with armed escorts, as they had in the final year of Austria-Hungary. Villagers in Hluk, Uherské Hradiště district, took umbrage at the appearance of the final requisitioning commission that arrived in March 1919: "They were armed to the teeth, like some kind of robbers."[56] At one of the first houses they stopped at, a local farmer assaulted the commanding officer. A furious crowd quickly assembled and forcibly disarmed the soldiers, throwing their rifles into the stream. Pitchfork-wielding locals chased the officer and his men out of Hluk.

Political parties with mostly rural constituencies tried to intervene on behalf of their voters. In January 1919, deputies of the Czechoslovak People's Party (Československá strana lidová) submitted a proposal to the national assembly for smallholders and cottagers to be represented according to their share of the population in requisitioning commissions, local provisioning councils, and other administrative bodies.[57] Soon after, the Czech Agrarian Party's representatives in the assembly proposed that smallholders and cottagers be allowed an "existential minimum" that would be exempted from requisitions. According to their plan, any family possessing three hectares (7.5 acres) or less of arable land would not have to yield agricultural products or livestock. Nor would small peasants who annually slaughtered a pig for family consumption be required to deliver lard; an exemption that was extended to two pigs for families of six or more.[58] While parliament approved the People's Party scheme, blanket exceptions for smallholders across the republic did not go into effect. Requisitions and price controls on agricultural products continued for the next two years to ensure supply at affordable prices for urban consumers, as in wartime under the previous regime, and to maintain favorable trade balances. Incidents in which peasants protested or resisted intrusions into the rural economy multiplied, peaking in 1920, a year of widespread social upheaval and strikes in Czechoslovakia.[59] In the middle of that year, a political fight over the prices paid to farmers for requisitioned products almost brought down Vlastimil Tusar's coalition government.[60]

Starting in the spring of 1920, peasants across the republic assembled to pass resolutions urging an end to the wartime economy in the countryside. In eastern Slovakia, over seventy villages sent identical eight-point lists of demands to the Slovak ministry in Bratislava, in which they called for an end to maximum prices, for requisitions to cease, and a for a return to the free market within state borders.[61] In Moravia, Czech and German peasants found common cause in pressing for similar changes. A June 5 assembly of three hundred Czech agriculturalists in Znojmo, southern Moravia, welcomed the arrival of fifteen hundred German farmers; their bilingual resolution called for "freedom in a free republic and for the agriculturalist the abolition of his present serfdom, embodied in central agencies [for agricultural products] and requisitions. We demand the abolishment of central agencies, requisitions, and the unshackling of agricultural production. We will not tolerate confiscation of the next harvest."[62] Elsewhere, German peasant anger against the "command economy" shaded into nationalist rejection of the republic itself. The six thousand people who converged in February 1920 on the (at that time) mostly German-speaking market town of Pohrlitz/Pohořelice sang the nationalist battle hymn "The Watch on the Rhine" and "Deutschland über Alles."[63] Two demonstrators died after a clash with Czech soldiers charged with keeping order. Some Slovak activists also channeled peasant discontent into anti-Czech nationalism. In July 1920, the priest Vavro Černý in the town of Šimonovany decried that "the Czechs take away our grain and pay us 80 crowns while in Bohemia and Moravia they pay 150 crowns and the French pay 580 crowns. And now they are preparing to again take the harvest to Prague from which they will sell us expensive flour. My dear brothers, the final hour has struck. [C]lose ranks and do not hand over one kernel."[64] But most instances of resistance to requisitions, and to the controlled economy more generally, possessed no nationalist agenda. Many self-described Czech patriots took part, including the pensioned Hluchý, who on August 1, 1920, exhorted assembled peasants in a village near Hodonín not to fulfill the state-mandated grain quotas.[65] State prosecutors later dropped the case against him, perhaps because of his popularity in the area.

As peasants in all parts of the republic challenged requisitions, southeast Moravia became the center of forceful land occupations and parcellization of large estates by radicalized peasants.[66] In early September 1920, inhabitants of villages around Hustopeče seized control of large estates in Velké Pavlovice and Židochlovice, formerly holdings of the imperial family. "Peasants (mostly cottagers), armed with household tools, are measuring out land for themselves and beginning to till it," reported the authorities in the local town.[67] The local state administration had previously divided up the estates along lines that the natives of Němčičky, Velké Pavlovice, Kobilé, and Bořetice found acceptable. But the Ministry of Agriculture subsequently undertook a revised distribution following the proposal of the estate manager, which resulted in many villagers receiving inferior land. Their written protests to the State Land Office went unanswered, and their deputation to Prague, supported by several parliamentary deputies, was ignored. After several months of waiting, they decided to take matters into their own hands. A local official who sympathized with peasant frustration warned that "a crackdown by the authorities would certainly lead to violence because there is great outrage among the people."[68]

In the eastern part of Slovácko near the town of Uherské Hradiště, several hundred peasants took part in the confiscation and redistribution of a large estate in Sušice. Their petitions to the State Land Office had also fallen on deaf ears, so between September 18 and 21 they began distributing among themselves, claiming that the current leaseholder (a certain Doctor Seifert from the town of Napajedla) was cultivating it poorly and that local smallholders did not have enough property to feed themselves.[69] While some of Seifert's laborers returned to work even after the seizure, they quickly bowed to the pressure of their covillagers, who, shouting from the edge of the estate fields, convinced them to stop plowing and return home. Local authorities tried to negotiate with the expropriators, perhaps because ex-legionaries were among their leaders. A delegate from the State Land Office agreed to increase the size of parcels distributed in the spring, which had already exceeded state standards, by nearly 100 percent, but villagers rejected the offer. Unlike his counterpart in Hustopeče, the district captain in Uherské Hradiště called up the gendarmerie to restore Doctor Seifert's tenancy by force, for, as he put it, "the three-day negotiation with the interested parties displayed their complete incomprehension of the legal situation."[70] Although land occupations occurred elsewhere in the republic, few were so premeditated or on such a scale as in southeast Moravia.

Rural unrest in the Slovácko region further complicated the already equivocal legacy of the volunteer army brigade that arose there and the Green Cadres that preceded it. The events of 1918–20 in southeast Moravia fitted poorly into Czechoslovakia's founding myth of cross-class national solidarity, unified resistance to Habsburg tyranny, and implicit trust in the Prague-based leadership of philosopher-president Tomáš G. Masaryk. The dilemma presented by Slovácko's recent past surfaced in municipal chronicles, which proliferated following a January 1920 law (no. 80) that made recordkeeping obligatory throughout the republic.[71] The statute required each parish to assemble a committee that would appoint a chronicler, ensuring that the person charged with recording local events was properly vetted. Josef Kazimour, curator of the Agricultural Museum in Prague, wrote the manual for prospective chroniclers, emphasizing the need for rural perspectives on the recent epochal transformations:

> Today's era, a serious era, the era of the world war whose events touch even the most remote cottages and hamlets, itself demands and also deserves to be captured for future memory in records and chronicles. Events of a general character have been abundantly recorded and are accessible to virtually everyone in the daily press, but the consequences caused by world events, their meaning for individual municipalities, need to be preserved for future times. And precisely such description of the influence of world events on the formation of conditions in our little villages is very necessary and essential.[72]

Kazimour's exhaustive guide made clear that official records were insufficient; "Documents are dry, but there is life in a chronicle," he wrote. Regarding whom to select as chronicler, he recommended that schoolteachers assume the role because of their education.[73] Though unstated, he doubtless knew that many Czech-speaking teachers in the countryside were, since Habsburg days, reliable middle-class nationalists.[74] Most teacher-chroniclers obligingly narrated local wartime events with reference to the dominant narrative of Czechoslovak democracy, unity, and anti-Austrian resistance emanating from the "Castle" controlled by Masaryk and his foreign secretary, Edvard Beneš.[75] Whenever possible, they remarked on the prewar national consciousness of the parish's inhabitants, the heroism of local legionaries, and the general enthusiasm that greeted the news of independence. The men who during the war joined the Czechoslovak legions in France, Italy, and above all Russia basked in state-sponsored adulation throughout the interwar period.[76] They had privileged access to employment and agricultural land, the benefits of membership in well-funded veterans' organizations, and were generally regarded as torchbearers of Czechoslovak democracy.

The triumphalist narrative needed to be adapted to local conditions, however, particularly in southeast Moravia where Green Cadres often outnumbered the local legionaries. In Hluchý's home village of Moravská Nová Ves, which boasted twenty-three legionaries but at least thirty Green Cadres, the head teacher and chronicler Vilém Rosendorfský wrote: "The Czech spirit had fully awakened. Soldiers on leave were reluctant to return to the battlefield and many disappeared—they hid in attics, hayracks, cellars, and forests. People sometimes brought them food to a specific place, or out of caution they came for it themselves. People called them the 'Green Cadres.'"[77] These bearers of the "Czech spirit" had, according to many accounts, contributed to the national cause by undermining the Austro-Hungarian army. That they "helped to accelerate the end of the war and the collapse of Austria-Hungary" was a common refrain in chronicles.[78]

But lionizing accounts of the deserters were not ubiquitous. Many viewed their actions with deep ambivalence or hostility. The chronicler of Hrušky concluded that "the Green Cadres did not benefit the area. Theft on the fields and in the area was rampant; when not in the fields, the soldiers committed armed robberies on trains in the station in Hrušky and nobody dared to stand against them. These armed gangs became the terror of the vicinity."[79] The phrase "terror of the vicinity" appeared in many such recollections, as did references to "robber gangs."[80] The teacher from neighboring Moravská Nová Ves who regarded the Green Cadres as a manifestation of the "Czech spirit" showed little sympathy for the gangs of "deserters"—likely the same men—that plundered freight trains in the vicinity following the revolution.[81] In 1927, the state prosecutor in Uherské Hradiště brought charges against former members of the Green Cadre in Hrušky for their involvement in train robberies before and after the revolution.[82] It was ultimately of little consequence that they had redistributed the looted goods to needy villagers, who sometimes arrived with empty wagons to prearranged meeting places.[83] Not until the first half of 1919 did the gendarmerie, in cooperation with army units and citizen militias, succeed in halting the thefts. With the war's end, socially minded redistribution transformed into blatant larceny, and some former Green Cadres, such as the Vylášek brothers in Vřesovice (today Březovice) near Kyjov, became hardened criminals.[84] One of the brothers, Jan, had been discharged from the Slovácko Brigade.[85] Sporadic press dispatches appeared with titles like "The Green Cadre Still Menaces," "Courtroom Report: The Třebíč Green Cadre," and "100 Months in Prison for Members of the 'Green Cadre.'"[86]

Moreover, desertion still plagued some rural areas of the republic, even if it never reached the same scale as in other post-Habsburg states such as Yugoslavia. After news of the revolution arrived in Hluk, deserters forced the closure of the gendarme station, attacking commander František Jančík's home, his wife, and his replacement, Metoděj Král. The Hluk chronicler, Josef Dufka, downplayed the attack, explaining that "the war had ended and there was freedom, which needed to be celebrated, and the evil and hatred need to be vented somehow."[87] The parish priest Karel Namyslov had allegedly emboldened them at a meeting, shouting "glory to the deserters." An official report on the incident underscored the lack of patriotic commitment among the perpetrators: "According to the judgment of more moderate elements, [Namyslov's interjection] strengthened the dissatisfied and unreliable portion of the population. This exclamation was certainly clumsy and unjust, because any sort of ideal Czech-national stance was foreign to the deserters in question."[88] Over the following months, their distance from acceptable Czech nationalism seemed only to increase. In late April 1919, the fearful gendarme commander in Hluk reported that the over three hundred deserters in the area refused to enlist in the Czechoslovak army or pay any heed to him and his men. "Among the deserters," he continued, "are those who, after the state revolution, perpetrated violence and theft on the wife of ranking commander František Janšík [*sic*] and a number of Jews."[89] Their ranks swollen by radicalized workers formerly employed in Lower Austria, the deserters constituted a "Bolshevik movement" that allegedly was preparing to plunder those who had prospered during the war on May Day 1919. The district gendarmerie commander in Uherské Hradiště assured authorities in Brno that steps were being taken to avoid social unrest. In early May, the Brno military command charged the Slovácko Brigade with investigating the situation more closely but insisted that no troops be garrisoned in Hluk.[90]

Peasant deserters posed a bigger threat in Slovakia. In June 1919, a "Green Cadre" of deserters established its stronghold in the forests near Levoča, located in the country's northeast.[91] The commander of the local garrison worried about the damaging effect they might have on the morale of his men and asked for reinforcements to raid their lair. On the morning of June 15, perhaps in response to the buildup in troops, a hand grenade was thrown expertly into one of the barrack buildings (empty at the time) and exploded. To cow the deserters, the garrison commander decided to take ten hostages from the local population, replacing them every forty-eight hours. Toward the end of the month, units under General Drobný raided the forests, arresting sixty members of the Green Cadre, but many more remained at large.[92] As during the war, villagers supported the deserters, either out of sympathy or fear. In the Zlaté Moravce district of western Slovakia, the mayor of Lavče, Štefan Hudec, initially refused to escort gendarmes who came in late August to round up deserters, having received death threats to prevent him from cooperating with the authorities.[93] Hudec relented under duress, but the house searches by gendarmes produced no results. The patrol and mayor then narrowly escaped with their lives when they were fired at with military rifles as they proceeded through the forest toward the village of Zlatno. The authorities could not locate the shooters, who, it was assumed, received supplies and warning from their families. In late 1919, General Mittelhauser, the French commander of Czechoslovak armed forces in the east of the country, announced that mobile units would be deployed to combat desertion and set high fines for aiding deserters (2,000 crowns), or for violently resisting their capture (20,000 crowns).[94]

The continuing menace of armed deserters, along with their disputed wartime record, cast a shadow over the Slovácko Brigade's legacy. The chronicler in the town of Hodonín itself, schoolmaster Josef Švábenský, noted that there were "many reasons" why the brigade "did not prove successful," but refrained from expatiating on them, likely out of respect to local sentiment, save that it "was organized from romantic elements by the complete romantic, captain Cyril Hluchý."[95] The teacher-chronicler in Lanžhot, Hynek Novotný, agreed: "These troops could have been good, but the leadership of brigade commander Cyril Hluchý was not to their advantage."[96] Both welcomed the arrival of well-armed and disciplined Czechoslovak legionaries from Italy to complete the pacification of the region. Even Hluchý's adjutant Jandásek admitted years later that there was more than a bit of naivety surrounding the entire venture.[97] Though, like other defenders of the brigade, he saw Hluchý's nonconformity as a strength rather than a weakness, some reservations notwithstanding. "There was something sort of Jánošík-ish in his physical presence and spirit," wrote Jandásek, referring to the legendary eighteenth-century Slovak bandit Juraj Jánošík, about whom more will be said in the next chapter.[98] Tall, thin, direct in speech and action, he was a typical product of the Slovácko region, according to his adjutant. He could be strict with his men, especially those coarsened by their time in the Green Cadre, but he had deep affection for them as well. One former brigade infantryman, Martin Ondryska, remained convinced that Hluchý had uniquely channeled a "tribal sense of belonging," which in the case of the brigade manifested itself in "Slovácko fearlessness and pugnacity."[99] Brigade Lieutenant (later Major) Lev Ecker speculated that a century prior, Hluchý would likely have enjoyed more success as an "*ataman*" at the head of his tribe.[100] Still, the Slovácko Brigade had resonated deeply in south Moravian society. At the end of October 1938, exactly a month after the Munich Agreement ceded the defensible, German-majority borderlands of Bohemia and Moravia to Nazi Germany, Slovácko author Vojtěch Rozner penned an encomium to Hluchý and his brigade in the Czech press, lamenting only that this national and regional hero had never received due recognition and lived in obscurity in his native village.[101]

Rozner had established himself as a writer a decade before with a novel celebrating the roles of the southeast Moravian peasantry and the Green Cadres in the 1918 Czechoslovak national revolution. His *Revolt of the Cottages* (1928) was among half a dozen such literary and theatrical works that appeared around the decennial celebrations of Czechoslovakia's founding. With varying motives and varying degrees of faithfulness to the historical record, authors tried to find in the deserter bands some clear Czech national meaning. Most, like Rozner, aimed to conjure for the new republic a usable past from the tumultuous and ambiguous events of the Czech countryside at the end of the world war. Most of them also insisted on the intrinsic value of hinterland desertion to the movement for Czechoslovak independence, or at least on its effect in sharpening popular anti-Austrian sentiment. Implicit comparisons with the Czechoslovak legions loomed behind all these works, though they diverged in how closely their peasant deserters conformed to the Czech national ideal broadcast by Masaryk and Beneš's regime.

Perhaps most loyal to the young republic's founding myth, the dramatist Josef Liška Doudlebský's play *The Green Guard* underscored the cooperation of Czechs from all backgrounds in undermining Austrian rule. In the foreword to his panegyric to Czech unity, he explained: "Much has already been written and said about our 'foreign resistance,' but relatively little about the internal one, so to speak; and yet how many conscious Czechs there were (and thank God there were so many!). . . . This play is dedicated to all those tiny grubs gnawing slowly but inexorably through the foundations of the Habsburg throne and rotten Austria, all those who through open or secret hostility fought for Our Republic."[102] Doudlebský's chief protagonist is the gentlemanly landowner and Czech patriot Emil, who becomes the protector of the local peasant lads of the Green Guard in the hills of northeast Bohemia. The deserters take cues from leaders of the Czech resistance and Emil is connected to the Prague-based anti-Habsburg Maffie organization.[103] In the final scene, the local Green Guards pay homage to their patron and, at Emil's encouragement, swear an oath of loyalty to the republic.[104]

Similarly, in Jan Václav Rosůlek's tragic novel *Noha, Colonel of the Green Cadre,* the eponymous main character, a recent returnee from Russian internment in 1918, muses that "the nation must also show its dissatisfaction at home—not just abroad."[105] The plot—based less on actual deserter bands than on the failed mutiny of a mostly Czech regiment in Rumburg/Rumburk in May 1918 (a rifleman named Noha was one of its leaders)—portrays Noha's desertion and assembling of a small fighting force that embarks on an ill-starred expedition to liberate Prague from Austrian rule.[106] He and the men who remain loyal to him are caught and killed, while other deserters abandon the cause early on to plunder the countryside. This Green Cadre is ultimately less of a fighting force on the ground than an expression of Noha's patriotic vision: an inchoate, less glamorous, do-it-yourself form of anti-Austrian resistance that is nonetheless resolutely Czech; in stark contrast to Rosůlek's portrayal of Russian Bolshevism and the brutal militarism of the multiethnic Habsburg army, embodied by the "Romanian gypsy" NCO who oversees Noha's execution at the Terezín/Theresianstadt prison.[107]

Czech military and social elites who had come into contact with the Green Cadres in wartime tended to corroborate Doudlebský and Rosůlek's depictions, as well as their own indispensability (like Doudlebský's Emil) in turning desertions by ordinary country folk into something more useful. An engineer from the northern Bohemian Železný Brod district remarked that there were two forms of domestic resistance in his area during the war: "One, tied to our circle, which was committed, patriotic, and religious; and the other, which arose from shirking [*ulejváctví*] and for a lark [*ze srandy*] but also from patriotic feelings. The 'Green Cadres' worked at home on the fields and in trades, while we worked with our intellect."[108] The deserters' lighthearted propensity to organize or attend village dance parties featured in some mainstream Czech interwar fiction, including a 1939 book by the hugely popular Karel Poláček.[109] Richard Sicha, the Brno-based officer and member of the conspiratorial Zádruha society, considered such antics and limited horizons to be only natural, since the Green Cadres manifested the resistance of the "simple Czech soldier."[110]

Because the deserters often seemed distant from, or oblivious to, the maneuverings of Czech independence movement leaders, some authors took a different tack than Doudlebský and Rosůlek, playing up their primitive nature. Josef Pavel's 1927 adventure novel *The Green Cadre* was less a Czech story than a Slavic one, featuring a Ukrainian deserter named Mychajlo Bunčuk. According to one approving reviewer, Pavel's novel faithfully described "the wartime sufferings and miserable life of the Slavic population in thrall to Austria."[111] Besides becoming an effective commander of Green Cadres in the Carpathian forests, Bunčuk steals from the rich to give to the poor, just like his putative eighteenth-century antecedents, Juraj Jánošík and the Ruthenian/Ukrainian Oleksa Dovbuš.[112] The novel trades heavily in anti-German and anti-Magyar sentiment, as well as in anti-Semitic stereotypes. Bunčuk's cadres are the obverse of such prejudices: a picture of Slavic solidarity, with Poles and Czechs fighting alongside the humble Ukrainian peasants against Habsburg oppression and militarism. But the pan-Slavic idyll is shattered after the war's end. The Ukrainian deserters form the core of the army that, as in reality, battles both General Józef Haller's Polish army and the Russian Bolsheviks to establish a Ukrainian state. While valorizing the Green Cadres, Pavel to an extent also exoticized them, locating them far from the Bohemian Lands in the misty Carpathian forests, where romantic bandit heroes still roamed. This was the territory of the renowned highwayman Nikola Šuhaj, who at the end of the First World War became widely feared and admired in the easternmost province of interwar Czechoslovakia, Subcarpathian Ruthenia. In Ivan Olbracht's famous 1933 novel *The Bandit Nikola Šuhaj*, the protagonist early on briefly considers joining the Green Cadres.[113]

The deserter bands of Rozner's *Revolt of the Cottages*, by contrast, were both noble savages and conscious Czechs. Unlike the authors above, Rozner doubtless had first-hand experience with the deserter movement. In 1918, he was a fourteen-year-old boy in the village of Hýsly in Kyjov district, where his father Benedikt was schoolmaster and, in the 1920s, municipal chronicler.[114] The teenage Vojtěch composed sentimental nationalist poetry for the 1922 unveiling of a monument to the eighteen war dead of Hýsly. Perhaps dissatisfied with his father's cursory treatment of the Green Cadres in the official history of the village (all of one sentence), he decided to write a novel describing how they energized villagers in southeast Moravia. His protagonist, the heroic "commander of the Green Cadre" Karel Zach, is also a nationalist who decorates his uniform with Slavic red-white colors and sports a green linden leaf (symbolizing Slavs, but also the Green Cadre apparently) in his buttonhole. The "army of deserters" that Zach commands is reminiscent of the Blaník knights, a legendary army of Czech warriors sleeping under a Bohemian mountain until it is called to deliver the nation in its hour of greatest need.[115] According to this depiction, the Green Cadres are ultimately at least as important as the émigré Czechs and legions in bringing about the collapse of the Austro-Hungarian army, "for not everyone had the opportunity to be captured [by the enemy]. Some had to carry out the revolution at home. It was often even more courageous and dangerous."[116] The verisimilitude of Rozner's portrayal lay in his clear familiarity with the cadres' modus vivendi in the final war year. The novel details their warning system against gendarme patrols, their secret candlelit village meetings, their control of an extensive territory centered on the Buchlov Forest. *Revolt of the Cottages* captured the sense of empowerment that humble Moravian villagers found in the Green Cadres movement, along with, crucially, how its national significance was refracted through the prism of regional identity. Toward the end, the hero Zach marvels at a map together with his tearful mother, remarking, "Slovakia [i.e., Slovácko] . . . it is all Slovakia . . . and it is ours."[117] Two sorts of national unity triumph in the conclusion: the peasant version, with Zach and his men enlisting in the Slovácko Brigade, and the Masarykian version, with the village priest converting from Catholicism to the Czechoslovak national church.

Only Michal Mareš, author of *Green Guard* (1927), invoked neither the Czechoslovak legions nor the interwar republic's master narrative. Born in 1893 to a working-class Social Democratic family in Teplice, north Bohemia, Mareš had a mostly German education, was bilingual in Czech and German, and gravitated toward internationalist anarchism before the First World War.[118] As a known antimilitarist, he was kept during wartime in low-level bookkeeping jobs, one of which was at a cannery in southwest Moravia. Here, in 1918, he joined the Green Cadres in the vicinity of Dačice; a source of considerable pride for him after the war. In 1924 while touring Italy, he by chance met General Luigi Cadorna—the disgraced commander of the Isonzo Army that lost the battle of Caporetto/Kobarid in October 1917—in a seaside restaurant. Cadorna asked him if he had ever fired on Italian troops, to which Mareš boasted that he had never spilt "enemy" blood and had only exchanged fire with gendarmes as a member of the Green Cadres. The general replied coldly, "in my view, it was your duty not to mutiny but to follow orders and go into battle."[119] While the exact circumstances under which Mareš joined the deserters on the Bohemian-Moravian border remain unclear, it is likely that he—like Luka, the main character in his novel—was impressed by their humble origins and David-like defiance of the militarized Austrian Goliath in the name of both national and social liberation.

Mareš's tale ends bitterly with social hierarchies resurrected under the new regime. Yet it also sounds a note of prophetic optimism—the forests harboring the pioneers of, and resources for, a more just system in the future: timber provides railroad ties, telegraph poles, but also materials for building revolutionary barricades. Green thus figures in his novel as "the color of hope."[120] Nonetheless, for at least a decade after the end of the First World War, red Communism seemed to the author a better alternative to "incomplete" democracy, though what he got after the Second World War was not to his liking.[121] Accidentally arrested in May 1945 by agents of the NKVD (the Russian People's Commissariat of Internal Affairs), Mareš raged in the press against the ruthless expulsion of ethnic Germans from the Sudetenland and after the February 1948 Communist takeover landed in prison for seven years. His interwar portrayal of the Green Guard resonated widely enough to be the basis of a 1928 stage adapation, called *The Lads of the Green Cadre,* by the socialist dramatist Felix Bartoš. The play contains many similar characters (the names are often only slightly changed), analogous scenes, some identical dialogue, and features the same radical song cited above in chapter 2.[122]

Peasant deserters and the Slovácko Brigade unsettled the official memory of the war years and their immediate aftermath in interwar Czechoslovakia. To some extent, the state's founding myth could accommodate them, a process facilitated by the efforts of authors and publicists, who found in their exploits a plausible, if unorthodox, rural genealogy for the republic. While Michal Mareš rejected the Masarykian master narrative altogether, most writers who addressed the Green Cadres tried to make them broadly acceptable to mainstream political sensibilities. Literary endeavors had their counterpart in public expressions of mutual goodwill among various former combatant communities in southeast Moravia. In the summer of 1938, for instance, veterans of the legions and the Slovácko Brigade in Lanžhot near Břeclav jointly celebrated twenty years of independence with a wreath-laying ceremony and a village festival.[123] This occurred a month after Lanžhot welcomed Robert William Seton-Watson—champion of Czechoslovak independence well before 1914, personal friend of the late president Masaryk, and professor of central European history in London—as he and his wife toured the republic.

The honors afforded to former deserters or brigade veterans did not always live up to their own expectations. Hluchý was a case in point. Added to the injurious treatment he endured while in active state service was the insult of being rejected dozens of times for other military and civilian posts that he requested. At the same time, he did little to help his own cause. In 1920, as we have seen, he nearly got into legal trouble for encouraging peasants to resist the controlled economy. Then, at some point in the next few years, he embraced the nascent, if small, Czech fascist movement. In June 1926, several months after the National Fascist Community (Národní obec fašistická) was established, a Moravian newspaper published a front-page article by Hluchý entitled "Fascism and Workers," in which he lauded the new ideology's ability to bridge class differences within the national community, unlike divisive socialism with its focus on class struggle: "Whereas the goal of just about all political parties is the division of the nation into progressives and anti-progressives, Hussites and non-Hussites, classes and estates, country and town, the goal of fascism is to unite the nation into one unity under the slogans: 'labor, discipline, courage' and 'Let the welfare of the homeland be the supreme law!'"[124] Hluchý's allegiance to a movement regarded by ruling circles as at best a nuisance and at worst a subversive threat did not endear him to potential state employers. Though no doubt guided in part by his own contrarian instincts, southeast Moravia supplied a disproportionate number of Czech fascists: by some accounts a reflection of deep-rooted anti-Semitism and the anti-Jewish violence that erupted there in 1918–19.[125] One early Moravian fascist leader even wrote that "fascism fits into the framework of Moravian Slovácko, its people, its temperament, and its art."[126] When German fascists took over a large portion of the republic after the 1938 Munich Agreement, Hluchý relocated back to his home village from Moravský Beroun/Bärn, where he had moved in the 1920s and which now found itself in Hitler's Reichsgau Sudetenland.

The Slovácko Brigade commander's enigmatic career can be read as a metaphor for the indeterminate position of peasant-soldiers in interwar Czechoslovakia as well as in other newly independent east central European countries. Committed nationalists though they were in many cases, peasant soldiers expected commensurate rewards, material and moral, for their loyalty to postimperial states. This applied especially to those who had deserted under the previous imperial regime. Often regional patriots, they balked at the centralizing policies of the new national capitals. But to the extent that they insisted on maintaining their "tribal" identities, they inadvertently strengthened the very tendencies that they tried to counter. As much as peasant conscripts would have wished it, and as much as their numbers would warrant it, the armies of the new states would not be constructed in their image. Some, like Hluchý, would turn to political extremism, though usually not before other avenues of parliamentary and democratic politics had been closed off; something that did not occur until late in the 1920s or the 1930s and never in the First Czechoslovak Republic.

6

The Band of Mountain Birds

FOR THE PEASANTS OF SLAVONIA, February 27, 1925, was the day Robin Hood died. His real name was Jovan Stanisavljević, nicknamed Čaruga, and his life ended on the gallows in Osijek, the region's principal town, before thousands of onlookers. Čaruga's capture and execution were the denouement in a tale of rebellion, crime, and altruism that in the early 1920s captivated eastern Croatia, and Yugoslavia as a whole. The year before his death, Čaruga's trial in Osijek witnessed raucous scenes as hundreds of people from all walks of life packed the courtroom gallery daily throughout weeks of proceedings to catch a glimpse of the bandit hero. While in jail, he received regular deliveries of fine food and drink from admirers in the public at large, as well as love letters from various women; one Osijek waitress even tried to arrange for his escape. According to the newspaper *Hrvatski list* (Croatian pages), Čaruga had become "the most popular personality in the state of Serbs, Croats, and Slovenes."[1] The famed Croatian academic painter Vladimir Filakovac drew his portrait as he sat in prison awaiting his fate. The Serbian journalist Predrag Milojević, later to achieve prominence for his interviews with Mussolini, Hitler, and Churchill, arrived from Belgrade as a young man to speak with him. None of his other interlocutors, Milojević claimed in advanced age, were as interesting as Čaruga.

Hailing from the tiny Slavonian village of Bare, the legendary outlaw had deserted from the Austro-Hungarian army in 1916 and then, in 1920, having already committed two murders, joined a revolutionary bandit gang called the Band of Mountain Birds (Kolo gorskih tića). He soon took over leadership of the group, assuming the mantle of *harambaša,* reserved for commanders of *hajduks*—the Balkan bandits celebrated for centuries as freedom fighters against the Ottoman Turks. Čaruga was the last great hajduk in southeastern Europe, whose actual deeds, like those of his eighteenth- and nineteenth-century predecessors, only occasionally lived up to his exalted reputation among the peasantry. The dissolution of the Band of Mountain Birds also marked the effective end of the post-1918 Green Cadre movement in the former Habsburg territories. Into the middle of the 1920s, bandits drawn from both wartime and postwar deserters continued to oppose new state authorities, especially, though not exclusively, in Yugoslavia. Čaruga achieved celebrity status because he excelled in so many of the roles that peasants attributed to bandits: avengers of injustice perpetrated on the rural poor, jaunty scourges of the rich and powerful, embodiments of liberty, benefactors of the peasantry, and, after the First World War, armed resisters to expanded and illegitimate state demands. He was, in other words, a consummate "social bandit," to use the term introduced and theorized by historian Eric Hobsbawm.[2]

The fact that so many Slavonian peasants looked up to Čaruga was a sign that other ways of pursuing revolution in the village had failed. Forest-based paramilitaries could not hold out indefinitely, local and regional republics could not contend with nation-states, and standing armies would not be federalized and decentralized to honor peasant understandings of nationalism. Banditry filled the void as an "archaic" and "primitive" form of rural resistance that had long flourished outside of revolutionary periods. Its efflorescence in the early 1920s was thus in some ways a return to the status quo in the countryside. The popularity of highwaymen reflected the smallholding peasantry's demoralization in the face of superior might, its disillusionment with forms of revolutionary action that had previously seemed viable. By the early 1920s, the new successor states found themselves on relatively stable footing, and fundamental challenges to their authority appeared futile. Support for outlaws may be read as a sign of widespread despair in rural society; a retreat into traditional, largely apolitical forms of defiance that had salved peasant feelings of humiliation and powerlessness for centuries. Through Čaruga's exploits, the villagers of Slavonia could find vicarious liberty and redress of perceived wrongs against them.

On the other hand, post-1918 banditry itself became more political. Rural society imputed to armed robber bands the power to force state reforms, going beyond a generalized rejection of reigning injustice. The nineteenth-century hajduks after whom many interwar bandits in southeastern Europe styled themselves had already enjoyed, deserved or not, a more politicized reputation as national liberators than brigands in other contexts.[3] Then, the rise of Green Cadres of deserters at the end of the First World War convinced many peasants of the revolutionary potential of forest- and highland-based bands, even as some increasingly resembled unprincipled freebooters. Some outlaws, including Čaruga himself initially, took their revolutionary mission seriously. The Band of Mountain birds was established expressly as a radical political organization that would continue the fight against the Yugoslav ruling class by underground means. Other bandit leaders saw themselves as auxiliaries of parliamentary political movements, such as Stjepan Radić's Croatian Peasant Party. Deeply rooted in rural mentalities, the interwar admiration for social banditry was doubtless a symptom of desperation, yet banditry could also figure as a desperate form of politics.

Bandits had been fixtures of peasant society and oral culture around the world for centuries. Unlike common robbers, who belonged to a criminal underworld distinct from mainstream society, "social bandits" hailed from the ranks of the peasantry, shared their fellow villagers' dialects and customs, and could, under the right circumstances, reenter the world of the village with little difficulty.[4] Wherever peasants still made up the bulk of the population in the early twentieth century, the exploits of legendary brigands continued to offer solace as well as models for concrete action. In Polish Galicia around 1900, recounting tales of outlaws—of their magical powers and their ability to liberate peasants from seigneurial oppression—was one of the most common forms of evening entertainment.[5] Each ethnically or linguistically defined people tended to have its own pantheon of social bandits, but some figures transcended national boundaries. Juraj Jánošík (1688–1713) was figure of remarkably widespread and lasting appeal in the territories of Austria-Hungary. A villager from what is today northwest Slovakia, Jánošík's cult extended beyond the Slovak population to Czech Moravia, Carpathian Poland, and even into the Hungarian heartland. Hungarians regarded him as a martyr of the uprising led by Ferenc Rákóczi against Hungary's reintegration into the Habsburg monarchy after the expulsion of the Turks. Although Jánošík's career as a bandit lasted just over a year from autumn 1711 to the winter of 1712–13, he achieved lasting fame as a benefactor of poor villagers and as a doughty nemesis of nobles, priests, burghers, and merchants.[6] The scant evidence there is suggests that he sometimes lived up to his reputation as a Robin Hood, at the very least lending money on favorable terms to impecunious peasants. While other lesser-known Carpathian bandits also displayed a munificent streak, Jánošík left an indelible mark on folk memory, perhaps because his exploits coincided with the turmoil and uncertainty associated with the final years of the Rákóczi rebellion. Apprehended in March 1713 while visiting the former leader of his band, Tomáš Uhorčík, he was swiftly tried and executed in gruesome fashion, hung on a hook stuck through his ribs.

Jánošík won admirers throughout the Slavic-speaking Carpathian region, but non-Slovaks had their own highland bandit heroes as well. Ruthenes celebrated the memory of Oleksa Dovbuš (ca. 1700–1745), a highwayman active from around 1738 in the borderlands of Poland, Hungary, and Moldavia, who over the course of his seven-year career targeted Jewish and Armenian merchants, along with nobles and rich peasants. Moravian Czechs recalled the exploits of Ondráš (1680–1715), leader of a band of brigands that robbed Jews as well as innkeepers, millers, and travelers.[7] Meanwhile, the ethnic Magyar inhabitants of the Hungarian Great Plain sang ballads about the *betyárs*, livestock-rustling social bandits, and above all their "king" Sándor Rósza (1813–76), whose decades-long career in robbery peaked in the years of administrative chaos that followed the 1848–49 revolutions.[8] The son of a poor peasant family in a village south of Szeged, Rósza typified the social type from which *betyárs* filled their ranks: landless cottagers and herdsmen squeezed by the advancing commercialization of agriculture. Finding reliable protection in the crossroads taverns (*csárda*) and isolated large farmsteads (*tanya*) of the southern Great Plain, Rósza and his followers committed dozens of robberies and several murders, as well as numerous unverified acts of kindness toward poor peasants. He was finally arrested in 1857 and sentenced to death, later commuted to life imprisonment. In 1868, he was released thanks to an imperial amnesty, but shortly thereafter he reassembled his *betyár* gang and a year later ended up again in prison, where he died in 1876.

In the south Slav lands, collective purposeful banditry against Turkish authorities dominated folk memory, though individual heroes were not unknown. In the Slovene-inhabited Lower Styria, which had never experienced Turkish rule, peasants hailed the deeds of Franc Guzej/Guzaj (1839–80), who committed many of his daring robberies in disguise.[9] Most Slovenes, however, found a more influential archetype in the *rokovnjači*—organized bands of highwaymen originally composed of deserters from Napoleon's armies, who were especially active in Upper Carniola.[10] In 1881, author Josip Jurčič published one of the first Slovene novels about them. Among Croats and Serbs, some individual hajduk leaders captured the popular imagination, such as Joco Udmanić (1843–67), a noble-minded robber from the central Croatian Moslavina region.[11] Yet hajduk bands were almost always conceived as—and perhaps also functioned as—egalitarian undertakings without clear leadership. Their collectivist character heightened the national meaning that Croat, Serb, Montenegrin, Macedonian, and Bulgarian activists attributed to them as they waged unceasing irregular warfare against the Turks.[12] In this respect, they resembled the highland Greek *klephts* (the word is related to the English prefix "klept-," meaning thief/thieving) who were valorized for their purportedly central role in the Greek War of Independence.[13] Not that charismatic Robin Hoods could not be claimed as national liberation fighters, as the cases of Jánošík, Rósza, and the Lithuanian social bandit Tadas Blinda (1846–77) attest.[14]

The peasant soldiers who abandoned the Austro-Hungarian army for the forests and hills of their home regions in 1917–18 sometimes consciously styled themselves as heirs of this rich tradition. As noted above, Green Cadres in Croatia and Slavonia often referred to themselves as *komitas* or *komitadjis*, invoking a nineteenth-century term used to describe anti-Turkish irregulars, particularly in Macedonia.[15] Some of their leaders cultivated the look of nineteenth-century *harambaše*, supplementing their traditional folk dress with bandoliers and flintlock pistols (*kubure*) in addition to their military rifles.[16] When the Slovene Alfonz Šarh overheard in a Maribor tavern a group of soldiers sent to capture him and his fellow deserters, he described his clever escape—slipping the waiter a note that read "I am Šarh from the Pohorje Green Cadre" to present to the soldiers when he was safely away—as giving them "a taste of *rokovnjaško*"; that is, outwitting them in the style of the *rokovnjači*.[17] The Slovak poet-activist Jozef Ferančík portrayed his friend Augustín Nuhál, the commander of a Green Cadre band in the Little Carpathians, as the ideal noble robber. When Ferančík deserted the army to join Nuhál in the hills above their home village of Veselé, Nuhál explained their selfless mission: "I live from the war, whoever renders unto Caesar must also render unto me and to you [;] take wherever there is enough and give wherever there is not. The people have nothing but misery, labor, and die on the fronts. Here is our front, here at home beneath the Tatra [mountains]."[18] Because of their band's magnanimity, Nuhál soon assumed mythic qualities in the minds of local villagers, metamorphosing into a towering giant of a man with a waist-length beard.[19] Confronting the local administrator in the village of Šterusy, Nuhál lifted him clear off the ground and barked, "I am Jánošík, do you know who that is?"[20] Ferančík maintained that his Green Cadre band lived up to their reputation, blending altruism with revenge. When they cleared out the Jewish merchant Markus's storehouse, they distributed the spoils among desperate villagers, keeping nothing for themselves.[21] They became, in effect, executors of divine justice: "At that time poor people said that we are supposedly God's scourge on the lords and Jews. Indeed, they were right because the lords and Jews did not go to war and were brutes toward the people, and indeed besides the Green Cadres no one knew how to settle scores with that rabble."[22] Such virtuous vigilantism outlived Habsburg rule, persisting into the early months and years of the Czechoslovak Republic and becoming a serious nuisance to the new state authorities. In the Záhorie region, a deserter named Ján Dulanský, who led the November 1918 plunder in Sološnica, later became a notorious bandit in western Slovakia.[23] Vavro Šrobár, "minister with full power for the administration of Slovakia," dismissed the Green Cadres as mere "gangs of Bolshevik bandits in the mountains who adorned their crimes with the Jánošík legend: with hatred toward the lords and generosity toward the people."[24]

Of all the successor states, the south Slav kingdom suffered the depredations of banditry the most. Apart from relatively orderly Slovenia, brigandage plagued virtually all its territories, reaching the level of protracted insurgencies in the southern regions of Montenegro, Metohija, Kosovo, and Macedonia. Even some veterans of the Serbian army who had fought loyally in two Balkan Wars and the world war turned to the hajduk life (*hajdučija*) out of opposition to the new state, and particularly its renewed conscription drives.[25] *Hajduk* was actually a legal category in interwar Yugoslavia, defined in the criminal code as "one who breaks away from the authority of the land and rebels against it such that he, by himself or in the company of others, begins to live by his own authority with the intention of committing punishable acts."[26]

In the former Habsburg lands, outlawry flourished in some of the same places where strong Green Cadre forces had assembled. Highwaymen lurked in the dense forests of Petrova Gora in the southern Croatian Kordun region, accosting travelers on the roads in early 1921.[27] The gendarmerie raided forests and villages in retaliation but had little to show for their efforts. Local peasants shielded the miscreants, either out of fear or for the material benefits they reaped for their support. Investigators found it difficult to pin blame on any particular villagers, "because all of the peasants in these situations are solidary among themselves and crafty."[28] The bandits themselves showed great resourcefulness in avoiding capture. Three of the most wanted—Rade Mijatović, Nikola Gogić, and Stojan Čučković, all local peasants—were known to don various disguises, including dressing up as women. The officer reporting on the situation in the Petrova Gora area called for a strengthening of gendarmerie, preferably with young, unmarried men who would not succumb to pressure from their wives. Experience had taught him that many of the married noncommissioned gendarme officers heard admonishments from their spouses of the sort, "go to work but look out for yourself first" or "beware of bandits and come home as soon as possible."[29] Such men had little incentive to jeopardize neighborly relations in the villages where they were stationed. He suspected that the brigands even had confederates in at least one of the local stations.

To the south, on the administrative boundary between the Croatian region of Lika and Bosnia, the ordeal of the Munižaba family illustrated the risks that officials took upon themselves in pursuing bandits. Mile Munižaba, a local gendarme sergeant in Martin Brod, attempted to force an end to robberies committed by an infamous hajduk called Stevan "Stevo" Obradović by arresting his wife, Milka.[30] With Mile away from home in mid-September 1921, Obradović burst into his dwelling, armed with a repeating military rifle and grenades, and threatened his wife Sofija and their children. Sofija Munižaba pleaded for mercy, at which point Obradović reached into his pocket and pressed twenty dinars (a large sum at the time) onto the chest of her six-month-old son Svetozar with the words: "Here you have forty forints, child, may the Bosnian gendarmes chase you to jail in Bihać too." He left the shaken family without further violence, though he took time to converse with admiring villagers before he crossed the Una River into Croatia, announcing his departure with five rifle shots in the air.

Peasants supported such men for various motives, not all of them "archaic" or apolitical. In the spring of 1921, a bandit leader named Ivan Vugrinović, who was active in the vicinity of central Croatian Garešnica, claimed, sincerely or not, to be working on behalf of Stjepan Radić's movement for a peasant republic.[31] On May 18, Vugrinović entered a tavern in the small village of Trnovitica at the head of between ten and fifteen bandits. He was dressed "elegantly" in civilian clothes, while most of his followers wore military uniforms, some topped with Austro-Hungarian caps and others with the trademark Serbian *šajkača* hat. Nearly all of them bristled with ammunition-filled bandoliers and some had knives in addition to their firearms. Vugrinović approached the quaking innkeeper, introducing himself courteously as the commander of the "Radić Republican Gendarmerie," whose aim was neither robbery nor theft but rather the establishment of an independent Croatian republic. While the "gendarmes" drank merrily, the innkeeper noted that two of them spoke to each other in flawless Viennese German, suggesting that some wartime deserters from the Habsburg army may have made a smooth transition to postwar banditry in the successor states. The following day, three outlaws entered the local school, impaled portraits of the king and regent with their knives, and then paraded them through the village, shouting anti-monarchist slogans.

The authorities predictably struggled to apprehend Vugrinović and his men. Local peasants sheltered them, at least partially out of sympathy for Radić's movement. One gendarmerie commander named Božin Marković alleged that the bandits targeted any known opponents of the Croatian Peasant Party, including ethnic Serbs, who were a small but significant majority in the Moslavina region.[32] Vugrinović's penchant for committing robberies disguised as a gendarme lieutenant also complicated efforts to bring him to justice. After some weeks, the gendarmes ingeniously turned the tables on him, disguising themselves as forest-based deserters. On June 7, they emerged from the woods near the village of Šmiljanica and instructed two local peasant women working in the fields to fetch their commander, who was then lunching at a local peasant's house. Vugrinović immediately detected the subterfuge, exclaiming to the messenger that "my green cadre is not in uniform!"[33] But his anger got the better of him and he set off to the forest's edge with three of his men, promising to capture the faux deserters and "crucify them like Christ"; he was shot and died of his wounds some twelve hours later. His bandit gang disintegrated immediately. Marković noted with satisfaction that "the death of Vugrinović has had a very great moral impact on the citizens in this area, a colossal change in the attitudes of peasants toward gendarmes can be observed."[34]

Vugrinović's demise was part of a broader, ultimately successful antibanditry campaign waged by the state in the early 1920s, which employed both more forceful actions by the gendarmerie and blanket amnesties.[35] Authorities gradually extinguished the rebellion of autonomist Montenegrin "Greens" (named after the color of the ballots they cast in late 1918 and unrelated to the Green Cadres further north) against what they regarded as unlawful annexation by Serbia. They also dampened the resolve of the Albanian separatist Kaçaks in Kosovo, who, with time, lost the backing of their patron, King Zog (Ahmet Zogu) of Albania.[36] In the former Habsburg Croatian territories, a series of gendarme victories against brigands in 1920 did not prevent a spike in banditry in 1921. Nonetheless, by the end of 1922, the miscreants in many areas had been either arrested or killed.[37]

The Band of Mountain Birds remained at large for some time after, thanks in part to Čaruga's cunning. It was Božidar "Božo" Matijević who had originally founded the Band of Mountain Birds in early 1919 in the forests around the town of Đakovo in eastern Slavonia. Born in 1896 to a prosperous farming family in the nearby village of Tomašanci, Matijević attended academic high school in Osijek. His schoolmate at the time, the future physician and World

War Two resistance fighter Lavoslav Kraus, recalled a "young man and comrade of exceptional character" who instinctively opposed any sort of injustice.[38] After an abortive attempt to volunteer for the Serbian army during the Balkan Wars, he was conscripted for Austria-Hungary's war against Russia on the Eastern Front. There, in 1915, he fell into enemy hands (or perhaps deserted to the enemy), eventually winding up in the Yugoslav Volunteer Corps that formed in Odessa beginning in 1916. He likely joined the Bolsheviks in 1917, after which, in 1918, he returned to Slavonia and found his way into the Green Cadres in the vicinity of his home village. Toward the end of the war, "Red Božo," as he was now known, met Ivan Ribar, a lawyer based in Đakovo who sought allies among peasant deserters to prepare for the postwar establishment of unified Yugoslavia.[39]

Ribar would go on to serve as president of the Belgrade parliament (*skupština*) after both world wars, showing an impressive talent for political self-preservation. In the immediate aftermath of Austria-Hungary's breakup, he spearheaded the establishment of the local National Council committee in Đakovo. As elsewhere in Slavonia at the end of October 1918, peasant violence led by Green Cadres threatened to engulf towns across the region. Ribar, exceptionally, decided to enlist Matijević's Green Cadre band for defense of Đakovo. On Ribar's invitation, Red Božo arrived with his men at a public meeting in town, informing those present that they had already begun settling scores with those who had profited from popular misery during the war.[40] Ribar proposed that the Green Cadres ally with the newly christened National Council as National Guards. While the deserters held counsel among themselves, most of the assembled townsfolk deserted the meeting hall, either out of fear or to protest Ribar's scheme. Some misgivings aside, Matijević's unit accepted the invitation and prevented further plundering in and around Đakovo for the entire turbulent month of November, though his early victims found little to praise in the arrangement. Red Božo proved more reliable than guard units made up of former deserters in other parts of Croatia-Slavonia. Many of the ten thousand or so volunteer National Guards paid little heed to the Zagreb-based National Council, joining in the plundering themselves.[41] Arms were withheld from them in some places, while other districts refused to establish guard units altogether. Matijević's men, by contrast, honored their pledge to Ribar until the first days of 1919, when the Đakovo National Council was dissolved under pressure from the government in Belgrade. On January 12, Ribar's recently launched newspaper *Glas slobode* (Voice of freedom) praised the former Green Cadres: "The National Council committee in Đakovo hereby extends its most sincere gratitude to Božo Matijević, as commander, and to his company for their selfless, energetic and above all diligent work in the interest of order and peace."[42]

Yet the incorporation of his homeland into the Karađorđević-ruled kingdom likely marked a point of no return for Red Božo. As the officials, gendarmes, and wealthy Slavonians who had fled the unrest in autumn 1918 returned home under the protection of the Serbian army, he decided to turn his back on the new order altogether. Ribar later wrote: "Božo Matijević, disappointed that among those [who came home] were also precisely those who should have been in jail instead of back at work, returned with his unit to the forest and his camp so that they could from there settle scores with them."[43] Calling themselves the Band of Mountain Birds, they retreated to the forests of Krdnija and Papuk to plan their punitive expeditions. Matijević may have also feared prosecution for his National Guard unit's indiscriminate killing of a suspected looter in the village of Trnava in November 1918.[44] By the winter of 1919, the Mountain Birds were well established in the highlands of Slavonia. Lavoslav Kraus eulogized his former schoolmate as a hero who, "like the mythological avenging god or the archangel Gabriel, hounded through Slavonia all those who mistreated and looted the poor during the war."[45] Persecuting state officials and robbing the rich, Matijević and his men distributed the spoils, or at least a portion thereof, to the rural poor.

More importantly for the Communist Kraus, Matijević headed "the first fighting force with an explicit revolutionary aim on the terrain of today's Yugoslavia."[46] He did not have to embellish the truth. The Band of Mountain Birds under Red Božo's command espoused radical politics and saw in its irregular warfare a means for furthering the Bolshevik cause. The group's handwritten "program" declared unambiguously that "this association is organized for revenge on the bourgeois capitalist party and [to avenge] the tyrannical misdeeds of its servants, the insolent gendarmerie, who, in breach of the law, carries out the worst terror on the popular masses as in the era of Turkish overlordship. . . . [The association will] institute counter-terror against the terror of the state, thus establishing the foundations of Soviet government in Yugoslavia."[47] The history of banditry contains few such overtly political statements. If Soviet rule in southeastern Europe was the goal, the decision to pursue it by means of a fancifully named bandit gang no doubt fitted its members' notions of justice. To them, such a course of action likely seemed both natural and legitimate. And the calculating Matijević no doubt knew the extent of popular approval that social bandits enjoyed in the south Slav lands.

Čaruga was a desperate and wanted man when he joined Red Božo's Mountain Birds in 1920. He had begun life on February 2, 1897, in promising circumstances as the heir to a livestock farm that had once been, under the direction of his great-grandfather and namesake Jovan, one of the largest in Slavonia, with around a thousand head of cattle. Under Čaruga's father Prokopije, the business declined precipitously, but the Orthodox Stanisavljević family still commanded respect in Orahovica district. Prokopije alienated his son when, after his wife's sudden death in 1907, he remarried within a month. Young Jovo left the village to learn the metalworking trade in Osijek, but soon returned home to work on the family farm. Mobilized in 1915 into the Twenty-Eighth Honvéd Regiment, he apparently turned to crime on the Eastern Front, selling counterfeit furlough documents to other infantrymen. In early 1916, he produced for himself false papers, according to which he was the wounded First Lieutenant Fett with permission to convalesce in his home district. Soon after arriving in his native region, he killed a Magyar soldier who had been courting the object of his affection, a tavernkeeper's daughter named Katinka, and who had defamed Čaruga as a "Vlach" (a derogatory term for Serbs). His life of outlawry thus appropriately and typically began with an affair of honor, in which most fellow villagers saw Čaruga on the side of justice.[48] For the rest of the war, he ranged through Slavonia, posing as a wounded officer, and making a living from forged documents.

In late October 1918, he again returned home to Bare and helped establish a National Guard detachment. Although most local peasants backed him, Čaruga's command of the volunteer force fanned preexisting resentments between his own kinsmen and the Bošnjak family.[49] The wartime village mayor Mirko Bošnjak had previously reported Čaruga to the gendarmerie as a deserter while he was visiting his home; Bošnjak had also allegedly encouraged officials to requisition the Stanisavljević family's cattle. Already in early 1918, Čaruga had threatened to kill him. Now, at the November 1 village assembly where the National Guard was organized, Andrija Stanisavljević, an older relative, accused Mirko Bošnjak of having betrayed the village. A scuffle broke out in which the former mayor's brother, Stanko, intervened roughly, enraging Andrija. When his son (also Andrija) and Jovo Stanisavljević arrived at the assembly, the Bošnjaks had left, but Andrija demanded they avenge him, saying: "Go and kill him [Stanko], and do not let Mirko remain alive either." The young men went immediately to the Bošnjak homestead, clamoring for Stanko to show himself. At gunpoint they forced Stanko to hand over his own rifle, at which point Čaruga told his cousin to "carry out the order"; Andrija shot

Stanko in the leg at close range. The Stanisavljevićes left without molesting Mirko, but the wounded man died of blood loss a week a later. Several months afterward, the perpetrators were arrested and found guilty of murder after a brief May 1919 trial. Andrija Stanisavljević the younger was sentenced to fifteen years in prison, while his father received a three-year sentence and Čaruga four years. The Osijek court also ordered them to pay the Bošnjak family twenty-six thousand crowns in damages. For Čaruga, this was a relatively lenient punishment, further mitigated by lax conditions in the Sremska Mitrovica prison. He escaped while chopping wood in December 1919, finding refuge in the forests of Papuk and Krndija and, according to his later testimony, eking out a living as a tobacco smuggler. He frequented the area's taverns, where he heard tales of a hajduk company known as the Band of Mountain Birds. In spring 1920, he caught up with them in the forest near Virovitica and asked to join.

Božo Matijević evidently took to their new comrade. Soon after Čaruga's initiation, Red Božo made him deputy commander of the group. Together they drew up the disciplinary statute of the Band of Mountain Birds, setting out strict rules of conduct for all members. The first three articles of this astonishing document outlined the basic principles of the group's leadership and membership: command of the group belonged to the "most experienced person," who nonetheless was obliged to listen to the counsel of his fellows; every new recruit was expected to familiarize himself with the responsibilities of membership and the consequences of not fulfilling his duty; membership counted as legally binding once an applicant signed his name on the statute, or marked it with an "X" if he was illiterate.[50] The statute's subsequent articles amounted to a bandit's code of conduct. Alongside obedience to the commander, the rules required solidarity and mutual respect among the men, constant maintenance of—and preparedness to use—firearms, bravery and perseverance in battle, vigilance and alertness on guard duty, and courtesy and dignity in dealings with the public. Infractions against the code were in many instances punishable by death, as were things like desertion (defined as more than twenty-four hours away from the group without leave) and betrayal to the authorities.

In the summer of 1920, the Mountain Birds committed a series of audacious and lethal robberies.[51] On the night of July 9, they arrived dressed as gendarmes at the home of Nathan Schlossberger, a wealthy Jewish merchant in the village of Bokšić, demanding access to his home and warehouse under the pretext of searching for army deserters. Matijević shot Schlossberger in the chest when he began to protest. On July 24, the gang accosted the forester Pavao Gašo in the woods near Vladislavci, robbing him of his rifle and holding him hostage until his wife handed over his binoculars and military rifle. As they waited for their accomplices to return with Gašo's valuables, Matijević and Čaruga treated the hapless estate employee to "an entire sermon on Bolshevism," encouraging him to join their movement instead of remaining clueless "like one of [his] dogs."[52] Two days later, the bandits ambushed shopkeeper Gejza Merkl on the road near his home in the village of Feričanci, taking the thousand crowns he had on him and releasing him only on condition that he pay the remainder of what they demanded (twenty thousand crowns) as soon as possible if he did not want to meet Schlossberger's fate. On August 1, they stopped a fine carriage in the forest near the village of Vraneševci, relieving passengers Robert Doležal, clerk to a local aristocrat, and notary Vašo Todorović not only of their firearms and cash but also of their coats and shoes. From there they made their way to the village of Kutovi, where, on August 2, the gang leader and his deputy entered Adolf Goldschmidt's shop in disguise—Matijević as an ordinary peasant and Čaruga as a gendarme—forcing the proprietor to hand over five thousand dinars, again brandishing the example of Schlossberger as a threat. The authorities declared a state of emergency in Slavonia.

The fortunes of the band started to turn. Red Božo dispatched a gang member called Mijo Rebić to rob the priest in Rebić's home village of Punitovci. Rebić lost his nerve before the disarmingly equanimous clergyman, returning to camp emptyhanded. His fellows condemned him to death for breaching the code; Matijević shot his weeping young comrade at close range with a revolver. Soon after, Božo was hunting alone in the forest when he chanced upon a gendarmerie patrol. His men heard the ensuing gun battle but could not arrive in time to rescue their commander, who died on the scene. The official report stated that a gendarme's bullet hit the grenade hanging from the bandit leader's belt, pulverizing his body. His tiny home village of Tomašanci later honored its famed son with an obelisk-shaped marble tombstone in the graveyard, the epitaph of which reads: "Many bitter torments / in the storm of life / and now without pain / you are in gentle peace" (figure 6.1).

The leaderless bandits scattered, fearing arrest or retribution, for the most part back to their home villages. Only Čaruga, it seems, stayed in the forests, contemplating ways to reestablish the group. By mid-October, he had found willing recruits among woodsmen from the village of Andrijevci. The reconstituted Mountain Birds plundered the warehouses of the Gutmann family, Slavonia's largest landowners, just outside the village of Nova Bukovica. The sale of the stolen tools, household items, shoes, and tobacco yielded enough money

FIGURE 6.1 Tombstone of Božo Matijević in the Slavonian village of Tomašanci. Author's photo

for Čaruga and his new accomplices to live comfortably for some time. But the gang had bigger prizes in their sights. At the end of the month, in the village of Poreč on the south slopes of Krdnija, they took almost fifty thousand dinars from the family of Stevo Šajn, a wealthy horse merchant of Roma background—their biggest haul to date. During the confrontation, the bandits mortally wounded Šajn's son with a shot to the abdomen. The following spring, the Mountain Birds came into another thirty-two thousand dinars when they plundered a railroad handcar belonging to the forestry firm Slaveks in the woods near the village of Vučjak; in addition to the lost cash box and camera, the firm suffered three casualties in the battle against Čaruga and his men, one of whom later died of his wounds.

Bolshevik revolution, still the ostensible goal under Red Božo's command, receded from view entirely. Čaruga thirsted for booty far more than societal transformation. Many of his larcenous deeds showed a sadistic streak. Without hesitation he drew his pistol and fatally shot a gendarme named Franjo Širola, who had the misfortune to enter the tavern where he and his comrades were carousing in June 1921. He hunted down gang member Jozo Matota, who had gone home without permission for more than a day, and executed him in the name of the group's statute. In summer 1922, they entered the village of Ostrošinci dressed again as gendarmes, first taking nine thousand dinars from the prosperous farmer Stjepan Planšćak, then extorting eighteen thousand dinars from the tavern-keeper Martin Kuritz, whom they later coerced into leading them to the home of wealthy Stjepan Kristek. Not finding anything of value in Kristek's house, they beat him to death. Authorities raised the price on Čaruga's head to ten thousand dinars.[53]

Such brutality did not stop Čaruga from becoming a folk hero among the region's peasants, surpassing by a wide margin the reputation Božo Matijević had enjoyed. Like many other social bandits, Čaruga possessed no program for reforming or revolutionizing peasant society; he accepted the status quo but wanted it to be more just, or simply less intolerable.[54] Even if peasants were to remain at the bottom of the social hierarchy, they ought to occasionally revel in the seemingly ill-gotten gains of those above them. Čaruga appears to have rewarded his village-level confederates handsomely and sometimes doled out stolen money, food, clothes, and shoes to the rural poor. The Slavonian gendarmerie identified ten villages in Našice district and two in Slatina district that unhesitatingly aided the Band of Mountain Birds.[55] Many of the bandits' crimes took place in these friendly villages, suggesting that local allies were instrumental in their execution. In the eyes of poor villagers, Jovo protected them from rich landlords; "the hand of god" protected him in return.[56] Already in his lifetime, peasants referred to him as the "Slavonian Robin Hood." Čaruga's fame spread, not least because he actively curated his own image. Stories circulated of how he decided not to plunder the rich Gašparac family in Pakrac because the family treated even the lowliest farmhands as equals; how he spared the prominent livestock veterinarian Doctor Vranić from Županja for allegedly "helping poor people."[57] In both instances Čaruga was known to the intended victims under a false identity, which he then theatrically cast aside to praise their conduct and guarantee their safety. Restraint could elevate a bandit's reputation as much as righteous appropriation. So too could generous payment for ordinary services.[58] A woman from an innkeeping family in the village of Vidovci near Požega recalled how, when she was ten years old, a group of well-dressed men came to her family's establishment and ordered abundant food and drink. After they had paid and left, one of the party returned, handing to the little girl a two-dinar coin with the words: "Now tell everyone that Čaruga was here."[59] With his fearsome and beneficent reputation at stake, the Slavonian Robin Hood could brook no imitators. In August 1921, the Mountain Birds hunted down and murdered another bandit chieftain called Rade Ratković who was committing robberies under Čaruga's name in the vicinity of Slatina.

Now a celebrity, Čaruga sought entry to high society in eastern Croatia. He lived lavishly for a time in a villa in the town of Vinkovci—as if the English Robin Hood had availed himself of a chic abode in Nottingham. He maintained amorous relations with multiple women, whom he showered with gifts of jewelry, clothing, and cash; he apparently was engaged to several of his lovers at the same time (no single Maid Marian for him). From autumn 1921, he began to need medical treatment for syphilis, which he obtained under false names in Osijek and even Zagreb. His condition precluded lengthy stays in the forested hills of Papuk. He resided for some time undetected in the Zlata Inn in Virovitica, posting a taunting letter to the local gendarmerie upon his departure. He did the same in Zagreb after his hospital stay there. But his most daring move was stealing the identity of Nikola Drezgić, a man who had many years before left southern Slavonia to learn the mechanic's trade in Belgrade and had never returned. At some point in early 1923, Čaruga began presenting himself as Drezgić, a military supplier (*vojni liferant*), and going as far as to contact Nikola's actual cousin, Marko Drezgić, a butcher in Donji Andrijevci. Under circumstances that remain unclear, Marko welcomed his long-absent relative. Perhaps Marko did not recall his kinsman well enough to doubt Čaruga's claim, or maybe Nikola's conspicuous wealth deterred him from voicing his doubts. In any case, "Nikola" persuaded Marko to relocate with him to Vinkovci and work as his livestock buyer. Marko's presence may have lent verisimilitude to Čaruga's cover, as he established genuine business relations with the Seventeenth Infantry Regiment garrisoned in Vinkovci and received treatment in the local hospital for syphilis. In the second half of 1923, having secured military discharge papers in Nikola Drezgić's name in the Lika region, Čaruga took up residence in a villa by the Bosut River, which he rented for four thousand crowns a month. He became a fixture of polite society in Vinkovci, strolling the town's main boulevard (*corso*) in fashionable attire and playing cards with officers and businessmen in elegant cafés.

Meanwhile, he surreptitiously reassembled the Mountain Birds from old veterans and new recruits. When not traveling around Slavonia on business as Nikola Drezgić, the bandit chieftain investigated new opportunities for plunder, building cordial relationships with local villagers while he reconnoitered a particular locality. Nikola's "cousin" Marko joined up at some point, perhaps under compulsion. The gang committed its last successful large-scale robbery in June 1923 near the eastern Slavonian village of Budimci. The previous month Čaruga had become acquainted with a local peasant called Nikola Mijić, at whose house he lodged, winning his trust before inquiring about wealthy locals and Jews whom they might rob.[60] Mijić proposed the forestry company Neuschloss, which every Saturday morning sent a handcar laden with cash to pay its employees in the nearby woods. The Mountain Birds recruited almost twenty peasants in Budimci and the neighboring hamlets of Bračevci and Kršinci in preparation for an attack. On the morning of June 16, Čaruga, with two of his most trusted followers—Pavao Prpić "Mali" (Small) and Pavao Prpić "Veliki" (Big)—and Mijić, lay in wait at a forested bend in the track between Budimci and Koška, across which the bandits had laid a large tree trunk. When the handcar stopped before the obstruction, Čaruga, dressed as a gendarme, leapt out of the undergrowth shouting "stop!" while his uniformed accomplices opened fire, hitting Simo Tintor, the only true gendarme present, who was providing armed escort. As the two Neuschloss employees fled on foot through the forest, the mortally wounded Tintor rebuked Čaruga for killing a "Serb brother" and told his murderers, "Brothers, you are doing worse than in Albania";[61] that is, in a place where violent banditry was perceived to be endemic. Unfazed by their victim's last words, the Mountain Birds remorselessly took Tintor's hat, rifle, bayonet, and watch and divided up the Neuschloss treasure of forty thousand dinars. Each of the four received seven thousand dinars, two local peasant allies who had helped prepare for the attack got a thousand apiece, and a gypsy named Luka Grebenar who had also assisted was paid four hundred dinars. The remainder went into Nikola Drezgić's bank account in Vinkovci.

Čaruga's final exploits ended in fiasco. In November 1923, the Mountain Birds in their gendarme disguises attempted to pillage two estates belonging to Count Eltz near Vinkovci, but they were repulsed by actual gendarmes on both occasions; they seized next to nothing and managed to kill an innocent forester. Authorities in the south Slav kingdom now raised the price on

Čaruga's head to 120,000 dinars, dead or alive. Soon after, the bandits set fire to an isolated barn near the village of Retkovci, hoping in vain that the diversion would prompt locals to leave their homes unguarded as they extinguished the blaze. The barn was left to burn down. Čaruga later referred to the incident in a letter he wrote to his lover in Retkovci, a woman named Božica "Manda" Smolčić, to whom he was acquainted under the name Mile Barić. He did not know that there were two women named Manda Smolčić in Retkovci, and his letter mistakenly reached an elderly widow who, baffled by its contents, reported it to the local notary. The authorities knew only that the letter was somewhat suspicious; they could not guess who lurked behind the sender's name. Around midnight on December 21, gendarmes arrived at the house of Manda Smolčić the younger, compelling her to furnish them with the address of her beau's dwelling in Vinkovci. Finding the riverside palazzo empty, they proceeded to Marko Drezgić's butcher shop, where they found Čaruga on the floor, sleeping off a night out. "Mile Barić" admitted that he knew Manda Smolčić but claimed that he was in fact Nikola Drezgić, further confounding gendarmes. They knew the suspicious and well-dressed stranger had something to do with the fire in Retkovci and arrested him. The next day, as the putative arsonist was escorted through the nearby village of Ivankovo, one of his victims recognized him. Over a week later he confessed, probably after torture, that his real name was indeed Jovan Stanisavljević. Gendarmes Stjepan Balatinac and Dimitar Milović split the 120,000-dinar reward.

Folk memory interpreted Čaruga's capture as the result of rank treachery by a jealous lover. A popular song that circulated at this time in Croatia ran:

They caught the 'Band of Mountain Birds'
They caught Jovo Stanisavljević
In Vinkovci in his abode
Where Jovo was having a rest
Hey gendarmes you are clever ones
Having captured Čaruga and tied his hands
When Čaruga awoke from sleep
And saw gendarmes beside him
[He said] My brothers, I am not Čaruga
My name is Nikola Drezgić
[They replied] You had better tell your father that the law is after you
Your young lover betrayed you
[He replied] If I could escape once more

They would never find me again
I would fight in the mountains
Until my last gasp of air[62]

The rustic bards who sang such verses conveyed peasants' wistful yearning for Čaruga to remain at large, a perpetual thorn in the authorities' side. If only Manda had not yielded to official pressure, or to her vindictive impulses upon learning of her sweetheart's other paramours. There is little evidence she knew much about him at all, though she was conspicuously absent among the bandit's long list of callers at his Osijek jail cell.

For the first months of 1924, prosecutors worked tirelessly to assemble the evidence against Stanisavljević. The rest of the Mountain Birds were caught and brought into custody. Surviving victims and witnesses of their crimes were interviewed. Bodies of murdered comrades were exhumed and examined. One such grisly mission involved Lavoslav Kraus, then the local doctor in Našice. As instructed by county authorities, Kraus boarded a train in the village of Markovac to which two special wagons had been attached; in one of them sat Čaruga, chained and surrounded by gendarmes. At Đurđenovac they transferred to a narrow-gauge train belonging to the state forestry company, which proceeded slowly northward through the forest as gendarme patrols marched alongside for added security. Owing to Čaruga's superb knowledge of the terrain, the officials located several corpses of men who had been shot at close range—evidence of the Mountain Birds' merciless group discipline. Kraus seized the opportunity to speak with Čaruga, thinking he might shed light on his old schoolmate Matijević's death. The doctor came prepared with expensive cigarettes to facilitate their communication in the heavily guarded rail wagon. What struck him most were the bandit's pretentions of grandeur. "He spoke with great affectation," Kraus recalled, "and tried to use as many foreign words and expressions as possible, as if he wanted to show the 'doctor' that he was not dealing with an 'ordinary peasant' but with a 'man of the world.'"[63] Hardly less surprising were some of Čaruga's outlandish claims. He told his traveling companion that Matijević had been an ideological fanatic who demanded slavish loyalty from his followers and aimed to establish Soviet rule in every Slavonian village. Čaruga supposedly resisted such antistate propaganda, only pretending to accept Red Božo's tenets, but in fact waiting for an opportunity to liquidate his own commander and safeguard the Yugoslav kingdom's future. The chance presented itself in late summer 1920, when gendarmes surrounded the Mountain Birds; Čaruga's lethal shot had been mistaken for a gendarme's bullet.

His ingratiating self-defense led nowhere in the courtroom. Čaruga's numerous crimes after Matijević's death glaringly belied his professed loyalty to the state. But it revealed much about the character of a man caught between the peasant world of his origins and the high life that he had enjoyed for several years under various aliases. While he may have continued to help the rural poor, he felt no attraction to their life of toil. His riches and celebrity had far removed him from the rank-and-file Green Cadres, who helped till their family plots whenever they could. The photograph taken of Čaruga in custody shows a dandy in a frockcoat, starched shirt, and fashionable hat (figure 6.2). He stares jauntily at the camera, surrounded by his captors, and by the other arrested Mountain Birds in another photograph (figure 6.3).

The spectators who crowded the courtroom for a month of proceedings beginning on May 12, 1924, saw a young cocksure man of foppish appearance wearing patent leather shoes, who smiled mockingly and vehemently denied committing the six murders and fifteen robberies he was accused of, even though he had previously confessed. His demeanor fed speculation that he would again somehow outwit the authorities and escape captivity. It appeared that he still had the support of dangerous elements beyond the jail walls. The presiding judges received an anonymous menacing letter dated May 19 that read: "In the name of my association, I warn you that you will all fall victim to my organization if you condemn any of us to death. . . . You must, like it or not, hand down sentences only for imprisonment, but you shall not sentence anyone to death. Your head is already in the bag. You do not see us, but we see you."[64] The letter was read aloud in the courtroom and given to the press for publication, but nothing followed from the sinister communique.

Čaruga's defenses crumbled as the trial wore on. The prosecution produced more witnesses, and the bandit leader's legal counsel could not stop him from making ludicrous statements in his own defense; for instance, that he stole one victim's bag because he thought it contained books that he might want to read. Meanwhile, his stay in jail was as comfortable as possible thanks to his many admirers, including an Orthodox priest from Virovitica named Jovan Božić, who believed Čaruga to be a "benefactor of the Serb people."[65] His accomplices began admitting involvement in the Mountain Birds' crimes, despite their former commander's furious tirades against them. On the nineteenth trial day, Čaruga also started to confess, incriminating his comrades in turn. On June 21, he was found guilty of all charges of murder and robbery and sentenced to death by hanging. His attorney's closing argument that the Great War had turned his client into a "trained beast" aroused little sympathy.

FIGURE 6.2 Čaruga after his arrest in 1924. Museum of Slavonia

FIGURE 6.3 Čaruga and other members of the Band of Mountain Birds in custody in 1924. Museum of Slavonia

Stanisavljević's right-hand man at the time of his capture, Pavao Prpić "Veliki," received the same punishment, as did two other gang members whose sentences were commuted weeks later. Upon hearing the court's verdict, Čaruga supposedly smirked and winked at a woman in the gallery above. He remained faithful to his audience to the very end. The approximately three thousand spectators who, on the cold morning of February 27, 1925, crowded into the yard of the Osijek royal courthouse, watched as guards led the impeccably turned out Čaruga to the gallows, where Prpić's body already dangled limply. He bowed deeply to the hangman before turning to the assembled throng, shouting, "Goodbye, people, Čaruga is departing!" He was buried in Osijek's Saint Ana cemetery in a grave that remains well tended to the present.

The Slavonian Robin Hood lived on in popular consciousness, celebrated in song, story, and eventually film. One of the very last movies made in socialist Yugoslavia before its bloody disintegration was Rajko Grlić's *Čaruga*,[66] which appeared in cinemas in spring 1991. The most expensive Croatian production to date, often referred to as the "last Yugoslav film," it was based on a screenplay cowritten by Grlić and the novelist Ivan Kušan and featured the acclaimed actor Ivo Gregurević in the title role. It faithfully portrayed Čaruga's principal misdeeds, beginning with his desertion from the Eastern Front, as well as his increasing vanity and delusions of grandeur. The filmmakers spiced up what could be gleaned from the documentary record with abundant sex scenes and gratuitous violence. They decided to depict Božo Matijević more like the ideologue of Čaruga's fanciful self-defense than the "archangel" of Lavoslav Kraus's ennobling recollection. Instead of a fresh-faced dreamer aged twenty-four in 1920, cinemagoers encountered a jowly, mustachioed blusterer. And the femme fatale of the story is not the village belle Manda, but rather the invented aristocratic seductress Svilena, who has a fetish for Lenin.

The film touched only obliquely on Čaruga's heroic stature among the peasants of his home region. Grlić, perhaps to counterbalance the liberties taken with the historical record in the feature film, made a documentary later in 1991 in which he interviewed surviving members of Čaruga's family and eyewitnesses in Orahovica district.[67] Croatian media authorities halted the project during post-production, maybe because the bandit hero by then counted as an enemy "Serb." The film reels were subsequently lost. Two documentaries on Čaruga then appeared in the first decades of the twenty-first century, one made for television and drawing on the expertise of historians, the other by an amateur filmmaker and featuring interviews with eastern Slavonian villagers.[68] The latter evoked the fame that Čaruga, irrespective of his birth religion, still enjoys in what remains of local peasant culture.

As enemies of rural injustice, social bandits have offered perennial inspiration, even if their actions have tended to be selfish, violent, and cruel. Their star often rises as more constructive and participatory peasant movements appear to have failed. The fame of Red Božo and especially Čaruga correlated inversely with the prospects of grassroots peasant revolution after 1918. Still, the Mountain Birds' initially earnest political aims caution against dismissing them as simply opportunistic criminals. Matijević probably hoped his gang could wage revolutionary irregular warfare against what they saw as illegitimate authorities in Croatia-Slavonia and inspire others to do the same. Some villagers who abetted him and his less principled successor likely nurtured similar hopes, though some no doubt assisted the outlaws out of fear or desire for material reward. After both world wars, banditry proliferated in parts of rural east central Europe, signaling not just lawlessness, but also widespread disillusionment with the new order, along with the faint belief that particularly unscrupulous and violent individuals drawn from peasant society might prevail against the authorities. In this way, it marked the transition from a radicalized countryside to a more stable state of affairs. The process after the First World War was distinct, however, since the peasants of central and eastern Europe were more drawn to revolution than during and after the Second World War. And significantly, even after the demise of Čaruga and his kind, they could still pursue their aims by other, more conventional means.

7

The Apogee of Peasantism

REVOLUTIONARY IMPULSES AT THE VILLAGE LEVEL in east central Europe enabled an explosion of agrarian parliamentary politics, leading some informed observers to believe that the First World War had ushered in the age of the peasant. Milan Hodža, Slovak agrarian leader and interwar Czechoslovakia's last prime minister before the country's dismemberment at the 1938 Munich Conference, was convinced that "in the ten states of Eastern Europe, the most bloodless, quiet, and yet most profound, social revolution in world history took place after World War I. The strongest social class of all time, the landed aristocracy, was destroyed at one blow and replaced with agrarian democracy."[1] Although this seismic transfer of political-social power to the peasantry was felt strongest in central, eastern, and southeast Europe, its shock waves reverberated around the world. In 1922, the maverick English philosopher and critic G. K. Chesterton wrote:

> The Green rising is a thing like the great war. It is a huge historical hinge and turning point, like the conversion of Constantine or the French Revolution. . . . What has happened in Europe since the war has been a vast victory for the peasants, and therefore a vast defeat both for the Communists and the capitalists. . . . In a sort of awful silence the peasantries have fought one vast and voiceless pitched battle with Bolshevism and its twin brother, which is Big Business, and the peasantries have won.[2]

Sharing Chesterton's aversion to communism, though not his antipathy to capitalism, the president of the University of Oklahoma William B. Bizzell borrowed the Englishman's phrase for the title of his 1926 *The Green Rising*, in which he discussed the "world-wide agrarian movement now in progress throughout most of the civilized countries of the world, and more particularly in the countries of western Europe and the United States."[3]

In hindsight, such pronouncements appear naïve, both with respect to eastern European peasants' ability to withstand Communist pressure and regarding agrarianism's long-term political prospects. But in the 1920s there appeared to be ample cause for the optimism of Chesterton, Hodža, and others. The energies of ordinary villagers who had survived the First World War flowed not only into the grassroots initiatives charted in the foregoing chapters. Their new resolve galvanized and expanded existing agrarian political movements and led to the establishment of new ones. Not that formal politics and local rebellion were always easily distinguishable. On the night of November 24, 1918, as Stjepan Radić made a last-ditch effort to dissuade his fellow deputies in the National Council of the State of Slovenes, Croats, and Serbs from virtually unconditional unification with the Kingdom of Serbia and Montenegro, he thundered, "You do not believe that our peasant was in a state of slumber before the war and that the said war has relentlessly shaken him, woken him up and made a man out of him. . . . You, gentlemen, do not care at all that our peasant, and especially the Croatian peasant, does not want to hear anything about the king or emperor, or about a state *that is being forced upon him*."[4] He spoke as much about Green Cadres and village republicanism as about his own Croatian People's Peasant Party, which several years later would count a million members, up from fifteen thousand on the eve of the war. His party's chief ideologue, Rudolf Herceg, theorized that the peasant irruption into postwar European politics marked the beginning of the final and most consequential stage of world historical development.[5] Like many other newly emboldened peasant movements, the Croatian Peasant Party also understood itself as a vehicle for national liberation—in its case from both dynastic rule and a fissiparous multinational successor state.

As peasant tribunes raised the standard of freedom, they refined agrarian ideology into a distinct, rural blueprint for modernity.[6] Political rivals and historians have often dismissed agrarianism as amorphous, contradictory, and myopic.[7] It appeared to them shapeless because it lacked a robust ideological tradition that could unite individual parties. At the same time, it seemed riven by contradictions: between an embrace of some aspects of modernity, such as agricultural technology and cooperative banking, and a rejection of others like cultural pluralism; and between commitments to government representing all of society's various interests and majoritarian impulses. Many perceived it as shortsighted since it tried to arrest the inexorable forces of urbanization and industrialization. Yet agrarianism offered a coherent, if flexible, program of sociocultural, political, and economic progress. The pillars of its platform were agricultural cooperation, parliamentary democracy, and land reform. Agrarians' key innovation was to see the countryside itself as a site of modernity, albeit a particular version thereof, rather than as the sclerotic relic of the past that liberal and Marxist commentators tended to see, or the deferential social ballast that figured in conservatives' wishful thinking. The main protagonist of their vision was the smallholding peasant, who, once furnished with access to voting rights, agricultural technology, education, and sufficient credit, would form the backbone of egalitarian and peaceful democracies.

Only in east central and southeast Europe after the First World War did self-styled peasant parties advocating a clear agrarian program achieve mass electoral support. And only in the Habsburg Empire's successor states did they constitute a significant political force throughout the era of world wars. Arguably, this was a "historical freak phenomenon," since, in global perspective, peasants have otherwise had little to no autonomous presence in modern politics.[8] Peasants, so one oft-recited narrative goes, have tended to involve themselves in conventional politics merely as opportunistic and unreliable allies of non-peasant parties and movements. But east central Europe after 1918 was less an outlier than the leading edge of a worldwide trend. Parties and organizations championing elements of agrarianism radically expanded or proliferated in the wake of the First World War across the globe, from the Mediterranean basin to Ireland and the United States. This reflected a new self-confident "peasantism," as interwar agrarianism was also known, as well as a bid by agrarian leaders to shape an emerging governmental agenda of rural governance, the centerpiece of which was control of agricultural production to accelerate modernization schemes.[9] The Great War had shown in stark relief the need for states to secure domestic food supply and manage rural populations. Small-scale agricultural producers around the world sensed that their interests no longer aligned with the bureaucratic governmental machines that had waged the world war, if indeed they ever had. In the 1920s, they put their trust in agrarian political movements to blaze a new trail forward. After over a century of debates over whether peasants were even capable of participating in modern politics *as peasants*, the answer of the interwar years was emphatically affirmative.

While medieval and early modern European peasant uprisings had arguably sometimes possessed political content, espousing visions of how society could be justly remade, the era of revolutions in the late eighteenth century raised new questions of whether villagers could grasp concepts like the nation, popular sovereignty, and representative democracy and act collectively upon on them.[10] Karl Marx was likely the most influential skeptic. In his *Eighteenth Brumaire of Louis Bonaparte* (1852), he dismissed the idea that peasants could articulate their own class-based, national politics and derided them for their adulation of patriarchal demagogues:

> In so far as there is merely a local interconnection among these smallholding peasants, and the identity of their interests begets no community, no national bond and no political organization among them, they do not form a class. They are consequently incapable of enforcing their class interest in their own name, whether through a parliament or through a convention. They cannot represent themselves, they must be represented. Their representative must at the same time appear as their master, as an authority over them, as an unlimited governmental power that protects them against the other classes and sends them rain and sunshine from above.[11]

At most, Marx famously sneered, their cohesion beyond individual localities was "much as potatoes in a sack form a sack of potatoes."[12] Peasants' apparent support for political reaction in the 1848 French presidential elections that swept the great Napoleon's nephew to power was merely a function of their doomed social position under the capitalist mode of production. In the *Communist Manifesto* (1848), Marx and Engels wrote that peasants, artisans, tradesmen, and shopkeepers "gradually sink into the proletariat, partly because their diminutive capital does not suffice for the scale on which Modern Industry is carried on, and is swamped in the competition with the large capitalists, partly because their specialized skill is rendered worthless by new methods of production."[13] This thesis took on the aura of scientific fact in subsequent decades, as Marx further elaborated on capitalism's inexorable tendency toward concentration in both industry and agriculture. Large, capitalized farms employing legions of wage-earning laborers represented the future; peasants tilling small, family-owned plots belonged to the past. Thus, even if peasants could overcome their fragmentation and achieve consciousness of a class *for itself* (a doubtful proposition, as far as Marx was concerned), their interests would translate into retrograde political programs aimed at arresting or reversing inevitable historical development by preserving small family farms.

Careful readers of Marx's oeuvre could find more sanguine assessments of the smallholding peasantry. These ranged from his remarks in the *Eighteenth Brumaire* about the French revolutionary villagers who recognized their common cause with urban workers to his later-life interest in the Russian *mir*, or village commune, as a proto-socialist social formation.[14] For some countries, such as Poland and Ireland, Marx and Engels saw "agrarian democracy" predicated on small private property as the appropriate initial goal of movements opposing despotism.[15] But the negative view of the peasantry, which reflected Marx and Engels's urban bias as much as their keen powers of social observation, set the tone for subsequent Marxian socialism. At the 1867 Lausanne congress of the International Workingmen's Association (the "First International"), delegates from England, Germany, and Belgium overrode objections of French and Italian representatives in articulating a socialist agricultural policy that pushed for collective ownership of cultivated land.[16] This position afterward attained the status of dogma for the mass socialist parties that arose across Europe in the latter half of the nineteenth century. Although parties sometimes considered tactical deviations from the official line as they attempted to woo rural voters, especially from the 1890s on, the impulse to dismiss smallholders' concerns as regressive often proved stronger. In 1895, for instance, leaders of German Social Democracy debated whether to promulgate a peasant-friendly program of communal rights, mortgage, and credit regulations. Karl Kautsky, the intellectual doyen of the movement, cut the discussion short, arguing that such a program would needlessly protect an outdated form of production, quickly being pushed to extinction by capitalism's spread.[17]

More charitable interpreters than Marx and Engels and their followers were faced, nonetheless, with an ambiguous record of peasant political action since the late eighteenth century. In France during the revolution, peasants had shown some interest in developments beyond their localities, and the pressure they exerted on Parisian assemblies—albeit primarily in the form of antiseigneurial violence, as during the "Great Fear" of summer 1789—yielded concrete results, notably the blanket abolition of feudal privilege in August 1789. From 1790, they expressed their demands for complete emancipation and access to large estate land in increasingly patriotic language.[18] Notions of the nation and even representative government achieved lasting popularity in large portions of the countryside. Yet by 1793, many embraced the counterrevolution, often in defense of their priests who refused to take an oath of loyalty to the secular regime in Paris.

Their ideological indeterminacy was more pronounced in the 1848 revolution. In the elections to the Constituent Assembly of the French Second Republic held in April 1848, many newly enfranchised peasants voted for a moderate version of the newly proclaimed French Second Republic, but more cast their ballots for royalist priests and nobles in the belief that the republic served exclusively urban workers' interests.[19] In the December presidential elections, they overwhelmingly supported the conservative demagogue Louis-Napoleon Bonaparte. However, from early 1849, increasingly large numbers of peasants backed the leftist republican Democratic Socialists, and numerous rural areas rose in revolt against Louis Bonaparte's December 1851 coup that established the French Second Empire.[20] In the Habsburg monarchy, where peasants had virtually no prior experience of representative government or freedom from seigneurial dues, they proved themselves to be committed revolutionaries, at least as far as their own economic interests were concerned. While Hungarian nationalist leaders abolished the remnants of feudalism by decree in the April Laws of 1848, which essentially made Hungary independent in domestic matters, peasants in the other lands of the monarchy played an active role in their own emancipation. Elections in June 1848 on the basis of nearly universal (though indirect) male suffrage brought 383 deputies into the new unicameral parliament, or *Reichstag*, of which ninety-three (24 percent) were peasants, some illiterate: thirty-five from Galicia, thirteen from Upper Austria, twelve from Lower Austria, ten from Bohemia, eight from Moravia, seven from Bukovina, six from Carinthia and Carniola, and two from Styria.[21] The peasant deputies pushed hard for an end to the *robot* and tithe without compensation. By the end of August 1848, they had secured emancipation legislation, along with only "cheap" compensation to former lords; it officially passed on September 7. This was likely the most important achievement of the revolution in east central Europe and one of the few that was not rescinded by the new Emperor Franz Joseph I after his ascent to the throne in December 1848. But peasants appeared to show little interest in the further course of the revolutions. And across Europe, villagers' participation in newly held elections did not preclude their use of traditional, ostensibly nonpolitical forms of collective action, some of them violent, such as forest occupations and attacks on manor houses.[22]

To many urban onlookers around 1850, and far more so than in 1918, a modern peasant political consciousness remained at most a hypothesis. For decades after 1848, central European villagers deferred to local large landowners and their societies for agricultural improvement that had arisen in the prerevolutionary period.[23] Their first efforts at self-organization in the 1870s were concentrated in the realm of economics. The flood of cheap grain imports from the Americas—a result of the newly globalized world economy in the final third of the nineteenth century—along with the 1873 economic crash, caused agricultural prices to plummet, exacerbating rural privation, indebtedness, and fragmentation of parcels. Governments responded to the plight of the countryside by raising tariff barriers to protect farmers and promoting agricultural technology, along with land reclamation schemes to lower their production costs. In central Europe, they sometimes encouraged farmers to establish their own organizations, above all cooperatives, which, in Austria, were given legal sanction in April 1873 and promoted by provincial diets. Alongside such economic initiatives was a rapid proliferation of more culturally and politically oriented agricultural clubs, which contributed to growing political awareness in the countryside.[24]

The rural political organizations that arose in central Europe at the end of nineteenth century under the stewardship of wealthy farmers or conservative magnates did little to convince skeptics that smallholding peasants had achieved autonomy in politics, however. These included the powerful German Agrarian League (Bund der Landwirte)—established in 1893 when Chancellor Leo von Caprivi dismantled some of the protectionist tariffs erected by his predecessor, Otto von Bismarck—and permanent agricultural lobbies within parties, such as the Catholic Center Party in Imperial Germany, the Catholic Party in Belgium, and the Austrian Christian Social Party in the German-speaking Alpine provinces.[25] Clerical leadership did not, in fact, rule out the adoption of programs increasingly friendly to smallholding peasants. In December 1905, Slovaks in Upper Hungary and Slovenes in the Austrian crownlands of Carniola and Lower Styria transformed existing Catholic nationalist parties into "People's Parties" that had almost entirely peasant constituencies and championed peasant interests, particularly through their affiliated cooperatives.[26] For instance, the Cooperative Union (Zadružna zveza) founded in 1903 by Slovene clerical nationalists counted 433 cooperatives a mere four years later, over half of which were in Carniola.[27] Although antimodern sentiments predominated among leaders of the Slovak and Slovene People's Parties, they both contributed to what Ernst Bruckmüller called the "conservative modernization" of their respective societies.[28] Peasants in these places were organized into effective economic self-help associations and schooled in the importance of state politics, even in Upper Hungary, where few Slovaks could vote.

As Miguel Cabo has argued, self-proclaimed "agrarian" or "peasant" parties with overwhelmingly peasant constituencies arose only where other strategies of mobilization (cooperatives, pressure groups, and intraparty lobbies) appeared to be insufficient, and where there was widespread discontent with existing parties.[29] Several of these dynamics were present in the Nordic countries, where, starting in the 1880s, small and medium farmers contested the conservative and socially elitist leadership of existing rural parties. But the parties they founded were often left liberal rather than explicitly agrarian in outlook, and sometimes eschewed class-specific labels, reflecting the early inclusion of Scandinavian and

Finnish peasants into national self-understandings and representative assemblies.[30] On a regional level, the liberal-leaning Bavarian Peasants' League (Bayerischer Bauernbund) seceded from the Center Party in 1893 and functioned from the start as an independent political party. It was in east central and southeast Europe around the turn of the twentieth century that the conditions identified by Cabo were most prevalent: between 1895 and 1904, peasantist agrarian parties were established by Bulgarians, Croats, Czechs, and Poles.

The Polish peasant representatives who established the People's Party (Stronnictwo Ludowe) in Rzeszów in 1895 aimed to cast off the influence of the nobility and clergy, which had dominated Galicia since it became semiautonomous in 1868, and the agricultural organizations that had proliferated since the late 1870s.[31] The program of the first genuine agrarian party called for protection of the peasant way of life, as well as modernization of the countryside through investment and the spread of industry. It demanded the abolition of remaining privileges enjoyed by the nobility, such as their exemption from having to pay for the construction and upkeep of roads and their right to hunt on peasants' fields, regardless of the damage caused. The emergence of the Czech Agrarian Party in Bohemia in 1899, meanwhile, was the result of a final, likely overdue split with the National Freethinking Party (known as the Young Czechs), which had long commanded the loyalty of the Czech countryside, but in the late 1890s refused to support a plan for agricultural defense and rural modernization drawn up by the Association of Czech Agriculturalists of the Kingdom of Bohemia.[32] A Moravian Agrarian Party emerged in 1904 with a less prosperous constituency than the sugar-beet farmers who formed the bedrock of Bohemia's rural economy, but both parties cooperated closely from the start and their executives formally merged in 1905.[33] Thanks to the adroit leadership of Antonín Švehla, scion of a prosperous farming family from the outskirts of Prague, much the Czech-speaking countryside quickly lined up behind the Agrarian Party and its dense network of cooperatives; in the 1907 elections they won twenty-eight mandates, the most of any Czech party. The year 1899 also witnessed the culmination of several years of mobilization by credit-starved, heavily taxed Bulgarian smallholders, who assembled the Bulgarian Agrarian Union from 250 independent agricultural associations. Under the command of peasant strongman Aleksandar Stamboliiski, the Bulgarian Agrarian National Union (as it was soon renamed) steadily increased its share of seats in parliament in the years before 1914.[34] In 1904, brothers Antun and Stjepan Radić founded the Croatian People's Peasant Party out of frustration with the urban-oriented Mladi (the Young) of fin-de-siècle

Croatian politics, who sought popular and practical alternatives to the legalistic question of Croatian state rights that had preoccupied Croatian activists since the 1860s. While most of the Mladi perceived latent national leadership in the growing urban working class, the Radićes saw it already manifest in the peasant masses. They founded their party in December 1904 with a far-reaching program of "peasant rights" in the economy (self-sufficiency and state protection from indebtedness and market volatility), in politics (universal suffrage and peasant representation in administrative organs), and in society and culture (respect and dignity, above all).[35] Stjepan, the more charismatic and mercurial of the siblings, soon became its undisputed leader.

Like other Slavic agrarian leaders, the Radićes drew inspiration from the Russian Narodniks, or Populists, who from the 1860s believed the solution to Russia's problems lay not in Marxian socialism, with its emphasis on industrialization and urbanization, but in Russia's indigenous forms of peasant egalitarianism, embodied above all in the peasant commune, or *mir*. If the *mir* figured for many Russian radicals as a precursor of a future socialist society—an inborn blueprint for revolution—the Narodniks saw it as the goal of the revolution itself: Russia reborn as an immense peasant commune without having to endure the agonies of capitalism and proletarianization.[36] The Russian Socialist Revolutionary Party established in 1900 was the obvious heir to this tradition; though ostensibly representing all toiling classes, in practice it focused on the peasantry by calling for the breakup and redistribution of large estate land. East central European peasantists like Radić and Stamboliiski subscribed to the Populist vision in its broad outlines but sought to specifically ennoble and empower the smallholding peasantry. While the continuing preponderance of the peasantry was implicit in hazy Narodnik imaginings, and the actual role of peasant actors in the revolution unclear, the agrarians of east central Europe made peasant class power their stated goal.[37]

Heterodox Marxian socialists similarly adapted the European social democracy to social conditions in the continent's eastern half. The Ruthenian-Ukrainian Radical Party, established in 1890 in Habsburg Lemberg (today Ukrainian Lviv), attempted to strike a delicate balance between commitments to "scientific socialism" and "the prevention of the creation of a proletariat" in the countryside. Primarily through their popular newspaper *Khliborob* (The farmer), the Ruthene Radicals swiftly garnered a mass following among the Ukrainian-speaking peasantry of the Habsburg Empire.[38] On the vast latifundia of the Hungarian plain, agricultural strikes for higher wages and better treatment erupted in the early 1890s in the southeast of the country, culminating in mass harvest strikes in 1897.

FIGURE 7.1 Stjepan Radić, founder and leader of the Croatian Peasant Party. Public domain

Frustrated with the Hungarian Social Democratic Party's unwillingness to condone the strikers' demands for land reform, renegade socialist István Várkonyi founded a new Independent Socialist Party, calling for the confiscation and redistribution of large estate land. It gained a sizable following among landless laborers and dwarfholders in the southeast "stormy corner."[39] Várkonyi was arrested, and in 1898 the Hungarian parliament passed the so-called "Slave Law," severely curtailing the rights of agricultural laborers and allowing draconian punishments of strikers. Three years later, Vilmos Mezőfi founded the agrarian socialist Reorganized Social Democratic Party. These initiatives in the Kingdom of Hungary remained small in influence owing to the restricted franchise, which denied over three-quarters of peasant men the right to vote.

Events in Russia in 1905 and Romania in 1907 cautioned neighboring states against turning a blind eye to rural misery or suppressing peasant politics altogether. The 1905 Russian Revolution had witnessed widespread rural violence against landowners, as well as a groundswell of rural politicization. This prompted Lenin to challenge the orthodox Marxist dismissal of the peasantry, arguing that the semiproletarian rural poor, along with some downwardly mobile middle peasants, could be decisive allies of the working class in a revolutionary situation.[40] In 1907, peasants in the Kingdom of Romania revolted with terrifying fury against a political-economic system dominated by oligarchical absentee landowners and their exploitative leaseholders (the *arendași*). The government called up 140,000 troops to crush the uprising, at the cost of up to 11,000 peasant lives.[41] In response, the Romanian socialist thinker and former Narodnik Constantin Dobrogeanu-Gherea wrote in 1910 that the peasants of his adopted country (he was born Solomon Katz in what is today Ukraine) were victims of "neo-serfdom," which was neither feudalism nor capitalism but an unhappy combination of the worst features of both. Because capitalist relations had yet to establish themselves fully, peasant demands for land redistribution had to be met, at least in the short run.[42]

In neither Russia nor Romania did social conflagration bring many peasants into electoral politics, though the upheavals of 1905 and 1907 presaged the revolutionary events of 1917 and after; and they may have augmented the bargaining power of fledgling agrarian movements in the Habsburg monarchy, Bulgaria, and other states in the region. By the eve of the First World War, smallholding peasants, particularly in east central and southeast Europe, had demonstrated a capacity for political organization and vision that Marx could not have foreseen sixty years earlier. For the time being, however, their movements did not pose a serious threat to the established political camps. Before 1914, radical rural politics menaced the status quo only on the other side of the Atlantic, where in 1892 the American People's Party (the "Populists") held its first convention in Omaha, Nebraska, with a program of direct democracy, state ownership of telegraph and telephone systems, and bimetallism to reduce financial strains on farmers. Its early center of gravity was in Kansas—"the mother of radical movements," according to William Bizzell in 1926.[43] They came close to national power in the fiercely contested 1896 presidential elections when the Democratic candidate, William Jennings Bryan, won their endorsement by adopting much of their program and chose a Populist running mate.

The climacteric of the First World War supercharged agrarian politics in Europe and beyond. Everywhere, narrow prewar understandings of citizenship bowed and buckled under pressure from previously excluded or marginalized groups: workers and peasants, as well as women, colonized peoples, and religious minorities. Access to political participation and civil rights widened in the countries that survived the war, as well as in the new states that took the place of those that did not. Peasant leaders understood their movements in revolutionary terms; not content with facilitating their followers' inclusion in the polity, they pursued wholesale societal transformation. A breakthrough appeared to be imminent in east central and southeast Europe, where peasantists saw their meteoric rise connected with, though distinct from, the volcanic eruption of revolution in Russia. Stamboliiski could be forgiven his hyperbole for writing early in 1923, "Today there are only two interesting social experiments: the experiment of Lenin and my own."[44]

Stamboliiski's party experienced the sharpest upturn of any agrarian organization in the immediate aftermath of the war.[45] When the Bulgarian front lines collapsed in September 1918, mutinous peasant soldiers around the village of Radomir, southwest of Sofia, were swiftly organized by the Bulgarian Agrarian National Union (BANU) activist Raiko Daskalov into the army of a newly proclaimed republic. Although Macedonian brigades and German reinforcements routed the mutineers as they advanced on the capital, the Radomir Rebellion gave the agrarians immense political clout.[46] Stamboliiski, recently released from prison after serving several years for his antiwar stance, joined the new government and was part of the delegation that in 1919 presided over Bulgaria's formal exit from the war, including acceptance of the punitive Treaty of Neuilly. Following the BANU's election victory in August 1919, he was invited by Tsar Boris to form a coalition government, which he attempted first with the Bulgarian Communists, then with the Socialists, and finally, and successfully, with the rightist parties. The number of BANU organizations doubled in 1919, while its membership shot up to 77,298. Backed up by paramilitaries of the party's newly established Orange Guard, Stamboliiski thwarted a wave of antigovernmental Communist agitation at the end of the year and called fresh elections in March 1920, which, with some manipulation, handed the BANU an absolute parliamentary majority.

From May 1920, Stamboliiski launched an ambitious reform program to remake Bulgarian society from the ground up. Arable land was already distributed relatively equally among Bulgarian peasants, but a new law set the maximum allowable holding at thirty hectares (74 acres), permitting the government to seize lands belonging to the Orthodox Church and local authorities. Educational reforms followed, expanding free compulsory schooling, and making agriculture a compulsory subject. Stamboliiski's party accelerated orthographical reforms of Bulgarian to simplify the written language and make it more accessible to the popular classes—a proposal that scandalized the literate elite. Though rescinded after Stamboliiski's fall, the agrarian-backed language reform returned as law under the post-1944 Communist regime. Most controversially, in June 1920, Stamboliiski instituted compulsory labor service: a year of manual labor building roads, harvesting state-owned forests, and performing other tasks for all men over age twenty, and six months for all women over age sixteen. The scheme was scaled back somewhat after objections from the Inter-Allied Control Commission on Disarmament, which saw it as a clandestine way of rebuilding the national army. The urban middle classes, many of whom supported the political right, reacted furiously to the program. Disgust with the BANU's radical reforms and its pacifist, nonexpansionist foreign policy, as well as with Stamboliiski's increasingly authoritarian rule, brought together disparate opposition groups, who backed a violent coup in June 1923 in which the agrarian chief was brutally murdered, and his regime toppled.

Nowhere in the post-Habsburg territories did an agrarian party wield as much power as the BANU in the years 1919–23, perhaps because of the relative insignificance of competing ethnic factors in Bulgaria that could fragment a class-based program. But the peasant parties of the former Habsburg lands all grew in influence and became fixtures of their respective domestic political scenes. Radić's Croatian Republican Peasant Party (HRSS) acquired a messianic character for its new legions of followers. Expanding from fifteen thousand prewar members to one million organized in two thousand local party organizations by the time of the first statewide Yugoslav elections, the HRSS became the foremost vehicle for Croatian national aspirations, along with the principal opposition force against Belgrade centralism. In 1921, the HRSS assumed leadership of the parliamentary Croatian Bloc, giving the peasantists unrivalled authority within the Croatian national movement, even if some villagers worried this would dilute its commitments to the countryside.[47] Radić himself boycotted the skupština until early 1925, when he ended his abstention after the British tentatively pledged support for the Croat cause and after having recognized that his passivity had not undermined the regime-maintaining Radical and Democratic Parties. His political zigzags in the years 1925–28 caused consternation in Belgrade, Zagreb, and abroad, but they did not lessen his stature among Croatian peasants, who regarded him as one of their own. Hailing from a poor household in the central Croatian village of Desno Trebarjevo, both Radić brothers received elite educations, beginning with academic high schools in Zagreb and Karlovac. Antun completed his doctorate at the University of Zagreb, while the younger Stjepan finished his

MAP 3. East central Europe between the wars

at Sciences Po in Paris after expulsions from universities in Zagreb and Prague for political provocations. But neither man ever lost his sense of indignation as a son of the village looked down upon by urban bourgeois society.

Despite his stature among Croatian peasants and in other agrarian movements, Stjepan Radić's leadership style repelled many. Milan Hodža regarded him as "the strangest mixture of the violent Balkan 'Chief' and the Sorbonne intellectual European."[48] The British writer and journalist Rebecca West, traveling through Yugoslavia in the 1930s under the tutelage of a patriotic Serb poet, compared Radić to Tolstoy, writing disapprovingly:

> He talked nonsense as often as not, but nobody minded; they all listened and felt exalted. It was his habit to speak in parables that were apt to be childish and obscure, and his speeches sometimes lasted for half a day and usually contained matter that was entirely contrary to human experiences; but his audiences adored him as a sage and a saint, and would have died for him. . . . The only practical step Raditch [*sic*] ever proposed was the abolition of a centralized Yugoslavian Government and the establishment of a federalism which would have left the economic position of the Croat peasant exactly where it was. The rest was a mass of violent inconsistencies. Probably nobody but St Augustine has contradicted himself so often or so violently.[49]

His antithesis was Antonín Švehla, the urbane and subtle leader of the Czech Agrarian Party, which in 1919 was renamed the Republican Party of the Czechoslovak Countryside and then, in 1922, after a merger with the much smaller, though influential, Slovak agrarians, the Republican Party of Farmers and Peasants. Though of peasant stock, Švehla's profitable family farm was in Hostivař, then a village on the edge of Prague, today a neighborhood of the city itself. His upbringing was thus both rural and urban; he felt as comfortable in the village tavern as he did among the city's lower middle classes who demanded affordable agricultural products and among the cultured and wealthy bourgeoisie of the Czech metropolis. Švehla's profile, along with the Republican Party's electoral base among prosperous, market-oriented sugar-beet growers, imbued the organization with a centrist patriotism straddling the rural and urban worlds. These attributes also pulled the party away from the antiurban populism that characterized many successful agrarian parties of the region. Its main postwar achievements were less conspicuous in the realms of organizational expansion or electoral majorities. By 1918, most Czech voters lived in urban areas or worked in industry, unlike the other "nationalities" of the former empire, apart from the Germans and Italians. Moreover, unlike Croatian peasants, Czech peasant men—rich and poor—had been able to vote in democratic elections since 1907. Instead, Švehla and his party were instrumental in the founding of the Czechoslovak Republic and shaped its political system in profound ways.[50] During the war, he had been the driving force in instituting formal cooperation among all Czech parties, including the ostensibly internationalist Social Democrats. Although the agrarians could not match the total socialist vote in independent Czechoslovakia—split initially between Social Democrats and National Socialists and after 1921 between these and the Communists—they formed, apart from a brief period in 1920–21, an integral part of all governing coalitions in the interwar years and provided four prime ministers: Švehla three times, František Udržal twice, Jan Malypetr twice, and Milan Hodža once.

Švehla did much to ensure stable Czech predominance in the multiethnic republic by initiating the *pětka*, an informal coordinating group of the five strongest Czech parties, minus the Communists. These were the Republicans, Social Democrats, National Socialists, National Democrats, and People's Party. He also fostered rapprochement with the German minority, bringing a German party—the Agrarian League (Bund der Landwirte)—into a governing coalition for the first time in 1926. The 1919 land reform law was his brainchild, and his party controlled the powerful Land Office, which implemented and oversaw the reform. As the lynchpin of Czechoslovak democracy, Švehla's agrarians could advance a program beneficial to the party's core constituency of medium to prosperous farmers, though smallholders and landless peasants had reasons to be dissatisfied. As discussed below, the first Czechoslovak Republic also offered a relatively safe home for peasant internationalism.

Elections in newly reconstituted Poland gave agrarians there a significant presence in the Warsaw sejm, even if it did not match the peasantry's demographic weight in Polish society. Internal divisions vitiated agrarian influence at the state level. A unique political culture had developed in each of the former partitions, hampering the integration of political parties even when interests broadly aligned. Peasant political activity was by far most advanced in former Habsburg Galicia, where elections to representative bodies had been held in 1848 and uninterruptedly between the 1860s and 1914. But even here, the Polish People's Party (as it was known since 1903) had split in 1913 into a rightist "Piast" party, named after Poland's first medieval dynasty and led by Wincenty Witos, and a "Lewica" (Left) party under Jan Stapiński.

In reestablished Poland, the Lewica and Piast groupings faced competition from the leftist Wyzwolenie (Liberation) faction, which had emerged in 1915 in the Russian partition. In the first statewide elections of January 1919, agrarians and rural-based Catholic people's parties won 62 percent of the vote in former Galicia, with Piast commanding a comfortable majority, but only 27 percent in the former Russian-ruled Kingdom of Poland and hardly any votes in former Prussian territory, where no autonomous peasant party existed. The result translated into 157 of 444 seats, or 35 percent in the first sejm, with most mandates divided between Wyzwolenie and Piast.[51] Many of the representatives who took their seats in parliament for the first time in February 1919 wore white peasant shirts, proudly signaling their background.[52] The challenges they faced were nonetheless evident in the divergent parliamentary blocs that their deputies belonged to: Wyzwolenie and Lewica to the left, Piast to the center, and the Catholic parties to the right. Witos's candidature to become first marshal of the sejm faltered when the leftist agrarians refused to endorse him. He subsequently held the position of prime minister three times, the first time in summer 1920, when his appointment was intended to rally rural support for the war effort against Soviet Russia. His Wyzwolenie and Lewica rivals never fully trusted him, however.

Despite its fractious nature, the agrarian political scene in Poland succeeded in fostering widespread, sometimes millenarian belief among millions of villagers in the ideal of a "People's Poland" (*Polska Ludowa*), or a Polish state serving peasant interests. Agrarian leaders could not agree on the form it should take, though its mobilizing power produced some critical moments of unity—for instance in 1925 when Wyzwolenie supported Piast's modest land reform bill; or in 1931, when all People's Party factions agreed to unite in the face of repression. From 1919 to 1928, the proportion of seats held by peasantist representatives hovered between a quarter and a third of the house, and at least one cabinet member was consistently drawn from the agrarian parties—invariably from Piast, except for Wyzwolenie's Stanisław Thugutt as minister of the interior.

While the internal politics of most states in the region had assumed some semblance of stability in the first half of 1919, turbulence in Hungary lasted until the 1920 consolidation of Horthy's conservative regency. Agrarian politicians had watched from the sidelines in late October 1918 when revolution broke out in Budapest, resulting in Mihály Károlyi's liberal republic, and again in March 1919 when Béla Kun's Councils Republic was established. This is not to say that the countryside did not shape the course of each regime; in both cases, peasants' dismay at delayed or abortive land redistribution schemes contributed to the demise of republican governments.[53] Disillusionment likewise strengthened counterrevolution, although Horthy's celebrations of the peasantry's national authenticity did not translate into effective reforms. Despite grassroots radicalism in November 1918, characterized by seizures of large estate land, and antiregime resistance in spring and summer 1919, Hungarian peasants struggled to unite around a coherent agrarian platform. One reason was the presence in Hungary of a massive wage-earning agricultural proletariat, absent in neighboring countries on the same scale. They tended more toward the inchoate agrarian socialism of the 1890s than toward István Szabó's moderate Smallholders' Party, originally established in 1909 as the National Independence and 48-er Smallholder Party.[54] As before, urban socialists, whether Communist or Social Democrat, generally turned a deaf ear to their demands.

Szabó's party did register some successes before oligarchical rule was cemented in 1922.[55] Included in Károlyi's government in early 1919, the Smallholders authored the initial land reform legislation of mid-February, whose implementation was cut short by the Communist takeover. They again joined the government in autumn 1919 and won the most seats in the 1920 elections, with 15 percent of the vote. Now championing a more moderate land reform aimed at the creation a self-sufficient class of middling peasants, they settled for a further-diluted version in exchange for the fulfilment of their antimonarchical demands (they were the heirs of the anti-Habsburg party of 1848) and Szabó's appointment as minister of agriculture. Outmaneuvered by conservative prime minister István Bethlen, Szabó's influence declined, and his party's fortunes plummeted after his sudden death in 1924.

Along with transforming the parties that had existed before 1914, the war led to the emergence of several wholly new peasant parties in east central and southeast Europe. In Serbia in October 1919, agrarian activists and cooperative movement veterans established the Union of Agriculturalists (Savez zemljoradnika) to challenge the hegemonic Radical Party in rural areas, offering a more clearly peasant-oriented program. The Radical Party, despite its roots in the Serbian countryside, had matured into a Belgrade-based electoral machine, and under the adroit and wily leadership Nikola Pašić had steered the process of south Slav unification in a manner that cemented its own dominance. Like their Serb counterparts, Slovene activists eager to dethrone the clerical Slovene People's Party founded the Independent Agrarian Party (Samostojna kmetijska stranka) in June 1919. In 1926, it was reconstituted as the Slovene Peasant Party (Slovenska kmetska stranka), with a stronger program of federalism and national autonomy. Bosnian agrarians in August 1919 established the Peasant Organization (Težačka organizacija) in Bosnia-Herzegovina, independent of national-religious influence, which the following year was renamed the Union of Peasants (Savez težaka) in Bosnia and Herzegovina.[56]

An agrarian party finally appeared in rural Romania: in December 1918, a month after the introduction of universal suffrage, the country schoolteacher Ion Michalache brought the Peasant Party into being. Based primarily among the villagers of Wallachia, it called for sweeping agrarian reform, and delegates at its first party congress in 1921 united around an unabashed program of peasant class struggle, while also seeking cooperation with political parties representing other productive classes. Intellectual leadership came from Virgil Madgearu, a German-trained economist, who, following the work of unorthodox Soviet agrarian economist Alexander Chayanov, argued for the long-term superiority of small peasant family farms over large-scale agricultural operations.[57] The Peasant Party wielded limited power, however, and its radicalism diminished as reformist intellectuals joined its leadership. Although Michalache served as minister of agriculture for a few months at the end of 1919 and beginning of 1920, his party remained in opposition until after its 1926 merger with the Transylvanian National Party, a cross-class alliance of Romanians that had existed in the historic province since Habsburg days. The new National Peasant Party, led by Iuliu Maniu from the Transylvanian wing, surprised observers by combining seemingly incompatible social elements. Nevertheless, it triumphed in the 1928 elections, perhaps the only unmanipulated democratic exercise in interwar Romania, winning around 78 percent of the vote and 348 out of 387 seats in parliament.[58]

Rural Catholic people's parties arose in Bohemia and Moravia, soon merging into the relatively progressive Czechoslovak People's Party under the skillful leadership of Monsignor Jan Šrámek. In pious Moravia, the People's Party deployed its rhetoric of "Christian solidarity" to outmaneuver Švehla's increasingly bourgeois Republican Party and become the primary representative of smallholders' interests, though its more radical land reform plan tellingly exempted ecclesiastical properties.[59] Germans in Czechoslovakia created their own Agrarian League (Bund der Landwirte) less than a month after the state's founding. Franz Spina, one of the League's foremost politicians, who served as justice minister in Švehla's second government, spoke for many peasantists in the aftermath of the war when he remarked that his party's emergence was a response to the "command economy system that heavily burdened agricultural production."[60]

Wartime exigencies invigorated rural politics far beyond the graveyard of multinational empires in central and eastern Europe. In Ireland, food crisis in the winter of 1917–18 triggered social radicalization in the nationalist Sinn Féin organization, whose lower functionaries were recruited mostly from the rural poor. In the western province of Connacht, a war over land erupted, reprising events of 1879–82, as tenant farmers and smallholders seized estate land belonging Anglo-Irish landowners.[61] The agrarian movement in the west and south fed directly into the violence of the Irish War of Independence (1919–21), during which 125 manor houses were burned to the ground.[62] The absence of redistribution provisions in the Anglo-Irish treaty that established the Irish Free State drove many smallholders to embrace the anti-treaty Irish Republican Army during the ensuing civil war, when another 130 manor houses were razed.[63] But the land reform bill that passed in May 1923 at the end of the civil war sapped much of the IRA's rural support by fulfilling peasant aspirations: final transfer of land from landlords to tenants and further redistribution.[64]

When the United States of America entered the war in 1916, the recently established Non-Partisan League rapidly expanded from its base in the northern Great Plains, broadcasting its program of "state ownership of terminal elevators, flour mills, packing-houses, and cold storage plants. State inspection of grain and grain dockage. Exemption of farm equipment from taxation. State hail insurance on the acreage tax basis. Rural credit banks operated at cost."[65] Whereas the smallholding peasants of Europe tended to want protection against the intrusive wartime state, the market-oriented farmers of middle America demanded that federal and state governments defend them against predatory transport monopolies, especially railroad companies, and market caprice. The League captured both houses of North Dakota's state legislature in 1918, but it suffered swift decline in 1920 when wheat prices fell precipitously. Its radical impulses flowed largely into the Farm Labor Party, which fielded Robert La Follette as a third-party candidate in the 1924 presidential election, winning 17 percent of the popular vote.

Even countries that remained neutral during the war witnessed a surge in peasant politics, as conflicts sharpened between rural producers and urban consumers. Sweden's two Farmers' Leagues (established 1913–14 and 1915 respectively) mushroomed and merged in 1921.[66] Both the Dutch Peasants' League (Plattelandersbond) and the Swiss (originally Bernese) Party of Farmers, Traders, and Independents were established in 1917.[67] Rudolf Minger, the Swiss agrarian activist who founded the latter, attributed his rise to the 1914–18 conflict:

> At the outbreak of the world war, earlier relationships experienced quite a sudden shift. The main concern of the people and the authorities concentrated naturally on domestic food production, with a stroke shifting

agriculture, previously despised in so many ways, to the foreground, and binding all the hopes and expectations of the Swiss people to this 'firm rock in a stormy sea.' The Swiss peasantry was from the beginning very conscious of its responsibility. . . . In the years of the world war it reconquered its self-confidence.[68]

In war-torn, socially polarized societies where no mass agrarian party arose, there was a strong tendency for peasants to drift, at least temporarily, toward the conservative or ultranationalist right. This was the case in Germany and Italy, where the antipeasant attitudes of many urban socialists accelerated the trend. Immediately after the cessation of hostilities, peasants in several German regions established revolutionary councils, but they were short-lived and isolated from contemporaneous workers' councils in the cities. So long as privation in urban centers persisted, which it did in many places until 1923, vitriolic socialist rhetoric against selfish rural hoarders showed no signs of abating; meanwhile the command economy stayed in place during the same period. Agrarian pressure groups expanded as they made concerted efforts, in spite of their patrician leaderships, to attract smallholding peasants and even landless laborers. In northwest Germany, for instance, membership in the Westphalian Peasant Association increased by 50 percent over prewar levels, in the Rhineland association by 85 percent, and in the Westphalian Agricultural Chamber by around 130 percent.[69] Facing hostility from urban parties, especially Social Democrats, the rank and file of such organizations proved receptive to antiurban, anti-Semitic, and antirepublican rhetoric nurtured in the right-wing of the Center Party. The stage was set for their post-1933 embrace of Nazism.

In Italy, peasants returning from the battlefield expected land in return for their sacrifices and had received promises to that effect following the 1917 military disaster at Caporetto. Although between 125,000 and 130,000 new peasant smallholdings were created and 300,000 existing small farms received additional land in the immediate aftermath of the conflict, peasant militancy remained high, and support for the Italian Socialist Party and its associated agrarian union, the Federterra, skyrocketed during the 1918–20 *Biennio Rosso* (two red years).[70] The tide turned against radical peasant movements as the postwar economic boom ended, and landowners enlisted the help of burgeoning fascist *squadre* to intimidate peasants who demanded better contracts on large estates or their own plots. But the *squadre* also won over many peasants by promoting Mussolini's vague rhetoric of a redistributive "democracy on the land," while the Federterra increasingly emphasized the necessity and benefits of collectivization.[71] The switch from socialism to fascism was particularly dramatic in late 1920 and early 1921 among the smallholders and tenant farmers in Emilia Romagna, who became a bastion of rural fascism.[72] Once firmly in power, Mussolini's agrarian policies clearly favored large landowners in the north, though his regime continued to herald a "ruralized" Italian nation of sturdy smallholding peasants.[73]

In the countries where agrarianism became a significant political force, its exponents sought radical change in politics, economics, and culture. They called for universal, equal, and direct suffrage for the entire adult population as a means of empowering the peasant majority. They generally upheld parliamentarism and respected democratic procedures with the confidence that such mechanisms would allow them to prevail through the sheer numbers of their followers. At the same time, they insisted that peasants be represented by their own kind in representative assemblies, as well as in administrative bodies. Undemocratic, unelected institutions—namely, the army and the often militarily organized gendarmerie—were to be significantly scaled back. Land reform, it was thought, would expand the ranks, and strengthen the viability, of small- to medium-holding villagers, who were to form the bedrock of agrarian democracy. Commitments to private property did not dampen their enthusiasm for cooperative labor systems and profit-sharing at the local level. In politics, as in other spheres, agrarians tried to chart a middle course between liberalism and socialism.

This "third way" was most developed in the realm of economics. Agrarian ideologues vehemently rejected the urban-centered programs of their liberal and socialist rivals, which privileged industry, and especially heavy industry, at the expense of other sectors.[74] In interwar Yugoslavia, where around three-quarters of the population was engaged in farming, the Ministry of Agriculture often received only 1 percent of the state budget.[75] East central European governments saw industry, not entirely unreasonably, as a panacea for the overpopulated, technologically backward, and undercapitalized countryside. By creating thousands of new and relatively well-paid jobs, factories could draw in surplus inhabitants of villages, reducing rural misery and augmenting national wealth. Yet industrialization was often pursued in ways that did not alleviate rural social-economic malaise, and in some cases even deepened it. Leaving aside Czechoslovakia, which inherited over two-thirds of the Habsburg Empire's industry, light manufactures such as paper and textiles (also strongly represented in the diversified Czechoslovak economy), along with food processing, accounted for most of east central Europe's industrial growth in the period. Governments still tended to favor heavy and extractive industry as a point of national prestige and, in the case of armaments production, a precondition of national defense. Such enterprises did little to solve rural overpopulation, geographically concentrated as they were and commonly—as in the case of Romanian oil production—heavily dependent on foreign capital and workers. Furthermore, textile production was often geared toward the tastes of a growing, nationally conscious, but proportionally small urban middle class rather than those of the practically minded peasant majority.

The peasantry's chronically low purchasing power fell further as they were effectively forced to subsidize domestic industry through indirect taxes levied on essential consumer goods, such as matches, salt, kerosene, and shoes.[76] Interwar east central European governments imposed tariffs on manufactured goods and distributed subsidies as part of their program of import-substitution industrialization, while they retained features of nineteenth-century export-led modernization by encouraging the cultivation of cereal crops.[77] This too was shortsighted, since the small farms predominating in the region could not produce wheat or maize efficiently enough to compete with grain arriving in Europe from overseas farms in the Americas and Australia. Traditions of peasant farming and diet also played their part, but governments bore significant responsibility in pushing cereal production—a policy that would prove disastrous during the collapse of agricultural prices at the end of the 1920s.[78]

Discerning agrarian activists recognized the manifold shortcomings of economic policy in post-1918 east central and southeast Europe. Although their insistence on redistribution of large estate land through sweeping reforms could not in itself solve rural overpopulation, and indeed often exacerbated peasant insolvency by increasing the number of small and dwarf holdings, their policies were arguably more farsighted than those of their rivals. They recognized, for instance, that for industry to benefit the rural population, manufacturing centers had to be spread evenly throughout state territory, which would also require state investment in improved transport links; peasants in many regions suffered the effects of not being able to cost-effectively deliver their products to national and international markets. They further reasoned that industry could under the right circumstances develop symbiotically with intensive agriculture on small, family-owned farms (Denmark's successful dairy farms were often cited as a model). Processed food products—milk and cheese, fruit for jams, sunflower and soya for industrial use—might then be profitably sold on domestic and international markets.[79] Such a reorientation would require investment in agricultural technology and education, neither of which state governments in the region showed great interest in.

The solution offered by agrarians in both the short and long term was cooperatives. Cooperatives, they maintained, would address peasant cultivators' immediate woes, as well as providing the foundation for a democratic, prosperous peasant society of the future. As the Romanian economist and agrarian activist David Mitrany wrote of the interwar peasantists, "It is not too much to say indeed that they had in mind a cooperative society, equally distinct from the Liberal capitalist society as from the collective society of Socialism."[80] The first rural cooperatives in the latter third of the nineteenth century had been either marketing societies, which allowed farmers to assert some control over the prices they could get for their products, or credit societies that, following the model devised by German author and small-town mayor Friedrich Wilhelm Raiffeisen, encouraged agriculturalists to pool their savings in local institutions offering affordable credit to members. Supported by provincial assemblies, the number of credit cooperatives in the western half of the Habsburg Empire exploded from thirty in 1888 to six thousand in 1908.[81] Over the same period, average cooperative membership rose from 53 to 131. Hungary experienced similar expansion, though the number of overall institutions was much lower and their memberships consequently higher. Cooperatives may have combatted overall rural indebtedness. They doubtless contributed to a rationalization of operations among the mostly middling peasants who joined; subsistence farmers often did not produce enough of a surplus to jointly market it. Production cooperatives modeling themselves on sophisticated arrangements that existed among dairy farmers in the Alpine provinces also took off. These spread agricultural knowhow among small cultivators and provided access to equipment that they would not have otherwise been able to afford. Consumer cooperatives, though more common in urban areas, permitted members purchasing goods in bulk to obtain lower prices of manufactured items and household essentials. In Czechoslovakia, Poland, and in some regions of Yugoslavia and Romania the cooperative movement advanced between the wars. In other places, it faced insuperable obstacles—one was state control of cooperatives, which rendered them utterly ineffectual; the other was that the local peasantry, mired in poverty, did not have sufficient resources to pool.[82]

Cooperativism challenged the individualist ethos of liberalism. At the same time many agrarians insisted on preserving the small, privately owned family farm as the basic unit of production, thereby rejecting socialist notions of collective ownership. Fedor Houdek, a prominent interwar Slovak agrarian politician and proponent of cooperatives, wrote that to arrest the baleful exodus of country folk to cities, "villages must become attractive for villagers. It is possible to reach this aim by various routes, but the most important of them will always remain *self-supporting and communal cooperation of villagers*, open to all irrespective of religion, property relations, social position, and cultural maturity."[83] Peasantists aimed to reward individual initiative and hard work, though they did not object to state ownership of large-scale operations where workers possessed little to no independence—for instance, in heavy industry and mining. They also, in some cases, advocated state ownership of banking to guarantee affordable credit to their village-level constituents. Implementing this vision would entail a wholesale reorientation of economists' and politicians' attention from the city to the countryside. Some hoped for rural areas to simply achieve parity in modernization schemes. Others, like Stamboliiski, sought the exaltation of village life at the expense of the city. Either way, agrarians demanded that the place of peasant producers in the modern era be radically rethought: no longer a hindrance to modernity, or a bulwark against its deleterious effects, they now figured as its vanguard. Their virtuous toil, independence, and instinctive egalitarianism would undergird a new social order. And crucially, they could derive new confidence and dignity from the central role that agrarian leaders cast them in, reversing centuries of prejudice. This was an urgent cultural task, for as Stjepan Radić wrote in 1896:

> In Croatia even a foreigner notices at first glance that there are two peoples here: the gentleman and the common people. . . . Everyone who wears a black coat has the right to the title of "gentleman," and only with this title can one in practice, in life, have any worth as a man. All of the others . . . are "peasants," "thick-headed," "vulgar people," or simply slaves, subjects. Neither the property, nor the personal honor, nor the individual freedom of any man from among the common people is secure. . . . Whoever says a single harsh word already sits in prison. A true reign of terror. In short: In Croatia only the *kaputaš* [frockcoat wearer], the "gentleman," and more recently only the bureaucrat, is a man, a person.[84]

To confront such injustice peasantist ideologues praised villagers' political and cultural potential, often in exaggerated terms, earning them the scorn of contemporaries as well as later historians. Their enthusiasm was perhaps forgivable given the historic neglect of the countryside. Agrarians' confidence that peasants could begin to correct this imbalance through the democratic franchise was matched by their belief that education would forever banish peasants' inherited inferiority complex. It is possible that rural education and technological instruction at levels advocated by agrarians would still not have been sufficient to overcome the fundamental demographic and economic challenges facing the east European countryside. But interwar states shortsightedly did not make such provision, instead incentivizing the production of ever more university law graduates to staff hypertrophied bureaucracies.

As if to disprove claims about peasant parochialism and political immaturity, agrarian leaders often declaimed their patriotism in loud tones or promised to lead emancipation of their oppressed nation, as in the case of Radić's Croatian Peasant Party. Yet this produced far less chauvinism and warmongering than in other political camps. On the contrary, international cooperation flourished between agrarian parties in the 1920s, for reasons of both practicality and principle. Peasantist leaders hoped that international support could bolster their domestic political positions, which were often precarious despite the solid demographic majorities that stood behind them. Internationalism also corresponded to basic tenets of agrarian ideology, especially that solidarity between pacifistic villagers of various nations was the best guarantor against future war. Slavic agrarians were confident that the old, nineteenth-century ideal of Slavic reciprocity was alive among the peasantries of central and eastern Europe. These ideas found clearest expression in the writings of Antonín Švehla, who in the early 1920s stated: "We are convinced that a great task arises here above all for the agriculturalists of Slavic nations, joined by the agrarian idea, that natural gospel of the land, to show the path to others. It is their duty, because precisely they form the basis and overwhelming majority of the population in their nations. Only thus can they fulfill the historic task of the Slavic race, since: whoever is a Slav is also an agriculturalist."[85] The Great War, Švehla maintained, had revealed the paramount importance of agricultural producers to society, along with their capacity to prevent war by defending their livelihoods. The peasant's natural egotism ensured peace.

Few peasant activists had looked beyond national borders in the years before the First World War. At most, there had been efforts to institutionalize international coordination of agricultural policy and expertise. The French minister of agriculture Jules Méline was the driving force behind the 1891 establishment of an International Commission of Agriculture (Commission internationale d'agriculture) to harmonize various national agrarian lobbies and served as its first president for thirty-two years. In 1905, representatives of forty countries at a conference in Rome founded the International Institute of Agriculture, forerunner of the United Nations' Food and Agriculture Organization (FAO), to aggregate information on world agriculture and disseminate agricultural expertise. The following year, an International Federation of Agricultural Cooperatives was launched, but mistrust between French and German leaders bedeviled it from the start.[86] The lives of smallholding peasants remained largely untouched by these organizations, notwithstanding the data on their output and practices that appeared in statistics compiled in Rome. Nor did peasant party leaders engage in any formal international or transnational cooperation before 1914. Agrarian Czech, Polish, and Slovene deputies in Vienna sometimes met, as did future agrarian Slovak and Romanian deputies in Budapest.[87]

The years after 1918 presented a very different picture. Over the course of 1921–23, Švehla and his party presided over the creation in Prague of the International Agrarian Bureau (Mezinárodní Agrární Bureau), unofficially known as the Green International, though the initial impetus came from Stamboliiski.[88] Aware of the fragility of his regime, the Bulgarian leader in March 1920 told Czechoslovakia's diplomatic envoy that he regarded Prague as the most important Slavic center and hoped to foster friendship between their countries, a sentiment that was then conveyed to Švehla in a letter. The overture was received hesitantly, since Bulgaria, as a defeated power and enemy of Romania and Yugoslavia (Czechoslovakia's allies in the Little Entente), carried little weight in the diplomatic considerations of President Masaryk and Foreign Minister Beneš. Stamboliiski followed up his suggestion with a visit to Prague in December 1920, during which he discussed his ideas with Švehla at an informal dinner. In spring 1921, he dispatched Aleksandar Dimitrov to Poland, receiving a pledge of support from Witos, despite the strained relations at that time between Czechoslovakia and Poland over border disputes. That autumn, Švehla's secretary Jiří Fiedler attended a congress of Yugoslav peasant parties near Belgrade and accompanied a Yugoslav delegation to Sofia. By the end of 1921, the bureau existed as an alliance between the Czechoslovak Republican Party, the Bulgarian BANU, the Polish People's Party "Piast," and the Serbian Union of Agriculturalists. In 1922, its Prague office (a department of the Republican Party organization until 1923) was home to six full-time employees, delegates of each of the four member parties, and seven officers for the various sections of the bureau's activity.

Stamboliiski's violent demise in June 1923 shook the fledgling Green International, as did the murder on Prague streets two months later of his lieutenant Raiko Daskalov by the same Macedonian terrorist organization that had orchestrated the coup in Sofia. The BANU remained a member of the organization, but the inspiring example of a peasant state in the Balkans was no more. Now more Czech-centered, the bureau did not waver from its program of Slavic peasant solidarity, agrarian mutualism, pacifism, and anticommunism. Over the next several years, it welcomed the Croatian Peasant Party into its ranks, but also non-Slavs from the Romanian National Peasant Party and the Finnish Agrarian League. Its main propaganda instrument was the monthly (from 1925, quarterly) *Bulletin*—a publication that sought to disseminate the bureau's views, present issues facing individual member parties, and generate interest in agrarian matters more broadly. Czech was the primary language of the *Bulletin*; contributions in Czech were accompanied by French translations, while articles in other languages appeared alongside Czech translations. From 1927, the *Bulletin* published articles in parallel Czech, French, and German versions. Besides its flagship periodical, the bureau sponsored conferences, exhibitions, and congresses of peasant and agricultural organizations.

Impressive though they were, the Green International's efforts in the early to mid-1920s did little to secure the political futures of member parties. Meanwhile, it faced competition from other internationalist ventures. The Swiss agronomist Ernst Laur, already active in agricultural internationalism before the war and head of the Swiss Farmers' League (Schweizer Bauernverband), joined the Paris-based International Commission of Agriculture and steered it toward a more active political stance.[89] At the commission's 1925 conference in Warsaw, a German, an Italian, and a Pole joined the executive, showing the organization's growing interest in defeated states and east Europeans. In 1927, the commission won official recognition from the League of Nations through its newly established subsidiary, the International Economic Conference, further raising its profile. Laur likely intended to compete with the Green International; indeed, since 1922 he had helped Austrian and Hungarian colleagues edit a rival Vienna-based periodical called the *Green International*, though this did not stop him from also sometimes contributing to the bureau's *Bulletin*.

The Czech leaders of the Green International felt compelled to change course, formalizing cooperation among member parties. Švehla and fellow Republican Party leader Karel Mečíř drew up statutes, dispatching them to agrarian parties across Europe, along with an appeal to formally join the Prague-based organization.[90] By 1928, membership encompassed parties from Austria, Bulgaria, Czechoslovakia (both "Czechoslovaks" and Germans), Estonia, Finland, France, Holland, Germany, Latvia, Lithuania, Poland, Romania, Switzerland (both Bern and Aargau organizations), and Yugoslavia

(Croat, Serb, and Slovene parties). In April 1929, the bureau's first general assembly convened and ratified twelve proposed statutes. The first among them declared that only those parties representing the inhabitants of villages and committed to parliamentary democracy could join. Each state was to be represented by one peasant party, although multinational states could send parties from each of their constituent nations. Membership of competing parties from the same nationality was discouraged, though permissible if other members consented. Thus, Piast would have to allow accession of Wyzwolenie and the leftist Peasant Party (Stronnictwo Chłopskie, established 1925), which had replaced Lewica. The point was rendered moot two years later when all Polish peasantists merged into the People's Party (Stronnictwo Ludowe). In the early 1930s, the Green International accepted membership applications from new agrarian parties in Greece (1930), Belgium (1933), and Spain (1934), while authoritarian takeovers meant the loss of parties from Germany (1933), Austria (1934), Estonia (1934), Latvia (1934), and Lithuania (1936).

The statutes redefined the Green International's core mission as political coordination among peasant parties. Reciprocal contacts between parties from various countries were to be established and maintained. The bureau acted as a clearing house for information about initiatives undertaken by individual peasant parties and committed itself to organizing joint action. Where disputes arose between member parties, it aimed to foster reconciliation. Along with a presidium and general secretariate, the bureau's main collegial body was a general assembly to which member parties sent between one and five delegates, depending on the size of their constituencies. Meeting not less than once biennially, it would decide by simple majority on all important questions facing the bureau. The meetings took place in Prague in the years 1928–33, after which economic crisis and political persecution curtailed many member parties' activities.

Relatively few villagers had direct contact with the Green International, but millions of them were affiliated with member parties that hailed cross-border solidarity among peasants, an ideal that resonated strongly with the rank and file. Despite peasants' proverbial narrow-mindedness and signs of deeply rooted ethnic prejudice among them, they showed more interest in building and maintaining international ties than adherents of many rival parties. They may have been inspired by what the authors discussed in chapter 1 described as an instinctive sense of fraternity among peasant soldiers in the Austro-Hungarian army, or between them and peasant soldiers in enemy armies. (Villagers around the world have often shared the conviction that those who till the land possess the same virtues and face the same obstacles whatever their background.) Of likely equal importance was east central European peasants' reserve toward the strident ethnic nationalism of the mostly urban-based parties they tended to oppose.[91]

Peasant youth organizations were among the most important expressions of grassroots internationalism. From 1924, the Slavic Federation of Village Youth drew together young peasant activists from Bulgaria, Czechoslovakia, Poland, and Yugoslavia, as well as from Russia and the Lusatian Sorbs, a Slavic-speaking minority in eastern Germany. At its founding congress, held September 5–8 in Ljubljana and at Lake Bled in Slovenia, Milan Hodža delivered a keynote address on the innate connections between Slavicness and agrarianism.[92] Although the federation remained in principle politically unaffiliated, in practice it functioned as the youth arm of the Green International. Alongside Hodža, who regularly spoke at their events, Švehla, Mečíř, and other leaders made appearances at youth events, promoting agrarianism, peasant democracy, and cooperatives. The federation grew symbiotically with national-level youth organizations that emerged in the early postwar years. In Poland, both the Central Union of Village Youth (Centralny Związek Młodzieży Wiejskiej), founded in 1919 in the former Russian partition, and the Union of Youth in Lesser Poland (Małopolski Związek Młodzieży) established in 1920 pursued a program of apolitical rural education; the former in informal partnership with Wyzwolenie, and the latter under the influence of Piast.[93] By the time of Piłsudski's May 1926 coup, each organization counted over fifty thousand members. The democratically inclined majorities among them responded in June 1928 to the authoritarian takeover by forming the Union of Village Youth of the Polish Republic (Związek Młodzieży Wiejskiej Rzeczpospolitej Polskiej), commonly known as the "Wici"—a name that invoked the democratic assemblies of the ancient Slavs. In 1929, the Wici, with its eponymous periodical, counted twenty-two thousand members in 746 circles, figures that had more than quadrupled by 1937. Like its predecessors, the Wici maintained contacts with agrarian youth movements in Czechoslovakia, Yugoslavia, and elsewhere. Its counterpart in the south Slav lands was the Slovene Union of Associations of Peasant Youths and Maidens (Zveza društev kmetskih fantov in deklet), which ensured that the founding congress of the international federation took place in Slovenia, and which forged strong regional ties with Croatian and Serbian rural youth. Prominent foreign representatives attended its September 1925 general assembly at Lake Bled, including Stjepan Radić, Milan Djordjević of the Serbian Union of Agriculturalists, and the Polish scouting leader, Piotr Olewiński.[94]

Many of its leaders had studied in Prague, where they imbibed the spirit of Slavic agrarian internationalism. But the real impetus, claimed the Slovene Union's ideologue Stanko Tomšič in 1933, came from the war: "If anywhere the world war forms a milestone between two eras, it forms it doubtless in the life of our young village. Peasant youth, before the war lacking any deeper, more serious movement of its own, without interest for the questions of public life, far more the object than the bearer of life in the Slovene countryside, now acts as its organization, the combative avant-garde shaping its content."[95]

Genuine internationalist spirit often coexisted unproblematically with antiurban bias or ethnic prejudice in the minds of many village-level activists. Peasants who gathered on September 7, 1919, in the Slovenian town of Krško passed a seventeen-point resolution demanding, among other things, that immediate elections be called on the basis of universal equal and direct suffrage for men and women; that salaries for bureaucrats and gendarmes be lowered; that the gendarmerie be reduced because of its unpopularity among the people; and that "excess land" be confiscated from large landowners.[96] The assembly rejected proposals that voting rights be extended only to "enlightened women" or that an "educated committee" implement school reform without "the people."[97] More stridently, they claimed, "We do not want agrarian reform to be solved by various doctors, who maybe know the laws well but not peasant needs and conditions. We demand that the minister for agrarian reform as well as the bosses in the ministry and in the regional government be agricultural experts." Xenophobic point 16 insisted that "all gypsies who do not belong in our municipality be removed by force from it."

The combination of peasant yearning for reform, or even revolution, with deep-seated social resentment in villages elicited various responses among agrarian leaders. While Švehla eschewed populist animus against cities, people's tribunes like Radić and Stamboliiski made it their trademark. The Radić brothers were reputed to conspicuously avoid Zagreb's fashionable restaurants and cafés, making it clear that, despite their cosmopolitan education, they did not belong among the urban bourgeoisie.[98] The Bulgarian leader, for his part, wrote uncompromisingly:

> The town and the village are centers of two different world views, two different cultures. . . . In the villages live a people who work, fight, and earn a living at the caprice of nature. In the towns live a people who earn their living not by exploiting nature, but by exploiting the labor of others. That is a rule to which there is no exception. These two basic principles are the

> primary cause of the unique and different interests, ideas, and world views that move society in these two areas. The way of life in the village is uniform, its members hold the same ideas in common. That accounts for the superiority of the village over the city. The city people live by deceit, by idleness, by parasitism, by perversion.[99]

Such sentiments shaded easily into anti-Semitism in countries where Jews made up a sizable portion of the urban financial elite—namely, Hungary, Romania, and Poland, as well as, to a lesser extent, in Croatia and Slovakia. While east European agrarian parties refrained from open anti-Jewish rhetoric in official publications and party programs, it was common enough among ordinary members. And it cropped up in speeches by leaders such as Stjepan Radić himself and, as discussed above, Polish peasant radicals and leaders of the Tarnobrzeg Republic Tomasz Dąbal and Eugeniusz Okoń. For such men, Jewish financial power correlated directly with village indebtedness and penury, reflecting the disproportionate, unjust influence of the city over the countryside.

It was in fact Dąbal who launched the Green International's principal rival institution in 1923 in Moscow. His checkered career in Polish parliament ended in July 1922 when he, now a Communist, was sentenced to six years in prison for agitating to abolish the sejm and establish a dictatorship of the proletariat.[100] None of his political rivals had forgotten the speech he delivered to the assembly on July 24, 1920, when, with the Red Army threatening to overrun Warsaw, Dąbal blasted the government for cynically dangling land reform before the peasant masses to win them for the war effort. Those who advocated for a "People's Poland," he went on, desired fundamental societal reform far more than a diversionary war with the Bolsheviks. Dąbal barely escaped the chamber unhurt after his unforgivable tirade.[101] It also estranged him from Okoń, though his stature among peasants in the former territory of the Tarnobrzeg Republic remained undiminished.[102] In any case, Dąbal did not serve the entirety of his sentence, leaving Poland for Russian exile in March 1923 as part of a prisoner exchange with the Soviets.

Dąbal's arrival in Moscow coincided with efforts by the Communist International (Comintern) to expand its influence beyond directly subordinate parties and trade unions. In late 1922, delegates at the Fourth World Congress of the Comintern had decided to establish an organization dedicated to political agitation among peasants. Stamboliiski's fall in June 1923 accelerated the process of forming the Red Peasant International, or "Krestintern"—a name derived from the Russian word for "peasant" (*krestian*).[103] Bulgarian Communists' decision to stay aloof during the bloody coup in Sofia earned them a severe reprimand from the Comintern, which now concluded that Communist parties should ally with progressive agrarian groups and seek to eventually exert control over them. With his firsthand experience in radical agrarian politics, Dąbal was poised to mold the Krestintern according to his own ideas. The founding conference of the Krestintern was held October 10–16, 1923, in Moscow in tandem with an International Agrarian Exhibition. Delegates from all over the world attended, demonstrating the global reach of Soviet internationalism. The efforts of the Green International in Prague appeared decidedly provincial in comparison. Alongside representatives from the Soviet Union, Poland, Bulgaria, and Hungary were delegates from the USA, Mexico, Japan, and Indochina, including a young Ho Chi Minh.[104]

Dąbal delivered the keynote address, in which he refuted any revolutionary hierarchy of the industrial proletariat over rural toilers. Lenin had defied European socialist orthodoxy by regarding the peasantry as a crucial, if temporary, component of any successful revolutionary movement in underdeveloped countries; a theoretical intervention seemingly vindicated by Bolshevik practice. Yet the primacy of the industrial proletariat in bringing the revolution to completion and building socialism remained uncontested. Dąbal now trampled on the distinction. In subsequent years, he even appeared to subordinate movements of the working classes to those of peasants. Such heresy caused remarkably little concern in the mid-1920s, when the New Economic Policy was at its zenith. Dąbal steered the Krestintern from his position as deputy to the organization's general secretary, Alexandr Petrovich Smirvov, who was also people's commissar for agriculture in the Russian Soviet Federative Socialist Republic. Until 1926, the Red Peasant International basked in the approval of the Comintern's top decision-makers.[105] Its initial patron was Grigory Zinoviev, who enthused over what an alliance between workers' and peasants' organizations could accomplish during the supposedly imminent repetition of the postwar revolutionary conjuncture. The more circumspect Nikolai Bukharin, the Krestintern's principal benefactor following Zinoviev, called for patient Communist infiltration of peasant parties and establishment of Communist-controlled agricultural unions. Along with covert bottom-up tactics, the organization pursued negotiation and alliances with existing peasant parties in eastern Europe.

Like the Comintern, the Krestintern was to hold biennial international conferences attended by representatives of peasant movements. Institutional governance fell to the General Council, whose presidium was composed of three leaders and a permanent secretariate. An International Peasant Information Bureau oversaw communication with affiliated parties, and for each target country a chosen "correspondent" was responsible for building contacts with agrarian parties, unions, and other rural organizations. The organization's eponymous monthly journal, *Krestianskii internatsional*, featured articles in Russian, English, French, and German, while the International Agrarian Institute, founded in 1925 under the Krestintern's auspices, conducted research on global agriculture as a Communist answer to the International Institute of Agriculture in Rome.[106]

Yet the accomplishments of the Red Peasant International were modest and fell short of its Prague-based rival. Most of its alliances with peasant parties proved ephemeral. In mid-1924, it appeared to score a significant victory when Stjepan Radić accepted an invitation to come to Moscow, consenting amid great fanfare to the accession of his party to the Krestintern. The Soviet commissar for foreign affairs, Georgy Chicherin, greeted him upon his arrival as "a peasant leader and intrepid fighter for the liberation of the Croat peasants."[107] Though opposed to communism in principle, Radić had expressed some sympathy for events in Russia since the revolution, showing admiration for the Soviet nationalities policy based on cultural autonomy. But his main motive in 1924 appears to have been frustration with the Green International, which he regarded as too closely aligned with Czechoslovak foreign policy and insufficiently supportive of Croatian independence. Seeking support from the Prague federation's competitor, he agreed to join only on the condition that his party's program be accepted as it was, without tempering its pacifism or adulterating it with notions of proletarian struggle. The partnership was short-lived and politically costly. The Comintern, no doubt deferring to Radić, duly made pronouncements in favor of Yugoslav federalism and obliged the Yugoslav Communist Party to grudgingly accept the Croatian Peasant Party as an ally. The Belgrade political establishment, already rabidly anti-Soviet, reacted irately, and Radić's Moscow sojourn provided them with a pretext for harsher measures against his party. When Radić less than a year later entered the Belgrade government, the Croatian Peasant Party's membership in the Krestintern was over. Tentative alliances with the Farm Labor Party and other progressives in the United States likewise came to naught. Probably the most significant achievement of the Red Peasant International was creating a Communist-friendly left wing of the post-Stamboliiski BANU, which lasted from 1924 until 1931.[108]

From the mid-1920s, the Krestintern suffered rapid demotion. Former patrons like Bukharin abandoned it, while Stalin, steadily consolidating his power at the time, had no patience for it. The Krestintern sat uneasily with his doctrine of "socialism in one country," and from 1928 appeared to be an anachronism with the end of NEP and the beginning of collectivization. Dąbal continued to author optimistic articles in *Krestianskii internatsional*, but his audience dwindled. The Comintern's "peasantist phase," as George Jackson described it, was over.[109] Mao Zedong's seminal 1927 "Report on an Investigation of the Peasant Movement in Hunan," penned when the Krestintern was already in terminal decline, caught the attention of few, if any, Communists outside China. The document that initiated the most serious revision of orthodox Marxist views on the countryside, elevating the peasantry to the revolutionary class par excellence in agrarian societies, came too late to rescue the Moscow-based organization.[110] After 1929, the Red Peasant International was never again mentioned in Comintern meetings. Dąbal sought refuge in Minsk, becoming vice-president of the Belorussian Academy of Sciences in 1932. In August 1937, he died as a victim of Stalin's purges. The Krestintern was formally dissolved in 1939.

The fate of the Red Peasant International was symptomatic of a broader crisis facing peasantist politics at the end of the 1920s. Peasants had proven that they could mobilize for modern political contests on an impressive scale, pursuing their own ideology. But even in post-Habsburg east central Europe, where their efforts produced resilient mass parties, a continental center of peasant internationalism, and an expansion of rural civil society, it seemed as though agrarianism was no match for the state repression and political violence spreading across Europe. Stamboliiski's 1923 murder had already cast a shadow over the movement. The establishment of dictatorial regimes in Poland (1926), Lithuania (1926–27), and Yugoslavia (1929) further dimmed its prospects. Then, in summer 1928, an incensed Serbian Radical Party deputy shot Stjepan Radić at close range on the floor of the Belgrade skupština, mortally wounding him.

Hope still flickered, however illusory it may appear in retrospect. The Romanian National Peasant Party had won a stunning victory in the 1928 elections, fueling optimism that salvation was nigh for the long-suffering Romanian peasantry. Nor did the onset of Stalin's brutal collectivization campaign in the Soviet Union immediately sow despair among agrarian leaders, who still believed the Russian peasantry would prevail in their contest with state power. As late as 1929, when Stalin's forced collectivization was already well underway, Milan Hodža wrote:

> Whoever at least somewhat critically follows events in Russia sees that it is in the first instance the farmer who pushes Bolshevism into capitulation. It is

> doubtless that the farmer cannot lose in his great struggle against Bolshevism. The Russian farmer is a guarantee that such development will come in Russia as is desirable for international peace policy and national progress. That which is valuable in the Russian Revolution for Russia and for humanity will be saved by a primitive form of Russian agrarian democracy.[111]

Some peasant activists even tolerated the new authoritarian regimes arising across central and eastern Europe, seeing them as superior to pre-1918 imperial rule despite their obvious shortcomings. Jan Słomka, the former mayor of Dzików near Tarnobrzeg, lauded the Polish government in 1929 for honoring him and many other villagers with the Golden Order of Merit, bestowed at a glittering Warsaw ceremony. "Surely," he wrote in his memoirs, "it was the first time that Poland recognized and rewarded so many obscure farmers—them who nourish and defend the nation. Such an act sealed the significance of the tiller of the soil. This was stated by the President himself, who declared that agriculture is the foundation of national well-being, but that the achieving of progress in that domain is harder than in any other."[112]

Such isolated symbolic victories did little to alter a growing sense of despondency among peasantist politicians. Some began to think that means more forceful than electoral politics would be needed to advance their cause. Their eager embrace of parliamentary democracy had rested on the assumption that they would progress inexorably toward political supremacy, given the demographic weight of the countryside. As circumstances disabused them of their optimism, they reinterpreted democracy in narrower terms. Albin Prepeluh, a Slovene agrarian socialist and member of the Slovene Peasant Party, closed his 1928 study of the peasant movement he had helped to build with the words: "Peasant democracy is in our country above all a political movement. Yet the final aim of this movement cannot be anything else than the complete predominance of peasant and working people in the state. . . . It can only reach its ultimate social and also cultural goal when it will be able, with its political might, to dictatorially assert its own social will."[113] Prepeluh's majoritarian notion of democracy, denigrating dissent and compromise, was already commonplace on the far right and left of European politics. With the Great Depression devouring rural livelihoods by the early 1930s, many convinced agrarians would embrace it as well.

8

Outcast Patriots

AT THE END OF 1933, in the depths of the Great Depression in Poland, a peasant farmer from the hilly south of former Austrian Galicia entered a memoir competition organized by the Institute of Social Economy (Instytut Gospodarstwa Społecznego) in Warsaw. The native of an unnamed village some twelve kilometers (7.5 miles) southeast of the market town of Jasło described the devastating effects of the world economic crisis on the Polish countryside.[1] Thirty-four years old at the time of writing, he recounted the rocky path trodden by many peasant veterans of the First World War: from Austro-Hungarian trenches to the chaotic birth of new or resurrected states in east central Europe, to their fragile consolidation in the mid-1920s and, eventually, to the social and economic collapse of the early 1930s. In spring 1918, after almost a year on the Italian Front, he had taken advantage of a furlough at home to desert the Habsburg army and assemble a local Green Cadre (*zielona kadra*) with thirty-five other soldiers. Although the unit was a relatively serious fighting force with a commanding officer and its own ground machine gun, gendarmes succeeded in ambushing and arresting the deserters; the memoirist received a deferred five-year prison sentence and was again dispatched to the Italian Front, where he again mutinied. From February 1919 to July 1922, he served in the Polish army, spending eighteen months on the front lines fighting against both Ukrainians and Bolsheviks, later returning to work on the family farm.

After his father's death in 1925, he inherited a modest two hectares (5 acres, or 3.5 *morgy*) of the family property, though as the eldest son he was expected to cultivate the remainder until his five younger siblings could claim their portions. Despite the financial burdens of medical care for infirm family members and payouts to siblings who desired cash instead of even punier holdings than the one he received, he managed to turn profits in the late 1920s, thanks in part to agronomic knowledge he imbibed through self-study and as a member of local agricultural associations. The collapse of agricultural prices at the end of the decade extinguished these fragile rays of hope. In 1930, he and his wife decided to forgo store-bought meat and rice, buying coffee and sugar only occasionally and matches not at all (a lighter would suffice). An avid reader, he discontinued two of his three periodical subscriptions and stopped purchasing any new books. Although harvests in 1931 and 1932 were not bad, miserably low prices for farm products required further belt-tightening. In 1932, the family of six—two parents, two children, and the memoirist's two dependent siblings—did not slaughter a single pig, buying bacon only on rare occasion and sugar only for major holidays. The farm's income in 1932–33 amounted to 790 złoty, mostly from the sale of butterfat and grain, while the family's expenditures totaled 1099 złoty. Since the largest expense was clothes (60 złoty per person), the memoirist decided to plant hemp so that they could manufacture their own garments "in the old way." He abandoned his evening reading altogether to save kerosene, rendering winter nights painfully long. Nonetheless, he concluded, their family had it better than many others who were reduced to begging and starvation.

The crisis of the early 1930s was all the more unpleasant because of the political marginalization of peasants that accompanied it. A supporter of the oppositional agrarian youth movement Wici, the Jasło-area contributor finished his life story to date on a defiant note: "The state is ours and even if we are now treated even worse than in a stepmotherly fashion, we have a right to demand and fight for our rightful position in this state. . . . We [peasants] will persevere, the only thing that's needed is work to raise the consciousness of the peasant masses, so that we will sooner achieve that which our contributions to rebuilding the state and our numbers entitle us to, i.e. People's Poland."[2] A smallholding memoirist from Rzeszów area was more fatalistic, reflecting bitterly on the failed integration of peasants into the resurrected Polish state after the Polish-Soviet War. Those, like him, who had joined up to fight the Red Army in 1920 after the government promised land reform and promoted agrarian leader Wincenty Witos to the position of prime minister, were later profoundly disappointed:

> Some got [land for fighting] but others didn't. Now in Poland there isn't enough land. At the time [in 1920] moreover Witos, the leader of the people, was put in charge of the government. And maybe it was just that which gave the huge masses of peasant sons the desire and courage to fight. Let's defend Poland till the final drop of blood, because it will be ours. Behold, a peasant at the helm of the government, there will be a People's Poland. How bitterly

> those who had hopes were disappointed. Now they think differently. And once again the same everyday chores await me as before.[3]

While agrarian parties of various stripes had channeled peasant hopes and energies in the 1920s across east central Europe, by the mid-1930s, apart from still-democratic Czechoslovakia, they could no longer fulfill this role owing to government repression or their own failures. Peasants in Poland and elsewhere found shelter from the cold winds of authoritarian government and economic crisis in new forms of activism. These ranged from left-leaning, nominally apolitical village youth movements to fascistic and ultranationalist opposition parties, and from paramilitary organizations to Communist or newly established rural socialist parties. In Hungary, Romania, Yugoslavia, and even Slovakia, many peasants appeared to metamorphose from reformist supporters of liberal democracy to adherents of increasingly radical right-wing oppositions. Yet nowhere did they subordinate themselves to new leaders who might hail their ethnic-national purity—or their instinctual hatred of capitalism, in the case of radical leftist movements, which also gained strength in rural areas—without hard evidence of said leaders' commitment to the countryside. Indeed, the new movements that proved most durable were built on preexisting agrarian foundations. Though often disoriented by the overlapping crises of the 1930s, peasants were neither unprincipled nor uncritical; they adapted the agrarian commitments of the 1920s to a political climate that seemed to demand extraparliamentary (or even antiparliamentary) action.

In all cases, villagers felt cruelly alienated from both state power and national leadership. Peasantists reasserted their claims on both. The memoirists cited above consciously or unconsciously echoed the rhetoric of the Polish People's Party, which unified from various competing factions in 1931, and in its December 1933 program proclaimed:

> Because of their numbers, their physical and moral strength, which derives from their association with the land and their value to nation and State, the rural population are justified in regarding themselves as the natural masters of Poland. And so the People's Party, as the political representative of this population, is concerned not only with the interests of the rural class but also with the interests of the whole Polish nation and State which has been created by the people through labors of a thousand years.[4]

Such rhetoric confronted the apparent hypocrisy of dictatorial regimes in the 1930s, which loudly trumpeted their devotion to a virtuous countryside at the same time as they clamped down on autonomous peasant activity in politics, economy, and culture. Mussolini had perhaps set the example for rightist authoritarians by proclaiming "agrarian democracy" and "land for those who work it" as cornerstones of fascism, at the same time that he silenced opponents and pursued economic policies shoring up the landlord class's power and striving for economic self-sufficiency at the expense of independent small farmers.[5] As peasants regrouped in various ways to oppose repression, oppositional intellectuals across the region redoubled their efforts to publicize rural misery and offer solutions.

The Great Depression magnified the weaknesses of agriculture in east central Europe, and across the world. Foremost of these was chronic overproduction of staple crops, especially grains, which had depressed prices throughout the 1920s. Whereas global wheat production increased by 17 percent between 1924 and 1929 over the prewar average, consumption rose by only 11 percent. Meanwhile, competition from cheaper overseas producers caused a sharp decline in east European countries' share of the global wheat market in the late 1920s.[6] With the failure of banking systems in the United States (1929) and then in Europe after the May 1931 collapse of Austria's Creditanstalt, world commodity markets went into freefall. By 1934, average aggregate agricultural prices had plummeted to 37 percent of their 1929 values; wheat sank to a third of its pre-Depression price, while meat was down to 40 percent of its previous worth.[7] Ivan Puntar-Štacnar, a relatively prosperous Slovene peasant from the village of Unec in Inner Carniola, described the situation in 1931 in his diary: "Terrible misery started to push down on the peasant in particular since he could not sell anything, if he did sell he didn't even reach half of the previous price."[8] Subsistence farmers, as Alexander Chayanov had pointed out in the 1920s, might weather such crises by retreating into self-sufficiency; certainly those who were net buyers of grain benefited from the staggering price drops.[9] But by the 1930s there were relatively few peasants in east central Europe who did not rely on the market. Thus, despite the glut of agricultural products, many smallholders attempted in the early 1930s to increase production and supplement their incomes, even though this had the effect of further depressing prices.

As the above testimony of the Jasło-area memoirist reveals, smallholding peasants had, by the 1930s, come to rely on the market less for food than for manufactured goods, such as shoes and clothes, which a century before they had still produced at home. He chose to plant hemp, in hopes that the family could revert to supplying their clothes "in the old way." The need to pay for such basic household articles explains peasants' seemingly irrational drive to increase agricultural output amid an acute crisis of overproduction. Worse still, the prices of manufactured goods did not experience the same slump. A disastrous "price scissors" opened to the detriment of agricultural producers. For example, while agricultural prices fell in Romania by 56 percent between 1929 and 1934, industrial prices fell by only 19 percent, effectively raising the prices of essential manufactured goods by 37 percent. In Yugoslavia and Poland, the gap between agricultural and industrial prices opened to 33 and 22 percent, respectively.[10] For peasants dependent on already exiguous profit margins, this was ruinous.

Indebtedness weighed on the rural population more unbearably than before. The collapse of banks on both sides of the Atlantic led to the recall of short-term loans by the principal creditor countries, above all the United States and France, which had underwritten the fragile recovery of central and eastern Europe in the mid- to late 1920s. The debt-ridden, mostly agrarian countries of east central Europe experienced a rapid contraction of their economies in summer 1931, to which they responded with deflationary measures to "rescue" their currencies, along with protective tariffs designed to shield their incipient industrial sectors. Loans could be obtained in the countryside only with the greatest difficulty and then at usurious rates. Governments attempted to alleviate the problem through various mechanisms, including a 1932 Yugoslav moratorium on all foreclosures and debt repayments, though this had the deleterious side effect of eliminating all sources of rural credit.[11] More farsighted and popular measures to assist peasants through the conversion and reduction of debts followed in the middle of the decade—for instance, in Romania (1934) and Yugoslavia (1935)—yet credit remained difficult to obtain.[12] Even in relatively prosperous Czechoslovakia, the burden of debt forced villagers to take unprecedented steps. In mid-June 1934, an eight-man delegation including members of the agrarian Republican Party, the rural-clerical People's Party, the leftist Social Democrats, and the center-right Party of Traders and Businessmen set out for Prague from the small southeast Moravian municipality of Prušánky bearing a petition signed by 203 villagers to present to the Ministries of the Interior and Agriculture:

> We undersigned peasants, cottagers, traders, and workers in Prušánky, Hodonín district, without party political distinctions, unable to further bear the burden of debts brought about by the catastrophic drop [in prices] of agricultural products and as a consequence of the unprofitability of

agricultural production, [and] being constantly at the mercy of repossessions and standing before the complete collapse of our farms, turn in the final instance to the decisive authorities in this state and demand:

1. Accelerated debt relief for agriculturalists.
2. A complete halt to all repossessions, if debt relief will not be carried out.
3. Securing of profitability for economic enterprise in general and thus the profitability of agricultural enterprise, because neither debt relief nor halting repossessions will rescue the agricultural estate, if profitability will not be guaranteed to [this estate].[13]

Governments took some steps to address the plight of the countryside, even if their priorities lay elsewhere.[14] Already in 1930, Romania and Yugoslavia had established state-subsidized or state-owned purchasing and sales organizations for grain producers, attempting to guarantee farmers' income as prices fell. In 1934, Hungary instituted a similar agency covering nearly all agricultural products. From 1932, at the suggestion of the Austrian National Bank, countries in southeast Europe began signing "clearing" agreements, or currency-less trade pacts based on barter. Germany, especially, committed itself to taking agricultural products and raw materials from the Balkans in exchange for manufactured goods, particularly machinery; a policy that was expanded under the Nazi regime's quasi-colonial *Grossraumwirtschaft* policies. Meanwhile, east European countries aimed to keep their agricultural exports competitive on the world market through what economic historian Ivan Berend described as hidden devaluation: maintaining official exchange rates for debt repayments and imports, while using a lower rate set by the central bank for exports of foodstuffs. Such policies were designed to keep agriculture alive while fostering industry behind tariff walls. But outside of Czechoslovakia, where an already solid industrial manufacturing base was reoriented toward heavy industry, little changed in the fundamentals of the region's economy. Between 1929 and 1938, the proportion of agricultural products and raw materials in the exports of Poland, Romania, and Yugoslavia remained constant at 76 percent, 83 percent, and 96 percent, respectively. Hungary's declined only slightly from 60 to 59 percent. And wheat exports continued to make up the bulk of these figures, even while governments encouraged expanded production of more marketable agricultural products, such as meat, dairy, oilseeds, and wine.

At the heart of state policies initiated around the world during the Great Depression was the idea of autarky. The collapse of agricultural prices convinced regimes across the political spectrum that overreliance on global markets led to fatal dependence on fickle commodity prices and potentially hostile foreign nations. Price fluctuations determined by banking events in distant capitals could, at a stroke, push the rural "heart of the nation" to the brink of starvation. At the same time, since a nation's ability to survive conflict in a hostile world depended, as the First World War had shown, on its industrial base, agriculture needed to be put at the service of industrial growth. The states that responded to these impulses during the world economic crisis most vigorously—and, on the surface, most successfully—were the Soviet Union and Nazi Germany. Virtually cut off from world markets in the early 1930s, Stalin's USSR experienced probably the most rapid and successful economic modernization in history, but at a staggering human cost. As part of Stalin's maniacal drive to transform the Soviet Union into an industrial powerhouse that could defend itself from attack by the capitalist West, his program of forced collectivization uprooted tens of millions of peasants and, under the pretext of eliminating class enemies in the countryside, resulted in famine and mass imprisonment, causing millions of deaths in Ukraine and Russia.[15] With reliable information about the extent of devastation hard to come by, many observers in depression-ravaged central and eastern Europe looked with admiration to the Soviet Union's self-sufficiency, its apparent immunity from crisis, and its capacity for rapid modernization.

While the Soviet regime had declared war on the peasantry to rescue Russia from backwardness, Hitler and his followers looked to the countryside in far more urban, industrial Germany as the bastion of a racially pure German identity. Not that agrarian backwardness did not vex them as well. The 1933 census counted 29 percent of the German population engaged in agriculture, with ratios of arable land per farmer closer to those of southern and eastern Europe than to western Europe.[16] In autumn of that year, the Nazi regime passed legislation to safeguard an idealized Aryan German farming class and to modernize agriculture. Walter Darré's September 1933 law on entailed farms (*Erbhofgesetz*) created indivisible and inheritable holdings of between 7.5 and 125 hectares (18.5–309 acres) owned by German proprietors who could demonstrate their non-Jewish lineage back to 1800. The farmers who enrolled in the scheme enjoyed debt relief and some protection from market caprice. Another law created a Reich Food Estate (*Reichsnährstand*), which brought the free market in agriculture to an end by introducing controls on prices and production. For many peasants, this brought back unpleasant memories of the command economy during and after the 1914–18 war. Although the agency contributed to raising German agriculture's productivity in the 1930s, these measures could not remedy the land hunger that afflicted up to 88 percent of the German farming population. Hitler and other leading Nazis became convinced that Germany would achieve autarky only with the conquest of sufficient "living space" (*Lebensraum*) in the east.[17]

The agrarian countries of east central and southeast Europe might have cast envious glances on Nazi and Soviet efforts at self-sufficiency and rearmament, but they lacked the resources or political will to undertake anything on the same scale. State interventionist schemes nonetheless multiplied and expanded over the course of the 1930s, even if, as noted above, they failed to alter the basic character of the region's economies. As we have seen, increased resources flowed into the rural colonization programs designed to benefit titular nations, though these too fell short of their objectives. By the mid-1930s, enthusiasts for colonization were calling for population transfers without parliamentary interference, citing the positive examples of Nazi Germany and the Soviet Union.[18] Regimes lauded the current and potential participants in such schemes as the healthy, martial, peasant core of their respective nations. Ruralism flourished in the halls of power in Belgrade, Bucharest, Budapest, Prague, and Warsaw, where statesmen prided themselves on the dubious achievements of postwar land reforms, and where considerable energies were expended to impress foreign visitors with colorful folk customs performed by cheerful, gaily costumed peasants.[19] That this façade contrasted with the bitter realities of the 1930s goes without saying. And such mostly urban enthusiasm was hardly limited to eastern Europe, as paeans to the rural basis of national life in western Europe reveal.[20]

Frustrated with the sham commitments of their governments, a new generation of educated, socially activist, oppositional intellectuals rose to prominence in east central Europe. Although many of the social scientists who made their names in the 1930s were associated with the political left, others embraced the ultra-nationalist right. Many drew inspiration from rural-themed novels that enjoyed their heyday in the interwar years. In Hungary, the oft-cited exemplar of this literature was Dezső Szabó's 1919 *The Swept Away Village*, which portrays a prototypical and idealized village besieged by alien influences of capitalism, liberalism, and socialism and their non-Magyar bearers, particularly Germans and Jews (though Szabó himself was neither particularly nationalist nor anti-Semitic). The hugely popular novel, which casts peasant intellectuals in the heroic role of national redeemers, inspired the movement of Hungarian populists (*népi*) in the 1920s and 1930s and their variously agrarian, socialistic, and radical right programs of rural renewal.[21] In a series of novels in the late 1920s and 1930s, Czech writer Václav Prokůpek unflinchingly described the plight of his native northeast Bohemian countryside, placing much of the blame for its woes on misguided, corrosive, and urban-directed reform schemes, from compulsory schooling to Czechoslovakia's post-1918 land reform.[22] Romanian novelist Liviu Rebreanu's much acclaimed and prize-winning novel *Ion* (1920), about an eponymous peasant in his native Transylvania, described personal ruin brought about by land hunger. Here too, east central Europe epitomized a global trend of surging literary interest in humble villagers. During the interwar years, no fewer than four Nobel Prizes in Literature went to authors who charted peasant life, including in 1924 Polish novelist Władysław Reymont for *The Peasants* (1904–9).[23]

Social scientists confronted the rural depredations of the Depression era with their own analytical tools. In Romania, history professor Dimitrie Gusti led a research team that charted the social, economic, and psychological problems of Romanian villages from the mid-1920s to the late 1940s in a series of monographs.[24] Some of Gusti's acolytes formed a left agrarian opposition after the collapse of the National Peasant Party government in the early 1930s. Others preferred the mystical ultranationalist program of rebirth proffered by Corneliu Zelea Codreanu's fascistic Legion of the Archangel Michael.[25] The contemporaneous work of Croatian economist and Peasant Party advocate Rudolf Bićanić drew attention to the economically stagnant, "passive regions" of Yugoslavia in the 1930s, where living standards had declined since the Habsburg period. Hungarian interwar intellectuals such as Géza Féja, Ferenc Erdei, and Zoltán Szabó found inspiration in *People of the Puszta* by left-populist writer Gyula Illyés, himself a devotee of Dezső Szabó, as they spread awareness of rural poverty in various print media. Efforts to chart the plight of the countryside were most extensive in Poland, where numerous well-publicized memoir competitions were held, including the one that attracted the testimonies cited above. These aimed to provide a window onto the conditions faced by the popular classes—an implicitly political challenge to the government's handling of the economic crisis in the 1930s.[26] While some criticized the left-leaning Institute for Social Economy for encouraging complaints from respondents to make a political point, a subsequent peasant memoir competition initiated by the politically neutral Institute for Rural Culture elicited similarly detailed grievances.

The rise of authoritarian regimes across east central Europe drove the peasantry from the terrain of parliamentary politics, but it did not cow them into submission or dampen their desire for fundamental societal change. Many villagers continued to nurture the revolutionary aspirations of the years immediately following the First World War in ostensibly apolitical organizations with their militant subcultures. In Poland and Slovenia, agrarian youth movements took the initiative in swinging peasantism toward closer cooperation with urban workers and the political left. For the Slovene Union of Peasant Youths and Maidens (before 1929 the Slovene Union of Associations of Peasant Youths and Maidens), such an outcome was not foreordained. In May 1932, just over three years after the proclamation of a royal dictatorship under King Aleksandar, prime minister Petar Živković attempted to shore up flagging support for the regime by forming a broad-tent governmental party called Yugoslav Radical Peasant Democracy. Among those enlisted for the quixotic venture was Ivan Pucelj, former chairman of the agrarian Slovene Peasant Party that had thrived between 1926 and 1929. The leadership of the Slovene youth union immediately expressed its support for the new government party, bringing official favor—queen Maria personally sent gifts to winners of peasant competitions—as well as attempts to control the union.[27] Despite the word "peasant" in its name, the government party accomplished little on behalf of struggling smallholders; its name change in June 1933 to the Yugoslav National Party, and its adoption of an unambiguously unitarist and centralist program dispelled any lingering doubts. Facing pressure from the rank and file, the Slovene Union disavowed its alignment with the government, reaffirming its political independence.

Some peasant youth leaders remained in the ranks of the government party, while most aligned themselves with antiregime movements.[28] The most important legal opposition party through the 1930s in Yugoslavia was the Croatian Peasant Party, which, since Stjepan Radić's death, was headed by Vladimir (Vladko) Maček. Already in the elections of the 1920s, Slovene peasants had often cast their votes for the Croatian Peasant Party, and Radić was a regular speaker at Slovene Union events. In 1933, youth activists had joined their Croatian counterparts in mass assemblies on either side of the Sutla River, which forms part of today's Croatian-Slovenian border, to commemorate the 360th anniversary of the great Croat-Slovene peasant uprising led by the "peasant king" Matija Gubec. The shared heritage of peasant rebellion convinced many Slovene Union members that their political fate was inextricable from that of Maček's party. In the 1935 elections that ended the Alexandrine dictatorship and ushered in the government of Milan Stojadinović, a significant portion of the Slovene Union membership voted for the Croatian Peasant Party.

In the final years before the Second World War, the Slovene Union drew closer to the Communist Party, interwar Yugoslavia's main illegal opposition movement, whose youth members began to join the ranks of the agrarian movement. Their motives were often tactical: in 1934, following Moscow's volte-face on cooperation with non-Communists in the interest of establishing "popular fronts" to combat fascism, alliances with progressive peasant groups were encouraged. With increasing numbers of Communist youth joining the Slovene Union, the administration of the Drava Banovina—one of the state's nine nonhistorical administrative units created in 1929, consisting of much of today's Slovenia minus the coastal region then under Italian control—clamped down on its expansion.[29] Facing suppression by the latest incarnation of the government party (the Yugoslav Radical Union) along with financial woes, the youth organization's growth to eighteen thousand members in 250 local branches by the eve of the Second World War was nothing short of remarkable.

The Slovene Union drew strength from the oppositional subculture that it fostered. Its main press organ, *Gruda* (The clod), celebrated a purportedly centuries-old Slovene peasant radicalism. Combative songs invoking the memory of Matija Gubec regularly appeared in its pages. In 1938, on the 365th anniversary of the Gubec uprising, *Gruda* drew a straight line between the 1570s and the present: "Still today we do not have that for which Gubec and thousands of peasants had to die—we do not have freedom or land. True, on paper we are free masters of our land. But in reality, we can barely say what we think; we have to do what they say, [and] the land is so indebted that we can hardly call ourselves its owners."[30] Complementing press activism was an expanding program of lectures on history, economics, sociology, and cooperativism. The courses offered by the Slovene Union were practically oriented, covering subjects like dairy and cheesemaking, animal husbandry, cooperative organization, and health care. Courses on housekeeping, sewing, and cooking aimed to attract its sizeable female membership; in 1934, ten years after the Slovene Union's establishment, women composed fully a third of the eleven thousand members. The "village maidens" of the union's name did not content themselves with tending home fires and occupied administrative and elected positions at all levels of the organization. As only men could vote in interwar Yugoslavia, young peasant women led the union's vocal campaign for women's suffrage.

Especially important for sustaining the peasantist vision were reaping and harvesting competitions (*tekme koscev in žanjic*), held annually in various parts of today's Slovenia. Inaugurated in summer 1928 in the Upper Carniolan town of Medvode, the outwardly apolitical games took on special significance during the years of the royal dictatorship. As union leader Vladimir Kreft wrote in 1933, "Reaping and harvesting games are not just ordinary games where youths and maidens compete for first place. Reaping and harvesting games are peasant Olympiads, where peasant work is exalted, where peasant self-confidence is strengthened and will for farming is fortified, where class consciousness is augmented and where new forces gather for the continued struggle of peasant youth."[31] The crowds that these events drew alarmed clerical rivals in the Slovene People's Party, which had returned to government under Stojadinović, with Monsignor Anton Korošec as interior minister. Clergymen affiliated with the People's Party denounced the reaping and harvesting games, which often took place on a Sunday, as sinful, threatening to excommunicate priests and parishioners who joined in.[32]

In Poland, the much larger peasant youth movement was from the beginning committed to agrarian democracy, though its adherents embraced increasingly militant, extraparliamentary means of activism as the decade progressed. As in Slovenia, the Wici initially faced mistrust from pious Polish villagers. When the memoirist from Jasło district recommended to younger villagers that they read the Wici's eponymous periodical, the schoolmaster denounced him as an atheist-communist, and the village priest summoned him to discuss his views.[33] Jan Stryczek, a smallholding peasant from the village of Wola Dalsza in Łańcut county, recalled that when he and other members of the Piast-affiliated youth circle (*koło młodzieży*) decided to ally with the recently established Wici, village women, incited by the priest, verbally abused them as Bolsheviks.[34]

Stryczek in many ways typified the generation of agrarian activists that rose to leadership positions in the 1930s. Born in 1897 to a land-hungry farming family, he attended more school than most people of his background and before the war worked seasonally in Lower Silesia. He fought on the Italian Front and was wounded twice, the second time seriously, after which he spent months in Austrian hospitals. In late summer 1918, he joined an armed band of deserters in the vicinity of his village. Having successfully evaded capture by gendarmes, he returned to farming after the establishment of independent Poland. As a war invalid, he received a gift of three *morgy* (1.75 hectares, or 4.3 acres) from the local grandee, Count Potocki. Stryczek regarded the land redistribution provisions of the 1920s as hopelessly inadequate, seeing any expropriation with compensation to former owners as unjust and faulting Potocki for redistributing only land that before emancipation had been commons. He predictably found little to praise in Wincenty Witos's premierships: "He was several times in the government and did not do anything for villages."[35] Although Stryczek had been involved in the peasant youth movement since 1923, he joined a political party only after the 1925 establishment of the leftist Peasant Party (Stronnictwo Chłopskie), the successor to the Lewica faction of the Polish People's Party. In his telling, the rich peasants (*kmiece*) remained in the Piast camp, while the medium- and smallholders in Wola Dalsza joined the new party. With the 1931 merging of the three main peasant parties—Piast, Wyzwolenie, and the Peasant Party—radicals gained the upper hand in the agrarian movement, which continued to enjoy its greatest support in former Habsburg Galicia.[36] In late autumn 1932, even the conservative-minded Witos came out in support of confiscation of estate land without compensation to landowners. The exigencies of the Great Depression induced many former moderates to voice radical demands for reform. Stryczek himself felt the crisis acutely on his small farm; in 1932, he could not afford to buy salt, matches, or kerosene.

As a Wici activist in Łańcut county in Lwów province, Stryczek belonged to one of the densest and most locally powerful youth movement organizations in the country. These were concentrated primarily in former Habsburg Galicia, as well as in formerly Russian Kielce, Lublin, and Warsaw provinces.[37] The Wici attracted growing numbers of followers both for their practicality—propagating agricultural knowhow and technology—and for their willingness to engage in radical direct action. These distinct streams of Wici activity converged in their tireless proselytizing of a new set of values for village youth centered on mutual respect and assistance, egalitarianism, patriotic duty, and peasant dignity. The flagship venture that touted such principles was Orkan's Village University, established in 1931 in the settlement of Gać, Przeworsk county (also former Galicia), under the direction of peasant youth activist Ignacy Solarz and named after the ruralist author Władysław Orkan.[38] The thousand or so students who passed through Solarz's institution during the 1930s attended courses on the history of Poland and of Polish peasants, literature, and the agricultural and technical sciences. Wici members spread their ideas in established academic settings as well, above all in the universities in Cracow and Lwów, where they formed societies with names like Polish Populist Academic Youth (Polska Akademicka Młodzież Ludowa) and Academic Association of Village Youth (Akademicki Związek Młodzieży Wiejskiej).[39] At the village level, the Wici offered a rich educational program. They established libraries, with the goal of each "circle" possessing its own library (around one-third of circles—over a thousand—had by the late 1930s); they promoted their weekly periodical; and they founded amateur theater and choral societies. Stryczek particularly enjoyed youth movement gatherings where participants engaged in passionate and heated debates on how to change the world. "Wici meetings [*zjazdy*]," he recalled, "had such absorbing and interesting proceedings that it was a pity when they ended."[40] At the same time, he extoled the yeoman service that his organization performed for villagers to mitigate the effects of the economic crisis: instruction in agricultural techniques, particularly for the cultivation of more profitable fruit and vegetable crops, and selective animal breeding.[41]

Officially, the Wici remained politically unaffiliated until 1931. The merger of peasant parties and the worsening effects of the Depression prompted them to ally with the unified People's Party (Stronnictwo Ludowe). In Wola Dalsza, tensions inevitably rose between them and the government-sponsored peasant youth movement, the Agricultural Society of Lesser Poland, colloquially known as the "Green Shirts" (Zielone Koszule). These were the "authorities' pets," according to Stryczek, though he conceded that both organizations cooperated in the volunteer firemen's association.[42] Wici ideology was formalized in December 1934 in the Cracow Theses, which called for expropriation of estate land without compensation, the socialization of industry, mining, banking, and commerce, and a reorganization of society on a cooperative basis.[43] Youth activists were also at the forefront of mass People's Party manifestations, such as the June 29, 1935, demonstration in the village of Nowosielce, Sanok county, in Lesser Poland at which 100,000–150,000 peasants demanded political democracy, guarantees of civil freedoms, and amnesty for political exiles, foremost of whom was Witos after October 1933.[44]

Not all activities undertaken by the Wici had approval from the People's Party leadership. In summer 1933, for instance, Stryczek was among the peasant volunteers who rushed to the village of Grodzisko Dolne to support the "revolution" there.[45] The events of June 22–27 came on the heels of several days of tension caused by a heated People's Party rally in Rakszawa, where Witos had spoken, and the subsequent brutal repression by the authorities, which resulted in around a dozen peasant deaths. In Grodzisko Dolne on June 22, thousands of villagers exiting church on the octave of Corpus Christi, an important local holiday, clashed with police sent to enforce a ban on firing of mortars. Several peasants were killed, and one policeman was beaten to death. The remaining village police barricaded themselves in the station—the same building attacked by Austro-Hungarian army deserters in summer 1918 with lethal results. A belligerent and growing peasant crowd surrounded the building. With peasants like Stryczek arriving from as far as twenty kilometers away, the embattled authorities again opened fire in an attempt to break the siege, killing several more civilians. A force of around four thousand peasants assembled that night on the wooded hill above the station, preparing for a morning attack, but state reinforcements arrived in time to evacuate the police trapped in the station and disperse the peasant force with machine gun fire. The actual death toll remains unknown. The "revolutionaries" held Grodzisko Dolne for several days until army units arrived, initiating two weeks of bloody pacification in the area.

In early 1937, with the government drifting increasingly toward the fascistic right in the wake of Piłsudski's 1935 death, the People's Party decided to put on a massive show of force. Cheered by the recent successes of workers' strikes, delegates at a party convention held in January in Warsaw resolved to stage a ten-day strike that summer for the restoration of democracy, for the "liquidation of the *Sanacja* system" (the term used for Poland's authoritarian government since 1926), and for "rights, bread, and work for all."[46] They set the strike's start date as August 15, to coincide with the anniversary of the great "peasant action" of 1920, when battalions of peasant volunteers had rushed to Warsaw, joining the Polish army at the decisive moment in its victorious war against the Soviets. For the military leaders of the Sanacja regime, there was no greater source of pride than Marshal Piłsudski's 1920 mobilization of the entire Polish nation, regardless of social class, to vanquish the Bolshevik foe. Sanacja—a Polish word for "healing"—had been invoked since the mid-1920s as a purportedly salubrious alternative to divisive parliamentarism. Independent commemoration of the "peasant action" appeared to its exponents as a provocation. The year before, on August 15, 1936, police had brutally suppressed peasant celebrations of their role in the 1920 war, killing nineteen and arresting over eight hundred.[47]

The populists' invocation of the "peasant action" embellished the historical record somewhat. In July 1920, after being forced to retreat to the gates of Warsaw by Red Army advances, Piłsudski had invited Witos to form a government in hopes of drumming up peasant support for the war, while the sejm committed itself to land reform. Witos threw himself into his new role of national savior with alacrity, spearheading a massive propaganda campaign to convince millions of war-weary, cynical peasants that they had a stake in the new Polish state. In his July 30 proclamation to the countryside, he urged them: "We need to take up this struggle of life or death, since even death is better than life in chains, death is better than wicked servitude. . . . You must save the Fatherland, you must give it everything, property, blood and lives, since this sacrifice will pay off a hundredfold when we save the state from bondage and dishonor."[48] However, it remains unclear how many peasants were among the seventy to one hundred thousand new recruits that the army secured by the middle of August. Peasants undoubtedly heeded calls to contribute their draft animals and food products to the war effort in far greater numbers than before.[49] Those who did volunteer, like the memoirist from Rzeszów county cited above, expected peasant fighters to be rewarded for their efforts. Disappointment with their treatment by the fatherland became a familiar refrain within the interwar peasant movement. For his part, Witos insisted after the stunning "Miracle on the Vistula" that peasants had "passed the test."[50] By pointing to the 1920 "peasant action," People's Party strike organizers in 1937 burnished their patriotic commitments while demanding that the state belatedly show its gratitude.

The strike on the August 15 anniversary began with placards posted in villages and towns listing peasant demands. Mass demonstrations took place throughout Poland, as hundreds of thousands of peasants gathered on town squares to hear antigovernment speeches. Officials counted 188 of them.[51] From August 16 to 25, millions stopped work, boycotted towns, and refused to ship food from their farms. The People's Party instructed its followers "not to buy nor to sell. Do not go to town, [and] work only to finish the chores on your farm."[52] Stryczek was among those from Wola Dalsza who manned the roadblock preventing traffic to the local seat of Łańcut. Throughout the boycott, they had to turn back only four basket-toting women from going to market along with two peasant carts; they allowed passage to one cart going to town for medical reasons.[53] Along with injunctions against violence or resisting arrest by the authorities, the People's Party underscored that "the strike is not to punish other social groups, nor is it aimed at starving the towns."[54] Socialist workers reciprocated by sending delegations to the demonstrations on August 15 and by staging large sympathy strikes in the final days of the boycott. Stryczek, like many Wici activists, regretted that the People's Party had refused Communist cooperation, despite the latter's willingness. Nor did the peasantists respond to overtures from the center-left Polish Socialist Party during its January convention to ally formally in the interest of a worker-peasant Poland.[55] Nonetheless, the strikers' conspicuous lack of hostility toward cities, along with workers' parallel actions, signaled a convergence of agrarian and socialist movements that distinguished Poland from other countries in the region.

The 1937 Peasant Strike was the largest mass protest action in interwar Poland. It encompassed 111 districts (46 percent of all districts, and the majority if urban districts are excluded) in twelve of sixteen provinces.[56] The People's Party discouraged its cadres in a few provinces—far western Pomerania, Upper Silesia,

FIGURE 8.1 Polish peasants marching to an assembly in the town of Jarosław on the first day of the Great Peasant Strike, August 15, 1937. Institute of the History of the Peasant Movement, Warsaw

and the eastern areas of Wilno/Vilnius and Volhynia—from participating for fear of inflaming ethnic tensions. Participation was strongest in former Habsburg Galicia, particularly in the Polish-majority areas of Cracow and Lwów provinces, with their high density of agrarian organizations and recent memories of peasant radicalism. Over one million peasants, or a third of all participants, went on strike in Cracow and Lwów provinces. Government repression was also fiercest in these areas. The authorities killed forty-four peasants in armed clashes and arrested four thousand more, of which two thousand stood trial.[57] Not until August 29 did the pro-regime *Gazeta Polska* even mention the strike. But although the strike did not achieve its stated goals, it forced some tangible governmental reform: several months after its conclusion, the government purged fascist sympathizers from its ranks; colonel Adam Koc, the totalitarian-inclined leader of the governing party, resigned his post; and Minister of Agriculture Juliusz Poniatowski began to address land reform in earnest.[58]

Elsewhere in east central Europe, peasants seemed to be more attracted to the political right. This did not mean that they had abandoned hopes of radical

FIGURE 8.2 Polish peasants marching to an assembly in the town of Jarosław on the first day of the Great Peasant Strike, August 15, 1937. Institute of the History of the Peasant Movement, Warsaw

change or embraced the conservativism of ruling parties. Rather, insurgent right-wing and fascistic movements appeared to offer more promising vehicles for their demands than the alternatives. Such movements garnered rural support in part for their extreme antiurban positions, which were, for their ideologues, inextricable from visceral anti-Semitism—an acceptable if secondary additive for many villagers. They also profited from a lack of competition from established agrarian parties. This was the case in Hungary, where the reintroduced limited franchise had excluded most peasants anyway, and in Romania, where the National Peasant Party (itself a precarious amalgam of contradictory elements) was discredited by its handling of the economic crisis. It applied to some extent to Slovakia as well, where the Republican Party appeared too Czech and bourgeois for a significant number of smallholders in Czechoslovakia's eastern half. That familiar tenets of the political left and right played a lesser role in determining peasants' political allegiances is borne out by the success that radical leftist movements, either communistic or heterodox agrarian socialist, enjoyed in some of the same places. Parallels could be found in other parts of Europe where agrarianism had not sunk deep roots in the

FIGURE 8.3 Polish peasants demonstrating in the town of Przeworsk on August 15, 1937. Institute of the History of the Peasant Movement, Warsaw

political landscape. Protestant farmers in northern Germany quickly became some of the staunchest supporters of National Socialism, as the 1920s slump in agricultural prices and later the Depression ruined their livelihoods.[59] In Spain, the economic crisis of the 1930s doomed the Second Republic's land reform, igniting competition among villagers for scarce resources and polarizing them between fractious left-wing organizations and those who sought protection from landowners and traditional elites.[60] The latter ultimately prevailed with the help of Franco's conservative right-wing Nationalists. In France too, fascism and communism both experienced a rural efflorescence in the 1930s as a reaction to Paris's apparent unconcern for the Depression-afflicted, culturally marginalized peasantry.[61]

In Hungary, an independent agrarian party had died with István Szabó in 1924, and arguably before that when he accepted a junior role for his Smallholders' Party in the government led by István Bethlen's conservative Unity Party. As the "Bethlen system" faltered at the end of the decade, and agricultural commodity prices plummeted, middling and prosperous farmers in 1930 revived the Independent Smallholders' Party with a program of moderate land reform and vague calls for suffrage expansion. This could hardly address the desperate conditions faced by wide segments of Hungarian society during the Depression, however. In 1933, 18 percent of Budapest's population was classified as destitute, and the national incidence of tuberculosis stood at over 15 percent, the highest in Europe. In the Hungarian countryside, millenarian and Pentecostal sects proliferated, with names like "Seedless Ones," "Starvers," "Tremblers," and "Devil Chasers."[62] With the Communist left banned since the Béla Kun episode, momentum belonged to the Hungarian far right. In 1932, Admiral Horthy appointed the hard-right anti-Semitic nationalist Gyula Gömbös as prime minister. The year before, the Budapest journalist Zoltán Böszörményi founded the radical-right National Socialist Party of Work, which soon became known, from its emblem, as the Scythe Cross (after its use of the swastika was prohibited). The Scythe Cross movement grew rapidly among farmhands and smallholders in the restive southeast of the country (the "stormy corner"), though found little support elsewhere. In 1936, thousands of Böszörményi's peasant followers hatched an abortive plan to march on Budapest and topple the regime.[63] The government responded by banning the party, arresting hundreds of rural activists, and staging a mass trial of the alleged ringleaders in Békés County. The movement went into terminal decline. Its leader's demagoguery notwithstanding, the Scythe Cross attracted some populist intellectuals who gravitated toward anti-Semitism and antiurbanism. It was not until 1939 that leftist populists established the National Peasant Party to confront German influence and domestic right-wing radicalization; their program of immediate confiscation of estate land without compensation won many adherents in the stormy corner as well.

The Depression did not hit neighboring Czechoslovakia as hard, but its effects were uneven, with German and Slovak regions much more seriously affected than Czech ones. While German industry endured severe overproduction and unemployment—in part because the Sudetenland had oriented itself culturally and economically toward Germany and Austria, which now sealed off their markets from external competition—the undercapitalized and backward Slovak countryside suffered acutely from the collapse of agricultural prices. The Slovak People's Party, which had consistently commanded over 50 percent of the ethnic Slovak electorate since 1923, remained wedded to its long-standing agrarian program of further land reform, action against usury, and increased investment in the countryside, alongside its nationalist autonomist and clerical demands.[64] Openly anti-Semitic and anti-Czech leaders of peasant stock rose to prominence, some of them doing little to hide their admiration for Nazi Germany and Fascist Italy. Nonetheless, through the

Depression years, nearly 20 percent of voters in Slovakia continued to support the state-maintaining Republican Party of Farmers and Peasants. And in overwhelmingly rural Subcarpathian Ruthenia, clear majorities voted for the Czechoslovak Communist Party between 1924 and 1935. Communists performed well in other economically marginal regions of east central Europe inhabited by nontitular nationalities—for instance, in Macedonia and in eastern Poland, where the Belorussian Workers' and Peasants' Hramada (1925) and the Ukrainian Peasants' and Workers Socialist Union (1927) arose under Communist tutelage.[65]

Fascism won its strongest rural mandate in Romania. Although the National Peasant Party had prevailed in the 1928 elections with over three-quarters of the vote, the economic crisis undermined much of its reform program, in particular its promise to expand rural credit. Indeed, the 1926 merger between the old Transylvanian National Party and the more left-wing Peasant Party established in 1918 had effectively neutered radical impulses in the new party. The National Peasant Party aimed to shore up the relatively prosperous minority of Romanian peasants by making it easier for them to acquire more land, often at the expense of their poorer neighbors, and by solidifying their control of rural cooperatives. Meanwhile, the party did almost nothing to fulfill its promised confiscation of large estates over one hundred hectares (250 acres) or encourage the rationalization of smallholdings by consolidating isolated strips.[66] King Carol II, who ascended to the throne in 1930, succeeded in splitting the National Peasants into a right wing, which supported him and his plans for royal dictatorship, and a left-center opposition, which included the party's most prominent leader, Iuliu Maniu, and the original Peasant Party founder Ion Michalache.

The chief beneficiary of the National Peasant Party's fragmentation in the early to middle 1930s was the Legion of the Archangel Michael, also known as the Iron Guard. Espousing a mystical, religiously tinged ultranationalism rooted in ideas of extreme anti-Semitism and national rebirth through sacrifice and martyrdom, the "legionary" followers of Corneliu Codreanu believed that the essence of Romanianness was to be found in the countryside, not in corrupt, allegedly Jewish-dominated cities. In a 1936 booklet, Codreanu asked rhetorically what his country consisted of, answering thus: "a bunch of some million peasants without any means of decent living, and poor; without culture, poisoned by alcohol and controlled by enriched Jews, who are masters of the Romanian cities; or of Romanians (prefects, mayors, police, gendarmerie, ministers) who are only pro forma in charge, since they are no more than humble executors of the Jewish plans."[67] Codreanu envisioned the future rise of a healthy, ethnically pure Romanian middle class in the country's cities, but for the time being Romania was to be found in the Christian peasantry.

Starting in autumn 1928, legionaries, themselves mostly urban students, though often of peasant stock, fanned out into rural areas to spread the gospel of their saintly leader. They began in the regions of Moldova, Bucovina, and Banat, and by 1930 their peregrinations covered Transylvania and Bessarabia.[68] Unlike the besuited National Peasant politicians who turned up in villages in cars, legionaries appeared on foot or on horseback, often dressed in traditional folk costume. Those who flanked Codreanu on his 1929 rides sported turkey feathers in their hats in the manner of *haiduc* outlaws—the Romanian equivalent of the south Slav hajduks discussed in chapter 6. These latter-day mendicants helped with farm work, lodging in the poorest peasant hovels without complaint and joining in folk festivities. Villagers began welcoming them with lit candles and reverent song. Government persecution of the Iron Guard added to their mystique at a time when politics and economics seemed to conspire against the peasantry. Codreanu himself wore traditional peasant garb in parliament.[69] In the December 1937 elections, amid widespread voter suppression and intimidation, the Iron Guard still came in a startling third place, with 16 percent of the vote, after the reigning National Liberals and the National Peasants, with whom Codreanu had concluded an electoral nonaggression pact. Evidence suggests that the Guard finished second in the elections before the results were manipulated.[70] Peasants composed a significant portion of the Guard's constituency, though most of its voters continued to hail from the urban middle classes. That such a considerable portion of the electorate chose Codreanu's nebulous and violent program of national rebirth likely had less to do with conviction than with their profound disillusionment with the mainstream parties. On the other hand, a left-wing peasant party established in 1933, the Ploughmen's Front, garnered minimal support, and virtually none outside of Transylvania.[71]

The Croatian Peasant Party retained some of its post-1918 revolutionary elan throughout the interwar period, though a more nationalist, rightward drift was detectable under Maček's leadership, and especially with the rise of its paramilitary arm, the Croatian Peasant Defense (Hrvatska seljačka zaštita, HSZ). Not officially established until spring 1936, Peasant Defense had its roots in the Yugoslav gendarmerie's persecution of Croatian villagers and in the more recent crackdown on the Croatian Peasant Party during the royal dictatorship.[72] King Aleksandar's autocracy, launched on January 6, 1929, and lasting until his assassination in 1934, not only suppressed political activity but also gave free reign to proregime paramilitary formations. Foremost of these were the Chetniks, which had links with the Serbian Radical Party as well as with state administrators and gendarmes throughout the kingdom. Marko Kostrenčić, the governor (*ban*) of the Sava Banovina that made up much of today's Croatia in the mid 1930s, noted that "fear of the chetniks was general, and when the cry 'chetnik' was heard in villages, psychosis immediately took hold, the alarm was sounded, people armed themselves and gathered for joint defense or closed themselves in their houses to defend themselves."[73] Numerous incidents were recorded in the early and mid-1930s of harassment and intimidation, sometimes violent, of Croatian peasants by Chetniks and gendarmes.

Peasants began to organize spontaneously for self-defense. Already from late May 1932, local clandestine units formed in the Croatian countryside without the knowledge of Peasant Party leaders. Vladko Maček realized that the party would have to take a firmer stance against what appeared to be government-sponsored terror. For a time, he cultivated links with exiled radical nationalist Ante Pavelić, whose fascistic Ustasha movement was launched around 1930. Many peasants supported one the Ustashas' first acts of antigovernmental terrorism in September 1932: an attack on a gendarme station in the Lika region (the later much-vaunted "Velebit Uprising"). But Maček's talks with Pavelić broke down after 1934 when the Ustashas helped murder King Aleksandar in Marseille. Maček's party could, under the right circumstances, be reconciled to the framework of the Yugoslav state, while the Ustashas refused any such compromise. In spring 1935, on the eve of the May elections to the skupština, the Peasant Party leadership approved the formation of self-defense committees in central Croatia to safeguard its voters from intimidation. Echoes of the revolt against livestock branding fifteen years prior could be heard when the police unmasked one conspiracy of party functionaries near Vojni Križ that aimed to arm all members and carry out a "slaughter of the gentlemen."[74]

Chetniks and gendarmes continued to harass the Croatian peasantry during the first year of Stojadinović's government, even murdering several Peasant Party members and one of its leaders, Karlo Brkljačić. The last straw, however, was a gathering on April 16, 1936, of Chetniks and youth members of the governing party at the estate of regime-friendly former *ban* Antun Mihalović in Kerestinec. Local peasants overheard some attendees say, "Where are those Maček supporters so we can kill them?" prompting the enraged crowd of two thousand people to assemble and demand that Mihalović hand over the offenders.[75] When he refused, the peasants stormed his estate, killing six. As tensions reached boiling point in the Sava Banovina, the Peasant Party publicly disavowed violence, though it decided in late April to organize armed "night patrols" to keep order in Croatian villages. Maček then issued instructions for the formation of Croatian Peasant Defense units to thwart intimidation by Chetniks and the government party. The government accepted assurances from Maček that the Croatian Peasant Defense would merely defend innocent peasants, initially tolerating the organization as a potentially useful bulwark against Communists and Ustashas. By the end of 1937, the authorities reported that Peasant Defense units counted fifty thousand members in the Sava and Primorska Banovina (the latter making up much of Dalmatia) with particular strength in the areas of southern Slavonia and central Croatia.[76] In these areas, units regularly numbered eight hundred to a thousand men.

Peasant Defense's autonomist, antiregime agenda came into clearer view. Its units clashed repeatedly with gendarmes in 1937 and 1938, while drilling of volunteers became commonplace in the countryside. In the village of Ždala near northern Croatian Koprivnica, one observer reported, drumming and trumpets at seven in the morning on February 24, 1937, mustered two hundred men armed with pitchforks and axes, who proceeded to train on an adjacent meadow for half an hour before dispersing.[77] The paramilitary organization came to resemble parallel authorities in large areas of the Croat-populated banovine, a development Maček encouraged as an important step toward Croatian autonomy. At a mass assembly of fifteen thousand people in June 1938 in Velika Gorica, he brazenly stated that "if the Serbs will not wish to cooperate with the Croatian peasant, we are today so strong that we can alone win secure freedom without the Serbs. The best guarantee of that [is] the political, economic, and educational organizations of the Croatian people, and especially the Croatian Peasant Defense."[78] In the late 1930s, a cult of personality formed around Maček himself, who tended to appear before his increasingly besotted followers on a white horse. From 1935, his birthday celebrations every July 20 occasioned mass gatherings in Zagreb; at the 1939 event, thousands of supporters chanted, incongruously, "Hail king Maček! Hail the president of the Croatian republic!"[79]

With the establishment of a semiautonomous Croatian banovina in August 1939, the fruit of negotiations between Maček and Prime Minister Dragiša Cvetković, peasant paramilitaries went on the offensive. Now the de facto authorities in the new Croatian substate, Peasant Defense units launched a campaign of retribution against their former oppressors. Between August 1939 and February 1940, they killed or wounded over two hundred people, particularly individuals associated with the government party.[80] In early 1940, an officer school opened in Zagreb under the aegis of the Peasant Defense, marking the organization's transformation into a professional fighting force, as well as its increasing distance from the village volunteers who had initially filled its ranks. A significant portion of the leaderships of both the Peasant Defense and the Peasant Party moved sharply to the right and forged closer ties with the Ustashas, who denounced Maček's *sporazum* (agreement) with Cvetković as a betrayal of Croatian self-determination. Peasantism receded into the background.

The German invasion that broke up Yugoslavia in early April 1941 led to the creation of the Independent State of Croatia under Ustasha rule. Yet Berlin turned to the radical nationalists only after Maček—far and away the most popular politician in Croatia, and thus the best candidate for an alliance—rebuffed German offers to lead a client state under their protection.[81] Aware of the divisions in his movement, Maček opted not to resist. In a radio broadcast on April 10, he called on all party members to obey the incipient Fascist authorities as they seized control of the Croatian capital. Some Peasant Defense units needed no encouragement. They secured key positions in the city and repulsed a trainload of Yugoslav Sokols and Slovene Chetniks who arrived early that morning to stop the takeover.[82] They also helped disarm loyal Yugoslav units and gendarmes throughout the new state. When Hitler decided that Bosnia and Herzegovina would be part of Croatian territory, Peasant Defense units accompanied the southward Ustasha campaign, participating in expulsions and massacres of Serb villagers. The experience horrified many of the peasant auxiliaries, whose loyalty to the new state was, in the eyes of Ustasha leaders, increasingly doubtful. After Peasant Defense members reaffirmed their allegiance to Maček in early May demonstrations, Pavelić and his allies began looking for excuses to eliminate the organization. For its part, even the right wing of the Peasant Defense found it hard to stomach Pavelić's May 18 cession of much of the Dalmatian coastline to Italy, a reward for Mussolini's years-long support of extreme Croatian nationalism. At the end of the month, the Ustashas began systematically disarming peasant paramilitary units, and in early June the organization was dissolved altogether. Numerous Peasant Party functionaries later died in the Independent State of Croatia's notorious concentration camps.

Amid the welter of east central European movements that from the late 1920s mobilized to counteract economic crisis in the countryside and authoritarianism, two broad trends were discernible. One was a realization that the parties that had represented rural interests in the 1920s could not, with the partial exception of those in relatively stable Czechoslovakia, solve the problems that beset peasants, at least not in the same forms as before. Hence the reinvention of peasant movements in Poland and Yugoslavia, often drawing on the energy of youth or paramilitary organizations. Another was a more insistent, aggrieved claim on national leadership in the face of regimes that hailed rural virtue but delivered few actual benefits to villagers. This could lead to integration into oppositional nationalist movements that were sometimes fascistic, as in Hungary and Romania; or it could lead to both competition and alliance with fascists, as illustrated by the ultimately tragic case of the Croatian Peasant Defense. It could even lead to an embrace of communism with overtones of national defense and liberation, as in far eastern Poland and Czechoslovakia and the southern regions Yugoslavia—all places inhabited primarily by ethnic minorities. The political nomadism of European peasants in the Depression decade was linked to their deep-seated belief, held more intensely than ever, that conventional parties of the right and left did not care much about them. Agrarian parties commanded sincere and consistent loyalties in the countryside, but in some east central European countries they had proven themselves unviable, and in parts of western Europe they had barely an impact on the political scene. In such places, the search for a reformist, rural-oriented nationalism, one that defined itself explicitly against the patriotism of governments ensconced in capital cities, even if these were festooned in peasant-friendly colors, often became paramount.

Although a younger generation of peasant activists with no memory of the Great War and the collapse of empires was moving to center stage, the continuities in people and places between the peasant revolution launched in 1918 and the strivings of the 1930s were striking. The southern Polish village of Grodzisko Dolne witnessed bloody clashes between peasants and authorities in both 1918 and 1933. Stryczek and the memoirist from Jasło area had both been in armed deserter bands late in the First World War, later joining the Wici in their respective villages. In the Moravian village of Prušánky, whence a multiparty deputation had departed in mid-1934 to air peasant grievances in Prague, unruly soldiers of the Slovácko Brigade had joined in the looting of Jewish shops in December 1918.[83] Such local stories suggest that the regions in which villagers mobilized most concertedly in the 1930s were some of the same ones where peasant violence and revolution progressed the furthest after the collapse of Austria-Hungary, among them former Habsburg west Galicia, southeast Moravia, much of central Croatia and Slavonia, and the southeast "stormy corner" of Hungary. The radical energies and memories of the immediate postwar period flowed into new initiatives and confrontations during the second decade of precarious peace.

The career of Alfonz Šarh, the Slovene Green Cadre leader from the Pohorje plateau near Maribor, demonstrated how twisting and unpredictable the paths trod by peasants in this era could be. A committed member of the Slavic nationalist gymnastics organization Sokol before 1914, he deserted from the Habsburg army during the war, emerging from the forests in 1918 to be feted as a fighter for south Slav liberation. While most Slovene peasants in the 1930s supported either the clerical People's Party or the left-leaning agrarian camp represented by the Slovene Union of Peasant Youths and Maidens, the contrarian Šarh joined Dimitrije Ljotic's fascistic, stridently anticommunist Zbor movement, which oscillated between extreme Serbian and Yugoslav nationalism. In the 1938 Yugoslav elections, he stood unsuccessfully as a Zbor candidate in the right-bank Maribor district and in 1940 was arrested for distributing Zbor fliers.[84] After Nazi German forces dismembered Yugoslavia in spring 1941, Ljotić was instrumental in establishing a violently anti-Semitic and anticommunist, though resolutely ruralist, Serbian quisling regime under his relative, General Milan Nedić.[85] Šarh himself, as we will see, would die heroically in January 1943 as a partisan commander in the Communist-led anti-German resistance movement, the National Liberation Front.

9

The Green Resistance

HITLER STARTED THE SECOND WORLD WAR in large part to conquer agrarian "living space" for the German nation. Like the other principal Axis powers, Fascist Italy and Japan, Nazi Germany believed it could avert terminal decline only by colonizing extensive agricultural land, which would be settled by ethnically pure farmers—allegedly the healthy and virtuous core of its people. Less romantically, all three countries saw land empire as the key to autarky, the only means to resist the rising global hegemony of the United States and its western European allies. Such calculations motivated Japan to occupy Manchuria from 1931 and Italy to seize Abyssinia in 1935.[1] The countryside of eastern Europe featured much more centrally in Nazi ideology. To Hitler and his followers, Germany's very survival depended on its acquisition of Poland and the territories of the western Soviet Union, not to mention the former Habsburg, mostly Czech provinces of Bohemia and Moravia, as well as, eventually, mostly Slovene Lower Styria and Carniola. The war that began in Europe on September 1, 1939, could not but have devastating consequences for the Slavic peoples that tilled these lands.

Subjected under German occupation to ethnic national persecution and economic exploitation, some peasants in east central Europe began to fight back. But they did so in large numbers only when Hitler's New Order became intolerable, which it often was not at first. Integration into Germany's *Großraumwirtschaft* offered tangible economic benefits to many villagers, at least initially, even under particularly ruthless occupation regimes, such as in Poland or Slovenia. Despite the radicalism of the Nazi project, wartime authorities' intrusion into the rural economy was not as shocking as it had been during the First World War, although it swiftly became more onerous and far more deadly. Peasants supported or joined resistance movements in increasing numbers, becoming, most consequentially, a critical factor in the victory of the

Communist-led Partisans in Yugoslavia. Facing widespread rural suspicion and hostility, Tito's Partisans revised their stance on the countryside over the course of the war to attract peasant support. Elsewhere, Communists made few if any concessions to peasant attitudes. Yet villagers often had little choice, since from mid-1941 Communists commanded the only effective domestic resistance to occupiers in many places. In Poland, exceptionally, agrarian politics flowed into an autonomous, peasant-led mass resistance movement with its own radical program for postwar society.

While social revolutionary visions animated some peasants during the Second World War, they had less purchase than in the previous conflict, and did not exceed the programs that had emerged in 1917–18. Survival became the foremost aim under exponentially better organized and more merciless wartime regimes. Paradoxically, however, alliance with revolutionary Communists presented villagers in some areas of the Nazi empire with their best chances of survival, which in turn nurtured radical expectations among a portion of them. Meanwhile, in striking instances rural resisters drew on models of resistance from the First World War. Scattered "Green Cadres" emerged in parts of the formerly Austro-Hungarian countryside, usually recruiting autochthonous peasants who desired some version of local self-determination and accepted integration into Communist-led resistance units only with the greatest reluctance. Elsewhere, Green Cadre veterans became Partisan leaders, employing the guerrilla tactics that they had honed during the previous war.

Occupied east central Europe also witnessed the rise of armed, mostly peasant movements so viscerally opposed to Communism that they willingly collaborated with Nazi authorities. The Organization of Ukrainian Nationalists, active in formerly Habsburg eastern Galicia, and the Slovene Home Guards in Carniola formed another pole of rural mobilization. There were also those peasants who volunteered for SS units, service in the Wehrmacht, and positions in other German organizations; a category encompassing the villagers who loyally served the Independent State of Croatia, which, to a much greater degree than other Axis satellite states, was utterly subordinate to the German military and economy. On balance though, most peasants in the region abhorred occupation, and could not bring themselves to actively support it, even if the majority often found it too risky to openly oppose it. The expanding influence of Communist organizations in German-ruled territories, particularly in dismembered Czechoslovakia and Yugoslavia, seemed to many the necessary price for liberation. Aware of the shifting dynamics on the ground, exiled agrarian politicians in London committed themselves in stronger terms to land reform, democracy, and anticommunism. Disappointingly for them, many peasants who lived through the occupation acquiesced in the establishment of Communist-steered "people's democracies" in exchange for land reform that went far beyond interwar legislation. It was the apparent betrayal of the postwar land reforms by Communist authorities, who from 1948 were bent on collectivizing agriculture, that prompted the final surge of "green" peasant resistance in east central Europe.

When German motorcycles roared through the village of Wola Dalsza one early autumn morning in 1939 on their way to Łańcut, most inhabitants regarded them with ambivalence. Jan Stryczek and a handful of other curious villagers journeyed to town to see for themselves what the occupiers were like. In his telling, the Germans treated the Polish population with respect upon their arrival, though they were visibly disappointed that local people could not be induced to rob or assault the town's Jews. Some Poles thought that the Germans, reputed to be civilized people, would behave well during the occupation. According to Stryczek, they had failed to reckon with "Hitlerite" Germans.[2] Conditions in Rzeszów County, now Reichshof County in the occupied Polish rump territory of the General Government, deteriorated swiftly. The new German administration imposed rapacious demands on Polish agriculture, which grew more severe over the course of the war. New hierarchies appeared in Wola Dalsza, empowering those with access to certain goods and privileges, while breeding enmity and distrust. At the same time, evasion of delivery quotas and illicit economic activities fostered solidarity among some villagers. Worsening shortages, along with the constant threat of violence, took their toll: alcoholism, despondency, and criminality gripped a significant portion of the population. Stryczek, like most east central European peasants, continued to farm as best he could under the changed circumstances. Although he had contacts with the burgeoning Polish resistance, he appears not to have strayed much from Wola Dalsza. In summer 1944, just before the Red Army pushed the Germans out of most of Lesser Poland, he went to Łańcut to market his surplus honey, as it had been an extraordinarily good year for beekeepers like himself. To his chagrin, the authorities took his honey but fled shortly thereafter—before he received the processed sugar he had been promised in exchange.[3]

Even in Poland, the country that arguably suffered more than any other during the Second World War, there were bright spots for agricultural producers. These were most obvious in the first year of the war, when demand for goods, which had plummeted in the late 1920s and remained low throughout the 1930s, now surged as the General Government was incorporated into the larger German economic zone.[4] Initial organizers of the Polish underground even feared the boom had made peasants unwinnable for the liberation cause.[5] Their fears proved unfounded, however. From the middle of 1940, the occupier required that villages meet delivery quotas (*kontyngenty*) of virtually all agricultural products and livestock; the new directives caused uproar in Wola Dalsza.[6] Quotas reached ruinously high levels in subsequent years: in 1942–43, they increased over the previous year by a factor of twelve for grain, by almost 1,000 percent on all fats, and were two and a half times higher for cattle. By 1943, total grain output in the territory of the General Government had dropped from prewar levels by almost 20 percent, and the potato crop had declined by over 35 percent.[7] Part of the decrease in yields could be attributed to loss of manpower, as 1.3 million inhabitants of the General Government—mostly smallholding peasants and agricultural workers—were forced to labor in the Reich.[8] All countries conquered by the Germans suffered economic exploitation, but eastern Europe, and Poland in particular, was targeted for deliberate plunder.

The sizable Polish territories swallowed in 1939 by Stalin's Soviet Union after the Molotov-Ribbentrop Pact did not even enjoy a temporary upturn in agricultural profitability. Following a short-lived redistribution of large estate land, the authorities press-ganged peasants onto collective farms. Villagers' purchasing power dropped as Polish złoty were converted to rubles at the unfavorable rate of 1:1 (before the war it had been 1:4). The new masters of the eastern kresy confiscated agricultural equipment, shipping it, along with dismantled industrial infrastructure, deep into the Soviet Union.[9] In light of the Communist authorities' blatant disregard for peasant livelihoods, it is little wonder that collectivized peasants welcomed Hitler's armies with open arms when they smashed into the USSR in the summer of 1941. Many peasants in northwest Russia greeted the Germans as liberators, undertaking a vast campaign of decollectivization under their watch.[10] Villagers were also among those civilians in the lands evacuated by the Red Army who murderously—and sometimes without Nazi encouragement—attacked numerous Jewish communities.[11] As in 1918–20, the Jews were held responsible for Communist abuses. But in much of the territory that came under German control as a result of Operation Barbarossa, collective farms were retained to ensure stable production; in Ukraine, for instance, the Germans allowed only 10 percent of *kolkhozy* to be dissolved.[12] After the euphoria of liberation from the Soviets wore off, the Nazis subjected peasants in Belarus, Ukraine, and the Baltic countries to extraordinarily savage exploitation.

In Wola Dalsza, Stryczek and his covillagers resorted to covert means of circumventing the controlled economy: "A silent war began with all directives of the occupier."[13] Peasants milled grain, churned butter, and slaughtered livestock under the cover of night, defying decrees that such activities be centrally controlled. When orders came to submit all quern stones to the authorities, villagers handed over their battered old equipment, keeping the newer stones for surreptitious milling. Butter churners were hidden in piles of grain, or in the snow during the winter. Stryczek built a special container under a brick pile to store bacon from his illicit pig slaughters. Although he maintained that "solidarity of all reigned in the village," he also described how dairy farmers attained unheard-of influence; the impossibly high quotas set for their products allowed them to become lords of the black market.[14] As in the previous war, townsfolk descended on the village to buy foodstuffs directly from farmers at negotiated prices or in exchange for manufactured goods. According to Stryczek, they were able to see that peasants, far from wallowing in plenty, had to sell virtually everything they produced just to survive.

If most Polish peasants survived occupation by wielding these "weapons of the weak"—that is, dissimulation, feigning ignorance, noncompliance, foot-dragging, pilfering, and so on against mightier authorities—growing numbers joined the armed resistance as well.[15] Uniquely in Poland, this took the form of a covert agrarian army, the Peasant Battalions (Bataliony Chłopskie), which was built on the radical People's Party activities of the 1930s.[16] Though they eventually made up nearly a third of the domestic Polish resistance, the Peasant Battalions had to contend with the consistent disapproval of the dominant Home Army (Armia Krajowa), as well as, initially, with the hesitancy of People's Party leaders.

From the moment the last of Poland's armed forces capitulated in early October 1939, Poles disagreed on who should lead the nation in exile and who should lead the domestic resistance to occupation. In some ways fortuitously, the Nazis accepted no Polish quisling, or high-level collaborators, instead murdering or imprisoning the Polish political class indiscriminately, which put all Polish political elites on equal moral footing. The situation was different for low-level Polish civil servants, many of whom were recruited into the German administration, and in the parts of Poland directly incorporated into the Reich ordinary Poles were conscripted into the Wehrmacht.[17] Those politicians who escaped from east central Europe gathered around the Paris-based government of General Władysław Sikorski, which later moved to London when France fell to Hitler's invasion. Along with representatives of the pre-1939

FIGURE 9.1 A standard of the Polish Peasant Battalions with the motto "[They] feed and defend". Museum of the History of the Polish Peasant Movement

Polish government, Sikorski's cabinet included People's Party leaders and Socialists, but prewar divisions in Polish politics proved intractable. All parties recognized that whichever political orientation prevailed in the resistance and in the exiled government would, if the occupier were defeated, shape Poland after the war.

In autumn 1939, rightist National Democrats and former Sanacja leaders began organizing the Union of Armed Struggle (Związek Walki Zbrojnej), which in 1942 would be renamed the Home Army. The peasantists felt they needed to have their own institutions within the Polish underground; a conspiratorial version of the People's Party (Stronnictwo Ludowe "Roch") was established in early 1940 at the initiative of Maciej Rataj, who fell victim to the Nazis a few months later. People's Party leaders in exile, such as Stanisław

Mikołajczyk, at first opposed the establishment of peasant armed forces separate from the Union of Armed Struggle. He and others grudgingly accepted the spontaneous formation of Peasant Guard (Chłopska Straż) units in the summer of 1940, approving in September the ideological-educational and operational aims submitted to London by the growing organization's leaders. Renamed the Peasant Battalions (Bataliony Chłopskie) the following year, the forces grew to 21,000 in 1942 and by mid-1944 had swollen to 157,000.[18] At that point the Home Army counted around 400,000 fighters.

Tensions existed on the ground between the rival organizations. Stryczek recalled an incident when Home Army recruits, mostly drawn from the prewar government-sponsored Green Shirts, and Peasant Battalion members exchanged fire during nocturnal drilling near Wola Dalsza.[19] Better armed and better staffed with professional military men, the Home Army conscripted many peasants too, though their morale sometimes fell short of expectations. At one oath-taking ceremony, peasants allegedly remarked: "If Poland will be like it was before the war, there is nothing to fight for."[20] Having attracted the lion's share of Poland's prewar officer corps, the Home Army had five times more officers than the Peasant Battalions to lead its conscripts. The *bechowcy*—as the peasant forces were colloquially known after the initials "B" and "Ch" of their name—established their own officer training school to remedy the shortage. Facing a dearth of battle-ready weapons, they set up workshops to refurbish arms left over from September 1939 and even manufactured some of their own.

The Peasant Battalions' strength derived in large part from their progressive vision for the Polish countryside of the future. Small- to medium-holding peasants owning between five and ten hectares (12–25 acres) predominated in their ranks, particularly in Lublin and Cracow provinces, where the organization was densest.[21] The social character of the *bechowcy* thus resembled that of the Green Cadres in the previous war. They assisted the People's Party by distributing its numerous illicit periodicals, one of which was called "Green Cadre"; by the end of the war 147 underground People's Party publications had been launched.[22] They undertook educational work at the village level to combat the effects of wartime social decay. The Wici youth organization played an important role in this and conducted its own autonomous campaign in Cracow province.[23] The Peasant Battalions also fostered and worked closely with a sister organization called the People's Union of Women (Ludowy Związek Kobiet). Established in 1942, the People's Union of Women counted twenty thousand members two years later, who were organized into nine departments devoted to various activities: organization, cooperative-economic

FIGURE 9.2 Volunteers of the Green Cross, the ambulance corps of the Peasant Battalions. Museum of the History of the Polish Peasant Movement

matters, propaganda, press and publishing, children, health and social care, women's education, the Green Cross, and legal matters.[24] Up to eight thousand of its members served in the Green Cross, the Peasant Battalions' principal ambulance corps, which operated hundreds of field medical stations and hospitals.

Altogether the Peasant Battalions fought 830 battles with occupying forces and carried out thousands of attacks on German police and administrators, as well as on the occupation economy's infrastructure: factories, railways, sawmills, mills, dairies, and milk collection points.[25] The dilemma of such actions, as everywhere in occupied Europe, was that they tended to provoke bloody reprisals by German authorities. Yet the severity of the occupation regime in Poland convinced many peasants that they had no choice but to resist. This was most starkly illustrated in Zamość region in 1942–43, where the Waffen-SS attempted to put into practice Heinrich Himmler's General Plan for the East (*Generalplan Ost*). Himmler's sinister design foresaw the Germanization of conquered territories in eastern Europe through forced deportations and deliberate starvation of tens of millions of Slavs and Balts alongside limited assimilation. It predicted the percentage of each targeted people that would need to be eliminated; the Poles, projected to lose between 80 and 85 percent of their population, were to be among the most devastated. To begin implementation of the plan, the Nazi leadership decided to clear the countryside around Zamość for German settlement, launching in November 1942 a nightmarish ethnic cleansing campaign against the Polish inhabitants. SS and German police units under the notorious Odilo Globocnik "pacified" 148 of the area's 686 villages, meaning that they were razed, usually by fire, with inhabitants rounded up and shot, or burnt alive in locked buildings, or else deported to camps. The Peasant Battalions were among the most active resisters of the campaign in late 1942 and early 1943. But a vicious counterinsurgency campaign in the summer of 1943 defeated them. By August 1943, over 110,000 people had been expelled from nearly 300 villages; 40,000 people in Zamość were murdered.[26] Many of the 10,000 Peasant Battalion fighters who perished during the war fell in this campaign.[27]

Polish peasants did not suffer only at the hands of Nazi occupiers. In the former eastern kresy, the Ukrainian Insurgent Army, established by the far-right Organization of Ukrainian Nationalists, recruited tens of thousands of Ukrainian villagers to rid their putative homeland of Poles. From spring 1943 to mid-1944, units of the Ukrainian Insurgent Army in Volhynia and later eastern Galicia slaughtered up to a hundred thousand mostly peasant Poles, often with shocking brutality. The insurgents, radicalized by successive Soviet and German occupations, sought to prepare the ground for an ethnically homogeneous Ukrainian nation-state; in Galicia they operated in concert with German overlords, but in Volhynia the followers of Stepan Bandera undertook a more murderous ethnic cleansing alone.[28] The forested, poorly connected tracts of the region favored their tactics.[29] Poles responded to the savage violence in kind, with Peasant Battalion units committing retaliatory atrocities against Ukrainian civilians in Lublin and Rzeszów regions.[30] In the apocalyptic conditions prevailing in Poland during the Second World War, the Peasant Battalions' claims to moral-political renewal did not preclude vengeful ethnic violence.

As German defeat appeared more likely, pressures mounted on the Peasant Battalions to integrate into the Home Army. Mikołajczyk, the new Polish premier-in exile after Sikorski's untimely death in July 1943, saw a united underground as imperative to safeguard Poland's future independence.[31] Many peasant units submitted to the Home Army, but a sizeable portion continued to fight on their own. Such frictions notwithstanding, the resistance forces, including the Communist-sponsored People's Army (Armia Ludowa), cooperated with one another successfully in some notable operations. In the summer of 1944, for instance, they jointly liberated a sizeable area around Pińczów in Kielce region (the so-called "Pińczów Republic").[32] The more serious challenges faced by the Polish underground in the countryside were to be found in rising social radicalism and despair. In May 1944, a high-ranking Home Army officer reported to London that "the leadership of the party must reckon with the radicalization of the masses, which in some areas takes on a disturbing character, not only socially, but also due to an overly favorable attitude toward Soviet saboteurs ([in] Podlasie and western Lublin region). The separatism of the Peasant Battalions and the revolutionary tendencies of their base [are] causing numerous conflicts with the Home Army in the field."[33] Not all of the problems had political implications. Stryczek, one of the relatively few Poles who viewed the westward Soviet advance with unalloyed optimism, was nonetheless alarmed by the growing influence of doomsday prophets in his village, a symptom of the broader apocalyptic mood in the Polish countryside.[34]

The Slavic peasants of east central Europe who were incorporated into the Third Reich before September 1939 endured tightening economic restrictions in wartime, but nothing like the regime instituted in occupied Poland and the western Soviet Union. To them, the worst features of life in greater Germany were campaigns to eradicate Slovene or Czech identity and forced enlistment into the German armed forces. In some areas of what is today Austria and the Czech Republic, the memory of the Green Cadres in the First World War inspired organized resistance. Willingly or not, these scattered groups would join the Communist-led Partisans by the latter years of the war.

The tactics of 1918 were most clearly deployed in the southernmost part of Austrian Carinthia, where Slovene villagers fled to the forests rather than serve in the Wehrmacht. While enlistment had begun already after Hitler's Anschluss of his homeland in spring 1938, it was the draft orders of December 1939 that caused hundreds of young men to desert in and around Bleiburg/Pliberk, Eisenkappel/Železna Kapla, and Zell/Sele.[35] In tiny, remote Sele alone, at least twenty young men refused to join Hitler's army. One of them, Pavel Male, remarked that his village, located on the other side of jagged peaks from today's Slovenia, "was always a republic unto itself. Only rarely did the count's gamekeeper or other oppressor come to us. They scrupulously avoided us."[36] Over 90 percent of the inhabitants of Sele had voted for union with Yugoslavia in the 1920 Carinthian plebiscite, in which most of the Slovene-speaking population (59 percent) had opted to remain in Austria.[37] National sentiment was only one of the motives for desertion. Jože Kelih, another inhabitant of Sele, feared the consequences of breaking the soldier's oath he had taken before God to Kurt Schuschnigg, the clerical-fascist dictator of Austria before the Anschluss.[38]

The Slovene deserters initially sought refuge in neighboring Yugoslavia, as yet untouched by the war. The harsh reception that awaited them quickly shattered their illusions of ethnic-national fraternity; Pavel Male and his brothers Ludvik and Feliks were sent to work in a quarry in Serbia. With the German invasion of Yugoslavia in April 1941, they escaped north to Slovenia and waited in hiding near the small town of Kamnik for the snow to melt before making their way over the mountain passes into Austria. Along with other returnees from occupied Yugoslavia, they formed a "Green Cadre" in the forests above Sele. According to Karel Prušnik, a peasant from Lobnig/Lobnik and subsequently a local Partisan leader known as "Gašper," the deserters were instrumental in fomenting resistance among Slovenes in Austria: "In the Carinthian forests they built themselves hideouts and as Green Cadres visited the valleys and ignited the rebellious spirit there."[39] Their presence in the woods no doubt left an imprint on the collective memory of the war in southern Carinthia, as a prize-winning 2011 novel by Železna kapla-native Maja Haderlap attests.[40]

Yet when the Partisans of the Communist-led Liberation Front (Osvobodilna fronta) first reached out to them in summer 1942, members of the *zeleni kader* balked. Having found out about the Slovene resisters near Sele, the Liberation Front dispatched Matija Verdnik-Tomaž, political commissar of the Upper Carniolan Detachment (Gorenjski odred), to recruit them. Pavel Male recalled that Tomaž approached his group, saying, "I came from the battalion with orders to visit the Green Cadre. . . . Lads, what sense is there in wasting away like this in a bunker [?] The Slovene nation needs soldiers."[41] Male was one of the few deserters who quickly resolved to join the Liberation Front. Others resented the defection. In September 1942, the Upper Carniolan District Committee reported that "the Green Cadre in the 'Chamois' district is very angry at their secretary Pavli [*sic*] because he established relations with Tomaž. They are building hidden bunkers to while away the winter."[42] Most struggled to make up their minds. The Sele peasant Tomaž Olip, nephew of an Austro-Hungarian deserter in the First World War, heeded the call of another Partisan activist, his friend Ivan Županc, alias "Johan," to join them in July. After participating for around a month in Partisan operations, including the murder of a forester, Olip decided to sever ties with the Liberation Front. He retreated to his forest bunker with a couple trusted friends.[43] It was here that the Gestapo ambushed him in early December, having ascertained the location of his hideout from a wounded Partisan who betrayed Olip under torture. Olip was arrested, interrogated, and then executed; the seizure of his diary, which he had kept since the summer, led to the capture of 200 other local Slovenes, of whom 134 were sentenced for various crimes. At the end of April 1943, the thirteen principal defendants—twelve men and one woman—were executed by decapitation in Vienna.[44]

The severity of repression drove more Slovene villagers in Carinthia into the arms of the Liberation Front. Even many among the local priesthood lent their support, notwithstanding their reservations toward any Communist-led organization.[45] By 1944, Prušnik-Gašper concluded, "the peasants were our zealous allies, local sons were mostly in the Partisans; many of them had previously been Green Cadres."[46] Prušnik-Gašper himself had arrived in the Liberation Front in August 1942 by a rather lengthy route, having oscillated between Austrian Social Democracy and Communism in the mid-1930s and spending the nearly two years' duration of the Nazi-Soviet Nonaggression Pact as a "lost sheep in Hitler's 'paradise.'"[47] Not all of the Carinthian Green Cadres reached the same destination. Olip's brother Janko, after having contacted the Partisans in early 1943, resolved to chart his own course. He survived the war in hiding, nurturing his Catholic faith and hopes in the royalist Yugoslav resistance led by Draža Mihailović's Chetniks.[48] Ultimately though, Prušnik-Gašper could stand by his pronouncement that "the Green Cadres were brave partisans. . . . These first resisters against Hitler were outstanding fighters, and many among them died a heroic death."[49]

The previous war's deserter movement echoed in the Protectorate of Bohemia and Moravia as well, if more faintly. The mostly gentle, rolling terrain in these provinces was far less conducive to guerrilla warfare than southern Austria, let alone Yugoslavia. Dense networks of roads, railways, and communication lines crisscrossed the Czech-inhabited territories since the nineteenth century, leaving far fewer areas distant from the state than in other countries.[50] The technologically advanced German occupiers exploited this infrastructure much more effectively than the Austro-Hungarian authorities had. Still, relatively small-scale Partisan groups established themselves in parts of the protectorate, particularly in southern and eastern Moravia.[51] "Green Cadre" was the name adopted by one of the very first armed resistance groups that arose in the protectorate, in the forested Hostýnské vrchy area of the Beskid Mountains of northeast Moravia.[52] It was initiated in late 1941, when activists from the regions of Prostějov, Kroměříž, and Ostrava began meeting at the cabin of a certain Josef Mastný above the village of Chomýž. The members of this Green Cadre were generally not peasants—laborers and at least one waiter joined its ranks—though some of the politically minded among them debated the respective merits of communism versus agrarianism.[53] With thirty men under arms, it relied on a support network of around ninety civilians in local towns and villages.[54] In late summer 1942, the Gestapo managed to suppress the conspiracy, arresting most of its members, of whom dozens were eventually executed. The group's name had literary rather than folk cultural origins: survivors attributed it to the name of Jan Václav Rosůlek's 1928 novel, discussed above.[55]

The Czech Green Cadres of the First World War had a more distinguished legacy in the exploits of the Roma guerrilla Josef Serinek. A veteran of the organized west Bohemian deserters described in chapter 2, Serinek ended up in the Lety concentration camp for gypsies in August 1942. He escaped in September along with several others, but his wife and children were not so fortunate: from Lety they were deported to Auschwitz, where they perished. Serinek's experience in 1916–18 shaped his involvement in the anti-Nazi Partisans, as his conversation with a Catholic priest who sheltered him in west Bohemian Potvorov reveals: "He [the priest] asked me if I would again join the Green Cadre and I said that I don't know what it will be called, but that they won't catch me alive, that at most they can murder me and that I want to fight."[56] Toward the end of 1942, Serinek attempted to put to use the know-how with explosives that he had gained "from that commander of ours in the Green Cadre" to destroy a bridge in central Bohemia, but the operation went wrong, leaving him badly burned and scarred.[57] He survived his injuries and made it in 1943 to the Vysočina region that straddles eastern Bohemia and western Moravia. Here, with the help of sympathetic villagers, he became a celebrated resistance fighter under the nom de guerre "Black Partisan."[58] Though unwaveringly devoted to Czechoslovak liberation, he was embittered both by the shabby treatment he received from resistance leaders and, above all, by the complicity of many ordinary Czechs in the Roma holocaust.[59] It was no doubt his Roma identity that condemned Serinek to relative obscurity in triumphalist Communist histories of the Second World War.

The destruction of the Kingdom of Yugoslavia in April 1941 presented peasants there with arguably the most difficult choices. A vicious, multisided conflict resembling a civil war afflicted many regions of the former multinational state.[60] On the one hand were the occupying German and (until mid-1943) Italian armies. Allied with them, but often reluctantly and unreliably, were collaborationist forces, such as the Ustasha Militia and the Croatian Home Guard (Hrvatsko domobranstvo) of the Independent State of Croatia, the security forces and government-affiliated paramilitaries of the rump Serbian territory under Milan Nedić, Slovene anticommunist volunteers, and a sizeable Bosnian Muslim SS division. Locked in a life-and-death struggle with all the aforementioned, and with each other, were the two principal resistance movements: the royalist and mostly Serb nationalist Chetniks under Dragoljub "Draža" Mihailović, who aimed to restore the prewar Kingdom of Yugoslavia, and the Communist-led Partisans under Josip Broz Tito, who pursued revolutionary reconstruction of the south Slav state. These labels, complicated enough on the surface, concealed much inner factionalism and side-switching, which turned former enemies into allies and vice versa in sometimes dizzyingly rapid succession. The mostly peasant recruits who found their way into various Yugoslav formations often changed allegiances over the course of the conflict, depending on who seemed most likely to safeguard their livelihoods or who appeared strongest at any given moment.

Slovenia found itself torn apart by rival camps in an otherwise ethnically and religiously homogeneous population. While Germany annexed Lower Styria and Upper Carniola (three-quarters of all Slovene-speakers), Italy extended its control from the Slovene-speaking Littoral over Inner and Lower Carniola, with the minor Axis player Hungary swallowing the eastern Prekmurje region. The Slovene nation was condemned to ethnocide: the systemic destruction of Slovene culture and forced assimilation, particularly under German rule. It was to his officers in Maribor, the principal city of Lower Styria, that Hitler uttered his famous phrase "Make this land German again!"—implying that its mostly Slavic character was a corruption of its original Germanic state. Young Slovene men in Styria were conscripted in their thousands into the Wehrmacht or German police units. Tens of thousands of those deemed inimical to the German nation or un-Germanizable were deported, or fled, to fascist Croatia and Serbia.

Resistance under Communist leadership had begun in Slovenia already in the summer of 1941, but peasants often tried to keep their heads down, attempting to weather the hostile circumstances as best they could, and in some cases profiting under the occupation. In the Italian zone, Partisan terror against passive rural communities along with fervent, religiously hued anti-Communism led to the formation in late summer 1942 of fascist-sponsored anti-Partisan forces made up chiefly of Slovene villagers. These Village Guards (*vaške straže*), which were expanded and renamed Home Guards (*domobranci*) under the Germans after Mussolini's fall in summer 1943, aimed to defend the rural population against Partisan encroachments and reprisals. Yet, following the line of some leading figures in the clerical Slovene People's Party, they also tried to secure a favorable position for the Slovene nation within the Axis system through ruthless anti-Communist violence.[61] In the final years of the war, a bloody fratricidal conflict consumed Slovenia, pitting around eighteen thousand Home Guards against thirty to forty thousand Partisans, most of whom were concentrated in the former Italian-ruled Province of Ljubljana.

Peasants made up significant portions of both forces, but they were particularly conspicuous among the collaborationist Village Guards and Home Guards. Anti-Communist parish priests exercised considerable influence over their rural congregations in many villages. In the Krim Massif south of Ljubljana, for instance, peasants made up 77 percent of the approximately 150 men who joined the Village Guards in summer 1943 after their release from Italian internment on the island of Rab.[62] Significantly, most of them hailed from certain Krim villages, rather than other superficially similar villages where the Liberation Front recruited its numerous fighters.[63] And while some villages displayed a clear preference for one side over the other, others were divided down the middle. In the developing civil war, local experiences of occupation and of dealings with Partisans determined loyalties more than class identities.[64] Some villagers who joined the Liberation Front early in the conflict did so out of political sympathies, having been members of the Yugoslav Communist Party or of the leftist agrarian youth movement.[65] Others were veteran village radicals—like Ivan Krajec, who at the end of 1918 had helped establish the short-lived "republican" authorities in Kandija near Novo Mesto.[66]

The Styrian Green Cadre veteran Alfonz Šarh joined the Liberation Front when he decided that it was his only chance of survival. As it became clear that the German occupiers were conscripting men for military and police units, Šarh's wife Elizabeta went to the local administration in Ruše to request an exemption for her husband; with nine children including a small baby at home, she could not run the family farm on the northern slopes of the Pohorje Massif alone.[67] She received a letter that she was instructed to deliver to German authorities in Maribor, but instead brought it home to Alfonz. Rather than containing a discharge, it advised Styria's new authorities to keep a close watch on Šarh, a known enemy of the German nation and a former deserter during the First World War. His recent affiliation with Dimitrije Ljotić's fascistic Zbor movement—whose members became prominent collaborators in

FIGURE 9.3 Alfonz Šarh and his family in the late 1930s. National Liberation Museum Maribor

both Serbia and Slovenia—carried little weight now. Realizing his predicament, he built a bunker in the forest and readied a hiding place under the floorboards of his house behind the wood stove.

German soldiers finally came for him and his family on the night of August 3, 1942. Alfonz, awake baking bread with Elizabeta, disappeared in time under the floorboards. The soldiers, accompanied by people whom his daughter Jelka described as "local traitors," arrested Elizabeta and all the children, sending them to Maribor and thence to a temporary camp for families of dangerous outlaws in Celje (all except for the infant Marija, who was given to relatives to care for). Alfonz escaped to the forest, where he joined the Ruše Company (Ruška četa) of Partisans. In the Celje camp, meanwhile, women over eighteen were separated from their children amid anguished screaming and then transported via Graz to Auschwitz; Elizabeta died there in mid-November 1942. The children spent several weeks in a transit camp in Frohnleiten near Graz. The three older boys—Lojzek (age sixteen), Jožef (age fourteen), and Ivan (age thirteen)—managed to abscond from the poorly guarded facility, making their way covertly back to their home village, where Alfonz's sister Terezija hid and fed them in the nearby forest. Soon after, Alfonz came to take his sons away to the Ruše Company, which by the end of the year had been integrated into a bigger unit called the Pohorje Battalion (Pohorski bataljon).[68] The five remaining children in Frohnleiten were divided by age and sex and sent to various camps in Bavaria, where they survived the end of the war.

Alfonz and his elder sons did not live to see liberation. In December 1942, the Gestapo caught Slavko Vigec, another escapee from Frohnleiten and a Partisan. Under torture he divulged the location of the Pohorje Battalion's winter camp in the hollow at Trije Žeblji. On the morning of January 8, 1943, numerous German police units arrived in Ruše by train and advanced into the hills in three columns. On the way to Trije Žeblji, the troops apprehended Lojzek along with several other members of a patrol, shooting them immediately. The approximately two thousand men in the German force encircled the seventy partisans in three lines. The Pohorje Battalion fought doggedly to the last man, or child—thirteen-year-old Ivan ("Vanček") was among the last killed. Nazi commanders forced local peasants to cart the maimed partisan corpses first to the village of Oplotnica and then to Maribor as a grisly warning to other potential resisters.

It was escalating violence of this sort that convinced Ivan Puntar-Štacnar, a prosperous farmer from Unec in Inner Carniola, to steer clear of both the Partisans and the collaborationist force raised in his village. A devout Catholic and staunch supporter of the clerical Slovene People's Party, Puntar-Štacnar recorded a solemn entry in his diary on December 15, 1940, the day after Anton Korošec died: "Death of the greatest most beloved dr. Anton Korošec . . . the true father of our nation."[69] From April 1941, the occupiers' ethnocidal policies against the Slovenes, particularly in the regions under German control, enraged him. In August of that year, he fumed against "the German, that inhuman brute [who] has conspired to eliminate our nation from the face of the earth . . . the barbarian has deported from Styria all priests, teachers, doctors, lawyers, and even wealthier landowners, took from them all their property, even clothes, [and taken] livestock from peasants."[70] He conceded that Italian occupation in Unec was considerably milder, despite the reintroduction of the command economy. Among other things, the new controls meant that for agricultural products "we get nothing or shamefully low prices."[71] But by the end of the year, Puntar-Štacnar could revel in his unexpectedly high earnings since Yugoslavia disintegrated. "1941 was a terrible year of war and horror," he wrote in the year-end summary in his diary, "but economically it was favorable, everything there was from the harvests was sold."[72]

The next year was even better:

> The year 1942 was with respect to weather exceptionally favorable, fine, dry, just the right amount of rain. . . . In this year there was so much profit for us that we received around 40,000 lire for livestock, and around 60,000 for harvested crops. True abundance in our house, in this year we built a cellar by the pigpens, we renovated the mill, built a kitchen by the pigpens, a silo, a fruit drying building, [we bought] a new mill with white stone and a husking machine, which cost 40,000 lire, all the other buildings cost around 60,000. In this year we also bought a machine for digging potatoes, a sprayer for fruit, a plow, a hay presser, and almost an entire trousseau for [our] daughter Ivana![73]

The occupier's repressive policies and indications of civil war brewing in the Slovene population cast a shadow over Puntar-Štacnar's wartime economic miracle. In mid-May 1942, he jotted down his first mention of "chetniks, called partisans [who] everywhere attack the Italian occupying army. Assembled in the forests, they dismantle railways, and with ambushes attack automobiles with which the army travels."[74] Dreadful reprisals resulted, as innocent people were beaten and killed, and villages torched. Although he did not confuse the Chetniks and Partisans again, he noted with alarm the escalating violence between the resistance and occupiers in the summer of 1942. He and other villagers in Unec had to endure stricter curfews and during weeks when the Italians conducted counterinsurgency offensives, travel beyond the village, or even one's own property, was prohibited.[75] In the autumn, he finally linked the Partisans with the Communists, whom, as a loyal People's Party member, he hated and feared. Peasant self-defense units formed in response, though he often referred to them using the pejorative term "white guard": "The army hunted the communists also called partisans, who were hiding in the forests and pillaged peasant holdings, killing their opponents. [B]ecause of the atrocities committed by these partisans, an armed organization was formed from the people called the White guard, [and] almost everywhere where there were not army units village guards were established."[76] These same Partisans, he noted reprovingly at the end of the year, were responsible for murdering fourteen priests in the Province of Ljubljana.[77]

However, like many peasants, Puntar-Štacnar stood by his fellow villagers whatever their political inclinations. At the end of 1942, he tried to intercede with the Italian district authorities for a woman neighbor who faced eviction orders because one of her sons had joined the Partisans (her husband and other sons had already been interned).[78] He managed to obtain only a short delay on her behalf and he blamed the occupier for pressuring young men against their will to join Village Guards, thus inciting a "fratricidal war, so they could rub their hands and destroy our people."[79] When his farmhand Jože received orders from the authorities to enlist in the Unec Village Guard at the end of January 1943, Jože furiously (and wrongly) accused his employer of passing his name to the Italians. Puntar-Štacnar, distraught after the commotion caused in his house, felt obliged to explain in his diary: "We are neither for the white guards nor for the partisans since it is an indescribable misfortune for our nation and we rejected all of them."[80] After his own son Rado was conscripted against his will into the Village Guard in February 1943, Puntar-Štacnar stopped keeping a diary.

He survived the war, dying in 1972 at the age of eighty-four. He did not record his thoughts on the remainder of the war or on the Communist regime. The Partisans eventually prevailed over their opponents on Slovenian soil, but at terrible cost. The anti-Communist militias came under German direction after the capitulation of Italy. As Home Guards they swore public oaths of loyalty to Hitler and the SS, irrevocably compromising themselves in the eyes of the western Allies. When the remnants of their army and their families tried to escape north to Austria, along with tens of thousands of Ustashas, British forces turned them over to Tito's Partisans. Nearly all the repatriated Home Guards—around twelve thousand people—perished in clandestine mass executions on the territory of today's Slovenia.[81]

The conflict was even more complex and brutal in Bosnia-Herzegovina. Incorporated into the Independent State of Croatia in April 1941, the former Austro-Hungarian territory immediately bore the brunt of the Ustashas' violent fantasies of a racially pure Croat state. Because Orthodox and Muslim populations far outnumbered Catholics in Bosnia, Ante Pavelić's regime decided that 750,000 Bosniaks were "Muslim Croats," making them a crucial element in the state's ethnic Croat "majority" as well as potential allies in a genocidal campaign against Serbs. Ustasha forces, augmented by local Muslim recruits in many places, massacred thousands of Orthodox villagers in the spring and summer of 1941 and forced thousands more to flee southward and eastward. Terrorized Serb peasants rose in revolt, committing retributive atrocities against Muslim villages and increasingly submitting themselves to Chetnik command or, especially in the west of the region, to the Communists. In the many ethnically and religiously mixed areas of Bosnia, the conflict took on features of a civil war. Although a relatively small proportion of the Bosnian Catholic population, and an even smaller segment of Muslims, took part in the

Ustasha atrocities, communities fractured along ethnic-religious lines, with each group suddenly countenancing—and, in horrifying instances, attempting to implement—the annihilation of the other.

Over the course of the war, a majority of Bosnian Muslim villagers came to support the Communist-led People's Liberation Movement (Narodnooslobodilački pokret). If any ideology undergirded their oscillations, which overall could be characterized as a shift from cautious acceptance of Fascist Croatia to allegiance with the Partisans, it was Muslim autonomism.[82] A Muslim-majority administrative unit had disappeared in prewar Yugoslavia with the 1929 introduction of banovine; Bosnia-Herzegovina had been divided between three Serb-majority banovine and one Croat-majority one. By the end of the 1930s, the Yugoslav Communist Party adopted virtually the same autonomist platform as the main prewar Islamic party, the Yugoslav Muslim Organization (Jugoslavenska muslimanska organizacija), becoming more vocal supporters of Bosniak demands in wartime. The route Bosnian Muslims took to the People's Liberation Movement was often circuitous. Wartime conditions and disillusionment with Ustasha-ruled Croatia prompted them to consider a wide range of alternative routes to autonomy. One of them was under direct Nazi patronage: the plan for a mostly Muslim SS division—the first with a non-German majority—received approval in late 1942. The thirteenth SS Division "Handschar" grew from around twelve thousand men in April 1943 to almost twenty thousand by the end of the year.

Peasant self-defense, sometimes drawing on preexisting models of resistance, motivated Muslim villagers on a more elemental level. In the second half of 1943 around Tuzla, northeast Bosnia, a "Green Cadre" formed, growing from a couple of hundred men in July 1943 to between eight and ten thousand fighters organized in loosely connected bands by spring 1944.[83] Its founder was Nešad Topčić, a university-educated former civil servant, economics teacher, and agricultural merchant. In 1943, he decided to confront the terror raining down on Muslim villages in northeast Bosnia from overwhelmingly Serb Chetniks and mostly Serb Partisans with his own Islamic defense force. Previously allied with the Ustashas, Topčić was known to their intelligence service as a man who "continues to claim that he is a Croat whose only goal is *to destroy the Chetniks and the Partisans* . . . [but who] follows the path exclusively of purely Islamic politics and its true realization in the goal of the *Autonomy of Bosnia-Herzegovina under the Green Banner*."[84] In Topčić's *zeleni kadar*, forest green merged with the color of paradise in the Quran; many recruits wore fezzes adorned with the crescent moon.

Nominally allied with the Croatian Home Guard from January 1944, the Tuzla-area Green Cadre waged its own war against the encroachments of Chetniks and Partisans on the Muslim-majority countryside. It won some victories in the winter of 1943–44 in tandem with a German counterinsurgency campaign, but a buildup of Partisan forces in spring 1944 resulted in harsh reprisals against Muslim villages that supported the Green Cadre. Topčić knew that his backwoods military operation could not alone liberate his followers. Exploiting his knowledge of German and his German connections, he made three trips to Berlin over the course of 1944 to lobby Hitler's regime. These came to naught.[85] From September 1944, the green forces held talks with the People's Liberation Movement on the terms of their unification. Negotiations broke down when the Communists rejected Topčić's demands that his men remain exclusively in the Tuzla region under their own commanders. He was assassinated in December 1944 by Partisans dressed as Home Guards. At this point, many of the Greens had already deserted to the Partisans, and many more would follow after Topčić's death.[86]

Other Muslim "Greens" established themselves around Cazin in northwest Bosnia, one of the province's poorest areas. These were remnants of Husnija "Huska" Miljković's self-defense militia, which had grown from the middle of 1943 to around three thousand men organized into two brigades and eleven battalions.[87] Miljković had joined the Partisan movement in 1941, but fell out with them in early 1943, taking his own force into alliance with the Ustashas and receiving materiel from the Germans. Although he rejoined the Partisans in February 1944 when it seemed that German defeat was inevitable, two former associates killed him in April.[88] Throughout his tergiversations, Miljković appears to have been motivated primarily to achieve local autonomy for the mostly Muslim farming population of Cazin region, which regarded him as a folk hero. Those of his followers who refused (re)integration into the People's Liberation Movement called themselves "Greens" and remained in the local forests harassing the incipient authorities well after May 1945. Still confronted with this menace in northwest Bosnia in August 1945, Communist officials alleged that opportunistic local councilors around Bihać "support groups of the Green Forces and provide them with intelligence; through their errors in work, they carry out open sabotage which they justify on the grounds of ignorance of their work, thereby compromising our government among the people."[89] Newly established armed forces proved themselves unreliable as well: "The People's Militia is extremely weak. It lacks the required number of militiamen. The role of the militia is not properly grasped by the military commands and into it are sent illiterate people, even those who had been in the Chetniks and Home Guard. We have cases at Cazin where the militiamen meet with the Green Forces and, instead of shooting at them, surrender their weapons to them without firing a shot."[90]

Promises of national self-determination similarly motivated Catholic villagers in Croatia to turn to the People's Liberation Movement from 1943 on. Though celebrated by Ustashas as the authentic core of the reborn Croat nation, most Catholic peasants had adopted a position of passivity early in the war, in line with most Croatian Peasant Party leaders who had not gone over to the Fascist camp. Orthodox peasants in Croatia had meanwhile faced extermination from spring 1941 and comprised the bulk of Partisan units in the Banija, Kordun, and Lika regions.[91] Threatened by the increasing anarchy and bloodthirstiness of the Ustasha regime, and frustrated with the passivity of Peasant Party leaders, ethnic Croat villagers began to join the Partisans in droves. The number of Partisan fighters in Croatia grew from twenty-five thousand at the end of 1942 to over a hundred thousand a year later, making up fully a third of the Partisan forces in Yugoslavia. According to data from late 1944, peasants made up 65 percent of the Croatian National Liberation Army.[92]

The Communists successfully ingratiated themselves with peasants throughout war-ravaged Yugoslavia by softening the Marxist line on rural economic transformation. They silenced their vitriol against "kulaks" and declared Soviet-style collectivization to be an "extreme left-wing deviation."[93] In increasing measure, they cast small and medium peasants as the true victims of capitalism, rather than the landless poor. Having been forced out of Yugoslavia's cities early in the conflict, the Communists shrewdly recognized that the support of middling peasants would be crucial in their multifront struggle. Although talk of socialist agriculture did not entirely disappear from their propaganda, many villagers believed that it simply meant greater egalitarianism in the countryside. The Partisans who made their home for years in rural areas promised to rebuild the farm economy after the unprecedented destruction wreaked by the Second World War. Throughout the state it was estimated that the war had destroyed 56 percent of fixed agriculture capital, 20 percent of houses, and 24 percent of orchards. Meanwhile, the number of horses had fallen by 60 percent, sheep by 63 percent, cattle by 56 percent, and pigs by 59 percent.[94]

The prominent agrarian politicians who fled east central Europe before Hitler's armies were aware that they would have to contend with much-strengthened Communist movements after the war's end. From London exile they drafted robust plans for the postwar reconstruction of their countries based on land reform, international regional federation, and unambiguous orientation toward the Western Allies. Not yet prepared to reject the Soviet Union's help as decisive battles on the Eastern Front still raged, they nonetheless reaffirmed their view that private property was sacrosanct and that geopolitical stability in central and eastern Europe required federative agreements within the region, not sociopolitical systems imposed from without.

Already in autumn 1940, exiled agrarians convened in London as an East European Discussion Group under the auspices of the Fabian Society.[95] They included Polish, Czech, Hungarian, Croat, Serb, and Bulgarian peasantist politicians, along with Mihály Károlyi, who had served as Hungarian prime minister in 1918–19. In early July 1942, many of the same men—together with Stanisław Mikołajczyk and representatives from Greece, Romania, Slovakia, and Slovenia—participated in an "International Agrarian Conference" at Chatham House in London.[96] The result was a twelve-point "Peasant Programme" signed by twelve of the conference attendees. Point 1 committed the signatories to far-reaching land reform based on private property: "'The Land for the Peasant' is our watchword. As we believe that the land should belong to those who work it, we cannot tolerate the existence of multitudes of landless men, or men with too little land, side by side with existence of large estates. We regard the expropriation of the large owners and the sub-division of their estates as an essential social reform in those regions where peasant proprietorship does not prevail."[97] Subsequent points called for structural reform of the agricultural economy, industrialization in service of peasant interests, as well as rural education. In the prologue and the final point, the manifesto foresaw significant involvement of the Allies—Britain, the United States, and the Soviet Union—in the postwar reconstruction of the region, but it reserved special praise for the "principle of Democracy and the Four Freedoms proclaimed by President Roosevelt."[98] Point 11 urged reconciliation between the nations of central and southeast Europe.

Milan Hodža, the last prime minister of the Czechoslovak First Republic and a prominent agrarian ideologue, elaborated at length on the idea of reconciliation in his 1942 book *Federation in Central Europe: Reflections and Reminiscences*.[99] Unlike Edvard Beneš, who headed Czechoslovakia's government in exile, Hodža preached extreme caution in all dealings with the Soviet Union.[100] Rapprochement between Czechoslovakia and Poland was to be the bedrock of his envisioned federation, which would encompass Hungary, Austria, Romania, Yugoslavia, Bulgaria, and Greece. Once they had recovered from the war, these countries would perforce "set up a Federal Treaty establishing common affairs and the mutual obligations by virtue of which their own constitutions are modified by transmitting the administration of those common affairs to the Federal Government."[101] The federation's common affairs would extend to a customs union (especially for agricultural produce) and a common currency, along with joint fiscal and trade policies, defense and foreign policy, and a robust legal basis for cooperation, in particular to implement reciprocal minority protection. The Danubian Club, founded in London in November 1942 by members of the East European Discussion Group, authored an analogous report in July 1943 called "Central and South-Eastern European Union." It outlined a federal union of the same countries plus Albania. A bicameral legislature composed of a union council and a council of states would govern the polity; elected officials would choose a council of ministers responsible for collective defense, foreign policy, and trade within and beyond the union.[102]

Such ideas were never realized, but at the war's end there remained ample cause for agrarians' optimism. The Polish People's Party had at its disposal a sizable army in the form of the Peasant Battalions. In places where free elections were permitted by the new Soviet authorities, revived agrarian parties performed well. In Hungary in November 1945, the Independent Smallholders Party led by Ferenc Nagy won 57 percent of the vote, far outpacing the rival Left Bloc, which itself included the socialist National Peasant Party. In Bulgaria, where Communists enjoyed genuine popularity and controlled local politics after 1944, the Bulgarian Agrarian National Union still won almost a third of the vote in relatively free elections held in October 1946. In other places, however, agrarians could not contest free elections. Neither Romania nor Poland experienced unmanipulated elections after their "liberation" by the Red Army. In Yugoslavia, Tito's victorious Communists lost no time in establishing a one-party state. Already before the Communist takeover in Czechoslovakia, President Beneš's decrees barred the once-mighty Republican Party from reestablishing itself because of its involvement in the collaborationist Second Republic (1938–1939) under Emil Hácha.

Although agrarianism could not immediately revive its prewar party existence, there were signs that peasants throughout liberated Europe would be receptive to its program. The peasants who powered Communist-led resistance movements in southern and southeastern parts of the continent appeared to gravitate more to leftist agrarian democracy than to Marxism-Leninism. This applied to the villagers who helped Tito win the "People's/National Liberation

Struggle."[103] It also held true for the Greek peasants who took up arms in the Communist-led National People's Liberation Army. The rural *andartes* of the Greek resistance often proudly called themselves Communists, yet they espoused more rough-hewn agrarian populist principles of direct democracy, local autonomy, just redistribution of large estate land, and just rewards for hard work.[104] In southern Italy after the fall of the Fascist regime, peasants in dozens of villages and small towns enacted "communism" according to their own script, establishing short-lived local "republics," redistributing large estate land, and setting up "people's courts" to try their former oppressors.[105] Not surprisingly, the Italian Communist Party had no place for such unruly experiments in its official histories of the Mezzogiorno.

Some east central European peasantist leaders reckoned that by cooperating with the Communists in the short run, they might secure agrarianism's political future in the region. The villagers who still made up marked demographic majorities had apparently not forsaken agrarianism, even if they now inclined toward a more radical version of it. Such calculations underestimated their rivals' uncompromising and single-minded quest for power, however. Stalin's satraps inexorably eliminated their would-be agrarian partners from postwar coalitions, often with considerable brutality. The Romanian scholar and agrarian political activist David Mitrany even claimed that the establishment of "People's Democracies" across east central Europe in the aftermath of the war had as its primary goal to "provide insurance against any possible recrudescence of peasant strength."[106]

There is some plausibility to his claim, for with the nationalist right tainted by collaboration and Social Democrats either associated with the failed interwar regimes or susceptible to influence from their left, Communists rightly regarded the peasantists as their chief competitors in the postwar political landscape. After infiltrating and fomenting division in agrarian organizations during the first two postwar years, escalating Cold War tensions in 1947–48 gave Communists the pretext to ruthlessly eliminate them. Hungarian Communists, alarmed by the 1945 election results, at first attempted to win over leftist agrarian activists in the burgeoning People's Colleges, a movement supported by Minister of the Interior László Rajk. Even after their integration into the Communist-controlled National Association of People's Colleges, the agrarian People's Colleges continued to multiply, though fears that peasantism would vitiate their adherence to Marxism led to their disbanding in 1948–49.[107] The independent-minded Rajk was executed after a notorious 1949 show trial. From 1948, the regime imprisoned leaders of the Smallholders Party or else forced them into exile; the National Peasant Party likewise ceased to exist in February 1949.

The process was especially cruel in Poland where, unlike in the Axis satellites of Hungary and Romania, many peasants had fought heroically against the occupation and felt entitled to have a say in the postwar state. As a speaker at the January 1946 People's Party congress grandiloquently declared, "Through the sweat of his brow and his blood shed amply in battle, the peasant won the right to the land, the right to share in ruling the state—the right to Poland. And this Polish land, soaked with the sweat and blood of the most earnest peasant, became all the dearer to him."[108] The Peasant Battalions together with the much larger Home Army had dwarfed the Communist-led People's Army, which many Poles regarded as Soviet pawns. Not that Polish peasants universally shunned the Red Army. Jan Stryczek was pleasantly surprised by the friendly, well-behaved soldiers and officers who passed through Wola Dalsza on their way to Berlin.[109] But he had little to say about the countless documented instances of theft and drunken rape that made Soviet units a despised presence in many parts of Poland after the initial thrill of liberation had worn off.[110]

Even the pro-Communist Stryczek would eventually rue the way in which the Soviet-sponsored Polish Workers' Party (established in 1942) eliminated its agrarian rival. In 1944, they set up their own rural party, the People's Party-"Wola Ludu" (Will of the people) to promote Communism among peasants and foster links with socialist workers. Mikołajczyk perceived Wola Ludu as a direct challenge to his party's authority in the countryside, but he decided in mid-1945 to return to Poland from exile and join the Communist-led Temporary Government of National Unity as deputy prime minister and minister of agriculture and land reform. His return to the homeland, along with the August 1945 reestablishment of the People's Party, convinced most of the peasant underground, thitherto wary of the new authorities, to finally emerge from hiding.[111] Their suspicions proved justified, however. Treated as enemies, thousands of former Peasant Battalion fighters were harassed and imprisoned by the authorities, and many of their leaders murdered. Communist chicaneries further undermined the People's Party; the rightists faced persecution as "kulaks," while the leftist faction ("Lewica") was induced to secede. Mikołajczyk fled the country in 1947. In 1948, Wola Ludu and Lewica merged into the United People's Party and subsequently formed an innocuous arm of the regime.[112]

A similar fate awaited the Wici. Revived in 1944 by the movement's left wing in areas liberated by the Red Army, the peasant youth organization held a congress in August of that year in Lublin. The six hundred pro-Communist delegates in attendance resolved to build close links with the working classes and with the Soviet Union, signaling their departure from prewar policy.[113] At the same time, they reactivated their activities at the village level; in Wola Dalsza, Wici activists put on the first postwar harvest festival (*dożynki*).[114] The reemergence of the Polish People's Party brought many Wici who had served in the Peasant Battalions out of hiding. They cast aside the pro-Moscow orientation of the Lublin congress, calling unequivocally at a December 1945 congress for political democracy. Although the organization boasted record membership of half a million by the end of 1945, it was riven by internal disputes. The Lublin faction got the upper hand over the course of 1946, often by infiltrating its opponents' circles. In the spring and summer of 1948, the Wici were forcibly incorporated into government-sponsored youth organizations.[115]

Some People's Party activists and former Peasant Battalion fighters returned to the forests to wage an antiregime guerrilla war, which lasted until 1947, with isolated units holding out into the 1950s. Others had never come out of hiding and now joined the "Second Resistance." In the Podhale region of the Carpathian foothills, for instance, former partisan commander Józef Kuraś, alias "Ogień" (Fire), recruited local peasants into a five-hundred-strong guerrilla unit called "Błyskawica" (Lightning).[116] He died in combat with police units in February 1947. For many villagers, the Communists' reintroduction of production quotas and requisitions impelled them to support the armed resistance. Some of the most concerted risings against the new authorities occurred in Rzeszów and Cracow provinces, as well as in Lublin province and the northeast of the country.[117] Although a few leaders like Kuraś had served in the Peasant Battalions, most notable rural resisters came from the Home Army and the nationalist right. Wealthy peasants and gentry were conspicuous in their ranks.[118] In many areas, their activities became indistinguishable from banditry (already a widespread problem in 1944–45), which especially targeted Jews who had survived the Holocaust.[119]

Stryczek was dismissive of such desperadoes. And he regarded as fools those who tuned in to Radio Free Europe and continued to hope for American or British salvation. In his view, on balance, the "people's state and party passed the test."[120] What offended him about the post-1945 "People's Poland" (the Communists appropriated the phrase *Polska Ludowa* from the peasantists) was the disregard shown by the new regime for the hard-won achievements of leftist agrarians like himself. The closure of the People's University in Gać particularly irked him. Whereas the Sanacja government and its allies had maligned Ignacy Solarz's venture in the 1930s as a nest of Bolshevism, the new authorities rebuked Stryczek's idol—who had been murdered by the Nazis in 1940—for his paternalistic approach and insufficient collectivism.[121] They then shuttered local cooperative associations, replacing them with centrally administered ones. Peasant activists watched with dismay as the authorities axed or restructured the Wola Dalsza village credit association, the cooperative store, the health cooperative in Markowa, and the cooperative hospital in Łańcut. "What is the use of establishing a cooperative if it is later liquidated[?]" Stryczek asked bitterly.[122] Even if inefficiency and lack of equipment had plagued the previous institutions, they had been the fruits of peasants' own labor and villagers took justifiable pride in them. Callous disrespect for local initiatives prompted Stryczek to utter one of his few condemnations of the Communist regime, albeit tempered by remarks on peasants' chronic reservations toward authority: "Previously [peasant activists] had sat in *sanacja* prisons for their militant activities. But under People's Poland, for which peasant blood had been shed before the war, the peasant was not treated as he should be. It was perhaps also his fault in some cases that he could not gain trust in the new government, which was hardly a surprise since, after all, the peasant had been cheated for ages, hence also his mistrust toward new things."[123] For Stryczek, as for many others, a sense of village-level autonomy embodied in peasants' own institutions took priority over free and fair elections.

Hounded out of eastern Europe, leading agrarian politicians turned to messianic anticommunism in Western exile. The Bulgarian agrarian leader Georgi M. Dimitrov had fled to the USA in 1945, where in 1946 he met the recently arrived Milan Gavrilović of the Serbian Union of Agriculturalists and Vladko Maček of the Croatian Peasant Party, persuading them to reestablish an international agrarian organization. Ferenc Nagy of the Hungarian Smallholders Party joined them the following year. At a press conference held ostentatiously on July 4, 1947—American Independence Day—in Washington, DC, they called the International Peasant Union into existence, inviting other agrarian parties to join them in a campaign to liberate the countries behind the Iron Curtain and reestablish them on a democratic, peasantist basis.[124] Representatives of Polish and Romanian parties added their names to the declaration, which sketched a plan for a United States of Europe. At the start of 1948, the Polish People's Party acceded to the International Peasant Union, with Mikołajczyk joining the executive committee alongside the founding members. At the union's first congress in May of 1948, the Polish leader became president of the Central Committee, while Dimitrov was appointed general secretary. The International Peasant Union did not stipulate its criteria for membership as clearly as the interwar Green International had done, though like its predecessor it welcomed democratic organizations that stood for parliamentary democracy, especially those "under communist occupation."[125] By 1952, it encompassed twelve member parties, representing Albanian, Bulgarian, Croatian, Czech, Estonian, Hungarian, Latvian, Lithuanian, Polish, Romanian, Serbian, and Slovak agrarians.

From the start, the International Peasant Union was a Cold War organization. In 1948, Jerzy Kuncewicz, one of its leading activists and a fixture of exiled agrarian circles in wartime London, came out with a pseudonymous pamphlet entitled *The Peasant International in Action*, in which he stressed the peasant's leading role in the Manichaean struggle for the fate of the world. "The present historical moment," he wrote, "is to decide the 'to be or not to be' of mankind. . . . The question arises as to whether this globe of ours is to be transformed into a house of bondage, ruled from Moscow by the Order of Communist Bureaucrats, or whether it is to be a home for free men."[126] While Social Democrats had collapsed before the Communist onslaught, the peasant had held firm:

> The only member of the community who does not retreat, who does not break down, is the countryman, he who for centuries has driven his roots into the soil, the man who represents an inexhaustible capital of spiritual and moral values. From the enormous store of the tens of millions of the peasants who in Europe and in Asia make up the fighting vanguard of the Peasant International, ever new leaders arise. They declare unconditional war on Red Tyranny which still attempts to disguise itself under the cloak of lofty phraseology and to conceal its totalitarian face behind the shield of fake democracy.[127]

Somewhat surprisingly given the Peasant Union's reliance on urbanized America and Britain, Kuncewicz resuscitated the antiurban prejudices of the interwar years, casting Soviet dictatorship as the culminating act in the unnatural domination of cities over the countryside. The village community, by contrast, "strives to imprint its own ideas on the epoch. It wants to breathe the revitalizing air of the countryside into the decaying cities. It has faith it its mission—the so far unfulfilled social and political mission of the wise and healthy ploughman."[128] Such ideas found their way into the Peasant Union's *Bulletin*, conceived as a continuation of the Green International's eponymous periodical and circulated globally.[129] Alongside the east European member parties, the Peasant Union cultivated ties with agrarian political organizations in France, China, Japan, and Korea.[130]

But even if the peasants then "under communist occupation" had had access to the *Bulletin*, which they generally did not, it remains questionable how persuasive they would have found such propaganda in the first years of the "people's democracies." Despite the misgivings many villagers harbored toward the Soviet system, the new Communist authorities swiftly implemented the land reform that had eluded radical agrarians for the entire interwar period. Sweeping redistribution legislation passed in most places during the period when Communists still worked through coalitions and did not yet possess a monopoly on power, although Tito's unchallenged party opted for similar changes in Yugoslavia. Coordinated by Stalin in countries with a Red Army presence, the campaign aimed to woo the poorer peasantry away from agrarian parties.[131] At the very least, many villagers became convinced that communism and agrarianism were compatible.

Beginning in 1944, Polish Communists authorized the expropriation of all estates over fifty hectares (124 acres) without compensation, at a stroke eliminating the landlord class.[132] Poland's geographical shift westward to the line formed by the Oder and Neisse Rivers opened vast agricultural lands—the so-called "Recovered Territories" (Ziemie Odzyskane), recently vacated by ethnic Germans—for colonization by, in the first instance, People's Army veterans. In the event, relatively few peasant soldiers took advantage of the scheme, and the recovered territories were settled primarily by Polish refugees from the former eastern kresy—now in Soviet Ukraine, Belarus, and Lithuania—or allotted to state farms.[133] The reform faced obstacles everywhere within Poland's new borders. Peasants were sometimes reluctant to accept new land because they thought it would again be taken away in the future, by either returning nobles or duplicitous Communists. The previously landless feared the responsibilities of independent farming, and many who accepted land struggled to cultivate it for lack of experience, capital, draft animals, seeds, and fertilizer.[134]

Stryczek noted these problems, along with persistent land hunger in Wola Dalsza, even after redistribution had been carried out. Nevertheless, he judged the "long desired reform" a boon to his village. The reform's most important effects were less economic than psychological. Above all, there was palpable relief that the aristocratic Potockis' centuries-old grip on the area was broken. After an initial period of uncertainty, farms and houses sprouted up on the count's former estate, and the manorial residence was turned into a museum. On the other hand, redistribution narrowed significant social-cultural gaps within the village, particularly between those who had previously possessed their own land and those who had not. The one-time landless poor of Jawornik district finally integrated into the village community: "Those former grooms and estate farmhands [drawn] from oppressed people, docile [people], who had not taken an interest in the life of the village, since they never had any time for it, now felt completely differently, they felt like people on a par with the rest of the village. Now they began to take an interest in the life of the village and did not have to fear anymore that someone would say 'wretch from Jawornik.'"[135]

The psychological impact of the reforms helped their Communist architects achieve a degree of legitimacy among east central European peasants. The amount of land expropriated was enormous, even if much of it ended up in state land funds; for instance, 1.4 million hectares (3.5 million acres) were taken from 154,000 landowners in Romania, and 1.5 million hectares from 160,000 landowners in Yugoslavia.[136] Of those dispossessed in Yugoslavia, 40 percent were ethnic Germans, who also faced expulsion from the country—a pattern repeated across the region, as millions of ethnic Germans were forced from Czechoslovakia, Hungary, Poland, and the Soviet Union. New plots often far exceeded those distributed in 1918: peasants in Yugoslavia, especially former partisans, could receive up to forty hectares (99 acres), while after the First World War the maximum applicants could hope for was under five hectares (12 acres), with the average allocation less than two and a half.[137] Those peasants of the titular nations that remained after the dust of war and population transfers had settled could thank the Communists for spearheading reforms and for population transfers that created new opportunities to colonize and own land, however imperfect they were in practice.

When the new masters of east central Europe introduced collectivization of agriculture in the late 1940s, it seemed that they had reneged on the promise they had fulfilled to the toiling rural masses. Collectivization ushered in the final act of Europe's peasant war, as villagers across the region resisted Communist authorities—usually passively, sometimes openly. Soviet-controlled regimes across the region had initially been instructed to champion land reform and avoid all mention of collectivization, but their unstated goal from the beginning had been implementation of Stalin's 1935 Model Charter on collective farms. The 1948 Tito-Stalin split appears to have accelerated their plans, as Moscow scolded Belgrade for hailing peasants as the "strongest pillar of our state" and for failing to appreciate "sharpening class struggle" in villages.[138]

Most east European regimes launched collectivization campaigns over the course of 1948–49, though East Germany did not begin until 1952 when Stalin's hopes for German unification were dashed. Convinced that they had the full backing of the Yugoslav peasantry, Tito and his followers also introduced an aggressive collectivization program in 1949.

Collectivization in the "People's Democracies" diverged from the Soviet pattern of the 1930s in key respects, however.[139] First, agricultural land in the USSR had been legally nationalized early on and then leased to peasants in perpetuity, while in east central Europe peasants remained the legal owners of arable land. This contrast had its correlate in the difference between the Russian peasantry's historical traditions of communal ownership versus the entrenchment of liberal-individualist understandings of property ownership in lands farther west in the wake of emancipation from serfdom. Second, no mass deportations accompanied collectivization in east central Europe.[140] Although the authorities used various forms of compulsion, they continued to stress peasant voluntarism and undertook no wholesale liquidation of kulaks as a class. Finally, peasants in east central Europe could choose from several models of collective farming, some of which apportioned rewards based on the amount of land that individual peasants contributed to the collective, while rewards in the Soviet Union were calculated exclusively on the basis of peasants' labor input.

Alongside the diversity of approaches allowed in theory, the implementation of collectivization was heterogeneous and inconsistent, particularly with respect to kulaks, or rural capitalists. The definition of "kulaks" almost always featured their employment of nonfamily labor. Yet it often included a property threshold, which varied widely from place to place. In some countries at certain times, kulaks were encouraged to join collective farms; at other times and in other places, they were excluded. Communist practice during the early "class war" phase of collectivization hinged on a flexible use of the term "kulak," which in reality referred to anyone who opposed the new course. In Hungary in 1949, for instance, 63,300 farms fell into the kulak category, while 71,600 families were designated kulaks, including 21,900 landless peasants and 36,300 whose holdings were smaller than the 14.25-hectare (35-acre) threshold (it was three hectares for vineyards and four for fruit orchards).[141] Recalcitrant peasants labeled as kulaks were sometimes put on trial and subject to a range of punishments, including expulsion from their home villages.

Formerly landless villagers tended to join the collective farms first, often out of frustration with several years of unsuccessful private farming on plots distributed after the war. A mixture of incentives, compulsions, and threats was deployed to bring established small- and medium-holders into the new cooperative schemes. Those who refused to participate in the new arrangements had to deliver quotas of agricultural produce set at punitive levels.[142] Under Tito's regime, this represented a harshening of measures introduced just after the fighting ended. Although agricultural land had been exempted from Yugoslavia's blanket nationalization of industry in 1945, wartime constraints on the economy continued in the form of the *Otkup* system, which obliged peasants to sell their products to the state at fixed prices.[143] A 1946 Law on Cooperatives approved all existing types of cooperatives (production, consumption, and credit), encouraging their expansion and privileging members over nonmembers. With Yugoslavia's expulsion from the Cominform in 1948, the regime adopted a more aggressive approach. The Basic Law on Cooperatives in 1949 charted a bold course toward socialist agriculture, introducing Soviet-style peasant work cooperatives (*Seljačke radne zadruge*).[144] The work cooperatives attracted some peasants who wanted to escape *Otkup* obligations, but they suffered from a lack of capital, equipment, and qualified labor. In most cases, they failed dismally.

Peasants resisted the new impositions across eastern Europe. Most of their resistance was passive, taking the form of black-market activities, underreporting of yields, withholding deliveries, hoarding, and the like.[145] Yet violent attacks on party activists, on new mechanized equipment, and on collectivized property flared intermittently into the mid-1950s.[146] In most countries of eastern Europe, this was a rearguard action against a fundamental transformation of the countryside then underway. In Yugoslavia, where resistance was particularly fierce, it undermined official policy on agriculture, as Melissa Bokovoy has shown.[147] Villagers sabotaged equipment, ruined crops, and slaughtered livestock rather than join the work cooperatives. Those who willingly joined faced ostracization. Serb peasants in Croatia refused to enter work cooperatives until their Croat neighbors did. Revolts erupted in Macedonia as well as in the mixed Serb and Croat Banija and Kordun regions. In Croatia, menacing slogans circulated, such as "There will be war, and those who are found in the cooperative will be hung."[148]

In the former territories of the Habsburg monarchy, the final major act of violent rural resistance against Communist authorities took place in spring 1950 in northwest Bosnia.[149] Starting in early March of that year, several locally respected peasants who had fought with the Partisans hatched plans for a rising against the regime and its detested agricultural policies. Mile Devrnja, a

Serb farmer from Koranski Lug in the vicinity of Slunj, began plotting with Milan Božić, another Serb villager, from Crnaja in Cazin district, after they were both expelled from the Communist Party for failure to attend meetings. Božić recruited the Muslim peasant Ale Čović, a former Partisan and officer in Huska Miljković's autonomist force. Over the course of March and April 1950, they met secretly several times amid a widening circle of confederates to coordinate a revolt of the ethnically mixed peasantry in Cazin, Kladuša, and Slunj districts. At the outset, Čović won pledges from his coconspirators that Serb peasants would not use the unrest as a pretext to turn their weapons on Muslim neighbors to avenge the atrocities of 1941. With intercommunal alliances sealed, the peasant veterans planned armed action for May 6—Orthodox Saint George's Day (Đurđevdan), observed in northwest Bosnia by the mostly Muslim peasantry as well. They planned to disarm Communist authorities, distribute grain, and restore the exiled King Petar II. The rebels entertained fantasies that they would be assisted by risings elsewhere in Yugoslavia, as well as the invasion of a royalist émigré army.

On the eve of Saint George's Day, hundreds of peasants from Cazin district assembled under the command of Božić and Čović to disarm the police station in Tržac. They proceeded overnight to Begove Kafane, looting work cooperatives along the way and destroying their records. On the morning of May 6, district authorities in Cazin learned of the uprising for the first time when they received written orders from the rebels to surrender. Božić and Čović's force of three hundred men thereupon besieged Cazin, but they could not penetrate the town. All they had to show for their efforts was a commandeered jeep, which they used to stay in contact with Devrnja. By the end of the day, most of the insurgents had dispersed to their home villages. The actions in Kladuša and Slunj districts yielded even sparser results, as the smaller forces assembled there managed only to storm a handful of work cooperative offices. But the authorities acted decisively: within several days, they had arrested between five and seven hundred villagers connected with the revolt, killing eight in the process.[150]

In the final tally, state police and army units arrested 714 people. Of these, 288 were tried in military courts; 17 of them received death sentences, while the rest faced prison terms of fifteen to twenty years. Civilian courts tried the remaining 426 rebels, sentencing most of them to several years of hard labor in the Breza coal mines. Six of the death sentences were carried out, including those of Božić, Čović, and Devrnja.[151] Others died in captivity. Investigators concluded that the revolt was "of a pure Chetnik/Ustasha/Kulak nature" and that the "ringleaders included the remnants of Chetnik and Ustasha elements, Greens and others who are often relatives of our enemies."[152] The investigators could point to the involvement of "Green" veterans of Miljković's brigade in Cazin district, as well as the prominent role of one pro-Ustasha village in Kladuša district.[153] Officially, then, the rebellion figured as the handiwork of the regime's class enemies and surviving foes from the National Liberation Struggle. Unofficially, the Yugoslav Communist Party knew otherwise, and news of the Cazin events was scrupulously suppressed. A 1986 novel by an eyewitness of the Cazin revolt captured the sentiments of harried peasants watching on as the rebels were rounded up by the authorities:

> We had no choice, we couldn't take it anymore, things were unbearable, the quotas will finish us, they already have, us and the livestock, peasants have to live too, stop the quotas or kill us, we have been led astray, you better shut up, it makes no difference now whether I shut up or not, we want to live like human beings as well, we're not livestock, we are now, we just happened to be here, down with the quotas, shut up you idiot, anything is better than looking at hungry children, we won't even be looking at them now, we came to carnival, fucking carnival, there's nothing to celebrate now.[154]

Faced with a groundswell of peasant anger in northwest Bosnia, the authorities reduced the quotas associated with the *Otkup* system there.[155] Three years later, the government in Belgrade abandoned collectivization altogether. The March 1953 Law on Property Relations and Reorganization of Peasant Work Cooperatives permitted members to leave work cooperatives individually or in groups and, if they wished, to dissolve the organizations altogether.[156] Six years later, Slovene Communist Edvard Kardelj stated unequivocally in a speech to the party leadership that there would be no return to "Stalin-type" collectivization.[157]

Peasants in Yugoslavia won their final open battle against the Communist authorities. The exceptional role played by villagers in the wartime struggle of Tito's Partisans meant that they could not be shunted so easily aside. In other countries of the region, Communists had far fewer reasons to identify with smallholders. Of the Soviet Union's eastern European satellites, only Poland abandoned its feeble collectivization program in 1956, at which point a mere 11 percent of cultivated land and 6 percent of peasant farms had been brought under the control of production cooperatives.[158] Widespread peasant resistance was just one factor in Władysław Gomułka's momentous October 1956 decision to make membership in cooperative farms voluntary. Returning that month to power after enduring persecution and imprisonment in the years 1948–54, he likely wanted to demonstrate his independence from Moscow by implementing the view he had held up to 1948.[159] Most Polish collective farms had dissolved themselves within a couple of months of his reforms. Elsewhere in the Eastern Bloc, agriculture had been almost entirely collectivized by the mid-1960s, with the biggest push initiated from 1957 on amid relatively little resistance. By the early 1950s, armed opposition to Communist rule had become a rarity. Only in the Baltic republics of the western Soviet Union did guerrilla units known as "Forest Brothers" hold out into the middle of the decade.[160]

For Communists, collectivization was a centerpiece of their postwar "revolution" in central and eastern Europe. Although they abandoned it in two major countries of the region, they congratulated themselves everywhere on presiding over revolutionary societies built on the emancipation of workers and peasants. They could point to the not-insignificant part played by peasant insurgents in defeating Nazism; though, as we have seen, rural opponents of occupation were far from unambiguously pro-Communist. And the new regimes could claim credit for finally abolishing large estates without compensation and distributing much of the land to peasants, even if they later obliged villagers to pool their labor and property. This was ultimately not the revolution that peasant radicals and rural resistance fighters of the Second World War had called for. Across east central Europe—including Poland and Yugoslavia, where smallholding peasants could continue to farm their own, sometimes expanded plots—Communists now possessed free hand to pursue their urban-centered, industrialized visions of the future.

10

Epilogue

AFTER 1950, the European peasants who had for nearly two generations waged a multifront struggle to secure the future on their own terms were in retreat. The revolution they had launched at the end of the First World War in the eastern half of the continent had been premised on the demographic preponderance of the peasantry and on the incompatibility of their way of life with urban centers. From the middle of the twentieth century, neither of these premises seemed to hold up anymore. The number of people making their living from agriculture plunged across Europe, even on the southern and eastern peripheries where they had previously far outnumbered urban dwellers. Crash industrialization and collectivization transformed the Communist east, while in the west industrial rebuilding and new agricultural technologies, in large part financed by the United States, spurred an economic miracle. Peasants flocked to expanding cities where new, secure livelihoods of diminished (or different) toil beckoned. The millions of villagers who left their ancestral homes after the Second World War for growing urban-industrial centers experienced the changes with perhaps less remorse than previous generations had. Like other social groups who had witnessed the horrors of the last war, they tended to value peace above all else and recognized that there could be no return to the prewar political, social, and economic order. For the urban prophets of progress, whether liberal or Marxist, this was modernization, plain and simple. For peasant activists, especially central and east European agrarian politicians, it marked the end of a certain vision of modernity.

Alongside a broadly shared post-1945 aversion to conflict, many gradually saw that the new order brought concrete material benefits. The livelihoods of those who remained in villages were more secure than they had been in the 1930s, and illiteracy plummeted alongside expanded rural education. From the 1960s, liberalizing reforms allowed farms—even collective farms—to earn greater profits, while those who tilled them enjoyed increasing social benefits, such as state pensions and free health care.[1] Farming became less onerous and more productive with the proliferation of agricultural machines, advanced cultivation techniques, and easier access to seeds, chemical fertilizers, and pesticides. In western Europe, the pace of mechanization was extraordinary.[2] In West Germany, for instance, the number of tractors spiked from 30,000 before the war to 462,000 in 1955.[3] In the Communist east, mechanization proceeded more slowly, but its effects were equally dramatic, especially considering the lower initial starting point of most economies in the region. Romania, with its notoriously backward agricultural economy, experienced an elevenfold increase in the number of tractors during the period of state socialism; the number of self-propelled combine harvesters rose from fewer than 50 around mid-century to 62,000 in 1989.[4] Not least, state-sponsored infrastructure projects remade villages (not always with posterity in mind, as any traveler to the post-Communist countryside can attest), bringing new amenities and conveniences to their inhabitants. Writing in the mid-1950s, Jan Stryczek hailed the recent appearance in Wola Dalsza of paved sidewalks, asphalted roads, a public park, and a swimming pool.[5]

Yet those who stayed in the countryside would soon be a minority. Between 1950 and 1970, 40 to 50 percent of the agricultural labor force in central and eastern Europe relocated to cities. By eliminating market mechanisms and channeling investment into industry—in part by keeping prices for manufactured goods high at the same time that they remained low for agricultural products—Communist regimes achieved rapid rates of growth and industrial expansion in predominantly agrarian countries. By the last quarter of the twentieth century, urban dwellers far outnumbered inhabitants of rural areas, many of whom commuted to towns for work. The agricultural population dropped most precipitously in Bulgaria, from 82 percent in 1950 to 32 percent in 1973, while in Hungary it fell from 53 percent to 24 percent, and in Czechoslovakia from 40 percent to 18 percent.[6] By the mid-1970s only Romania still had a bare majority (53 percent) living in the countryside. For the established inhabitants of cities, the influx of millions of villagers was often a jarring experience. They bemoaned the low cultural and educational levels of the immigrants, along with their lack of personal hygiene. In some places, nostalgia for the refinements of interwar urban life—that is, before places like Belgrade, Bucharest, and Warsaw underwent "ruralization"—survived into the twenty-first century.[7]

Although many city natives feared that their home turf had been overrun by uncouth peasants, the newcomers differed in essence from previous generations of villagers. For alongside fundamental demographic and economic shifts was a sea change in rural attitudes toward land. Previously seen as the sine qua non of peasant identity and imbued with quasi-spiritual qualities, the family farm was gradually losing its mystique. Collectivization and the attractions of urban life were matched by the diminishing cultural value ascribed to the peasant's own parcel of land. The generations that came of age after the middle of the twentieth century, and even more so after the fall of Communism in eastern Europe, increasingly saw land as an asset to be bought and sold, and less as something that needed to be kept within the family at all costs.[8] From mid-century, not only was there a nose-dive in the number of peasants defined by economic activity, but the peasant consciousness that had crystallized in the era of world wars was being eroded. For Europe at least, historian Eric Hobsbawm could justifiably write in 1994 that "the most dramatic and far-reaching social change of the second half of this century, and the one which cuts us off for ever from the world of the past, is the death of the peasantry."[9] It appeared as though European peasants had offered their most sustained, coordinated, and revolutionary challenge to the world of cities on the eve of their disappearance. While many peasants remain in today's Europe, they are a tiny fraction of those who populated the continent's countryside a century ago.

For their part, the Communist regimes in central and eastern Europe deliberately suppressed alternative visions of society. Agrarianism and autonomous peasant revolutionism were among their primary targets, since their very existence belied a core tenet of Marxism-Leninism: revolutionary concert of workers and peasants with the former leading the latter. By the mid-1950s, peasant movements in central and eastern Europe had been either defeated or fought to a standstill. After the Second World War, Communists facilitated the redistribution of large estate land that villagers had coveted since their emancipation in the middle decades of the nineteenth century. The countryside became more socioeconomically equal than it had ever been. But this was just the prelude to a concerted campaign, beginning with collectivization, to eliminate peasant society and its representatives as obstacles to modernization. Although peasants won genuine victories in Yugoslavia and Poland, where their resistance contributed to the abandonment of collectivization, Communists effectively neutered their politics in the long run.

Persecution of agrarians crescendoed until Stalin's death in 1953. In Czechoslovakia, for instance, an infamous 1952 show trial in Brno convicted fifteen ruralist intellectuals, including the author Václav Prokůpek, as subversive "lackeys" of the Green International and sentenced them to long prison terms.[10]

The International Peasant Union—the real "Green International"—founded by exiled agrarian leaders in the West naturally posed no threat to the Soviet bloc, and after the middle of the 1950s it receded into obscurity.[11] Its conferences were held only sporadically after 1956, and the circulation of its main publication, the *Bulletin*, became incrementally less frequent. From the mid-1960s, the organization's foremost leaders died—Maček (1964), Mikołajczyk (1966), Dimitrov (1972), Nagy (1979)—leaving few who were willing to carry the torch of agrarian democracy into the future. After sending a delegation to an international agricultural conference in 1986, the International Peasant Union appears to have ceased its activities altogether.

On the academic front, scholars working under the auspices of state socialist regimes folded the grassroots peasant revolutionism embodied by the Green Cadres into the prehistory of triumphant Communism.[12] This was part of a broader intellectual effort to subordinate the long history of peasant unrest to the inevitable historical triumph of the proletariat.[13] Only those peasant deserters who had later joined the Communist Party or the Partisan struggle in the Second World War were fit for commemoration; for instance, the mercurial Alfonz Šarh had several streets named after him in Slovenia. By contrast, the Slovak Jozef Ferančík, who had worked for the collaborationist Slovak state during the Second World War, felt cruelly ostracized under the Communist regime, which he claimed to have prepared the ground for with his socially radical poetry and subversive activities as a Green Cadre commander during the end phase of Austria-Hungary.[14] After his request for a state subvention from the Slovak Literary Foundation (Slovenský literárný fond) was denied, the elderly and penurious Ferančík—"the oldest living Slovak writer," in his own words—blasted the "snobs" and "gentlemanly vermin" of the literary establishment in a scathing letter.

Agrarian politicians were able to reclaim modest influence in Hungary during the 1956 revolution, and more durably in Poland following Gomułka's return to power the same year. At a Central Committee meeting in autumn 1956, Gomułka stated: "Erasing the mistakes of the past, our Party will change its policy towards its ally, the ZSL [Independent People's Party]. We recognize ZSL as an independent party and we will progressively confirm this attitude in practice."[15] The following year, he took the significant step of attending a ceremony in Kasinca Mała to commemorate the victims of the 1937 Peasant Strike alongside People's Party chairman Stefan Ignar.[16] By the end of the 1960s, Independent People's Party deputies made up over a quarter of the sejm (117 of 460) and filled various ministerial, deputy ministerial, and other senior government positions.[17] Under its aegis, the Museum of the History of the Polish Populist Movement was founded in 1984, giving Polish agrarianism a foothold in official history and memory culture.[18] Though unable to challenge the dominant Polish Workers' Party on anything of substance, the semiautonomous party ensured a modicum of continuity for Polish peasantism through the state socialist years. The Bulgarian Agrarian National Union (BANU) likewise functioned under "real existing socialism" as a toothless ally of the ruling party; in other countries, agrarian parties were unceremoniously disbanded.

With the fall of state socialism, east central European peasant parties were revived in Croatia, Romania, Hungary, and Latvia, while the Bulgarian and Polish parties reclaimed their autonomy. They had some impact on post-Communist politics in the 1990s and early 2000s but have since faded in importance.[19] The Polish People's Party achieved the best results of all, winning just over 15 percent of the vote in 1993 parliamentary elections. While reborn agrarian parties invoked pre-Communist political traditions, rural people in central and eastern Europe were often drawn to the more recent past, casting their votes for Communist successor parties. Ironically, given the assault on their way of life at the start of the state socialist period, by the 1980s villagers were among the most loyal supporters of the regime, owing to the economic protections and comfortable standard of living they enjoyed.[20] Politicians who after 1989 heralded an alleged return to liberal-individualist landholding patterns overlooked the fact that Communism had achieved some of its legitimacy by intensifying the nationalist and collectivist approaches to land ownership initiated after the First World War.[21] Agriculture's declining profitability in the first decade of democracy also contributed to wistfulness for the old order, though farmers have fared better on average since accession to the European Union.

The twentieth-century Communist victory over peasant movements in central and eastern Europe was so complete that the active role played by peasant revolutionaries in shaping the era of world wars has become inconceivable to many in the early twenty-first century. Certain protagonists and organizations are remembered, though not as part of a broader struggle to reframe modernity in line with the values, aspirations, and lives of peasant villagers. Many initiatives described in the pages above—from armed rural deserters in the former Austro-Hungarian and Russian Empires to agrarian parties in east central and southeast Europe—are commemorated in narrowly national terms: as opponents of both oppressive dynastic empires and their tyrannical internationalist successors, the Communists. Other leaders and experiments have slid into the role of regional curiosities, such as Čaruga, the Slavonian Robin

Hood; the Slovácko Brigade; and the peasant republics established in 1918–20. Peasant rebelliousness has faded from collective memory, notwithstanding sporadic evocations of this heritage in antiestablishment and anarchist-leaning subcultural scenes. In 1999, for instance, the Croatian folk-rock group Cinkuši released their album *Zeleni kader* (Green cadre), and in 2018 a Polish folk-punk group called Hańba (Disgrace) played a concert in Tarnobrzeg on the centenary of the peasant republic's founding there.[22]

What is most forgotten, or occluded, is the animus toward cities that these movements and figures usually shared. Antiurbanism is of course an awkward legacy, not just because most Europeans now live in cities but because in the first half of the twentieth century it fused with various forms of ethnic antagonism, especially anti-Semitism. As we have seen, much of the violence associated with the peasant revolution of 1917–21 was directed against Jews, and Jews often appeared as dangerous outsiders in the emancipatory blueprints of agrarian ideologues. Other groups were also identified as exploiters or enemies of the peasantry, above all the class of noble estate owners and, depending on the place and time, ethnic-national others who were concentrated in towns and appeared indifferent to villagers' lives: Hungarians in Slovakia and Croatia, Germans in Moravia and Slovenia, and Poles or Russians in much of Ukraine, to take a few examples. Jews, on the other hand, were everywhere cast as an alien presence in the overwhelmingly Christian countryside of central and eastern Europe. Yet nowhere was ethnic animosity at the core of the peasantist vision, which strived for an egalitarian redistribution of rural property, local autonomy (or at least the decentralization of states), a cooperative economy, and the subordination of modern technology and industry to the needs of agriculture. Even in the 1930s, when many peasants gravitated toward fascist politics premised on ethnic-national struggle and hatred, they often did so conditionally, accepting xenophobia so long as it did not compromise their own priorities. The same could be said for those peasants who, during the Second World War, allied themselves with urban Communists and their program of proletarian revolution.

Though ultimately defeated, the rural mobilizations described in this book illuminate broader histories of the modern era. One is the global story of peasant revolutionism in the last century, theorized by anthropologist Eric Wolf in his seminal *Peasant Wars of the Twentieth Century* (1969), which nonetheless disregarded Europe outside of Russia. Unlike in Europe, Communists in the Global South embraced peasant radicalism, and sometimes adapted their ideology and tactics to it—at least as long as the fight against the "capitalist-imperialists" was not yet won. During the Cold War, the American-led "free world" joined the game of supporting rural insurgencies on the condition that they framed their programs in terms of anti-Communism and "liberty." The worldwide contest between the Soviet Union and the United States raised the stakes of political change astronomically, in even the most marginal countries. As a result, peasant rebels benefited from more external support in the form of supplies, military expertise, and arms than they had before. The obverse was that the superpowers, along with Maoist China, felt entitled to dictate political outcomes, ensuring that peasant action did not impinge on their own designs for any one country's future. In a small number of cases, such as Vietnam and to some extent Algeria and Cuba, peasant rebellions flowed more or less organically into socialism.[23] The ability of Vietnamese villagers to successfully challenge American military might inspired the Western political left, bringing contemporary rural insurgencies to the attention of scholars and activists.[24] But in many cases, peasants opposed the centralizing, high modernist state in both its Communist and capitalist forms, just as they had in Europe in the years 1914–50. Tragedy ensued as a mixture of sophisticated and primitive weapons were deployed by the superpowers or their proxies against recalcitrant subsistence farmers in South Vietnam, Indonesia, Ethiopia, Angola, and many other countries.[25] In some places, like Afghanistan, rural insurgents consciously rejected all ideologies of Western origin, opting instead for religious fundamentalism or ethnic exclusivism—a trend that seemed to accelerate in the early twenty-first century.[26]

As in Europe, the peasant population of the Global South has declined in relative terms, although it remains immense. The United Nations' population report in 2007 estimated that, for the first time in world history, inhabitants of urban areas outnumbered inhabitants of the countryside.[27] Yet there are still an estimated 2.5 billion peasants, a figure equal to the entire world population in 1950, and no current plans to tackle "underdevelopment" in the Global South feature industrialization on a scale capable of absorbing such a mass of humanity.[28] For the foreseeable future, a sizeable portion of the world population will continue to till small plots of land in Africa, Asia, and Latin America. Since the end of the Cold War, new forms of internationalist peasant activism have emerged to challenge the globalized neoliberal economy, which is characterized by trade liberalization, decreased state subsidies for family farms in poorer and indebted countries, and the financialization of agricultural commodity markets. This system has given large agribusinesses concentrated in the wealthy Global North a decisive advantage over most of the world's remaining agricultural population, 97 percent of which lives in the Global South and is made up overwhelmingly of peasants working small family farms.[29] In some ways heir to the interwar Green International in east central Europe, La Vía Campesina (The Peasant Way) was initiated in 1992 at a conference in Managua, Nicaragua, to confront such inequities. It has lobbied for increased rights and security for small agricultural producers, along with gender equality and sustainable farming practices.[30] A fruit of its efforts was the December 2018 United Nations Declaration on the Rights of Peasants and Other People Working in Rural Areas.[31]

Peasant revolution in the first half of the twentieth century also fits into a longer history of antiurban populism, a "recurring mentality" whose recrudescence has profoundly shaped early twenty-first century politics.[32] Movements that rail against the alleged plutocracy, corruption, and moral or ethnic-racial decay of cities have proliferated across the globe. Their rhetorical debt to peasantism is at most indirect; nonetheless, peasantist politics bequeathed a rich repertoire of antiurban speech, symbols, and dispositions that can be mobilized by the political right or left. In central and eastern Europe, rural citizens could not but notice that changes in the economy and society since the fall of Communism have disproportionately benefited urban areas, some of which have achieved western European levels of prosperity.[33] Populist animus is directed toward a certain type of city in particular: the growing, wealthy, often multicultural hubs that have been the principal beneficiaries of economic globalization since the 1970s. As a result, parties trading in antimetropolitan sentiment have gathered supporters not only from the depopulated countryside but from depressed, postindustrial, provincial towns and cities as well. A new geography of class pits the global metropolis, defined by its strategic location in worldwide supply chains as well as its by its ability to attract creative, upwardly mobile professionals, against an undercapitalized and exploited "hinterland."[34] The downtrodden of "metropolized" global capitalism appear to be defined less by what they do for a living than by where they live.[35]

In the first decades of the twenty-first century, the main political beneficiaries of these geographically inflected class resentments were right-wing movements led by strongman types. Invoking rural authenticity and virtue in ways reminiscent of interwar authoritarianism, they have won support in hollowed-out rural and small-town communities. They have also tended to represent the extractive mining and agribusiness firms that further degrade the rural environment but provide jobs that many people in the countryside value most in the short term. Established, putatively left-wing parties (though more accurately liberal or center-left parties) have concentrated almost exclusively on winning urban votes. In Europe and North America, their supporters—primarily educated middle classes, along with some ethnic and racial minorities—have found their prejudices against rural areas confirmed and deepened by the racist, xenophobic, and antimigrant attitudes of right-wing populism, which they commonly take to be its central feature. Yet, as was the case with bygone peasant movements, such unsavory sentiments are often less expressive of the ideological commitments of the hinterland's inhabitants than of a widespread belief that the bien-pensant media and artistic establishment lavish undue attention on minorities while their own struggles go unnoticed or are denigrated. Stjepan Radić might have been the mouthpiece of such perceived injustice, faulting Croatia's intellectuals and newspapers in 1907 for "writ[ing] more about our 20,000 Jews than our 2 million peasants. Every year they can write against the peasantry whatever they wish . . . and no one will complain, but if only one newspaper writes something against the Jews, entire studies would be written, how this is unworthy of enlightened people, how it is criminal to hate someone because of their faith."[36] As with those who lined up behind Radić's Croatian Peasant Party and other radical agrarian groups, it is often difficult to place the masses of people who oppose, or feel left behind by, contemporary global capitalism on a conventional left–right political spectrum. Nostalgia, self-pity, and bitterness sometimes characterize their outlooks, but so too do radical yearnings premised on wholesale rejection of the reigning system.

It took the blast furnace of the First World War to extract the peasant revolution of the years 1917–21 from the ore of rural defiance and despair. To many observers at the time and since, the smelting process did not eliminate impurities, such as regionalism, folk Christianity, ethnic hostility, and banditry. The result did not look like genuine revolution in their eyes; nor, for them, did the emerging rural politics qualify as modern. This book has taken a different approach, one that has sought to comprehend, on their own terms, the actions and views of people who are usually not inclined to openly challenge existing authorities and who are not accustomed to imagining or sketching plans for a society fundamentally different from the one in which they live. Their strivings were all the more momentous because of this. As Antonio Gramsci scribbled in his notebook in a Fascist prison in 1930, "The history of the subaltern classes is necessarily fragmented and episodic. . . . Subaltern classes are subject to the initiatives of the dominant class, even when they rebel; they are in a state of anxious defense. Every trace of autonomous initiative is therefore of inestimable value."[37]

ACKNOWLEDGMENTS

ANY HISTORIAN WRITING about peasants immediately runs into the problem of sources. As inhabitants of oral cultures, and mostly illiterate until relatively recently, peasants have left sparser written records than other people. To tell their story across the diverse lands of east central Europe would have been impossible without the help and advice of colleagues possessing intimate knowledge of sources in local languages and particular regions. I am grateful to those who have brought to my attention archival and published primary sources that proved critical in reconstructing the views of peasants and rural deserters: Juraj Benko, Lukáš Fasora, Lucian George, Roman Holec, Žarko Lazarević, Lukáš Lexa, Adam Lupták, Claire Morelon, Oskar Mulej, and Vitězslav Sommer. Many others shared literature tips, their own publications, or sent me photocopies of sources I could not obtain in the UK; they include Pavlina Bobič, Jochen Böhler, Tim Buchen, Miguel Cabo, Thomas Chopard, Zdenko Ďuriška, Brigitte Entner, Frank Grelka, Iskra Iveljić, Jernej Kosi, Jaroslav Slezák, Rok Stergar, Danilo Šarenac, Jakub Štofaník, and Piotr Szlanta—to name a few. Jasmin Nithammer located useful sources in Poland on a research assistantship enabled by the John Fell Fund at Oxford, and Jani Santarius provided me with digital copies of documents in the Moravian Provincial Archive in Brno as part of his Laidlaw Scholarship at University College London. Archivists in Břeclav, Hodonín, Maribor, Mikulov, Osijek, and Zagreb did far more than they had to for me. Tamás Révész was invaluable in finding and translating Hungarian sources, while on a postdoctoral fellowship on the Arts and Humanities Research Council project under my direction in 2021–23. He and my main project partner Petra Svoljšak deserve special thanks for our many enlightening discussions over the past several years. The AHRC project was also enriched by significant input from Gregor Antoličič and museum curators Martin Hoferka in Skalica and Petra Marincel in Varaždin.

I am indebted to colleagues at the three universities I have worked at since I started the research for this book for their generosity and insights. I would like to thank Jonathan Gumz, Simon Jackson, and Klaus Richter at the

University of Birmingham and my Oxford colleagues Robert Evans, Robert Gildea, Abigail Green, Adrian Gregory, David Hopkin, and Oliver Zimmer. The School of Slavonic and East European Studies at UCL, where I have worked since 2019, has provided the ideal environment for completing the project. Bojan Aleksov, Richard Butterwick-Pawlikowski, Simon Dixon, and Diane Koenker have been particularly supportive. I am very grateful to Tom Lorman and Rebecca Haynes for reading parts of the manuscript and offering their feedback, especially on Hungary and Romania. My PhD mentor Bill Hagen was, as always, both incisive and encouraging. Too numerous to name individually are those who gave useful comments on my work at conferences and seminars in Birmingham, Boston, Bratislava, Ljubljana, London, Oxford, Paris, Philadelphia, Prague, Uppsala, Cres, and elsewhere.

The book project benefited from excellent professional support from when I began planning it through to the end of the production process. My agent James Pullen at Wylie provided early enthusiasm and astute feedback on the proposal. I have been most fortunate to have in Ben Tate such a perceptive, encouraging, and good-humored editor. My sincere thanks also go to the anonymous readers of the manuscript, Maia Vaswani for her unusually attentive copyediting, and to Jenny Wolkowicki and the rest of the outstanding production team at Princeton University Press.

My loving family has sustained me throughout the research and writing process. I could not have done it without my eternally patient wife Maja, our delightful son Kajetan, my witty and energetic siblings Era and Martin, and my ever-enthusiastic, historically minded parents Jan and Vera, to whom this book is dedicated. Finally, and not least, I thank the people of Gomilsko and Poggi del Sasso for initiating me, a native of the San Francisco Bay Area, into village life.

ABBREVIATIONS

AHMP	Archiv hlavního města Prahy
AHOB	Allerhöchster Oberbefehl
AMH	Archiv města Hodonín
ARS	Arhiv Republike Slovenije
AVA	Allgemeines Verwaltungsarchiv
BSI	Boje na Slovensku I
CH	Cyril Hluchý collection
DAOS	Državni arhiv Osijek
DAZD	Državni arhiv Zadar
FS	Fond Franček Saje
HDA	Hrvatski Državni Arhiv
KA	Kriegsarchiv
KM	Kriegsministerium
KSSO	Kraljevski sudbeni stol Osijek
LA	Literárny archív
LAPNP	Literární archiv Památníku národního písemnictví
MDI	Ministerium des Innern
MKSM	Militärkanzlei Seiner Majestät des Kaisers
MMH	Masarykovo muzeum Hodonín
MPSP	Minister Československej republiky s plnou mocou pre správu Slovenska, Prezidium II/4
MRP/R	Prezídium ministerské rady Vídeň
MZA	Moravský zemský archiv, Brno
NA	Národní archiv, Czech Republic
ND	Namjesništvo za Dalmaciju
OESTA	Österreichisches Staatsarchiv
OPWR	Odvjetnička pisarnica Walter Radivoj
OSM	Okrožno sodišče Maribor
OUH PS	Okresní úřad Hodonín—presidiální spisy

OUPZV IV-B	Odsjek IV-B za pogranična redarstvena satništva
OUTPS	Okresní úřad Třebíč, Presidiálné spisy
PA	Präsidium Akten
PAM	Pokrajinski arhiv Maribor
PB	Präsidialbüro
PM	Prezidium místodržitelství
PS	Politička situacija 1910–1940
PŠPRS	Pobune štrajkovi i pokreti radnika i seljaka
RMM	Regionální muzeum v Mikulově
SBVS	Slovácká brigáda, Velitelství spisy
SNA	Slovenský národný archív
SNK	Slovenská národná knižnica, Martin
SOKAB	Státní okresní archiv Břeclav
SOKAH	Státní okresní archiv Hodonín
SOKAJH	Státní okresní archiv Jindřichův Hradec
SOKAT	Státní okresní archiv Třebíč
SOKABUH	Státní okresní archiv Uherské Hradiště
SPVS	Slovácký pluk, Velitelství spisy
VHAB	Vojenský historický archív, Bratislava
VHAP	Vojenský historický archiv, Prague
VMHO	Vlastivědný materiál hodonínského okresu
VSS	Velitelství skupiny Schöbl
ZČV	Zemské četnické velitelství
ZVV	Zemské vojenské velitelství
ZVVO	Zemské vojenské veliteľstvo, 1919–39

NOTES

Notes to Introduction

1. Djilas, *Wartime*, 22.

2. Hajdu, "Socialist Revolution," 108–9.

3. This contrasts with scholarship emphasizing peasants' perpetual desire to escape the reaches of the state or the notion that they exist in a mental universe largely untouched by the state and its agents. See James Scott's "Hegemony and the Peasantry" (270–71), *Weapons of the Weak*, and *Domination*. Nonetheless, Scott also concedes that "not all peasant movements are incipiently secessionist. A great many appear to aim rather at a renegotiation of peasant links to elites" ("Peasants and Commissars," 116).

4. Cf. Guha, *Elementary Aspects*, 18–20.

5. Edward P. Thompson pioneered this approach to class in the early 1960s. See, programmatically, his *Making of the English Working Class* (9, 10) and "Eighteenth-Century English Society" (149). For an elaboration of Thompson's notion of class as an oppositional social relation, see chapter 3 of Ellen Meiksins Wood's *Democracy against Capitalism*. Joan W. Scott initiated an analogous, though more linguistic and textualist (and therefore less socially grounded), approach to gender in her seminal "Gender: A Useful Category of Analysis," especially pp. 1067–69, which she then applied to the question of class in history in "On Language, Gender, and Working-Class History." Similarly, Rogers Brubaker issued an influential call to scholars of nationalism to regard nationhood as a "contingent event" in *Nationalism Reframed* (pp. 7, 13–20). An application of the Thompsonian method in race studies can be discerned in David R. Roediger's *Wages of Whiteness*. Debates over the salience of class since the "linguistic turn" seemed to have passed the peasantry by. For instance, not one of the forty-seven chapters in Patrick Joyce's *Class* is concerned with peasants. Nonetheless, the notion that the peasant class is at least somewhat a product of oppositional relations and perceptions—of separation from and unjust subordination to nonpeasant groups—was expressed already by Teodor Shanin in his introduction to *Peasants and Peasant Societies* (15) and by Eric J. Hobsbawm in "Peasants and Politics" (5–6).

6. Shanin, "Peasantry," 240; Hobsbawm, "Peasants and Politics," 3–4.

7. On "agriculturalization" in Germany, see Robert G. Moeller's *German Peasants and Agrarian Politics* (9). On Poland, see Jacek Kochanowicz's "Changing Landscape of Property" (35). A discussion of the literature on this phenomenon in France is provided by Edward Berenson in "Politics and the French Peasantry" (215–16).

8. The mutual interdependence of social experience or facts of class on the one hand and the "cultural and political postulate" of class on the other is posited in Geoff Eley and Keith Nield in *The Future of Class in History* (56, 167, 171).

9. Wolf, *Peasant Wars*, 276–92.

10. Wolf, 202, 293; Wolf, "On Peasant Rebellions," 268–70.

11. Hobsbawm, *Age of Extremes*, part 1.

12. Gerwarth, *Vanquished*, 13, 254, 258; Böhler, "Enduring Violence."

13. Schulz and Harre, *Bauerngesellschaften auf dem Weg*, esp. chapters by Schulz, Harre, and Holec; Müller and Harre, *Transforming Rural Societies*, esp. the introduction; Toshkov, *Agrarianism as Modernity*; Bideleux, "Peasantries and Peasant Parties."

14. Hobsbawm, *Age of Extremes*; Mazower, *Dark Continent*; Tooze, *Deluge*.

15. United Nations Department of Economic and Social Affairs, *Demographic Yearbook 1952*, 168, 179–85.

16. Spengler, *Decline of the West*, 245, 25–26.

17. On boisterous popular religiosity, see, for instance, David Blackbourn's *Marpingen Visions*. On popular indifference to the nation, see, for instance, Pieter Judson's *Guardians of the Nation*, Tara Zahra's *Kidnapped Souls*, and James Bjork's *Neither German nor Pole*.

18. Chakrabarty, *Provincializing Europe*, 8–11.

19. Moore, *Social Origins*, 453.

20. Moore, 480.

21. Trouillot, *Silencing the Past*, 70–107.

22. Van Molle, "Political Parties," 216.

23. James Scott, *Seeing like a State*.

Chapter 1

1. For context on *The Croatian God Mars* and its author, see John Paul Newman's "Croat Iliad." On *The Living Whip* and its author, see Joseph A. Mikus's *Slovakia and the Slovaks*, 112–16.

2. Krleža, *Hrvatski bog Mars*, 98.

3. Offer, *First World War*.

4. Urban, *Živý bič*, 238.

5. See, e.g., Státní okresní archiv Hodonín (SOkAH), Archiv obce Nenkovice, pamětní kniha, pp. 54–55, Archiv obce Hýsly, pamětní kniha (unpaginated), Archiv obce Čeložnice, pamětní kniha, p. 14; Státní okresní archiv Břeclav (SOkAB), Archiv obce Vrbice, pamětní kniha, p. 25; Zacharová, "Pramene k dejinám . . . II," 209 (recollections about the war in Lozorno).

6. SOkAH Vlastivědný materiál hodonínského okresu (VMHO), inv. č. 9 Hrušky, VC 1, 2.

7. C. Clark, *Sleepwalkers*, 402–3, 407, 423, 517–18.

8. On the Austro-Hungarian decision for war and the ultimatum to Serbia, see Clark's *Sleepwalkers* (423–30, 451–7) and Watson's *Ring of Steel* (7–51).

9. Clark, *Sleepwalkers*, 96.

10. Quoted in Connelly, *From Peoples into Nations*, 318.

11. Słomka, *From Serfdom to Self-Government*, 203. See also Watson, *Ring of Steel*, 68–69.

12. Hluk chronicle available at Hlucké Kroniky, http://www.kronikahluk.cz/. SOkAH VMHO, inv. č. 14 Kuželov, VC 1; inv. č. 40 Hrubá Vrbka, VC 1; inv. č. 18 Nová Lhota, VC 1.

13. In 1900, it was estimated that there were 5.65 million farms in the monarchy as a whole, of which the majority were under two hectares. The percentage of the population engaged in agriculture in 1910 was estimated at 56 percent (Bruckmüller, "Landwirtschaftliche Arbeitswelten," 277–80, 298–99).

14. Ermacora, "Rural Society."

15. Cole, *Military Culture*, 13–14.

16. Cole, 10–11.

17. On the development of the Habsburg Monarchy's recruitment system, see Cole's *Military Culture* (110–21).

18. Macartney, *Habsburg Empire*, 564.

19. Jeřábek, "Eastern Front," 151–52; Rauchensteiner, *First World War*, 55.

20. Rothenberg, *Army of Francis Joseph*, 160.
21. Cole, *Military Culture*, 121, 308–22.
22. Krleža, *Harbors Rich in Ships*, 20–21.
23. Frevert, *Nation in Barracks*, 178.
24. Słomka, *From Serfdom to Self-Government*, 156.
25. Cole, *Military Culture*, 113–14, 118.
26. Rauchensteiner, *First World War*, 57.
27. See Houlihan, *Catholicism*; Bobič, *War and Faith*.
28. Watson, *Ring of Steel*, 140.
29. Tunstall, *Austro-Hungarian Army*, 118.
30. Rumpler and Schmied-Kowarzik, *Habsburgermonarchie*, 162. The total losses of 949,895 includes soldiers missing in action as well.
31. Watson, *Ring of Steel*, 91.
32. Ress, " Königreich Ungarn," 1114.
33. Deak and Gumz, "How to Break."
34. Watson, *Ring of Steel*, 155.
35. Rumpler and Schmied-Kowarzik, *Habsburgermonarchie*, 204. See also Šedivý, *Češi*, 229–32.
36. Rumpler and Schmied-Kowarzik, *Habsburgermonarchie*, 205. The figures for 1913 and 1917 were 6,270,090 and 6,002,832.
37. Ermacora, "Rural Society."
38. Rumpler and Schmied-Kowarzik, *Habsburgermonarchie*, 204.
39. Słomka, *From Serfdom to Self-Government*, 225–28.
40. Watson, *Ring of Steel*, 344.
41. Scheer, "Kriegswirtschaft," 465.
42. SOkAB, Archiv obce Vrbice, pamětní kniha, 31.
43. SOkAB, Archiv obce Vrbice, pamětní kniha, 26.
44. SOkAH VMHO, inv. č. 14 Kuželov, VC 14; inv. č 40 Hrubá Vrbka, VC 11; see VC 11 section for other villages too. SOkAH, Archiv obce Sobůlky, pamětní kniha, 5; Romsics, "War in the Puszta," 48.
45. See, e.g., Zacharová, "Pramene k dejinám . . . I," 198; SOkAH, Archiv obce Věteřov, pamětní kniha, 6–8.
46. SOkAB, Archiv obce Vrbice, pamětní kniha, 30.
47. See, for instance, Řeháček, "Život venkovského."
48. Moeller, *German Peasants*, 48–49, 69–74; Ziemann, *War Experiences*, 191–96; Šedivý, *Češi*, 257.
49. See, e.g., Kučera, *Rationed Life*, 28–30.
50. Státní okresní archiv Jindřichův Hradec (SOkAJH), Archiv obce Sumrakov, pamětní kniha, 12.
51. SOkAB, Archiv obce Vrbice, pamětní kniha, 38.
52. Heumos, "Kartoffeln" 257.
53. Heiss, "Andere Fronten," 160.
54. Martan, "Nemiri u Hrvatskoj," 9.
55. Scheer, "Kriegswirtschaft," 466.
56. SOkAB, Archiv obce Vrbice, pamětní kniha, 39.
57. Romsics, "War in the Puszta," 48.
58. Kubů and Šouša, "Z časů," 61–69.
59. Hluk chronicle available at "1917," Hlucké Kroniky, http://www.kronikahluk.cz/index.php?id=1917.
60. Quoted in Kovačević, "Nemiri u Moslavini," 109.

61. Scheer, "Kriegswirtschaft," 466; Heiss, "Andere Fronten," 163; Romsics, "War in the Puszta," 48; Watson, *Ring of Steel*, 360–62.

62. Ermacora, "Rural Society."

63. This section is based on Moeller's *German Peasants* (43–67) and Ziemann's *War Experiences* (168–81).

64. Quoted in Moeller, *German Peasants*, 68.

65. This section is based primarily on Peter Gatrell's *Russia's First World War* (72–76, 154–72).

66. A. Adams, "Peasantry in Russia," 2.

67. Gatrell, *Russia's First World War*, 163–64; Retish, *Russia's Peasants*, 59–60.

68. Baker, *Peasants, Power, and Place*, 14–15, 30–37.

69. Retish, *Russia's Peasants*, 14, 55–57.

70. Plaschka, Haselsteiner, and Suppan, *Innere Front*, 1:211–33.

71. Morelon, "Sounds of Loss," 213.

72. Sršan, *Povijest petrijevačke župe*, 172–73.

73. Hluk chronicle available at "1917," Hlucké Kroniky, http://www.kronikahluk.cz/index.php?id=1917; quote by Josef Dufka.

74. Urban, *Živý bič*, 103–9.

75. SOkAH, Archiv obce Sobůlky, pamětní kniha, 5. See also Morelon, "Sounds of Loss," 205.

76. Hluk chronicle available at "1917," Hlucké Kroniky, http://www.kronikahluk.cz/index.php?id=1917.

77. Zacharová, "Pramene k dejinám . . . I," 233.

78. Romsics, "War in the Puszta," 45.

79. Zacharová, "Pramene k dejinám . . . I," 198.

80. *Pamiętniki chłopów*, 2:384.

81. Słomka, *From Serfdom to Self-Government*, 222.

82. Watson, *Ring of Steel*, 153–54.

83. James Scott, *Weapons of the Weak*.

84. Arhiv Republike Slovenije (ARS), C. Kr. Ministrstvo za Notranje Zadeve Dunaj, Predsedstveni spisi II, signature 22, box 20, no. 19352.

85. Urban, *Živý bič*, 96.

86. Plaschka, Haselsteiner, and Suppan, *Innere Front*, 1:216, 231.

87. Plaschka, Haselsteiner, and Suppan, 1:232.

88. This case is recorded in Pokrajinski arhiv Maribor (PAM), Okrožno sodišče Maribor (OSM), Kazenske zadeve 1918–19, case against Ačko and co.

89. Hrvatski Državni Arhiv (HDA), 79 Zemaljska vlada Odsjek IV B, box 89, no. 827-2990.

90. HDA 1363 Politička situacija 1910–1940 (PS), box 4, no. 207.

91. PAM OSM, Kazenske zadeve 1918–19, case against Mlakar.

92. Romsics, "War in the Puszta," 39–47; Tomasevich, *Peasants*, 230–31.

93. Baker, *Peasants, Power, and Place*, 29.

94. Urban, *Živý bič*, 152.

95. Rozner, *Vzpoura chalup*, 155.

96. Krleža, *Hrvatski bog Mars*, 99.

97. Urban, *Živý bič*, 236.

98. Urban, 138.

Chapter 2

1. Zlobec recounts his time in the Green Cadre in *V viharju prve svetovne vojne* (158–74).

2. Zlobec, 166.

3. Zlobec, 173.

4. On desertion of Black and White southern conscripts from the US army in 1917–18, see Jeanette Keith's *Rich Man's War, Poor Man's Fight.*

5. See, for instance, Österreichisches Staatsarchiv (OeStA), Kriegsarchiv (KA), Zentralstellen, Kriegsministerium (KM), Hauptreihe, Akten, box 13821 [previously no. 754], 64-46/27, July 5, 1918, report from Bosnia-Herzegovina and Dalmatia.

6. Überegger, "Auf der Flucht," 360.

7. Überegger, 360–61.

8. Plaschka, Haselsteiner, and Suppan, *Innere Front,* 2:63.

9. Holotík, *Sociálne a národné hnutie,* 261–64.

10. HDA 79, Odjel za unutarnje poslove Zemaljske vlade, Odsjek IV-B za pogranična redarstvena satništva (OUPZV IV-B), box 89, no. 827-1026. See also Hrabak, *Dezerterstvo,* 105. For population statistics, see Rumpler and Schmied-Kowarzik's *Habsburgermonarchie.*

11. The ban's circular is in HDA 79 OUPZV IV-B, box 89, no. 827-7955. For responses, see document nos. 827-995, 827-1026, 827-1346, 827-1519, 827-1863, 827-2718.

12. KA KM, box 13820 [previously no. 753], no. 64-46/16-26.

13. Holotík, *Sociálne a národné hnutie,* 177–78.

14. Holotík, 261–64.

15. KA KM, box 13820, no. 64-46/16-34.

16. KA KM, box 13820, no. 64-46/16-34. Hrabak, *Dezerterstvo,* 138–39.

17. On the summer 1918 raids organized by Cracow, Graz, Leitmeritz, Poszony, Lemberg, and Sarajevo military commands, see KA KM, box 13820, no. 64-46/16-34. For more detailed reports on raids in Przemyśl command's jurisdiction, see nos. 64-46/16-17, 64-46/16-26. On raids organized by Poszony and Vienna military commands, see no. 64-46/16-25. On raids organized by Zagreb military command, see no. 64-46/16-10. On spring raids in western Slovakia, see Holotík's *Sociálne a národné hnutie* (177–78, 229–30). On raids in Syrmia in the spring, see box 13821, no. 64-46/35; and in the late summer and autumn, see box 13820, no. 64-46/23-11. On spring raids in Dalmatia and Bosnia-Herzegovina, see KA KM, Präsidialbüro (PB) Akten, box 2429, no. 53-16/11. On late summer raids in Moravia, see *Sborník dokumentů* (290–95).

18. KA KM, box 13820, no. 64-46/16-34.

19. KA KM, box 13820, no. 64-46/16-17; *Sborník dokumentů,* 237, 293; Státní okresní archiv Třebíč (SOkAT), Pobočka Moravské Budějovice, Okresní úřad Moravské Budějovice, box 1, 761; Državni arhiv Zadar (DAZD), 88 Namjesništvo za Dalmaciju (ND), Prezidijalni spisi, file 707, nos. 3033, 4957; HDA 79 OUPZV IV-B, box 89, 827-4027.

20. DAZD ND file 707, nos. 3033, 4957.

21. KA KM, box 13820, no. 64-46/23-5; SOkAT, Okresní úřad Třebíč, Presidiálné spisy (OUTPS), box 21, no. 893.

22. KA KM PB box 2428, no. 52-5/32

23. HDA 79 OUPZV IV-B, box 89, nos. 827-2991, 827-3253.

24. HDA 79 OUPZV IV-B, box 90, no. 827-4269. For similar resentment in Czech lands, see the municipal chronicle for the village of Hluk, year 1918 ("1918," Hlucké Kroniky, http://www.kronikahluk.cz/index.php?id=1918); SOkAH, VMHO no. 14 Kuželov VC 15.

25. Archiv hlavního města Prahy (AHMP), Vojtěch Berger, Denní zápisky v době světové války 1914–1918, book IV, 143–44, 148, 175–76.

26. KA KM, box 13818, no. 64-20/16.

27. AHMP Berger 1914–1918, book IV, 150–51.

28. KA KM, box 13820, nos. 64-46/23-2, 64-46/16-26, 64-46/16-17.

29. HDA 79 OUPZV IV-B, box 90, no. 827-4260.

30. AHMP Berger 1914–1918, book IV, 157.

31. Rachamimov, *POWs,* 31, 39; Plaschka, Haselsteiner, and Suppan, *Innere Front,* 1:278; Leidinger and Moritz, *Gefangenschaft,* 649.

32. Plaschka, Haselsteiner, and Suppan, *Innere Front*, 1:279–80.

33. Roth, *Hotel Savoy*, 77.

34. Leidinger and Moritz, *Gefangenschaft*, 652.

35. Národní archiv, Czech Republic (NA), Prezidium místodržitelství (PM) 1911–1920, box 5108, 13073/18; Holotík, *Sociálne a národné hnutie*, 102–4. On the Hungarian would-be assassins, see NA Prezídium ministerské rady Vídeň (MRP/R), box 83, no. 8604.

36. Centrih, "'Govorile so celo strojnice!'" 317.

37. OeStA Allgemeines Verwaltungsarchiv (AVA), Ministerium des Innern (MdI), Präsidium Akten (PA), box 2077, no. 11325. See also AVA MdI PA, box 2076, no. 8021, and box 2077, no. 12659; NA PM 1911–1920, box 5107, no. 11488/18; Holotík, *Sociálne a národné hnutie*, 111–12, 130–35, 322, 339–40.

38. AVA MdI PA, box 2074, no. 9705; NA PM 1911–1920, box 5105, no. 1625/18.

39. This paragraph draws on Plaschka, Haselsteiner, and Suppan, *Innere Front*, 1:280–90.

40. KA KM, box 13821, no. 64-46/27, July 5, 1918, report from Bosnia-Herzegovina and Dalmatia.

41. Plaschka, Haselsteiner, and Suppan, *Innere Front*, 1:287–88.

42. KA KM, box 13821, no. 64-50/16.

43. Holotík, *Sociálne a národné hnutie*, 183–90; see also ibid., 257, and KA KM, box 13821, no. 64-50/16-6.

44. Słomka, *From Serfdom to Self-Government*, 210. See also Martan, "Nemiri u Hrvatskoj," 15; Holotík, *Sociálne a národné hnutie*, 183–90.

45. Przeniosło, *Narodziny niepodległości w Galicji*, 222.

46. Plaschka, Haselsteiner, and Suppan, *Innere Front*, 1:324–400; Pichlík, "Vzpoury navratilců."

47. Hronský, *Struggle for Slovakia*, 43.

48. KA KM, box 13820, no. 64-46/23-12, June 20, 1918, report from Ruma; AVA MdI PA, box 2078, no. 15250; HDA 79 OUPZV IV-B, box, 89, nos. 827-2858, 827-3238; Holotík, *Sociálne a národné hnutie*, 314–15.

49. AVA MdI PA, box 2078, no. 16040.

50. Hanák, " Volksmeinung," 63.

51. J. Beneš, *Workers and Nationalism*, chapter 6.

52. KA KM, box 13821, no. 64-46/27, May 24, 1918, report. I thank Tamás Révész for translating this document.

53. AVA MdI PA, box 2078, no. 16492.

54. NA PM 1911–1920, box 5111, unnumbered report from August 12, 1918, in file 30008/18-31650/18.

55. KA KM, box 13820, no. 64-46/10.

56. KA KM, box 13820, no. 64-42/4.

57. NA PM 17705; SOkAH, Okresní úřad Hodonín—presidiální spisy (OUH PS), box 725, no. 735/18; Janković and Krizman, *Građa o stvaranju*, 290.

58. Holotík, *Sociálne a národné hnutie*, 184–86, 188–90.

59. KA KM, box 13819, no. 64-26/29; Juriga, *Blahozvesť kriesenia*, 141–44, 251–53; Hronský, *Slovensko na rázcestí*, 53. On the origins of the phrase, see Konštantín Palkovič's *Ohoľ ho! Rozprávky zo Záhoria* (153).

60. Bimka, "Trnitou cestou k svobodě," 266. This slogan features in prose fiction: Kepka, *Vojna*, 53; Ljubotrn, *Vojno povol, hej rup!*. It also appears in the title of the drama by J. L. Doudlebský, *Zelená garda (Vojno, povol!)*. See also AHMP Berger 1914–1918, book IV, 193.

61. AVA MdI PA, box 2078, no. 18658, report from July 26, 1918.

62. KA KM PB, box 2429, no. 53-16/11-3.

63. KA KM, box 13821, no. 64-46/35.

64. *Sborník dokumentů*, 234–38.

65. KA KM, box 13821, no. 64-46/27, report from July 22, 1918.

66. KA KM PB box 2429, no. 53-15/27.

67. For information on this case, see AVA MdI PA, box 2078, no. 16704, and box 2079, no. 19537; NA MRP/R box 83, no. 8386; KA KM, box 13821, no. 64-46/27, late July 1918 report from Hauptmann Otto Wittmayer.

68. KA KM, box 13821, no. 64-46/27, circular from September 6, 1918.

69. KA KM, box 13820, no. 64-46/10-6.

70. HDA 79 OUPZV IV-B, box 92, no 4247; cf. box 90, no. 827-4168 and KA KM, box 13821, no. 64-47/27 July 5, 1918, report.

71. HDA 79 OUPZV IV-B, box 90, no. 827-4571.

72. HDA 79 OUPZV IV-B, box 89, no. 827-1519; box 90, no. 827-4934. On the ease of Bosnian deserters moving around Croatia-Slavonia, see the testimony of Salko Humo in box 90, no. 827-4168.

73. AVA MdI PA, box 2078, no. 15031.

74. KA KM, box 13821, no. 64-46/27, September 6, 1918, circular, Wittmayer's late July report; Holotík, *Sociálne a národné hnutie*, 198; SOkAH OUH PS, box 726, no. 949.

75. KA KM, box 13821, no. 64-46/27, report from July 22, 1918.

76. "Zelená garda v buchlovských lesích," *Nová doba*, August 10, 1918, p. 2.

77. "V Boj," *Československá samostatnost*, July 13, 1918, p.6 [published in Paris]. On July and August articles in the Swiss press based on reports from Reuters in London, see NA MRP/R, box 83, no. 8790 and AVA MdI PA, box 2079, no. 19362.

78. Hrabak, *Dezerterstvo*, 187.

79. NA PM 1911–1920, box 5111, no. 31588; DAZD ND file 708, no. 3044.

80. See, e.g., KA KM, box 13820, no. 64-46/10; KA KM PB, box 2429, no. 53-14/3/3. See also Landis, "Who Were the 'Greens'?," 33–34.

81. Janković and Krizman, *Građa o stvaranju*, 248.

82. Hrabak, *Dezerterstvo*, 81, 140; HDA 79 OUPZV IV-B, box 90, no. 827-4468.

83. Pivko, *Proti Rakousku*, book 1, 270–71; Pichlík, "Vzpoury navratilců," 587. See also KA Allerhöchster Oberbefehl (AhOB), Militärkanzlei Seiner Majestät des Kaisers (MKSM), Hauptreihe Akten, box 1369, telegram from May 29, 1918; KA KM, box 13820, 64-46/10-3; and Plaschka, Haselsteiner, and Suppan, *Innere Front*, 2:81.

84. KA KM, box 13821, no. 64-46/27, July 5, 1918, report; Pivko, *Proti Rakousku*,book 1, 271; Hrabak, *Dezerterstvo*, 96, 101.

85. Hrabak, *Dezerterstvo*, 125.

86. Moslavina is the setting of the romantic Croatian Green Cadre novel by M. Kaić entitled *Zeleni kader: Ljubavni i pustolovni roman iz prevrata 1918*.

87. KA KM, box 13821, no. 64-46/27, July 5, 1918, report; Janković and Krizman, *Građa o stvaranju*, 249–50; Pivko, *Proti Rakousku*, book 1, 271; Hrabak, *Dezerterstvo*, 102–3, 180; HDA 79 OUPZV IV-B, box 89, no. 827-1519.

88. Janković and Krizman, *Građa o stvaranju*, 250; Hrabak, *Dezerterstvo*, 97.

89. In general: AVA MdI PA, box 280, no. 23238, October 5, 1918, report from Dalmatian governor; Janković and Krizman, *Građa o stvaranju*, 250. On Korčula: DAZD ND file 706, no. 3033, and file 707, no. 4957; Hrabak, *Dezerterstvo*, 130. On Betina: Jakovčev, "Zeleni kadar Betine 1918," 137–47; Hrabak, *Dezerterstvo*, 134.

90. Hrabak, *Dezerterstvo*, 98, 110–11.

91. Bruckmüller, "Landwirtschaftliche Arbeitswelten," 298.

92. Glaise-Horstenau, *Katastrophe*, 249.

93. Prepeluh, *Pripombe k naši prevratni*, 136–37; Pleterski, *Prva odločitev*, 230–33.

94. Šarh, "Spomini na Zeleni kader," 229–40. Cf. KA KM PB, box 2429, nos. 53-16/22, 53-16/2.

95. On recruitment: Bimka, "Trnitou cestou k svobodě," 266. In general: Bimka, "Trnitou cestou k svobodě"; Žižlavský, "Chřibský Zelený kádr," 7; Adolf E. Vašek, "Z doby zelených kádrů (Před 15 lety)," *Moravská orlice*, September 3, 1933, p. 2; Hlucké Kroniky, Hluk chronicle for 1918, http://www.kronikahluk.cz/.

96. Lexa, "Slovácká brigáda," 162.

97. Ferančík, *Rozpomienky*; Pál, "Významu činnosti 'zeleného kádra,'" 9–21. Cf. Holotík, *Sociálne a národné hnutie*, 178–79, 191–93, 235–37; Juriga, *Blahozvesť kriesenia*, 120–21.

98. Juriga, *Blahozvesť kriesenia*, 143–45.

99. Poseł, *Przewrót w Polsce*, 10.

100. Poseł, 10; Słomka, *From Serfdom to Self-Government*, 242; *Pamiętniki chłopów*, 1:682; Cimek, *Tomasz Dąbal*, 36. On desertion in Brzesko district, see Przeniosło's *Narodziny niepodległości w Galicji* (221). See also Szlanta, "Unter dem sinkenden Stern," 149–51.

101. Kossowski, *Zielona Kadra*, 11.

102. Plaschka, Haselsteiner, and Suppan, *Innere Front*, 2:92.

103. Šarh, "Spomini na Zeleni kader," 232.

104. This account is taken from Josef Serinek's *Česká cikánská rapsodie* (19–32).

105. Zlobec, *V bojih*, 18.

106. Mareš, *Zelená garda*, 29.

107. Mareš, 30.

108. SOkAJH, Archiv obce Sumrakov, Pamětní kniha, 13.

109. Hrabak, *Dezerterstvo*, 186–87.

110. SOkAH OUH PS, box 725, no. 601, June 17, 1918, report from the gendarmerie in Uherské Hradiště.

111. SOkAH OUH PS, box 726, no. 995/18.

112. SOkAB, František Sedláček personal fond, war memoir, 13.

113. Sedláček, 17.

114. SOkAB, Archiv obce Vrbice, pamětní kniha, 42.

115. Bimka, "Trnitou cestou k svobodě," 264.

116. "Z bojů o Slovensko: K sjezdu dobrovolců první železnobrodské setniny," *Lidové noviny*, July 26, 1928, 1; Livonský, "Železnobrodsko za války," 127–28.

117. Václav Šlesinger, "Brňáci bojují ve Světové válce: Zelený kádr na Moravě," *Lidové noviny*, September 10, 1932, 1–3; Šlesinger, "Četnictvo," 251–54; Hosák, *Státní převrat*, 9. On similar activity on Dalmatian Korčula, see DAZD ND file 707, no. 4957.

118. HDA 79 OUPZV IV-B, box 89, no. 827-3931; box 90, no. 827-4839.

119. *Sborník dokumentů*, 236; SOkAB, Archiv obce Morkůvky, pamětní kniha, 20.

120. Hrabak, *Dezerterstvo*, 118.

121. KA KM, box 13820, no. 64-46/16-34

122. Slezák, "Němčičští," 121.

123. HDA 79 OUPZV IV-B, box 89, no. 827-1519.

124. Državni arhiv Osijek (DAOS), Kraljevski sudbeni stol Osijek (KSSO) 1850–1945, box 2094, case I-1924; HDA 79 OUPZV IV-B, box 90, no. 827-4913.

125. Wolf, *Peasant Wars*, 291–93.

126. SOkAH VMHO, no. 41 Malá Vrbka, 74.

127. HDA 79 OUPZV IV-B, box 89, 827 res. 1918 (inventory no. missing), 16.

128. HDA 417 Odvjetnička pisarnica Walter Radivoj (OPWR), box 174, case against Panić.

129. HDA 417 OPWR, box 142, case against Čavić and co. See also box 197, case K372 against Vračević.

130. Ferančík, *Rozpomienky*, 24.

131. Slovenská národná knižnica, Martin (SNK), Literárny archív (LA), fond Jozef Ferančík (1885–1972), accession nos. 803, 889, 1058, 1329, 1620.

132. SNK LA Ferančík, no. 803.

133. Livonský, "Železnobrodsko za války," 127–28; SOkAH VMHO, no. 16 Lanžhot VC 15; SOkAH, Archiv obce Blatnički, pamětní kniha (inv. č. 56), p. 63; "Převrat na Vojně," *Zájmy českomoravské Vysočiny*, September 14, 1933, p. 6.

134. SOkAT, OUTPS, box 21, nos. 550, 5214, "Deserteursunwesen in Hartwikowitz."

135. Stryczek, *Chłopskim piórem*, 231.

136. KA KM, box 13821, no. 64-46/46-2. Cf. Hrabak, *Dezerterstvo*, 118, 121.

137. Ćosić Bukvin, *Vrbanjci u 'Velikom ratu,'* 115; Banac, "'Emperor Karl," 295.

138. DAZD ND file 707, no. 4957.

139. Watson, *Ring of Steel*, 538–39.

140. HDA 79 OUPZV IV-B, box 89, no. 827-3785; see also KA KM, box 13820, 64-46/23-12.

141. HDA 79 OUPZV IV-B, box 89, no. 827-3785. On the aftermath, see box 92, no. 3785.

142. HDA 79 OUPZV IV-B, box 90, 827-4281; see also KA KM, box 13820, 64-46/23-12.

143. HDA 79 OUPZV IV-B, box 90, 827-4909. On Agić's widow's claims for compensation, see HDA 1352 Pobune štrajkovi i pokreti radnika i seljaka (PŠPRS), box 8, no. 384.

144. KA KM PB, box 2428, no. 50-20/1.

145. Vidmar, "Prilozi građi za povijest," 61–62. See also Bogdanović, "Kategorije zelenog kadra 1918." Such agitation was rumored to be underway in Moravia as well. See AVA MdI PA, box 2078, no. 16704, July 16, 1918, report.

146. HDA 79 OUPZV IV-B, box 89, no. 827-3114.

147. HDA 79 OUPZV IV-B, box 90, no. 827-5050.

148. HDA 79 OUPZV IV-B, box 90, no. 827-4934.

149. Žižlavský, "Chřibský Zelený kádr," 7.

150. HDA 79 OUPZV IV-B, box 90, nos. 827-4598, 827-4943.

151. Adolf E. Vašek, "Z doby zelených kádrů (Před 15 lety)," *Moravská orlice*, September 3, 1933, 25; Sicha, *Český vojín*, 13–14.

152. Rošický, *Rakouský orel padá*, 36.

153. Rošický, 59.

154. Janković and Krizman, *Građa o stvaranju*, 186–89, 247–50, 287–91.

155. Pivko, *Proti Rakousku*, book 2, 184–87.

156. Janković and Krizman, *Građa o stvaranju*, 252–54; Hrabak, *Dezerterstvo*, 181.

157. Janković and Krizman, *Građa o stvaranju*, 316–21.

158. Janković and Krizman, 381–82.

159. Quoted in Wade, *Russian Revolution*, 242.

160. Serge, *Memoirs of a Revolutionary*, 87.

161. Brovkin, "On the Internal Front," 558.

162. Landis, "Who Were the 'Greens'?," 35.

163. Landis, "Waiting for Makhno" and *Bandits and Partisans*.

164. Quoted in Landis, *Bandits and Partisans*, 3.

165. Hrabak, *Dezerterstvo*, 187; KA KM 64-41/8-72, 64-41/8/43, 64-46/44-2.

166. Glaise-Horstenau, *Katastrophe*, 249.

167. HDA 79 OUPZV IV-B, box 90, no. 827-4122. On conditions in Syrmia: box 89, nos. 827, 827-3114, 827-4093, box 90, nos. 827-4304, 827-4323, 827-4468; KA KM, box 13821, nos. 64-46/35, 64-46/46-2; Hrabak, *Dezerterstvo*, 142, 144; Janković and Krizman, *Građa o stvaranju*, 264–65.

168. HDA 79 OUPZV IV-B, box 90, no. 827-4891 September 12, 1918, report from Veliki Bastaji.

169. Plaschka, Haselsteiner, and Suppan, *Innere Front*, 2:12; Tunstall, "Military Collapse."

170. Zlobec, *V viharju*, 174.

171. HDA 79 OUPZV IV-B, box 90, 827-4838.

Chapter 3

1. Maroslavac, *Donji Miholjac kroz stoljeća*, 191.

2. Maroslavac, 192.

3. Maroslavac, 193.

4. Hagen, *Anti-Jewish Violence.*

5. Urban, *Živý bič*, 274.

6. Narkiewicz, *Green Flag*, 22.

7. Dobos, "Nagodba," 85. These statistics are for "Civil Croatia" without Slavonia and the Military Frontier.

8. Macartney, *Habsburg Empire*, 462–63; Okey, *Habsburg Monarchy*, 167.

9. Bruckmüller, "Landwirtschaftliche Arbeitswelten," 319–20.

10. On the expansion of the Habsburg state bureaucracy after 1848, see John Deak's *Forging a Multinational State.*

11. Dobos, "Nagodba," 88.

12. Hagen, *Anti-Jewish Violence*, 30–47, 507–9, 517. On Polish peasant superstitions and cosmology in general, see William I. Thomas and Florian Znaniecki's *The Polish Peasant in Europe and America* (205–88).

13. E.g., Petrungaro, *Kamenje i puške*, 75–76. On Jewish settlement in the Kingdom of Hungary, see Michael Silber's "The Making of Habsburg Jewry in the Long Eighteenth Century" (765–70).

14. Révész, "Soldiers in the Revolution."

15. Holquist, "Violent Russia, Deadly Marxism?," 648–50.

16. "Denní zprávy," *Moravská orlice*, November 5, 1918, 3.

17. Janković and Krizman, *Građa o stvaranju*, 394. See also 378, 381.

18. Quoted in Čulinović, *Odjeci oktobra*, 92.

19. Šišić, *Postanku Kraljevine Srba*, 211.

20. Krizman, "Građa o nemirima," 118

21. Krizman, 114, 116, 118, 125.

22. Krizman, 115.

23. Krizman, 113.

24. Krizman, 113.

25. Ferančík, *Rozpomienky*, 36.

26. Medvecký, *Slovenský Prevrat*, 3:58.

27. Juriga, *Blahozvesť kriesenia*, 145. On their role in the "revolution" in Kostolište, see Mária Zacharová's "Pramene k dejinám" (2:237).

28. Hlucké Kroniky, Hluk chronicle, year 1918, http://www.kronikahluk.cz/.

29. Mareš, *Zelená garda*, 106.

30. Saje, "Revolucionarno gibanje," 143–44. They also attacked gendarmes in Lower Carniolan Semič.

31. Krizman, "Građa o nemirima," 112, 119.

32. Vidmar, "Prilozi građi za povijest," 103–5.

33. Vidmar, 107.

34. Vidmar, 121.

35. Kraus, *Susreti i sudbine*, 99.

36. Hagen, *Anti-Jewish Violence*, 129–34. On the role of the Green Cadres, see also pp. 255–56, 287–88. See also Przeniosło's *Narodziny niepodległości w Galicji* (156–57 on Rozwadów; 219–20 on Brzozów; 220–26 on Brzesko).

37. Przeniosło, *Narodziny niepodległości w Galicji*, 206–7.

38. Hagen, *Anti-Jewish Violence*, 130–31.

39. Słomka, *From Serfdom to Self-Government*, 256.

40. Przeniosło, *Narodziny niepodległości w Galicji*, 124.

41. Przeniosło, 222.

42. Przeniosło, 123. Similarly, for Tarnobrzeg district see p. 158, and p. 208 for Limanowa.

43. Przeniosło, 121.

44. Przeniosło, 221–25.

45. Purivatra, *Nacionalni i politički razvitak*, 142.

46. Purivatra, 219–29; Užičanin, "Agrarni nemiri," 36–44.

47. Bergholz, *Violence*, 38–39.

48. Medvecký, *Slovenský Prevrat*, 3:110–11, 4:146–50, 180.

49. Saje, "Revolucionarno gibanje," 143–44.

50. On the potential for peasant anti-Jewish violence on market days, see Tim Buchen's *Antisemitism in Galicia* (128) and Klaus Richter's *Antisemitismus in Litauen* (76–83, 306).

51. Státní okresní archiv Uherské Hradiště (SOkAUH), Archiv města Uherský Brod, box 118, Kronika města I, 25.

52. Zacharová, "Pramene k dejinám," 1:235–36.

53. For instances in western Slovakia: Zacharová, "Pramene k dejinám," 1:241 (in Holíč), 2:205–6 (Stupava), 2:224 (Sološnica), 2:231–35 (Záhorská Ves).

54. This paragraph is based on Hrvoje Volner's *Od industrijalaca do kažnjenika* (45–51).

55. Volner, 53, 60.

56. DAOS KSSO, 1850–1945, box 2092, no. 1712-18. This paragraph is based mostly on the November 25, 1918, testimony of Ivan Bendek.

57. DAOS KSSO, box 2095, I-1956/18, March and June 1919 statements by Engelman.

58. Volner, *Od industrijalaca*, 53.

59. DAOS KSSO, box 2098, I-56/1919.

60. This case is contained in DAOS KSSO, box 2093, I-1875/18.

61. Lexa, "Skupinové násilí," 141–42, 175–76.

62. Lexa, 150–53, 157, 170, 172.

63. Hagen, *Anti-Jewish Violence*, xiii.

64. On the importance of communities defining themselves through public performance and ritual, see Clifford Geertz's "Deep Play" (esp. 82–85). On the importance of events in the crystallization of class consciousness, see the introduction.

65. Bergholz, *Violence*.

66. The founding text of historical "moral economy" studies is E. P. Thompson's "Moral Economy of the English Crowd in the Eighteenth Century." Its most forceful application to peasant studies is by James C. Scott in *The Moral Economy of the Peasant* and "Hegemony and the Peasantry" (279–81).

67. DAOS KSSO, box 2093, I-1875/18, February 2, 1919, deposition of Max Schlesinger.

68. Zacharová, "Pramene k dejinám," 1:205–6.

69. SNK LA Ferančík, box 2, no. 1329/1970.

70. DAOS KSSO, box 2107, I-415/19.

71. HDA PS, box 1, no. 26 (quotes in an unpaginated report from November 8, 1918); cf. Kovačević, "Nemiri u Moslavini," 82–95.

72. Kovačević, "Nemiri u Moslavini," 108.

73. HDA PS, box 1, no. 26, December 2, 1918 report.

74. Richter, *Antisemitismus*, 73–75; Hagen, *Anti-Jewish Violence*, 61.

75. Burke, *Popular Culture*, 190, 203–4. See also Bercé, *History of Peasant Revolts*, 26–34; Guha, *Elementary Aspects*, 30–36.

76. Cf. Davis, "Rites of Violence," 84–85. See also Hagen, *Anti-Jewish Violence*, 152, 158–61, 507.

77. Medvecký, *Slovenský Prevrat*, 3:82.

78. Zacharová, "Pramene k dejinám," 2:212, 221, 225–27.

79. Medvecký, *Slovenský Prevrat*, 3:98.

80. Medvecký, 3:5.

81. Zacharová, "Pramene k dejinám," 2:222.

82. Hagen, "Moral Economy."

83. DAOS KSSO, box 2097, I-2050/18.

84. HDA, PŠPRS, box 9, no. 390, p. 47.

85. HDA, PŠPRS, p. 47.

86. Cf. Schnell, *Räume des Schreckens* and "Tear Them Apart"; Baberowski, "Kriege in staatsfernen Räumen"; Böhler, "Enduring Violence."

87. Mitrany, *Marx against the Peasant*, 81.

88. Keep, *Russian Revolution*, 196, 209–16.

89. Veidlinger, *In the Midst*, 16–18.

90. Babel, *Red Cavalry*, 63.

91. Quoted in Chopard, "L'ere des atamans," 60.

92. Schnell, "Tear Them Apart," 209.

93. For an anatomy of the concept, see Paul Hanebrink's *Specter Haunting Europe*.

94. Chopard, "L'ere des atamans," 63–67; Gilley, "Ukrainian Anti-Bolshevik Risings," 123–24; Veidlinger, *In the Midst*, 188–216.

95. Veidlinger, *In the Midst*, 24–25.

96. Hagen, *Anti-Jewish Violence*, 512.

97. Banac, "Emperor Karl," 303.

98. Kraus, *Susreti i sudbine*, 132; Volner, *Od industrijalaca*, 60.

99. Feletar, *Dva seljačka bunta*, 9.

100. Medvecký, *Slovenský Prevrat*, 3:57.

101. Medvecký, 3:88.

102. Medvecký, 3:81.

103. Medvecký, 3:5.

104. Medvecký, 1:63–64.

105. Zacharová, "Pramene k dejinám," 1:201.

106. Zacharová, 1:200 (Brodské), 2:229 (Plavecký Mikuláš in 1919), 2:230 (Plavecký Peter).

107. SOkAB, Četnická stanice Lanžhot, book 1: památník.

108. NA, Zemské četnické velitelství (ZČV), box 283, no. 19347.

109. HDA, Odvjetnička pisarnica Walter Radivoj, box 138, Bara Blažinčić i dr. iz Peščenice—radi sudjelovanja u buni 31 listopada 1918, pljačke i zlobne oštete tudjeg vlasništva.

110. DAOS KSSO, box 2091, I-1642/1919; box 2097, I-2033/18.

111. SOkAH VMHO no. 9 Hrušky VC 16.

112. Šišić, *Postanku Kraljevine Srba*, 247–48.

113. Šišić, 256–57.

114. Quoted in Banac, *National Question*, 131.

115. Krizman, "Građa o nemirima," 121.

116. Šišić, *Postanku Kraljevine Srba*, 228–29.

117. Krizman, "Građa o nemirima," 127–28.

118. Krleža, *Hrvatski bog Mars*, 347.

119. Zorec, *Zeleni kader*, 172–73.

120. Zorec, 97.

121. Banac, *National Question*, 12–13.

122. Hronský, *Struggle for Slovakia*, 77–79.

123. Lexa, "Skupinové násilí," 133.

124. Hronský, *Struggle for Slovakia*, 70–71; Vojenský historický archiv, Prague (VHAP), Boje na Slovensku I (BSI), box 2, nos. 19/16, 19/17

125. Medvecký, *Slovenský Prevrat*, 3:36–45.

126. Medvecký, 3:119, 4:77–8, 93, 121–22.
127. VHAP BSI, box 2, no. 15, report by Emil Špatný, Cyrill Dušek, Jan Pocisk, 2.
128. Szabó, "'Rabovačky.'"
129. Medvecký, *Slovenský Prevrat*, 4:95.
130. See, e.g., Zacharová, "Pramene k dejinám," 1:197 (Kúty).
131. Zacharová, 1:211, 241, 2:206, 225; Medvecký, *Slovenský Prevrat*, 3:7, 56–57, 98, 155, 171–72, 4:78–79, 122.
132. Zacharová, "Pramene k dejinám," 2:211–13.
133. Juriga, *Blahozvesť kriesenia*, 121, 145.
134. Lexa, "Skupinové násilí," 45.
135. Hronský, *Struggle for Slovakia*, 134–35.
136. Quoted in V. Beneš, "Czechoslovak Democracy," 74.
137. See, e.g., VHAP BSI, box 1, no. 54, December 2, 1918, order from Schöbl; VHAP Slovácký pluk, Velitelství spisy (SPVS), box 1, no. 259, and box 3, no. 10, Vojenský historický archív, Bratislava (VHAB), Zemské vojenské veliteľstvo 1919–1939 (ZVVo), box 1, no. 22.
138. Kučera, "Exploiting Victory."
139. Bandoľová et al., *Od Uhorského kráľovstva*, 402–3.
140. Slovenský národný archív (SNA) Minister Československej republiky s plnou mocou pre správu Slovenska, Prezidium II/4 (MPSP), box 259, nos. 5626, 5256; box 271, no. 1864, report from March 22, 1919.
141. SNA MPSP, box 269, no. 420/1919.
142. SNA MPSP, box 10, no. 7660/1920.
143. Fink, *Defending the Rights*, 237. For an overview of the minority treaties, see Gerwarth's *The Vanquished* (216–19).
144. On these episodes see Hagen's *Anti-Jewish Violence*, chapters 3 and 7.
145. Fink, *Defending the Rights*, chapters 4 and 6.
146. Quoted in MacMillan, *Peacemakers*, 227.
147. Quoted in Fink, *Defending the Rights*, 257.
148. Fink, 260.
149. Fink, 269.
150. On the League of Nations' raison d'être, see Susan Pedersen's *The Guardians* and chapter 1 of Mark Mazower's *No Enchanted Palace*.
151. Rothschild, *East Central Europe*, 39.
152. Hagen, *Anti-Jewish Violence*, 135–42.
153. SNA MPSP, box 5, no. 5258/1920.
154. Lexa, "Skupinové násilí," 261.
155. DAOS KSSO, box 2107, I-415/19.
156. Geiger, "Povijest Đakova i Đakovštine," 57, 61; Kovačević, "Nemiri u Moslavini," 89; Hagen, *Anti-Jewish Violence*, 133.
157. Tolkatsch, "Lokale Ordnungsentwürfe," 109.
158. SNA MPSP, box 9, no. 5085.
159. SNA MPSP, box 5, no. 8601/1920. On limited compensation for Jewish victims in interwar Czechoslovakia, along with authorities' tendency to blame them, see Lukáš Lexa's "Skupinové násilí" (146–48).

Chapter 4

1. On Germans in Bohemia and Moravia and Vorarlberg, see John C. Swanson's *Remnants of the Habsburg Monarchy* (29–36).
2. On the Bavarian initiatives in Munich, see Eliza Ablovatski's *Revolution and Political Violence in Central Europe*.

3. On the Banat Republic, see Ladislav Heka's "Posljedice Prvoga svjetskog rata" (125–28). On the Black Diamond Republic, see Anca Glont's "Revolution of the Black Diamond Republic." Heka also discusses other self-proclaimed statelets on the territory of historic Hungary in 1919 and 1921.

4. Zacharová, "Pramene k dejinám," 2:230.

5. Weitz, "Self-Determination."

6. Manela, *Wilsonian Moment*.

7. Bugge, "Making of a Slovak City."

8. Lansing, *Peace Negotiations*, 97.

9. Schneer, "Markovo Republic."

10. S. Jones, "Marxism and Peasant Revolt."

11. Shanin, *Russia, 1905–7*, 99–119; A. Adams, "Peasantry in Russia," 6–9. On Russian Poland, see Robert E. Blobaum's *Rewolucja* (123–35, 148–46).

12. For example, in Kharkov/Kharkiv region, now in the Ukraine. See Baker, *Peasants, Power, and Place*, 64.

13. Figes, *Peasant Russia*, 72–73.

14. Tolkatsch, "Lokale Ordnungsentwürfe," 97.

15. Tolkatsch, 104.

16. Šovagović and Cvetković, *Valpovština u revoluciji*, 11.

17. Šovagović and Cvetković, 11.

18. Kraus, *Susreti i sudbine*, 129. On the date of the republic's fall: Vidmar, "Prilozi građi za povijest," 151. See also Sršan, *Povijest petrijevačke župe*, 21, 175–76.

19. Vidmar, "Prilozi građi za povijest," 124.

20. Kraus, *Susreti i sudbine*, 132.

21. Feletar, *Dva seljačka bunta*, 63–64.

22. Vidmar, "Prilozi građi za povijest," 156.

23. Hrabak, *Dezerterstvo*, 211.

24. Vidmar, "Prilozi građi za povijest," 140.

25. Quoted in Martan, "Nemiri u Hrvatskoj," 11.

26. ARS, fond Franček Saje (FS), box 26, no. 5, article by Franček Saje, "Notranjska rdeča republika: Odmev Oktoberske revolucije v Loški dolini," in *Slovenski poročevalec*, November 6, 1957.

27. ARS FS, box 26, no. 5, November 7, 1957, typescript recollections of Ivan Krajec; Franček Saje, "Revolucionarno gibanje kmečkega ljudstva v Sloveniji 1917–1919," *Prispevki za novejšo zgodovino* 7, nos. 1–2 (1967), 144–45.

28. An excellent biography is Cimek's *Tomasz Dąbal*.

29. My account of the Tarnobrzeg Republic is based on Henryk Cimek's *Tomasz Dąbal 1890–1937* and Marek Przeniosło's "Republika Tarnobrzeska (1918–1919)." Unless otherwise stated, events are reconstructed from these sources. For an overview in English, see Zachary Mazur's "Mini-states and Micro-sovereignty," 9–12.

30. Cimek, *Tomasz Dąbal*, 35.

31. Stankiewicz, *Konflikty społeczne*, 139.

32. Cimek, *Tomasz Dąbal*, 38.

33. Przeniosło, "Republika Tarnobrzeska," 479.

34. Przeniosło, ed., *Narodziny niepodległości w Galicji*, 158.

35. Słomka, *From Serfdom to Self-Government*, 253–54.

36. Quoted in Cimek, *Tomasz Dąbal*, 38. I thank Lucian George for his assistance in translating these verses, here rendered in the original Polish:

Wy nas nie straszcie sądem i kulą,

Jaśnie wielmożni z tej PKL,
Bo my pod zgrzebną chłopską koszulą

Nosimy piersi, które na cel
Stawialim, idąc w bój—straże przednie—

Za was i wasze Berliny i Wiednie.

Nas nie ogłupi, ludzi od młocki,

Krakowski kołtun, paskarz czy szlagon
Ani przechera "hrabia" Lasocki,
Że się dostanie nam z łaski zagon—
Jeno nie teraz, później, po sejmie,

Gdy Witos rządy w Polsce obejmie.

37. Cimek, 40.
38. Cimek, 48–49.
39. Przeniosło, *Narodziny niepodległości w Galicji*, 144.
40. Przeniosło, 155, 166. See also reports on pp. 151–52, 164, 165, 169.
41. Przeniosło, 168.
42. Przeniosło, 166.
43. Słomka, *From Serfdom to Self-Government*, 256–57.
44. Przeniosło, *Narodziny niepodległości w Galicji*, 169.
45. Słomka, *From Serfdom to Self-Government*, 259.
46. Hagen, *Anti-Jewish Violence*, 262–69, 289.
47. Hagen, 290.
48. Cimek, *Tomasz Dąbal*, 86, 97.
49. Unless otherwise stated, this section on the Hutsul Republic is based on Fedinec and Szakál's "Hucul Köztársaság." I am grateful to Tamás Révész for translating the findings of this new study into English.
50. Magocsi, *Backs to the Mountains*, 5.
51. Magocsi, "Ukrainian Question," 96–97.
52. On the western Lemkos' republic, see Magocsi's "Ukrainian Question between Poland and Czechoslovakia" (97–99).
53. Unless otherwise stated, the account of the Mura Republic and its origins is based on Julij Titl's *Murska republika 1919*.
54. For an eyewitness account, see Ivan Jerič's *Moji spomini* (40–41).
55. For Tkalec's biography, see László Göncz's "'Kalandor Vállalkozás' a Mura Mentén." I thank Tamás Révész for translating this work's findings into English for me.
56. Romsics, "Great War," 192.
57. Biondich, *Stjepan Radić*, 164.
58. Weiss, *Viniška republika*, 8, 12–13. This source is also the basis of the account of the Vinica Republic below.
59. Weiss, 10.
60. Weiss, 27.
61. Weiss, 37.
62. Paver, *Zbornik građe*, 62–63. See also HDA, fond 1363 Politička situacija 1910–1940, box 4, no. 191, May 23, 1919, report.
63. Paver, *Zbornik građe*, 149–52.
64. Paver, 157.
65. HDA PŠPRS, box 8, no. 387, report from Sveti Ivan Zelina district.
66. Paver, *Zbornik građe*, 282–83.
67. HDA PŠPRS, box 8, no. 357, report from Grubišno Polje district.

68. My account is based on Paver's *Zbornik građe za povijest radničkog pokreta i KPJ 1919–1920* (282–385); HDA PŠPRS, box 8, no. 357; and Banac's *The National Question in Yugoslavia* (248–60). Banac's discussion is based primarily on Paver's collection of documents.

69. Paver, *Zbornik građe*, 367.

70. HDA PŠPRS, box 8, no. 357, report from Dugo Selo district; Paver, 294.

71. Đerek, "Dezerterstvo i zeleni kadar," 206; see also HDA PŠPRS, box 8, no. 357.

72. E.g., HDA PŠPRS, box 9, no. 388.

73. HDA PS, box 5, no. 226, September 23, 1920, report from Virovitica.

74. HDA PŠPRS, box 8, no. 357, introduction and conclusion.

75. These figures are quoted in Banac's *National Question* (254).

76. HDA PŠPRS, box 9, no. 390.

77. HDA PŠPRS, box 9, no. 395, report from November 14, 1921.

78. HDA PŠPRS, box 9, no. 395, reports from November 7 and 11, 1921.

79. HDA PŠPRS, box 9, no. 395, report from November 14, 1921.

80. Saje, "Revolucionarno gibanje," 146.

81. HDA PŠPRS, box 9, no. 396, April 4, 1921, report from Čakovec; HDA PS, box 6, nos. 343: February 11, 1921, report from Sisak; 349: January 1921, reports from western Slavonia; 393: February 5, 1921, report from Varaždin county.

82. Đerek, "Dezerterstvo i zeleni kadar," 203–6.

83. HDA PŠPRS, box 9, no. 398, reports from May 24–25, 1921.

84. HDA PŠPRS, box 9, no. 398, letter from May 20, 1921.

85. HDA PŠPRS, box 9, no. 403.

86. HDA PŠPRS, box 9, no. 406.

87. Banac, *National Question*, 227.

88. Biondich, *Stjepan Radić*, 175–76.

89. Klaus Richter, "Orgy of license," 794. In the Baltic states, large-estate land accounted for nearly half of all arable land.

90. Romsics, "Great War," 194.

91. On the Polish reform, see Dietmar Müller's "Property between Delimitation and Nationalization" (124–25, 128) and "Colonization Projects and Agrarian Reforms in East-Central and Southeastern Europe, 1913–1950" and Jacek Kochanowicz's "Changing Landscape of Property" (137).

92. Müller, "Property between Delimitation," 120.

93. On the Romanian reform, see Keith Hitchins's *Rumania, 1866–1947* (347–55).

94. On the Yugoslav reform, see Tomasevich's *Peasants, Politics and Economic Change in Yugoslavia* (345–80). The text of the decree is on pp. 347–49.

95. On the Czechoslovak reform, see Václav Beneš's "Czechoslovak Democracy and Its Problems" (90–92), Mark Cornwall's "'National Reparation'?" (259–80) and Daniel E. Miller's "Colonizing the Hungarian and German Border Areas during the Czechoslovak Land Reform."

96. Cornwall, "'National Reparation'?," 261.

97. Miller, "Colonizing," 307–8.

98. Quoted in Tomasevich, *Peasants*, 347–49.

99. Quoted in Müller, "Colonization Projects," 54. On the reform, see Christhardt Henschel's "Front-Line Soldiers into Farmers" (145–49).

100. Müller, "Colonization Projects."

101. Bideleux, "Peasantries and Peasant Parties," 301–5.

102. SNK LA Ferančík, box 1, no. 903/1960.

Chapter 5

1. Regionální muzeum v Mikulově (RMM), Cyril Hluchý collection (CH), no. 26, June 12, 1930, letter to Jan Moterský.

2. Lexa, "Slovácká brigáda," 162.

3. Šarh, "Spomini na Zeleni kader," 229; Zlobec, *V bojih*, 40–63.

4. Šmidrkal, "Abolish the army?"; Zückert, "Vojáci republiky?"

5. SOkAH, Archiv města Kyjov, no. 163, p. 47.

6. SOkAH, Archiv obce Sobůlky, no. 19, p. 7; Archiv obce Dambořice, no. 53, p. 71; VMHO no. 3, Dolní Bojanovice (part 16); no. 16,Lanžhot (part 16); no. 38, Velká nad Veličkou (part 16).

7. Lexa, "Slovácká brigáda," 159–60.

8. The 1910 census counted 3,244 Czechs and 4,482 Germans; 60 of the local Jewish community claimed Czech nationality, based on their "language of daily use," while 262 identified as Germans. See Hosák, *Státní převrat*, 7. On the revolution there, see ibid. (10–16) and Lexa's "Slovácká brigáda" (160).

9. On the rise of the brigade, see especially Lexa's "Slovácká brigáda" and Lev Ecker's *Slovácká brigáda*.

10. SOkAH, Archiv města Hodonín (AMH), no. 296 Pamětní kniha 1914–1928, p. 151.

11. SOkAH, Archiv obce Ždánice, no. 73 Pamětní kniha, 67.

12. SOkAUH, Archiv města Uherské Hradiště, box 412, no. 502.

13. SOkAB, František Sedláček, war memoirs, 15.

14. VHAP SPVS, box 4, name registers. A total of 791 men were listed as peasants, while 294 were workers. The next largest professional group was cobblers, with 82 men.

15. VHAP, Slovácká brigáda, Velitelství spisy (SBVS), box 3, no. 96.

16. Figures from Lexa, "Slovácká brigáda"; Masarykovo muzeum Hodonín (MMH), D882/DJ150, memoirs of Martin Ondryska, 2.

17. Ecker, *Slovácká brigáda*, 6.

18. MMH Ondryska, 2.

19. For details, see Lukáš Lexa's "Vojenská ochrana demarkačních linií na Mikulovsku a Valticku v letech" (77–80).

20. VHAP SBVS, box 3, no. 96. See also VHAP Zemské vojenské velitelství (ZVV), Presidium, box 2, no. 814.

21. VHAP SBVS, box 3, no. 181.

22. Jandásek, "Z počátků Slovácké brigády," 277.

23. VHAP ZVV, box 2, no. 6423, November 27, 1918, order.

24. VHAP ZVV, box 1, no. 364, December 8, 1918, report; box 3, no. 212, January 3, 1919, order.

25. VHAP SBVS, box 3, no. 416, March 28, 1919, report.

26. Ecker, *Slovácká brigáda*, 13–14.

27. SOkAH AMH, no. 296 pamětní kniha 1914–1928, pp. 173–74.

28. VHAP ZVV, box 4, no. 2283, February 13, 1919, report.

29. Lexa, "Slovácká brigáda," 173.

30. SOkAH, Archiv obce Ždánice, no. 73 pamětní kniha, 68.

31. SOkAB, Četnická stanice Břeclav, Památník četnické stanice v Břeclavě, book I, part V.

32. Ecker, *Slovácká brigáda*, 5. See also Lexa, "Skupinové násilí," 159–60.

33. Medvecký, ed., *Slovenský Prevrat*, 4:97.

34. On Slovakia, see VHAP BSI, Velitelství skupiny Schöbl (VSS), box 1, no. 62, report from December 4, 1918. On Moravia, see VHAP ZVV, box 1, no. 26, November 17, 1918, report from Moravian provincial command; no. 122, November 19, 1918, report from Jihlava; no. 200, November 23, 1918, report from Jihlava.

35. VHAP ZVV, box 2, no. 1153, December 19, 1918, report; VHAP SBVS, box 3, no. 136, report from December 12, 1918.

36. VHAP ZVV, box 3, no. 46, January 2, 1919, report; see also no. 52, January 5 report to Prague.

37. VHAP ZVV, box 3, no. 46, January 2, 1919, report, marginal note.

38. VHAP SBVS, box 3, no. 5, November 15, 1918, report; VHAP ZVV, box 1, no. 13, overview report from November 13.

39. VHAP SBVS, box 3, no. 28, November 30, 1918, report; VHAP BSI VSS, box 2, report from Špatný et al., 19–20.

40. VHAP ZVV, box 1, no. 230, November 27, 1918, report to Prague.

41. VHAP ZVV, box 1, no. 386, December 4, 1918, report.

42. See in particular, VHAP BSI VSS, box 2, report from Špatný et al.; VHAP ZVV, box 1, no. 150, November 22, 1918, report. For a personal testimony, see František Šmída's *Vzpomínky z vojny* (149–51, 156).

43. VHAP SBVS, box 3, no. 443, April 4, 1919, order.

44. VHAP SBVS, box 3, nos. 60, 64 (November 16–17, 1918, messages).

45. VHAP SBVS, box 3, no. 364, December 8, 1918, report.

46. VHAP ZVV, box 1, no. 464, December 8, 1918, order; box 3, no. 696, January 22, 1919, proposal.

47. VHAP SBVS, box 3, no. 303, February 18, 1919, order; nos. 302/303 March 1, 1919, response; no. 431, April 5, 1919, report from Hluchý.

48. VHAP SBVS, box 3, no. 485, April 10, 1919, order.

49. On the brigade's renaming and subsequent life as the Slovácko Regiment, see VHAP SPVS, box 1, nos. 335/a, 77/1920; box 3, no. 89. Ecker, *Slovácká brigáda*, 12–13; MMH Ondryska, 3–4.

50. Quoted in Zückert, "National Concepts of Freedom," 333. On the motives for the new policy, see Zückert's "Vojáci republiky?" (160–63).

51. SOkB, František Sedláček, war memoirs, 15.

52. RMM CH, no. 26.

53. Mareš, *Zelená garda*, 109.

54. SOkAB, Archiv obce Vrbice, pamětní kniha, 47–48.

55. Quoted in Knaibl, *Vzpomínky státního zástupce*, 32.

56. Hluk municipal chronicle for 1919 ("1919," Hlucké Kroniky, http://www.kronikahluk.cz/index.php?id=1919; Josef Dufka quoted).

57. César and Otáhal, *Hnutí venkovského lidu*, 378.

58. César and Otáhal, 379.

59. See César and Otáhal's *Hnutí venkovského lidu* (454–55) for tabular data on 47 incidents of protest against, or resistance to, requisition: 7 in 1919, 28 in 1920, 12 in 1921; these data do not include some of the incidents documented in section 4 of the volume.

60. Miller, *Forging Political Compromise*, 68–69.

61. SNA MPSP, box 9, no. 5883.

62. César and Otáhal, *Hnutí venkovského lidu*, 393–97.

63. César and Otáhal, 385–87.

64. SNA MPSP, box 10, no. 7660, October 12, 1920, charges brought by state prosecutor.

65. SOkAH OUH PS, box 730, nos. 5017, 5033. I am grateful to Lukáš Lexa for sharing this source with me.

66. César and Otáhal, *Hnutí venkovského lidu*, 16; Nekuda, *Břeclavsko*, 158.

67. César and Otáhal, *Hnutí venkovského lidu*, 367.

68. César and Otáhal, 367.

69. César and Otáhal, 368–69.

70. César and Otáhal, 368.

71. *Sbírka zákonů a nařízení státu československého*, part XVI, February 17, 1920, p. 135.

72. Kazimour, *Návod*, 1.

73. Kazimour, 4.

74. Zahra, *Kidnapped Souls*, ch. 2.

75. Orzoff, *Battle for the Castle*.

76. On the legionaries' position in interwar Czechoslovakia, see Nancy M. Wingfield's "National Sacrifice and Regeneration" and Katya Kocourek's "'In the Spirit of Brotherhood United We Remain!'"

77. SOkAH VMHO, no. 37, Moravská Nová Ves (part 15).

78. SOkAH, Archiv obce Strážovice, no. 11, p. 106; Archiv obce Nenkovice, no. 58, p. 65; Archiv obce Věteřov, no. 68, p. 10.

79. SOkAH VMHO, no. 9, Hrušky (part 15).

80. SOkAH, Archiv obce Dambořice, no. 53, p. 68; Archiv obce Skalky, no. 38, p. 35; Archiv obce Vřesovice, no. 44, p. 64; Archiv obce Žarošice, no. 22, p. 39; Archiv obce Ždánice, no. 73, p. 62.

81. SOkAH VMHO, no. 37, Moravská Nová Ves (part 18).

82. MZA C 12 Krajský soud trestní Brno, III. Manipulace, box 1935, no. VII 3668/27 Jan Brzák a spol.

83. On the organized thefts, see ibid., and SOkAH VMHO, no. 22, Mikulčice (part 15); SOkAB, Četnická stanice Moravská Nová Ves, Památník, part V; SOkAB, Četnická stanice Lanžhot, Památník part V; "Denní zprávy. Po stopách starých zločinů," *Lidové noviny*, April 26, 1927, p. 2; Hosák, *Státní převrat*, 16–17.

84. On the Vylášek case, see MZA, C 48 Krajský soud Uherské Hradiště, no. 502/22; "Soudní síň. Tři bratři loupežníci," *Lidové noviny*, October 16, 1922, p. 3; SOkAH, Archiv obce Skalky, no. 38, p. 40. For a similar case see, Lexa, "Skupinové násilí," 157–58.

85. Lexa, "Vojáci Slovácké brigády," appendix A, "Databáze příslušníků Slovácké brigády."

86. "Zelený kádr ještě straší," *Lidové noviny*, November 15, 1923, p. 2; "Soudní síň. Třebíčský zelený kádr," *Lidové noviny*, June 8, 1925, p. 3; "Soudní síň. Třebíčský zelený kádr," *Lidové noviny*, June 15, 1925, p. 3; "100 měsicců žaláře členům 'zeleného kádru,'" *Národní politika*, October 5, 1932, p. 6.

87. Hluk municipal chronicle for 1918 ("1918," Hlucké Kroniky, http://www.kronikahluk.cz/index.php?id=1918).

88. SOkAUH, Okresní úřad Uherské Hradiště, box 490d, no. 577/18, report from November 15, 1918; the phrase "glory to the deserters" (*sláva desertérům*) also appears in Rozner's *Vzpoura chalup* (186).

89. VHAP SBVS, box 3, no. 576, April 24, 1919, report.

90. VHAP SBVS, box 3, no. 576, order from May, 5 1919.

91. VHAB ZVVo, box 6, nos. 2665, 2886, 2888.

92. VHAB ZVVo, box 7, no. 3337.

93. VHAB ZVVo, box 59, no. 64-24/31.

94. VHAB ZVVo, box 59, no. 64-24/1.

95. SOkAH VMHO no. 7 Hodonín VC 16.

96. SOkAH VHMO no. 16 Lanžhot VC 18.

97. Jandásek, "Z počátků Slovácké brigády," 278.

98. Jandásek, 276.

99. MMH Ondryska, 4.

100. Ecker, *Slovácká brigáda*, 14.

101. RMM CH, no. 27, Vojtěch Rozner, "Před 20 lety byla založena Slovácká brigáda," [unknown periodical], October 30, 1938, p. 6.

102. Doudlebský, *Zelená garda*, 4 (capitalization in original).

103. Doudlebský, 44–45.

104. Doudlebský, 63.

105. Rosůlek, *Noha*, 41–42.

106. On the Rumburg mutiny and the real Noha: Plaschka, Haselsteiner, and Suppan, *Innere Front*, 1:357–70. Noha's Czech nationalist aspirations are much less clear in the empirical record. His sole motivations were apparently "peace, end of the war, and home" (358).

107. Rosůlek, *Noha*, 24, 192.

108. Livonský, "Železnobrodsko za války," 128.

109. Poláček, *Vyprodáno*, 97–102. See also the story "Invalida Josef Jaroš" in Kepka's *Vojna* (7–30).

110. Sicha, *Český vojín*, 12, 15.

111. "Práce osvětová a spolková," *Horažďovický obzor* 6, June 10, 1927, p. 50.

112. Pavel, *Zelený kádr*, 20–21, 215. On these Robin Hood figures, see Adam Votruba's *Pravda u zbojníka* (18–23).

113. Olbracht, *Nikola Šuhaj Loupežník*, 28.

114. SOkAH, Archiv obce Hýsly, no. 29.

115. Rozner, *Vzpoura chalup*, 188, 228.

116. Rozner, 226.

117. Rozner, 234.

118. For biographical information, see Pavel Koukal's "Spisovatel a novinář Michal Mareš" (esp. 9–13).

119. Literární archiv Památníku národního písemnictví (LAPNP), Prague, Michal Mareš, box 7, Vzpomínky (draft typescript).

120. Mareš, *Zelená garda*, 109–10.

121. Mareš, 109.

122. Bartoš, *Hoši ze zeleného kádru*, 42.

123. SOkAB, Archiv obce Lanžhot, kronika, 98–99.

124. Cyril Hluchý, "Fašismus a dělnictvo," *Moravská orlice*, June 2, 1926, p. 1.

125. Vykoupil, *Český fašismus na Moravě*, 39–40, 48.

126. Robert Mach, quoted in Vykoupil, 48.

Chapter 6

1. Smiljanić, "Zločin i kazna," 36–37. My account of Čaruga's rise and fall is based on Smiljanić's article and his monograph *Čaruga*, as well as on the following unscholarly but well-researched works, which draw above all on contemporary newspapers and court records: Zurl, *Knjiga o Jovi Čarugi*; Rašeta, *Čaruga*. The following novelistic account also contains reproductions of some original documents relating to the Band of Mountain Birds: Kušan, *Čaruga pamti*.

2. Hobsbawm, *Bandits*. See also his *Primitive Rebels*.

3. Hobsbawm, *Bandits*, 77–89; Bracewell, "Proud Name."

4. Hobsbawm, *Bandits*, 19–30, 42–43, 107.

5. Dobrowolski, *Studia nad życiem społecznym*, 87.

6. For an overview, see Adam Votruba's *Pravda u zbojníka* (18–19).

7. On Dovbuš and Ondráš, see Votruba's *Pravda u zbojníka* (20–23).

8. On Rósza and the phenomenon of *betyárs*, see Shingo Minamizuka's *A Social Bandit in Nineteenth Century Hungary*.

9. See, for instance, SAMA Navitas, "How Did Franc Guzej Become the Outlaw Guzaj?," Outlaw Guzaj (website), accessed April 18, 2024, https://www.guzaj.si/o-guzaju/?lang=en. I thank Anton Rančigaj for bringing Guzej to my attention.

10. Zupan, "Dezerterstvo na Slovenskem," 18–20.

11. See Zurl, *Knjiga o Jovi Čarugi*.

12. Hobsbawm, *Bandits*, 81–83.

13. Van Boeschoten, *From Armatolik*.

14. On the last, see Tomas Balkelis's "Social Banditry and Nation-Making."

15. Hrabak, *Dezerterstvo*, 121, 190; Banac, "Emperor Karl," 285, 295; Ćosić Bukvin, *Vrbanjci u "Velikom ratu,"* 115, 188.

16. Hrabak, *Dezerterstvo*, 84, 97.

17. Šarh, "Spomini na Zeleni kader," 235–36.

18. SNK LA Ferančík, box 2, no. 1329/1970, "Nuhál: Rozpomienky na Zelený Káder" (original unpublished typescript), 9.

19. Ferančík, *Rozpomienky*, 10.

20. SNK LA Ferančík, box 2, "Nuhál," 21.

21. SNK LA Ferančík, box 2, "Nuhál," appendix, 9.

22. Ferančík, *Rozpomienky*, 31.

23. Zacharová, "Pramene k dejinám," 2:224–25.

24. Šrobár, *Osvobodené Slovensko*, 369–70.

25. Šarenac, "Serbia's Great War Veterans."

26. Alimpić, *Policiski rečnik*, 591. I am grateful to Danilo Šarenac for providing me with this reference.

27. HDA PS, box 6, no. 332, reports from February 23, March 14, and April 29, 1921.

28. HDA PS, box 6, no. 332, report from March 14, 1921.

29. HDA PS, report from March 14, 1921.

30. HDA PS, box 6, no. 330, reports from September 15 and 24, 1921. On Obradović, see also Bergholz's *Violence as a Generative Force* (40).

31. HDA PS, box 6, no. 364, report from May 20, 1921.

32. HDA PS, box 6, no. 364, reports from May 31 and Jun 18, 1921.

33. HDA PS, box 6, no. 364, reports from June 11 and 18, 1921.

34. HDA PS, box 6, no. 364, report from June 11, 1921.

35. Šarenac, "Serbia's Great War Veterans," 111–12.

36. On these two bandit insurgencies, see Banac's *National Question in Yugoslavia* (271–306).

37. See, for instance, HDA PS, box 5, no. 321; box 6, no. 421; box 7, nos. 471, 501.

38. Kraus, *Susreti i sudbine*, 119.

39. Geiger, "Povijest Đakova i Đakovštine," 21.

40. These events are based on Ribar's own memoirs and other contemporary sources (Geiger, 14–16, 20, 22, 35, 52–54, 56).

41. Zorko, "Narodne straže," 369, 372–73.

42. Quoted in Geiger, "Povijest Đakova i Đakovštine," 48.

43. Quoted in Geiger, 58.

44. DAOS KSSO, box 2104, no. I-312/1919, October 21, 1919, interrogation of Matijević in Đakovo.

45. Kraus, *Susreti i sudbine*, 121.

46. Kraus, 121.

47. The document is reproduced in Kušan's *Čaruga pamti* (59).

48. Hobsbawm, *Bandits*, 47–48.

49. For the details of this case, see DAOS KSSO, box 2091, no. I-1702/1918.

50. The text of the statute is reproduced in Zurl's *Knjiga o Jovi Čarugi* (17–18).

51. This discussion of Čaruga's crimes is based on the previously cited works by Smiljanić and Zurl, as well as on the court documents contained in DAOS KSSO, box 2160, no. I-2065/20, and box 2244, I-101/24, nos. 394, 414, and 415.

52. DAOS KSSO, box 2160, no. I-2065/20, testimony of Pavao Gašo.

53. HDA PS, box 7, no. 492. The report also addresses the bloodshed in Ostrošinci.

54. Hobsbawm, *Bandits*, 29–30.

55. HDA PS, box 7, no. 492, report from July 19, 1922. The villages were Bokšić, Bare, Ostrošinci, Zdenci, Gazije, Kutovi, Budimci, Poganovci, Kršinci and Šumeđe in Našice district, along with Mikleuš and Miljevci in Slatina district.

56. Rašeta, *Čaruga*, 11.

57. Rašeta, 136; Zurl, *Knjiga o Jovi Čarugi*, 100–104.

58. Hobsbawm, *Bandits*, 50–51.

59. Interview with Rajko Grlić in Rašeta, *Čaruga*, 218.

60. On this case, see DAOS KSSO, box 2234, I-1034/1923.

61. DAOS KSSO, box 2234, I-1034/1923, January 28, 1924, deposition of Čaruga.

62. Zurl, *Knjiga o Jovi Čarugi*, 94. I am grateful to Bojan Aleksov for his assistance in translating this song. Another, more current version is here: "Sremacki Tamburasi—Caruga Jova tekst," Tekstovi-Pesama.com, https://tekstpesme.com/tekstovi/sremacki-tamburasi/caruga-jova/.

63. Kraus, *Susreti i sudbine*, 125.

64. Zurl, *Knjiga o Jovi Čarugi*, 66.

65. Smiljanić, "Zločin i kazna," 35.

66. Maestro film Zagreb, Hrvatska radiotelevizija, and Viba film Ljubljana coproduction.

67. Interview with Rajko Grlić in Rašeta, *Čaruga*, 226.

68. *Legenda o Čarugi*, YouTube, posted by Antun Smajic (director), March 27, 2009, https://youtu.be/bwFDgQRmPGc?t=351; *Čaruga: Ogledalo vremena* (dokumentari film), directed by Boris Šeper, YouTube, posted by Sk Metak, June 29, 2015, https://www.youtube.com/watch?v=8Ye3L4XaWWA&t=2290s.

Chapter 7

1. Quoted in Jackson, "Peasant Political Movements," 263.

2. Quoted in Mitrany, *Marx against the Peasant*, 131.

3. Bizzell, *Green Rising*, 1.

4. Radić, "Speech," 156.

5. Gollwitzer, "Europäische Bauerndemokratie," 64; Jackson, *Comintern and Peasant*, 40.

6. Toshkov, *Agrarianism as Modernity*; Cabo, "Agrarian Parties in Europe," 319–22. See also Jackson, "Peasant Political Movements" and Mitrany, *Marx against the Peasant*.

7. See, e.g., Rothschild, *East Central Europe*, 16–18. For a critique of such thinking, see above sources, along with Daniel Brett's "Indifferent but Mobilized."

8. Hobsbawm, "Peasants and Politics," 19.

9. Dickinson, *World*, 153–54; Van de Grift and Forclaz, *Governing the Rural* (esp. the editors' preface and the chapter by Kiran Klaus Patel).

10. On the eighteenth-century sea change, see Laurent Brassart's introduction to part 1 of Brassart et al.'s *Making Politics in the European Countryside* (23–24). On an epochal peasant revolt with demonstrably political content, see Peter Blickle's *Revolution of 1525* (esp. 18–22).

11. Marx, *18th Brumaire*, 124.

12. Marx, 124.

13. Marx and Engels, *Communist Manifesto*, 228.

14. Marx, *18th Brumaire*, 125; Shanin, *Late Marx*. Positive assessments of the *mir* appeared in Marx and Engels's prefaces to Russian editions of the *Communist Manifesto*.

15. Hammen, "Marx," 697–704.

16. Mitrany, *Marx against the Peasant*, 43.

17. Eley, *Forging Democracy*, 93.

18. For an overview of the peasantry's role in the revolution, see Noelle Plack's "Peasantry, Feudalism, and the Environment." See also Peter M. Jones's *Peasantry in the French Revolution* and the 1932 classic by George Lefebvre, *The Great Fear*. For a case study of modern political concepts' mobilization in the revolution, see Jean-Pierre Jessenne's "Consensus or Conflict?"

19. Turnout was 84 percent (Tombs, *France 1814–1914*, 381).

20. A survey of the now-extensive literature on French rural politics during the period 1848–51 would include: Margadant, *French Peasants in Revolt*; Agulhon, *Republic in the Village*; Berenson, *Populist Religion*.

21. Bruckmüller, " Bauernstand," 784–85.

22. Brassart et al., *Making Politics*, part 2 and thematic introduction; Bruckmüller, "Bauernstand," 784–85; McPhee, "Popular Culture."

23. Drobesch, "Vereine und Interessenverbände," 1063–64.

24. Drobesch, 1065.

25. Cabo, "Agrarian Parties in Europe," 314; Bruckmüller, " Bauernstand," 804–10.

26. Lorman, *Slovak People's Party*, 103–124; Rahten, *Slovenska ljudska stranka*, 57. For a comparison of Slovak and Slovene politics in the period, see Tone Kregar's *Med Tatrami in Triglavom*.

27. Rahten, *Slovenska ljudska stranka*, 14.

28. Bruckmüller, *Landwirtschaftliche Organisationen*.

29. Cabo, "Agrarian Parties in Europe," 315.

30. See chapters by Tertit Aasland (Norway), Claus Bjørn (Denmark), Kari Hokkanen (Finland), and Gustaf Jonasson (Sweden) in Gollwitzer's *Europäische Bauernparteien*, as well as chapters by Jesper Lundsby Skov (Denmark) and Erik Bengtsson and Josefin Hägglund (Sweden) in Brassart et al.'s *Making Politics in the European Countryside*. Finland, part of Sweden until the Congress of Vienna, followed the Scandinavian model, as did, to an extent, the Estonian and Latvian peasant movements (Gollwitzer, "Europäische Bauerndemokratie," 3–4).

31. On Galician Polish peasants' entry into Polish national politics, see Keely Stauter-Halsted's *Nation in the Village* (esp. 216–38). On the origins of the People's Party, see also Dyzma Galaj's "Polish Peasant in Politics" and Olga Narkiewicz's *The Green Flag* (64–71).

32. Miller, *Forging Political Compromise*, 17–22.

33. Řepa, "Between the Nation."

34. On the origins of the BANU and Stamboliiski's rise, see John D. Bell's *Peasants in Power* and R. J. Crampton's *Aleksandur Stamboliiski* (24–43). Bulgarian agrarians won a surprising 23 seats in 1901, were virtually eliminated from parliament in 1903, reorganized and again won 23 seats in 1908, and in 1913 increased their share of the electorate to 21 percent and 48 seats.

35. Biondich, *Stjepan Radić*, 42–61, 67–68.

36. Mitrany, *Marx against the Peasant*, 54–60.

37. Ionescu, "Eastern Europe," 98–99.

38. Himka, *Socialism in Galicia*, 166–69, 171–72.

39. On agrarian socialism in Hungary, see Gyula Borbándi's *Der ungarische Populismus* (66–74), Keith Hitchins's "Hungary" (362), and Bruckmüller's "Landwirtschaftliche Arbeitswelten" (322).

40. Mitrany, *Marx against the Peasant*, 68.

41. Eidelberg, *Great Rumanian Peasant Revolt*; Marin, "Rural Social Combustibility."

42. Trencsényi, "Thinking Dangerously," 90; Mitrany, *Marx against the Peasant*, 52–54.

43. Bizzell, *Green Rising*, 171.

44. Quoted in Toshkov, *Agrarianism as Modernity*, 6.

45. This discussion of Bulgaria is based on Bell's *Peasants in Power*, Toshkov's *Agrarianism as Modernity* (28–32, 77–85, 108–9), and R. J. Crampton's "The Balkans" (251–52).

46. A detailed account of the Radomir Rebellion is in Bell's *Peasants in Power* (130–39).

47. Biondich, *Stjepan Radić*, 179–81.

48. Hodža, *Federation in Central Europe*, 115.

49. West, *Black Lamb*, 101.

50. Miller, *Forging Political Compromise*, esp. 11–15.

51. Leblang, "Polnische Bauernparteien," 298.

52. Leblang, 299.

53. Romsics, "Great War," 190–93; Janos, "Agrarian Opposition."

54. Fischer-Galati, "Peasantism," 105.

55. For an overview, see Bela Kiraly's "Peasant Movements in the Twentieth Century," 322–26.

56. On the origins of the new parties in Serbia and Bosnia-Herzegovina, see Toshkov's *Agrarianism as Modernity* (34). On Slovene agrarianism, see Albin Prepeluh's *Kmetski pokret med Slovenci po Prvi svetovni vojni*.

57. Hitchins, *Rumania, 1866–1947*, 320–30.

58. Hitchins, 391–95, 407, 414–16.

59. Trapl, "Zemědělská politika," 93–94.

60. Quoted in Gollwitzer, "Europäische Bauerndemokratie," 10.

61. See Campbell, *Land and Revolution*, esp. chapter 6.

62. Dooley, *Burning the Big House*, 108.

63. Dooley, 122.

64. For an overview, see Terrence Dooley's "Land and the People" (118–20).

65. Quoted in Bizzell, *Green Rising*, 183.

66. Bengtsson and Hägglund, "Agrarian Politics in Sweden," 303.

67. Gollwitzer, "Europäische Bauerndemokratie," 9–10.

68. Quoted in Gollwitzer, 10.

69. On Westphalia, see Moeller's *German Peasants and Agrarian Politics* (68–79, 116–17, 154–57). On Bavaria, see Ziemann's *War Experiences in Rural Germany* (168–191).

70. Absalom, "Peasant Experience," 140.

71. Absalom, 134; Corner, *Fascism in Ferrara*, 145–49.

72. Corner, *Fascism in Ferrara*, ix–xi, 137–44.

73. Absalom, "Peasant Experience,"134–40.

74. On the disproportionate emphasis on industry in the successor states, see Hugh Seton-Watson's *Eastern Europe between the Wars* (116) and Mitrany's *Marx against the Peasant* (118–22).

75. Rothschild, *East Central Europe*, 210.

76. Seton-Watson, *Eastern Europe*, 83; Mitrany, *Marx against the Peasant*, 119; Rothschild, *East Central Europe*, 273; Bideleux, "Peasantries and Peasant Parties," 276.

77. On import-substitution in the region, see Ivan T. Berend's *Decades of Crisis* (234–39).

78. On cultivation of cereals in Yugoslavia, especially for subsistence, see Tomasevich's *Peasants, Politics and Economic Change in Yugoslavia* (473–83).

79. See esp. Bideleux, "Peasantries and Peasant Parties"; Seton-Watson, *Eastern Europe*, 87–89, 107–10, 116.

80. Mitrany, *Marx against the Peasant*, 127.

81. Bruckmüller, "Bauernstand," 794–96.

82. Seton-Watson, *Eastern Europe*, 112; Mitrany, *Marx against the Peasant*, 118, 127.

83. Houdek, *Družstevné budovanie*, 7–8 (emphasis in original).

84. Quoted in Biondich, *Stjepan Radić*, 62.

85. Quoted in Kubů and Šouša, "Sen o slovanské agrární spolupráci," 38.

86. For an overview, see Juan Pan-Montojo and Niccolò Mignemi's "International Organizations and Agriculture," 241–46.

87. Indraszczyk, *Zielona Międzynarodówka*, 44.

88. On the origins of the Green International: Indraszczyk, 47–53; Kubů and Šouša, "Sen o slovanské agrární spolupráci," 39–40; Toshkov, *Agrarianism as Modernity*, 41–51.

89. On Laur's role in agrarian internationalism, see Pan-Montojo and Mignemi's "International Organizations and Agriculture" (242), Indraszczyk's *Zielona Międzynarodówka* (39–40,

55, 8), and Angela Harre's "Demokratische Alternativen und autoritäre Verführungen" (26–28).

90. On the Green International's formalization and expansion: Indraszczyk, *Zielona Międzynarodówka*, 55–79.

91. Mitrany, *Marx against the Peasant*, 149–51.

92. Košmrlj, "Društva kmetskih," 62–63; Indraszczyk, *Zielona Międzynarodówka*, 81–82.

93. Pasiak-Wąsik and Gmitruk, *Młodzi idą!*, 12–19.

94. Prepeluh, *Kmetski pokret*, 33.

95. Quoted in Košmrlj, "Društva kmetskih," 60.

96. Centrih, "'Govorile so celo strojnice!'," 319–20.

97. The full text is in ARS FS, box 26, no. 5, typed transcript of September 7, 1919, assembly.

98. West, *Black Lamb*, 101.

99. Quoted in Jackson, "Peasant Political Movements," 289.

100. Cimek, *Tomasz Dąbal*, 122–27.

101. Cimek, 98–99; Stankiewicz, *Konflikty społeczne*, 320.

102. Cimek, *Tomasz Dąbal*, 73, 101–5.

103. On the establishment of the Krestintern see Wim van Meurs's "Red Peasant International," Jackson's *Comintern and Peasant* (66–76), and Toshkov's *Agrarianism as Modernity* (56–57).

104. Jackson, *Comintern and Peasant*, 68–69.

105. Jackson, 78–97.

106. On the Krestintern's structure, see Van Meurs's "Red Peasant International" (265–66) and Toshkov's *Agrarianism as Modernity* (57).

107. Quoted in Biondich, *Stjepan Radić*, 196.

108. Toshkov, *Agrarianism as Modernity*, 58.

109. Jackson, *Comintern and Peasant*, chapter 4.

110. Lovell, *Maoism*, 32–34.

111. Quoted in Gollwitzer, "Europäische Bauerndemokratie," 64.

112. Słomka, *From Serfdom to Self-Government*, 272.

113. Prepeluh, *Kmetski pokret*, 44.

Chapter 8

1. *Pamiętniki chłopów*, 1:675–94.

2. *Pamiętniki chłopów*, 1:694.

3. *Pamiętniki chłopów*, 2:401–2.

4. Quoted in Mitrany, *Marx against the Peasant*, 147.

5. Absalom, "Peasant Experience," 138.

6. Clavin, *Great Depression in Europe*, 80.

7. Berend, *Decades of Crisis*, 255.

8. Puntar-Štacnar, *Moje delo*, 250.

9. Bideleux, "Peasantries and Peasant Parties," 288–89.

10. Berend, *Decades of Crisis*, 256.

11. Rothschild, *East Central Europe*, 270–71.

12. Seton-Watson, *Eastern Europe*, 83.

13. MZA, Zemský úřad Brno 1918–1945, box 218, no. 25219/34.

14. This paragraph is based on Berend's *Decades of Crisis* (258–65, 267–72).

15. Andrea Graziosi estimated that one million died during the deportations and repressions of the early 1930s, and seven million died in the 1932–33 famine (*Great Soviet Peasant War*, 2, 64, 66).

16. Tooze, *Wages of Destruction*, 167, 175–76. Tooze provides the following ratios of hectares per agriculturalist: 2.1 in Germany, 2.8 in France, 1.8 in Poland, 1.6 in Italy, 1.5 in Romania and Bulgaria, 12.8 in the USA, 3.8 in Britain, 3.1 in the USSR.

17. See Tooze's *Wages of Destruction* (178) on German land hunger. The laws discussed are detailed on pp. 182–91.

18. Müller, "Colonization Projects," 53.

19. Seton-Watson, *Eastern Europe*, 75–76.

20. See, e.g., Lynch, "Interwar France"; Griffith, "Saving the Soul."

21. Borbándi, *Ungarische Populismus*, 91–92, 101, 106–7.

22. Chitnis, "Zbraně slabých?"

23. The other peasant-focused Nobel laureates were Knut Hamsun (1920) on Norway, Pearl Buck (1938) on China, and Frans Eemil Sillanpää (1939) on Finland.

24. For an overview of the work of Gusti, Bićanić, and others, see Trencsényi's "Thinking Dangerously" (92–93).

25. R. Clark, *Holy Legionary Youth*, 131–32; Sandu, "Model of Fascism," 206.

26. Lebow, "Autobiography as Complaint."

27. Košmrlj, "Društva kmetskih," 114–17.

28. Vidovič Miklavčič, *Mladina*, 199; Košmrlj, "Društva kmetskih," 119–29.

29. Vidovič Miklavčič, *Mladina*, 245.

30. Quoted in Košmrlj, "Društva kmetskih," 87.

31. Quoted in Košmrlj, 97.

32. Košmrlj, 123.

33. *Pamiętniki chłopów*, 1:694.

34. Stryczek, *Chłopskim piórem*, 262–63.

35. Stryczek, 251.

36. Przybysz, *W konspiracji*, 22.

37. Pasiak-Wąsik and Gmitruk, *Młodzi idą!*, 19–21.

38. Pasiak-Wąsik and Gmitruk, 21–22; Przybysz, *W konspiracji*, 24. The university in Gać was the successor of a similar institution under Solarz's direction in Szyce, Cracow county.

39. Przybysz, *W konspiracji*, 24.

40. Stryczek, *Chłopskim piórem*, 301.

41. Stryczek, 291.

42. Stryczek, 292.

43. Pasiak-Wąsik and Gmitruk, *Młodzi idą!*, 24–25. See also Galaj, "Polish Peasant in Politics," 334.

44. Gmitruk and Pasiak-Wąsik, *Bądźcie solidarni!*, 6, 24, 95.

45. Stryczek, *Chłopskim piórem*, 311–18. My account of the Grodzisko events is based on Lucian George's "Comparative Study of Two Peasant Revolts in 1930s Poland" (28–40).

46. T. Adams, "'Rights, Bread," 1, 63.

47. Gmitruk, "Geneza Wielkiego Strajku Chłopskiego," 34.

48. Quoted in Nowak, "Udział chłopów," 102.

49. Stankiewicz, *Konflikty społeczne*, 316–17; Nowak, "Udział chłopów," 102–3.

50. Stankiewicz, *Konflikty społeczne*, 319.

51. Gmitruk, "Geneza Wielkiego Strajku Chłopskiego," 37.

52. Quoted in T. Adams, "Rights, Bread," 61.

53. Stryczek, *Chłopskim piórem*, 342.

54. Quoted in T. Adams, "Rights, Bread," 62.

55. T. Adams, 35–39.

56. On the numerical and geographic extent of the strike, see Thomas Adams's "'Rights, Bread and Work for All'" (60–61, 65–77) and Przybysz's *W konspiracji* (23).

57. On repression: T. Adams, "Rights, Bread," 90–93.

58. Seton-Watson, *Eastern Europe*, 169; T. Adams, "Rights, Bread," introduction.

59. Evans, *Coming of the Third Reich*, 208–11.

60. Simpson and Carmona, *Why Democracy Failed*, 5–7, 10–11, 247–50.

61. Paxton, *French Peasant Fascism*; Boswell, *Rural Communism in France*. On the small French agrarian movement (Parti agraire et paysan français) that existed 1927–39 and allied with Dorgères's movement, see Miguel Cabo's "Farming the Nation" (3, 12–13).

62. Rothschild, *East Central Europe*, 170–71. See also Borbándi, *Ungarische Populismus*, 58, 60–61.

63. Borbándi, *Ungarische Populismus*, 61; Nagy-Talavera, *Green Shirts and Others*, 108–9.

64. Lorman, *Slovak People's Party*, 187–217.

65. Jackson, "Peasant Political Movements," 272.

66. Hitchins, *Rumania*, 369–70; Fischer-Galati, "Jew and Peasant," 204–5.

67. Quoted in Sandu, "Model of Fascism," 207.

68. R. Clark, *Holy Legionary Youth*, 77–83.

69. Sandu, "Model of Fascism," 213.

70. Haynes, "Reluctant Allies?," 120.

71. Hitchins, *Rumania*, 395.

72. On the HSZ, see Sabrina P. Ramet's "Vladko Maček and the Croatian Peasant Defense in the Kingdom of Yugoslavia" and Željko Karaula's *Mačekova vojska*.

73. Karaula, *Mačekova vojska*, 91. On Chetnik terror, see pp. 87–91.

74. Karaula, 80.

75. Karaula, 91.

76. Karaula, 127.

77. Karaula, 132.

78. Quoted in Karaula, 135.

79. Karaula, 138.

80. Karaula, 291–93.

81. Tomasevich, *War and Revolution*, 49–50.

82. On the HSZ right's support for the Ustashas, as well as the organization's dissolution, see Karaula's *Mačekova vojska* (441–47, 457–69) and Tomasevich's *War and Revolution in Yugoslavia* (55–57).

83. Lexa, "Skupinové násilí," 80.

84. *Delavska politika*, December 15, 1938, p. 2; *Večernik jutra*, March 27, 1940, p. 4. I am grateful to Gregor Antoličič for finding these articles. On Zbor, see John Paul Newman's *Yugoslavia in the Shadow of War* (228–30).

85. Hoare, "Yugoslavia," 420–21. On the Nedić regime's ruralism, see Milan Ristović's "Rural 'Anti-utopia,'" 181–85.

Chapter 9

1. Tooze, "War of the Villages," 394–95.

2. Stryczek, *Chłopskim piórem*, 362–63.

3. Stryczek, 396–97.

4. Tönsmeyer, "Farming under Occupation," 138–39.

5. Przybysz, *W konspiracji*, 30.

6. Stryczek, *Chłopskim piórem*, 371.

7. Tönsmeyer, "Farming under Occupation," 136–38.

8. Przybysz, *W konspiracji*, 31.

9. Przybysz, 32–33.

10. Enstad, *Soviet Russians*, 113–18.

11. Prusin, "'Zone of Violence,'" 371–73; Struve, "Tremors in the Shatterzone," 473–74; Veidlinger, *In the Midst*, 360–62; Gross, *Neighbors*.

12. Tönsmeyer, "Farming under Occupation," 139.

13. Stryczek, *Chłopskim piórem*, 372.

14. Stryczek, 373–74.

15. James Scott, *Weapons of the Weak*, xvi.

16. See, in particular, Janusz Gmitruk's "Bataliony Chłopskie."

17. On administration, see, for instance, Tönsmeyer's "Farming under Occupation" (139–40).

18. Gmitruk, "Bataliony Chłopskie," 175–76.

19. Stryczek, *Chłopskim piórem*, 385.

20. Przybysz, *W konspiracji*, 38.

21. Przybysz, 84.

22. Przybysz, 129, 163, 167.

23. Pasiak-Wąsik and Gmitruk, *Młodzi idą!*, 27–28; Stryczek, *Chłopskim piórem*, 378–81; Przybysz, *W konspiracji*, 84–85.

24. Korneć, "Udział Ludowego Związku Kobiet," 187–91.

25. Gmitruk, "Bataliony Chłopskie," 182; Przybysz, *W konspiracji*, 183, 201–6.

26. Przybysz, *W konspiracji*, 188–93.

27. Gmitruk, "Bataliony Chłopskie," 184.

28. Snyder, "Ukrainian-Polish Ethnic Cleansing 1943."

29. Stojar "Venkov,"42–43.

30. Snyder, *Reconstruction of Nations*, 175–76.

31. Gmitruk, "Bataliony Chłopskie," 181–83.

32. Przybysz, *W konspiracji*, 195.

33. Quoted in Przybysz, 85.

34. Stryczek, *Chłopskim piórem*, 390; Zaremba, *Entangled in Fear*, 7–8.

35. Entner, "Zwischen Erinnern und Vergessen," 33–34; Turk, "Gorska vas," 18–19; Rausch, *Partisanenkampf*, 12–13.

36. Quoted in Prušnik-Gašper, *Gamsi na plazu*, 41.

37. Baum, *Im Käfig eingesperrter Vogel*, 93.

38. Entner, "Zwischen Erinnern und Vergessen," 33.

39. Prušnik-Gašper, *Gamsi na plazu*, 39.

40. Haderlap, *Engel des Vergessens*, 85.

41. Quoted in Prušnik-Gašper, *Gamsi na plazu*, 42.

42. Quoted in Prušnik-Gašper, 43.

43. Baum, *Im Käfig eingesperrter Vogel*, 97, 126–28; Entner, "Zwischen Erinnern und Vergessen," 34–36.

44. Entner, "Zwischen Erinnern und Vergessen," 32, 37–38; Turk, "Gorska vas," 21.

45. Entner, "Zwischen Erinnern und Vergessen," 35–36.

46. Prušnik-Gašper, *Gamsi na plazu*, 298.

47. Prušnik-Gašper, 16–19, 20–25, 37–39, 57.

48. Entner, "Zwischen Erinnern und Vergessen," 34; Turk, "Gorska vas," 23.

49. Prušnik-Gašper, *Gamsi na plazu*, 44.

50. On the notion of areas distant from the state, see Baberowski's "Kriege in staatsfernen Räumen" (291–310).

51. Stojar, "Venkov," 45–46.

52. Přikryl, *První partyzánská skupina*, 10–17.

53. MZA, B-340 Gestapo, box 61, no. 3934, signature 100-61-17: Karel Koláček (especially pp. 46–52, interrogation from October 9, 1942), and box 63, no. 4075, signature 100-63-35: Ladislav Kopečný (see pp. 8–11, interrogation from November 11, 1942).

54. Moravské zemské muzeum (MZM) in Brno, archive no. 12908, December 5, 1987, letter from Miroslav Neumann to Jan Břečka. I thank Lukáš Lexa for locating this source for me.

55. Přikryl, *První partyzánská skupina*, 17.

56. Serinek, *Česká cikánská rapsodie*, 1:73. On the fate of his family, see pp. 7, 10–11.

57. Serinek, 1:81–82.

58. On the solidarity of Vysočina peasants, see Serinek's *Česká cikánská rapsodie* (1:122–23).

59. Serinek, 1:10–11, 216–17.

60. For a concise account, see Stevan K. Pavlowitch's *Hitler's New Disorder*.

61. For a balanced assessment, see Gregor Kranjc's *To Walk with the Devil* (esp. 238–54).

62. Gestrin, *Svet pod Krimom*, 195–96.

63. Gestrin, 262.

64. Kranjc, *Walk with the Devil*, 108–110, 207.

65. Košmrlj, "Društva kmetskih," 146–49.

66. ARS FS, box 26, no. 5, November 7, 1957, typescript recollections of Ivan Krajec.

67. This account of the Šarh family's fate during the Second World War is based on Jelka Šporin Šarh's *Kronika družine Šarh* (19–37).

68. For a brief history of the Pohorje Battalion and its fate, see Metod Mikuž's *Pregled zgodovine Narodnoosvobodilne Borbe v Sloveniji* (199, 203).

69. Puntar-Štacnar, *Moje delo*, 477.

70. Puntar-Štacnar, 494.

71. Puntar-Štacnar, 495.

72. Puntar-Štacnar, 502.

73. Puntar-Štacnar, 530.

74. Puntar-Štacnar, 513. On reprisals, see pp. 514–15.

75. Puntar-Štacnar, 518–19, 521.

76. Puntar-Štacnar, 527.

77. Puntar-Štacnar, 530.

78. Puntar-Štacnar, 528.

79. Puntar-Štacnar, 531.

80. Puntar-Štacnar, 534.

81. Kranjc, *Walk with the Devil*, 9, 227.

82. Hoare, *Bosnian Muslims*, 7–12.

83. Hoare, 188–94; Jahić, *Muslimanske formacije*, 99–113.

84. Quoted in Hoare, *Bosnian Muslims*, 189.

85. Hoare, 247.

86. Jahić, *Muslimanske formacije*, 117–18; Hoare, *Bosnian Muslims*, 257.

87. Kržišnik-Bukić, *1950 Peasants' Revolt*, 19–25. This is a faithful translation of her *Cazinska buna 1950*.

88. Hoare, *Bosnian Muslims*, 232–41.

89. Quoted in Hoare, 371.

90. Quoted in Hoare, 371–72.

91. Nasakanda, *Klase, slojevi i revolucija*, 50–51, 94, 114.

92. Nasakanda, 120; Jelić, *Hrvatska u ratu i revoluciji*, 283, 285.

93. Luković, "Country Road to Revolution," 165–68; Bokovoy, *Peasants and Communists*, 1–2, 8, 27–28.

94. Kržišnik-Bukić, *1950 Peasants' Revolt*, 5.

95. Rutaj, *Peasant International in Action*, 10–11; Indraszczyk, *Zielona Międzynarodówka*, 106–7; Bideleux, "Peasantries and Peasant Parties," 298–99.

96. Royal Institute of International Affairs, *Agrarian Problems*, 23.

97. Royal Institute of International Affairs, 19.

98. Royal Institute of International Affairs, 18.

99. Hodža, *Federation in Central Europe*, esp. 161–78.

100. Indraszczyk, *Zielona Międzynarodówka*, 94–98.

101. Hodža, *Federation in Central Europe*, 172.

102. Rutaj, *Peasant International in Action*, 11; Indraszczyk, *Zielona Międzynarodówka*, 107.

103. *Narodnooslobodilačka borba* in Serbo-Croatian; *Narodna osvobodilna borba* in Slovene. *Narod* means "people" or "nation" in Serbo-Croatian but only "nation" in Slovene.

104. Van Boeschoten, *From Armatolik*, 7–8, 268, 272, and "Peasant and the Party," esp. 625–30; Mazower, *Inside Hitler's Greece*, 312–15.

105. Forlenza, "Europe's Forgotten Unfinished Revolution."

106. Mitrany, *Marx against the Peasant*, 205.

107. Borbándi, *Ungarische Populismus*, 273–76.

108. Quoted in Gmitruk, "Bataliony Chłopskie," 184.

109. Stryczek, *Chłopskim piórem*, 401–4.

110. Zaremba, *Entangled in Fear*, 69–71.

111. Gmitruk, "Bataliony Chłopskie," 185.

112. For an overview, see Galaj's "Polish Peasant in Politics" (337–39).

113. Pasiak-Wąsik and Gmitruk, *Młodzi idą!*, 33.

114. Stryczek, *Chłopskim piórem*, 417–18.

115. Pasiak-Wąsik and Gmitruk, *Młodzi idą!*, 34–36.

116. Charczuk, "Udział wsi i chłopów, 185.

117. Charczuk, 251, 253.

118. Charczuk, 254–56, 260.

119. Zaremba, *Entangled in Fear*, 159–62, 164, 166–70.

120. Stryczek, *Chłopskim piórem*, 434.

121. Stryczek, 430–31.

122. Stryczek, 431–32.

123. Stryczek, 429.

124. Indraszczyk, *Zielona Międzynarodówka*, 117–20.

125. Indraszczyk, 123.

126. Rutaj, *Peasant International in Action*, 5. Indraszczyk describes a London-based "Peasant International" established in 1947 by Kuncewicz and others as a short-lived initiative independent of the American-based IPU (*Zielona Międzynarodówka*, 169–70), but the 1948 pamphlet refers to Kuncewicz's circle as the organization's "European section," and treats peasant international activities on both continents as proceeding in tandem.

127. Rutaj, *Peasant International in Action*, 4.

128. Rutaj, 16.

129. Toshkov, *Agrarianism as Modernity*, 160.

130. Rutaj, *Peasant International in Action*, 12–14.

131. Swain, "East European Collectivization Campaigns," 510; Mitrany, *Marx against the Peasant*, 187–88.

132. Kochanowicz, "Changing Landscape of Property," 39–40.

133. Henschel, "Front-Line Soldiers into Farmers," 150–55; Zaremba, *Entangled in Fear*, 97.

134. Stryczek, *Chłopskim piórem*, 410–12; Kochanowicz, "Changing Landscape of Property," 39; Zaremba, *Entangled in Fear*, 203, 225–27.

135. Stryczek, *Chłopskim piórem*, 416. On the expropriation of Potocki, see pp. 412–13. On continued land hunger, see p. 432.

136. Müller, "Colonization Projects," 57–58.

137. Luković, "Country Road to Revolution," 172.

138. Swain, "East European Collectivization Campaigns," 499.

139. This discussion of collectivization is based primarily on Swain's "East European Collectivization Campaigns" (498–504, 515–23).

140. With partial exceptions of Romania in 1949 and 1951 (Swain, 502–3).

141. Swain, 516, 519.

142. Kochanowicz, "Changing Landscape of Property," 41; Kržišnik-Bukić, *1950 Peasants' Revolt*, 10–12.

143. Luković, "Country Road to Revolution," 169–70, 173–76; Bokovoy, *Peasants and Communists*, 42–43.

144. Luković, "Country Road to Revolution," 177–81; Bokovoy, "Collectivization in Yugoslavia," 299–302.

145. E.g., Bokovoy, *Peasants and Communists*, xv.

146. Swain, "East European Collectivization Campaigns," 523–25.

147. See especially Bokovoy's "Collectivization in Yugoslavia" (302–9, 313–15).

148. Bokovoy, 304.

149. My account of the "Cazinska buna" is based on Kržišnik-Bukić's *1950 Peasants' Revolt*.

150. Kržišnik-Bukić, *1950 Peasants' Revolt*, 122.

151. On the victims of the repression, see Kržišnik-Bukić's *1950 Peasants' Revolt* (152–53, 311–22) and Bokovoy's "Collectivization in Yugoslavia" (315–16).

152. Kržišnik-Bukić, *1950 Peasants' Revolt*, 147–48.

153. Kržišnik-Bukić, 24, 128–36.

154. Sabljaković, *Omaha 1950*, quoted in Kržišnik-Bukić, *1950 Peasants' Revolt*, 113.

155. Bokovoy, "Collectivization in Yugoslavia," 316–17.

156. Bokovoy, *Peasants and Communists*, 151, 153–59.

157. Bokovoy, "Collectivization in Yugoslavia," 294.

158. Jarosz, "Collectivization of Agriculture," 113.

159. Swain, "East European Collectivization Campaigns," 526. See also Jarosz, "Collectivization of Agriculture," 120, 135–38.

160. Lieven, *Baltic Revolution*, 87–90; Stojar, "Venkov," 42.

Chapter 10

1. Kochanowicz, "Changing Landscape of Property," 41–43; Cieplak, "Private Farming," 32–33.

2. Warriner, "Changes," 448–50.

3. Tooze, "War of the Villages," 394.

4. Murgescu, "Agriculture and Landownership," 53.

5. Stryczek, *Chłopskim piórem*, 419–28.

6. Berend, *Economic History*, 169–70.

7. See, e.g., Brzostek, "Ruralization of Bucharest"; Dobrivojević, "Changing the Cityscapes"; Horváth, "Ruralization."

8. Siegrist and Müller, introduction to *Property in East Central Europe*, 20; Kochanowicz, "Changing Landscape of Property," 45; Swain, "East European Collectivization Campaigns," 527.

9. Hobsbawm, *Age of Extremes*, 289.

10. Anev, "Proces s údajnými přisluhovači"; Chitnis, "Zbraně slabých?," 661, 664.

11. Indraszczyk, *Zielona Międzynarodówka*, 122–24, 162–64.

12. See, e.g., Čulinović, *Odjeci Oktobra*, 91–126; Pichlík, "Vzpoury navratilců," 584; Holotík, *Sociálne a národné hnutie*, introduction.

13. See, e.g., Godeša, "Kmečki punti," 216; Volgyes, introduction to *Peasantry of Eastern Europe*, vii–viii.

14. SNK LA Ferančík, accession no. 1329, December 15, 1960, letter. For Ferančík's biography, see *Biografický lexikon Slovenska* (vol. 2, *C–F*, 533).

15. Quoted in Galaj, "Polish Peasant in Politics," 339.

16. Gmitruk and Pasiak-Wąsik, *Bądźcie solidarni!*, 6.

17. Galaj, "Polish Peasant in Politics," 345–46.

18. Gmitruk, "Bilans działalności," 219.

19. See Gmitruk, "Bilans działalności"; Indraszczyk, "Partie chłopskie."

20. Swain, "East European Collectivization Campaigns," 528–29; Kochanowicz, "Changing Landscape of Property," 43–44; Rychlík, "Collectivization in Czechoslovakia," 202–3; Kaneff, "Work, Identity," 187–91.

21. Müller, "Property between Delimitation," 117–18.

22. "Koncert na 100-Lecie Republiki Tarnobrzeskiej," Tinfo, November 4, 2018, https://www.tarnobrzeg.info/2018/11/04/koncert-na-100-lecie-republiki-tarnobrzeskiej/.

23. Westad, *Global Cold War*, 399; Wolf, *Peasant Wars*, 157–273.

24. Skocpol, "What Makes Peasants Revolutionary?," 352. An important role was also played by Frantz Fanon's *The Wretched of the Earth*.

25. Westad, *Global Cold War*, 399–400.

26. Westad, 400–401.

27. "More than Half the World Is Now Urban, UN Report Says," World Bank, July 11, 2007, https://www.worldbank.org/en/news/feature/2007/07/11/more-than-half-the-world-is-now-urban-un-report-says.

28. Vanhaute, *Peasants in World History*, 3, 137.

29. Vanhaute, 113. Vanhaute calculates on the basis of FAO statistics that, of the 600 million farms worldwide, 550 million are family farms and 500 million of these are two hectares (5 acres) or less.

30. Borras, "La Vía Campesina"; Rosset, "Re-thinking Agrarian Reform"; Nicholson and Borras, "Wasn't an Intellectual Construction," esp. 610–11.

31. UN General Assembly, Declaration on the Rights of Peasants and Other People Working in Rural Areas, A/HRC/RES/39/12 (Sept. 28, 2018), https://digitallibrary.un.org/record/1650694?ln=en.

32. Gellner and Ionescu, introduction to *Populism*, 3. On recent developments, see Ian Scoones et al.'s *Authoritarian Populism and the Rural World*.

33. Ther, *Europe since 1989*, 132–44, 207–8.

34. Neel, *Hinterland*, 17, 95, 97, 111, 116, 119–20.

35. In addition to Neel's work, see Christophe Guilluy's *Twilight of the Elites* (viii–x, 2, 58–60, 85).

36. Quoted in Biondich, *Stjepan Radić*, 77.

37. Gramsci, *Prison Notebooks*, 2:21.

BIBLIOGRAPHY

Archives

Archiv hlavního města Prahy (AHMP)
Arhiv Republike Slovenije (Ljubljana) (ARS)
Državni arhiv Osijek (DAOS)
Državni arhiv Zadar (DAZD)
Hrvatski Državni Arhiv (Zagreb) (HDA)
Literární archiv Památníku národního písemnictví (Prague) (LAPNP)
Masarykovo muzeum Hodonín (MMH)
Moravské zemské museum (Brno) (MZM)
Moravský zemský archiv (Brno) (MZA)
Národní archiv (Prague) (NA)
Österreichisches Staatsarchiv—Allgemeines Verwaltungsarchiv (Vienna) (AVA)
Österreichisches Staatsarchiv (OeStA)—Kriegsarchiv (Vienna) (KA)
Pokrajinski arhiv Maribor (PAM)
Regionální muzeum v Mikulově (RMM)
Slovenská národná knižnica (Martin) (SNK), Literárny archív (LA)
Slovenský národný archív (Bratislava) (SNA)
Státní okresní archiv Břeclav (SOkAB)
Státní okresní archiv Hodonín (SOkAH)
Státní okresní archiv Jindřichův Hradec (SOkAJH)
Státní okresní archiv Třebíč (SOkAT)
Státní okresní archiv Uherské Hradiště (SOkAUH)
Vojenský historický archív (Bratislava) (VHAB)
Vojenský historický archiv (Prague) (VHAP)

Published Primary Sources

Alimpić, Dušan, ed. *Policiski rečnik*. Vol. 3. Belgrade: Izdavačka knjižarnica Gece Kona, 1927.

Babel, Isaac. *Red Cavalry*. Translated by Boris Dralyuk. London: Pushkin, 2014.

Bartoš, Felix. *Hoši ze zeleného kádru: Hra o čtyřech jednáních*. Prague: Fr. Švejda, 1928.

Bimka, Marcel. "Trnitou cestou k svobodě." In *Domov za války (Svědectví účastníků)*, vol. 5, *1918*, edited by Alois Žipek, 263–67. Prague: Pokrok, 1931.

Bizzell, W. B. *The Green Rising: A Historical Survey of Agrarianism, with Special Reference to the Organized Efforts of the Farmers of the United States to Improve Their Economic and Social Status*. New York: Macmillan, 1926.

César, Jaroslav, and Milan Otáhal, eds. *Hnutí venkovského lidu v českých zemích v letech 1918–1922*. Prague: Nakl. Československé akademie věd, 1958.

Djilas, Milovan. *Wartime*. Translated by Michael Petrovich. London: Martin Secker a Warburg, 1977.

Doudlebský, J. L. *Zelená garda (Vojno, povol!): Hra z našeho předpřevratového odboje o 3 děstvích*. Prague: Evžen K. Rosendorf, 1929.

Ecker, Lev. *Slovácká brigáda (Říjnový vojenský převrat na moravském Slovácku 1918)*. Břeclav, Czechoslovakia: Nákladem Musejního a vlastivědného spolku v Břeclavi, 1930.

Ferančík, Jozef. *Nuhál, Rozpomienky na Zelený káder*. Myjava, Czechoslovakia: self-published, 1920.

Glaise-Horstenau, Edmund. *Die Katastrophe: Die Zertrümmerung Österreich-Ungarns und das Werden der Nachfolgestaaten*. Zürich: Amalthea, 1929.

Gramsci, Antonio. *Prison Notebooks*. Edited and translated by Joseph A. Buttigieg. New York: Columbia University Press, 2011.

Haderlap, Maja. *Engel des Vergessens*. Göttingen, Germany: Wallstein Verlag, 2011.

Hodža, Milan. *Federation in Central Europe: Reflections and Reminiscences*. London: Jarrolds, 1942.

Holotík, Ľudovít, ed. *Sociálne a národné hnutie na Slovensku od Októbrovej revolúcie do vzniku československého štátu (Dokumenty)*. Bratislava: Veda, 1979.

Hosák, Ladislav. *Státní převrat v Břeclavi roku 1918*. Břeclav, Czechoslovakia: Musejní a vlastivědný spolek, 1930.

Houdek, Fedor. *Družstevné budovanie: Hospodárska a sociálna svojpomocná práca slovenského ľudu*. Bratislava: Družstvené nakladateľstvo, 1942.

Jandásek, L. "Z počátků Slovácké brigády." In *Brno v boji za svobodu*, vol. 2, *Zborník vzpomínek*, edited by Josef Kudela, 276–78. Brno, Czechoslovakia: Moravský legionář v Brně, 1937.

Janković, Dragoslav, and Bogdan Krizman, eds. *Građa o stvaranju jugoslovenske države (1. I–20. XII 1918)*. Belgrade: Institut društvenih nauka, 1964.

Jerič, Ivan. *Moji spomini*. Murska Sobota, Slovenia: Zavod sv. Miklavža, 2000.

Juriga, Ferdiš. *Blahozvesť kriesenia slovenského národa a slovenskej krajiny*. Trnava, Czechoslovakia: Urbánek, 1937.

Kaić, M. *Zeleni kader: Ljubavni i pustolovni roman iz prevrata 1918*. Zagreb: Romana, 1927.

Kazimour, Josef. *Návod k vedení pamětních knih*. Prague: Československé zemědělské muzeum, 1920.

Kepka, Rudolf. *Vojna*. Prague: F. S. Frabša, 1922.

Knaibl, Jan. *Vzpomínky státního zástupce*. Olomouc, Czechoslovakia: self-published, 1932.

Kossowski, Jerzy. *Zielona kadra*. Warsaw: Ludowa Spółdzielnia Wydawnicza, 1963.

Kraus, Lavoslav. *Susreti i sudbine: Sjećanja iz jednog aktivnog života*. Osijek, Yugoslavia: Glas Slavonije, 1973.

Krizman, Bogdan, ed. "Građa o nemirima u Hrvatskoj na kraju g. 1918." *Historijski zbornik* 10, no. 1–4 (1957):149–57.

Krleža, Miroslav. *Harbors Rich in Ships: The Selected Revolutionary Writings of Miroslav Krleža, Radical Luminary of Modern World Literature*. Translated and edited by Željko Cipriš. New York: Monthly Review, 2017.

———. *Hrvatski bog Mars*. Split, Yugoslavia: Logos, 1985.

Lansing, Robert. *The Peace Negotiations: A Personal Narrative*. Boston, MA: Houghton Mifflin, 1921.

Livonský, Josef. "Železnobrodsko za války." In *Domov za války (Svědectví účastníků)*, vol. 2, 1915, edited by Alois Žipek, 121–28. Prague: Pokrok, 1930.

Ljubotrn, Savo [František Brázda]. *Vojno povol, hej rup! Příběhy Tondy Knihy, landveráka ulejváka*. Drietoma, Czechoslovakia: self-published, 1930.

Mareš, Michal. *Zelená garda: Revoluční román z r. 1918*. Prague: Lípa, 1927.

Marx, Karl. *The 18th Brumaire of Louis Bonaparte*. New York: International, 1963.

Marx, Karl, and Friedrich Engels. *The Communist Manifesto*. London: Penguin, 2002.

Medvecký, Karol A., ed. *Slovenský Prevrat*. 4 vols. Bratislava: Komenský, 1930–31.
Olbracht, Ivan. *Nikola Šuhaj Loupežník*. Prague: Melantrich, 1933.
Palkovič, Konštantín, ed. *Ohoľ ho! Rozprávky zo Záhoria*. Bratislava: Ofprint, 1999.
Pamiętniki chłopów. Edited by [Ludwik Krzywicki?]. 2 vols. Warsaw: Instytut Gospodarstwa Społecznego, 1935–36.
Pavel, Josef. *Zelený kádr: Román z války*. Prague: Vilímek, 1927.
Paver, Josipa, ed. *Zbornik građe za povijest radničkog pokreta i KPJ 1919–1920*. Sisak, Yugoslavia: Historijski arhiv Sisak, 1970.
Pivko, Ljudevit. *Proti Rakousku*. Vol. 2, *Bok po boku*. 2 books. Translated by František Roubík. Prague: Nákladem Památníku odboje, 1926.
Poláček, Karel. *Vyprodáno*. Prague: Československý spisovatel, 1958.
Poseł, E. K. [Jędrzej Moraczewski]. *Przewrót w Polsce*. Vol. 1, *Rządy Ludowe*. Cracow: Nakładem redakcyi tygodnika Prawo Ludu, 1919.
Prepeluh, Albin. *Kmetski pokret med Slovenci po Prvi svetovni vojni*. Ljubljana: Kmetijska matica, 1928.
———. *Pripombe k naši prevratni dobi*. Ljubljana: Založba univerzitetne tiskarne J. Blasnika, 1938.
Prušnik-Gašper, Karel. *Gamsi na plazu: Zapiski in spomini*. Ljubljana: Založba Borec, 1958.
Przeniosło, Marek, ed. *Narodziny niepodległości w Galicji: Wybór dokumentów z archiwów lwowskich*. Kielce, Poland: Wydawnictwo Akademii Świętokrzyskiej, 2007.
Puntar-Štacnar, Ivan. *Moje delo, doživetja in pogledi: Dnevnik 1923–1943*. Edited by Franc Perko. Ljubljana: Jutro, 2009.
Radić, Stjepan. "Speech at the Night Assembly of the National Council on 24 November, 1918." Translated by Iva Polak. In *Modernism: The Creation of Nation States*, edited by Ahmet Ersoy, Maciej Górny, and Vangelis Kechriotis, 151–60. Budapest: Central European University Press, 2010.
Rebreanu, Liviu. *Ion*. Translated by A. Hillard. London: Peter Owen, 1965.
Rošický, Jaroslav. *Rakouský orel padá: Jak byla naše revoluce doma připravena a 28. října 1918 provedena vojensky*. Prague: Nakl. M. Forejt, 1933.
Rosůlek, Jan Václav. *Noha, plukovník zeleného kádru*. Prague: Sfinx, 1928.
Roth, Joseph. *Hotel Savoy*. Translated by John Hoare. New York: Overlook, 2003.
Royal Institute of International Affairs. *Agrarian Problems from the Baltic to the Aegean: Discussion of a Peasant Programme*. London: Royal Institute of International Affairs, 1944.
Rozner, Vojtěch. *Vzpoura chalup*. Prague: Vydavatelství přítel knihy, 1928.
Rutaj, J. [Jerzy Kuncewicz]. *Peasant International in Action*. London: Peasant International Central Committee—European Section, 1948.
Sabljaković, Dževad. *Omaha 1950*. Belgrade: Kniževne nove, 1986.
Šarh, Alfonz. "Spomini na Zeleni kader v pohorskih gozdovih." In *Boj za Maribor 1918–1919: Spominski zbornik ob sedemdesetletnici bojev za Maribor in severno mejo na slovenskem Štajerskem*, edited by Janez J. Švajncer, 229–40. Maribor, Yugoslavia: Obzorja, 1988.
Sbírka zákonů a nařízení státu československého. Prague: Státní tiskárna, 1920.
Sborník dokumentů k vnitřímu vývoji v českých zemích za 1. Světové války 1914–1918. Vol. 5, *Rok 1918*. Edited by Kolektiv pracovníků SÚA. Prague: Státní ústřední archiv v Praze, 1997.
Serge, Victor. *Memoirs of a Revolutionary, 1901–1941*. Translated by Peter Sedgwick. London: Oxford University Press, 1963.
Serinek, Josef. *Česká cikánská rapsodie*. Edited by Jan Tesař. 3 vols. Prague: Triáda, 2016.
Sicha, Richard. *Český vojín a říjnový převrat: Příspěvek k dějinám národního odboje domácího*. Brno: Barvič a Novotný, 1933.
Šišić, Ferdo, ed. *Dokumenti o postanku Kraljevine Srba, Hrvata i Slovenaca 1914–1919*. Zagreb: Matica hrvatska, 1920.

Šlesinger, Václav. "Četnictvo a zelené kádry na Moravě." In *Brno v boji za svobodu*, vol. 2, *Zborník vzpomínek*, edited by Josef Kudela, 251–54. Brno: Moravský legionář v Brně, 1937.

Słomka, Jan. *From Serfdom to Self-Government: Memoirs of a Polish Village Mayor, 1842–1927*. Translated by William J. Rose. London: Minerva, 1941.

Šmída, František. *Vzpomínky z vojny, 1914–1919*. Olomouc, Czech Republic: Poznání, 2014.

Spengler, Oswald. *The Decline of the West*. Translated by Charles Frances Atkinson. Oxford: Oxford University Press, 1991.

Šrobár, Vavro. *Osvobodené Slovensko: Pamäti z rokov 1918–1920*. Vol. 1. Prague: Čin, 1928.

Stryczek, Jan. *Chłopskim piórem*. Warsaw: Ludowa Spółdzielnia Wydawnicza, 1957.

United Nations Department of Economic and Social Affairs. *United Nations Demographic Yearbook 1952*. New York: Statistical Office of the United Nations Department of Economic Affairs, 1953.

Urban, Milo. *Živý bič*. Bratislava: Perfekt, 2003.

Vidmar, Josip, ed. "Prilozi građi za povijest 1917.–1918. s osobitom obzirom na razvoj radničkog pokreta i odjeke Oktobarske revolucije kod nas." *Arhivski vjesnik* 1 (1958):11–173.

West, Rebecca. *Black Lamb and Grey Falcon: A Journey through Yugoslavia*. Edinburgh: Canongate, 2006. Originally published 1942.

Zacharová, Mária, ed. "Pramene k dejinám 1. svetovej vojny a prevratu v roku 1918 na Záhorí I." *Zborník Záhorského múzea* 7 (2014):195–251.

———, ed. "Pramene k dejinám 1. svetovej vojny a prevratu v roku 1918 na Záhorí II." *Zborník Záhorského múzea* 8 (2017):202–51.

Zlobec, Andrej. *V bojih za severno in južno mejo*. Ljubljana: self-published by D. Kunaver, 2009.

———. *V viharju prve svetovne vojne*. Ljubljana: self-published by D. Kunaver, 2010.

Zorec, Ivan. *Zeleni kader: Povest iz viharnih dni našega narodnega osvobajanja*. Ljubljana: J. Blasnikovi nasledniki, 1923.

Secondary Sources

Ablovatski, Eliza. *Revolution and Political Violence in Central Europe: The Deluge of 1919*. Cambridge: Cambridge University Press, 2021.

Absalom, Roger. "The Peasant Experience under Italian Fascism." In *The Oxford Handbook of Fascism*, edited by R.J.B. Bosworth, 127–49. Oxford: Oxford University Press, 2010.

Adams, Arthur E. "The Peasantry in Russia, 1900–1917." In *The Peasantry of Eastern Europe*, vol. 2, *20th Century Developments*, edited by Ivan Volgyes, 1–14. New York: Pergamon Press, 1979.

Adams, Thomas P. "'Rights, Bread and Work for All': The Polish Peasant Strike of 1937." PhD dissertation, University of California Davis, 1995.

Agulhon, Maurice. *The Republic in the Village: The People of the Var from the French Revolution to the Second Republic*. Translated by Janet Lloyd. Cambridge: Cambridge University Press, 1982.

Anev, Petr. "Proces s údajnými přisluhovači Zelené internacionály." *Paměť a dějiny* 6, no. 4 (2012):23–34.

Baberowski, Jörg. "Kriege in staatsfernen Räumen: Russland und die Sowjetunion 1905–1950." In *Formen des Krieges: Von der Antike bis zur Gegenwart*, edited by Dietrich Beyrau, Michael Hochgeschwender, and Dieter Langewiesche, 291–310. Paderborn: Schöningh, 2007.

Baker, Mark R. *Peasants, Power, and Place: Revolution in the Villages of Kharkiv Province, 1914–1921*. Cambridge, MA: Harvard University Press, 2016.

Balkelis, Tomas. "Social Banditry and Nation-Making: The Myth of a Lithuanian Robber." *Past & Present* 198 (2008):111–45.

Banac, Ivo. "'Emperor Karl Has Become a Comitadj': The Croatian Disturbances of Autumn 1918." *Slavonic and East European Review* 70, no. 2 (1992):284–305.

———. *The National Question in Yugoslavia: Origins, History, Politics*. Ithaca, NY: Cornell University Press, 1984.

Bandoľová, Margita, Erik Dulovič, Mária Feješová, Ivan Guba, Peter Chorvát, Jozef Meliš, and Lucia Tokárová, eds. *Od Uhorského kráľovstva k Československej republike: Dokumenty z fondov slovenských regionálných archívov k udalostiam v rokoch 1918–1919*. Bratislava: Ministerstvo vnútra Slovenskej republiky, 2018.

Baum, Wilhelm, ed. *Wie ein im Käfig eingesperrter Vogel: Das Tagebuch des Thomas Olip*. Klagenfurt, Austria: Kitab, 2010.

Bell, John D. *Peasants in Power: Alexander Stamboliski and the Bulgarian Agrarian National Union, 1899–1923*. Princeton, NJ: Princeton University Press, 1977.

Beneš, Jakub S. *Workers and Nationalism: Czech and German Social Democracy in Habsburg Austria, 1890–1918*. Oxford: Oxford University Press, 2017.

Beneš, Václav L. "Czechoslovak Democracy and Its Problems, 1918–1920." In *A History of the Czechoslovak Republic, 1918–1948*, edited by Victor S. Mamatey and Radomír Luža, 39–98. Princeton, NJ: Princeton University Press, 1973.

Bengtsson, Erik, and Josefin Hägglund. "Agrarian Politics in Sweden, c. 1850–1950." In *Making Politics in the European Countryside, 1780s–1930s*, edited by Laurent Brassart, Corinne Marache, Juan Pan-Montojo, and Leen van Molle, 293–312. Turnhout, Belgium: Brepols, 2022.

Bercé, Yves-Marie. *History of Peasant Revolts: The Social Origins of Rebellion in Early Modern France*. Translated by Amanda Whitmore. Ithaca, NY: Cornell University Press, 1990.

Berend, Ivan T. *Decades of Crisis: Central and Eastern Europe before World War II*. Berkeley: University of California Press, 1998.

———. *An Economic History of Twentieth-Century Europe*. Cambridge: Cambridge University Press, 2006.

Berenson, Edward. "Politics and the French Peasantry: The Debate Continues." *Social History* 12, no. 2 (1987):213–29.

———. *Populist Religion and Left-Wing Politics in France, 1830–1852*. Princeton, NJ: Princeton University Press, 1984.

Bergholz, Max. *Violence as a Generative Force: Identity, Nationalism, and Memory in a Balkan Community*. Ithaca, NY: Cornell University Press, 2016.

Bideleux, Robert. "The Peasantries and Peasant Parties of Interwar East Central Europe." Chapter 9 in *Interwar East Central Europe: The Failure of Democracy-Building, the Fate of Minorities*, edited by Sabrina Ramet. Abingdon, UK: Routledge, 2020.

Biografický lexikón Slovenska. Compiled by Kolektiv pracovníkov NBÚ SNK v Martine. Martin, Slovakia: Slovenská národná knižnica, 2004.

Biondich, Mark. *Stjepan Radić, the Croat Peasant Party, and the Politics of Mass Mobilization*. Toronto: University of Toronto Press, 2000.

Bjork, James. *Neither German nor Pole: Catholicism and National Indifference in a Central European Borderland*. Ann Arbor: University of Michigan Press, 2008.

Blackbourn, David. *The Marpingen Visions: Rationalism, Religion and the Rise of Modern Germany*. Oxford: Oxford University Press, 1993.

Blickle, Peter. *The Revolution of 1525: The German Peasants' War from a New Perspective*. Translated by Thomas A. Brady and H. C. Erik Midelfort. Baltimore, MD: Johns Hopkins University Press, 1981.

Blobaum, Robert E. *Rewolucja: Russian Poland, 1904–1907*. Ithaca, NY: Cornell University Press, 1995.

Bobič, Pavlina. *War and Faith: The Catholic Church in Slovenia, 1914–1918*. Leiden: Brill, 2012.

Bogdanović, Tomislav. "Kategorije zelenog kadra 1918. godine i osvrt na na njihovo djelovanje u Podravini i Prigorju." *Podravina* 12, no. 23 (2013):96–108.

Böhler, Jochen. "Enduring Violence: The Postwar Struggles in East-Central Europe, 1917–21." *Journal of Contemporary History* 50, no. 1 (2015):58–77.

Bokovoy, Melissa K. "Collectivization in Yugoslavia: Rethinking Regional and National Interests." In *The Collectivization of Agriculture in Eastern Europe: Entanglements and Transnational Comparisons*, edited by Arnd Bauerkämper and Constantin Iordachi, 293–328. Budapest: Central European University Press, 2014.

———. *Peasants and Communists: Politics and Ideology in the Yugoslav Countryside, 1941–1953*. Pittsburgh, PA: University of Pittsburgh Press, 1998.

Borbándi, Gyula. *Der ungarische Populismus*. Mainz: Hase und Koehler, 1976.

Borras, Saturnino M., Jr. "La Vía Campesina and Its Global Campaign for Agrarian Reform." In *Transnational Agrarian Movements Confronting Globalization*, edited by Borras, Marc Edelman, and Cristobál Kay, 91–121. Malden, MA: Wiley-Blackwell, 2008.

Boswell, Laird. *Rural Communism in France, 1920–1939*. Ithaca, NY: Cornell University Press, 1998.

Bracewell, Wendy. "'The Proud Name of Hajduks': Bandits as Ambiguous Heroes in Balkan Politics and Culture." Chapter 2 in *Yugoslavia and Its Historians: Understanding the Balkan Wars of the 1990s*, edited by Norman Naimark and Holly Case. Stanford, CA: Stanford University Press, 2003.

Brassart, Laurent, Corinne Marache, Juan Pan-Montojo, and Leen van Molle, eds. *Making Politics in the European Countryside, 1780s–1930s*. Turnhout, Belgium: Brepols, 2022.

Brett, Daniel. "Indifferent but Mobilized: Rural Politics during the Interwar Period in Eastern and Western Europe." *Central Europe* 16, no. 2 (2018):65–80.

Brovkin, Vladimir N. "On the Internal Front: The Bolsheviks and the Greens." *Jahbücher für Geschichte Osteuropas* 37, no. 5 (1989):541–68.

Brubaker, Rogers. *Nationalism Reframed: Nationhood and the National Question in the New* Europe. Cambridge: Cambridge University Press, 1996.

Bruckmüller, Ernst. "Der Bauernstand: Organisationsbildung und Standeskonsolidierung." In *Die Habsburgermonarchie 1848–1918*, vol. 9, *Soziale Strukturen: Von der feudal-agrarischen zur bürgerlich-industriellen Gesellschaft*, pt. 2, *Von der Stände- zur Klassengesellschaft*, edited by Ulrike Harmat, 783–811. Vienna: Verlag der Österreichischen Akademie der Wissenschaften, 2010.

———. "Landwirtschaftliche Arbeitswelten und ländliche Sozialstrukturen." In *Die Habsburgermonarchie 1848–1918*, vol. 9, *Soziale Strukturen: Von der feudal-agrarischen zur bürgerlich-industriellen Gesellschaft*, pt. 1, *Lebens- und Arbeitswelten in der industriellen Revolution*, edited by Ulrike Harmat, 251–322. Vienna: Verlag der Österreichischen Akademie der Wissenschaften, 2010.

———. *Landwirtschaftliche Organisationen und gesellschaftliche Modernisierung: Vereine, Genossenschaften und politische Mobilisierung der Landwirtschaft Österreichs vom Vormärz bis 1914*. Salzburg, Austria: Neugebauer, 1977.

Brzostek, Błażej. "The Ruralization of Bucharest and Warsaw in the First Post-War Decade." In *Mastery and Lost Illusions: Space and Time in the Modernization of Eastern and Central Europe*, edited by Włodzimierz Borodziej, Stanislav Holubec, and Joachim von Puttkamer, 99–120. Berlin: De Gruyter Oldenbourg, 2014.

Buchen, Tim. *Antisemitism in Galicia: Agitation, Politics, and Violence against Jews in the Late Habsburg Monarchy*. New York: Berghahn, 2020.

Bugge, Peter. "The making of a Slovak City: the Czechoslovak Renaming of Pressburg/Pozsony/Presporok, 1918–19." *Austrian History Yearbook* 35 (2004):205–27.

Burke, Peter. *Popular Culture in Early Modern Europe*. Aldershot, UK: Ashgate, 1994.

Cabo, Miguel."Agrarian Parties in Europe prior to 1945 and Beyond." In *Making Politics in the European Countryside, 1780s–1930s*, edited by Laurent Brassart, Corinne Marache, Juan Pan-Montojo, and Leen van Molle, 313–31. Turnhout, Belgium: Brepols, 2022.

———. "Farming the Nation: Agrarian Parties and the National Question in Interwar Europe." *Studies on National Movements* 8, no. 1 (2021). https://doi.org/10.21825/snm.85272.

Campbell, Fergus. *Land and Revolution: Nationalist Politics in the West of Ireland, 1891–1921*. Oxford: Oxford University Press, 2005.

Centrih, Lev. "'Govorile so celo strojnice!' Boljševizem v prevratni dobi na Slovenskem: Med preprostim ljudskim uporništvom in vplivi ruske revolucije." In *Slovenski prelom 1918*, edited by Aleš Grabič, 311–27. Ljubljana: Slovenska matica, 2019.

Chakrabarty, Dipesh. *Provincializing Europe: Postcolonial Thought and Historical Difference*. Princeton, NJ: Princeton University Press, 2000.

Charczuk, Wiesław. "Udział wsi i chłopów w podziemniu niepodległościowym po 1945 r." In *"Żywią i bronią": Wieś i chłopi w obronie ojczyzny*, edited by Janusz Gmitruk and Piotr Matusak, 251–64. Warsaw: Muzeum Historii Polskiego Ruchu Ludowego, 2009.

Chitnis, Rajendra. "Zbraně slabých? Představa rolnického odporu v díle a životě Václava Prokůpka." *Česká literatura* 61, no. 5 (2013):661–96.

Chopard, Thomas. "L'ere des atamans: Politique, guerre civile et insurrections paysannes en Ukraine (1917–1923)." *20 & 21. Revue d'histoire* 141, no. 1 (2019):55–68.

Cieplak, Tadeusz N. "Private Farming and the Status of the Polish Peasantry since World War II." In *The Peasantry of Eastern Europe*, vol. 2, *20th Century Developments*, edited by Ivan Volgyes, 25–38. New York: Pergamon, 1979.

Cimek, Henryk. *Tomasz Dąbal, 1890–1937*. Rzeszów, Poland: Wyższa Szkola Pedagogiczna, 1993.

Clark, Christopher. *The Sleepwalkers: How Europe Went to War in 1914*. London: Penguin, 2012.

Clark, Roland. *Holy Legionary Youth: Fascist Activism in Interwar Romania*. Ithaca, NY: Cornell University Press, 2015.

Clavin, Patricia. *The Great Depression in Europe, 1929–1939*. Basingstoke, UK: Macmillan, 2000.

Cole, Laurence. *Military Culture and Popular Patriotism in Late Imperial Austria*. Oxford: Oxford University Press, 2014.

Connelly, John. *From Peoples into Nations: A History of Eastern Europe*. Princeton, NJ: Princeton University Press, 2020.

Corner, Paul. *Fascism in Ferrara, 1915–1925*. Oxford: Oxford University Press, 1975.

Cornwall, Mark. "'National Reparation'?: The Czech Land Reform and the Sudeten Germans 1918–38." *Slavonic and East European Review* 75, no. 2 (1997):259–80.

Ćosić Bukvin, Ivan. *Vrbanjci u "Velikom ratu."* Vrbanja, Croatia: self-published, 2014.

Crampton, R. J. *Aleksandur Stamboliiski*. London: Haus, 2009.

———. "The Balkans." In *Twisted Paths: Europe 1914–1945*, edited by Robert Gerwarth, 237–70. Oxford: Oxford University Press, 2007.

Čulinović, Ferdo. *Odjeci Oktobra u jugoslavenskim krajevima*. Zagreb: Izdavačko poduzeće 27. Srpanj, 1957.

Davis, Natalie Zemon. "The Rites of Violence: Religious Riot in Sixteenth-Century France." *Past & Present* 59 (1973):51–91.

Deak, John. *Forging a Multinational State: State Making in Imperial Austria from the Enlightenment to the First World War*. Stanford, CA: Stanford University Press, 2015.

Deak, John, and Jonathan E. Gumz. "How to Break a State: The Habsburg Monarchy's Internal War, 1914–1918." *American Historical Review* 122, no. 4 (2017):1105–36.

Đerek, Domagoj. "Dezerterstvo i zeleni kadar u Hrvatskoj poslije Prvoga svjetskog rata i nemira krajem 1918. Godine." In *1918.–2018. Povijesni prijepori i Hrvatska danas: Zbornik radova sa znanstvenoga skupa*, edited by Vlatka Vukelić, Mijo Beljo, and Vlatko Smiljanić, 191–222. Zagreb: Fakultet hrvatskih studija Sveučilišta u Zagrebu, 2020.

Dickinson, Edward Ross. *The World in the Long Twentieth Century: An Interpretive History*. Oakland: University of California Press, 2018.

Dobos, Manuela. "The Nagodba and the Peasantry in Croatia-Slavonia." In *The Peasantry of Eastern Europe*, vol. 1, *Roots of Rural Transformation*, edited by Ivan Volgyes, 79–107. New York: Pergamon, 1979.

Dobrivojević, Ivana. "Changing the Cityscapes: The Ruralization of Yugoslav Towns in Early Socialism." In *Mastery and Lost Illusions: Space and Time in the Modernization of Eastern and Central Europe*, edited by Włodzimierz Borodziej, Stanislav Holubec, and Joachim von Puttkamer, 139–58. Berlin: De Gruyter Oldenbourg, 2014.

Dobrowolski, Kazimierz. *Studia nad życiem społecznym i kulturą*. Wrocław, Poland: Zakład Narodowy imienia Ossolińskich, 1966.

Dooley, Terrence. *Burning the Big House: The Story of the Irish Country House in a Time of War and* Revolution. New Haven, CT: Yale University Press, 2022.

———. "Land and the People." In *The Oxford Handbook of Modern Irish History*, edited by Alvin Jackson, 107–25. Oxford: Oxford University Press, 2013.

Drobesch, Werner. "Vereine und Interessenverbände auf überregionalen (cisleithanischer) Ebene." In *Die Habsburgermonarchie 1848–1918*, vol. 8, *Politische Öffentlichkeit und Zivilgesellschaft*, pt. 1, *Vereine, Parteien, und Interessenverbände als Träger der politischen Partizipation*, edited by Helmut Rumpler and Peter Urbanitsch, 1029–132. Vienna: Verlag der Österreichischen Akademie der Wissenschaften, 2006.

Eidelberg, Philip Gabriel. *The Great Rumanian Peasant Revolt of 1907: Origins of a Modern Jacquerie*. Leiden: Brill, 1974.

Eley, Geoff. *Forging Democracy: The History of the Left in Europe, 1850–2000*. New York: Oxford University Press, 2002.

Eley, Geoff, and Keith Nield. *The Future of Class in History: What's Left of the Social?* Ann Arbor: University of Michigan Press, 2007.

Enstad, Johannes Due. *Soviet Russians under Nazi Occupation: Fragile Loyalties in World War II*. Cambridge: Cambridge University Press, 2018.

Entner, Brigitte. "Zwischen Erinnern und Vergessen: Ein Dorf und seine widerständige Vergangenheit." *Treatises and Documents, Journal of Ethnic Studies / Razprave in Gradivo, Revija za Narodnostna Vprašanja* 70 (2013):31–43.

Ermacora, Matteo. "Rural Society." *1914–1918 Online: International Encyclopedia of the First World War*, version 1.0, last updated January 6, 2015. https://encyclopedia.1914-1918-online.net/article/rural_society.

Evans, Richard J. *The Coming of the Third Reich*. New York: Penguin, 2004.

Fanon, Frantz. *The Wretched of the Earth*. Translated by Constance Farrington. New York: Grove, 1963.

Fedinec, Csilla, and Imre Szakál. "A Hucul Köztársaság: Történelem és emlékezet." In *Kérészállamok: Átmeneti államalakulatok a történelmi Magyarország területén (1918–1921)*, edited by Veronika Szeghy-Gayer and Csaba Zahorán, 201–24. Budapest: Ludovika Egyetemi Kiadó, 2022.

Feletar, Dragutin. *Dva seljačka bunta (Kunavečka buna 1903. i krvavu međimurski studeni 1918. godine)*. Čakovec, Yugoslavia: Zrinski, 1973.

Figes, Orlando. *Peasant Russia, Civil War: The Volga Countryside in Revolution (1917–1921)*. Oxford: Clarendon, 1989.

Fink, Carole. *Defending the Rights of Others: The Great Powers, the Jews, and International Minority Protection, 1878–1938*. Cambridge: Cambridge University Press, 2004.

Fischer-Galati, Stephen. "Jew and Peasant in Interwar Romania." *Nationalities Papers* 16, no. 2 (1988):201–8.

———. "Peasantism in Interwar Eastern Europe." *Balkan Studies* 8, no. 1 (1967):103–14.

Forlenza, Rosario. "Europe's Forgotten Unfinished Revolution: Peasant Power, Social Mobilization, and Communism in the Southern Italian Countryside." *American Historical Review* 126, no. 2 (2021):504–29.

Frevert, Ute. *A Nation in Barracks: Modern Germany, Military Conscription and Civil Society*. Translated by Andrew Boreham and Daniel Brückenhaus. Oxford: Berg, 2004.

Galaj, Dyzma. "The Polish Peasant in Politics: 1895–1969." In *Rural Protest: Peasant Movements and Social Change*, edited by Henry A. Landsberger, 316–47. Basingstoke, UK: Macmillan, 1974.

Gatrell, Peter. *Russia's First World War: A Social and Economic History*. Harlow, UK: Longman, 2005.

Geertz, Clifford. "Deep Play: Notes on the Balinese Cockfight." *Daedalus* 134, no. 4 (2005):56–86.

Geiger, Vladimir. "Skica za povijest Đakova i Đakovštine u vrijeme Države Slovenaca, Hrvata i Srba 29. listopada–1. prosinca 1918." *Zbornik muzeja Đakovštine* 11, no. 1 (2013):7–84.

Gellner, Ernest, and Ghiţa Ionescu. Introduction to *Populism: Its Meanings and National Characteristics*, edited by Ionescu and Gellner. London: Weidenfeld and Nicolson, 1969.

George, Lucian. "A Comparative Study of Two Peasant Revolts in 1930s Poland." Master's thesis, Central European University, 2016.

Gerwarth, Robert. *The Vanquished: Why the First World War Failed to End, 1917–1923*. London: Allen Lane, 2016.

Gestrin, Ferdo. *Svet pod Krimom*. Ljubljana: Založba ZRC, 2016.

Gilley, Christopher. "The Ukrainian Anti-Bolshevik Risings of Spring and Summer 1919: Intellectual History in a Space of Violence." *Revolutionary Russia* 27, no. 2 (2014):109–31.

Glont, Anca. "The Revolution of the Black Diamond Republic: Negotiating Socialism and Autonomy in the Jiu Valley, 1918–1919." *Nationalities Papers* (2023):1–18.

Gmitruk, Janusz. "Bataliony Chłopskie: Armie chłopska Państwa Podziemnego." In *"Żywią i bronią": Wieś i chłopi w obronie ojczyzny*, edited by Gmitruk and Piotr Matusak, 173–86. Warsaw: Muzeum Historii Polskiego Ruchu Ludowego, 2009.

———. "Bilans działalności Polskiego Stronnictwo Ludowego 1989–2009." In *Partie chłopskie i ludowe w Polsce oraz Europie Środkowo-Wschodniej (1989–2009)*, edited by Gmitruk, Arkadiusz Indraszczyk, and Stanisław Stępka, 213–34. Warsaw: Muzeum Historii Polskiego Ruchu Ludowego, 2010.

———. "Geneza Wielkiego Strajku Chłopskiego w sierpniu 1937 roku." In *Wielki Strajk Chłopski w 1937 roku: Uwarunkowania i konsekwencje*, edited by Wacław Wierzbieniec, 29–55. Rzeszów, Poland: Wydawnictwo Uniwersytetu Rzeszowskiego, 2008.

Gmitruk, Janusz, and Dorota Pasiak-Wąsik, eds. *Bądźcie solidarni! Wielki Strajk Chłopski 1937 r.* Warsaw: Muzeum Historii Polskiego Ruchu Ludowego, 2007.

Godeša, Bojan. "Kmečki punti in partizansko gibanje." In *Leukhup! Kmečko uporništvo v obdobju predmoderne zgodovine, vzporednice, (re)prezentacije*, edited by Sašo Jerše, 208–22. Ljubljana: Slovenska matica, 2017.

Gollwitzer, Heinz. "Europäische Bauerndemokratie im 20. Jahrhundert." In *Europäische Bauernparteien im 20. Jahrhundert*, edited by Gollwitzer, 1–80. Berlin: De Gruyter, 1977.

———, ed. *Europäische Bauernparteien im 20. Jahrhundert*. Berlin: De Gruyter, 1977.

Göncz, László. "'Kalandor Vállalkozás' a Mura Mentén." In *Kérészállamok: Átmeneti államalakulatok a történelmi Magyarország területén (1918–1921)*, edited by Veronika Szeghy-Gayer and Csaba Zahorán, 309–38. Budapest: Ludovika Egyetemi Kiadó, 2022.

Graziosi, Andrea. *The Great Soviet Peasant War: Bolsheviks and Peasants, 1917–1933*. Cambridge, MA: Harvard University Press, 1996.

Griffith, Wil. "Saving the Soul of the Nation: Essentialist Nationalism and Interwar Rural Wales." *Rural History* 21, no. 2 (2010):177–94.

Gross, Jan T. *Neighbors: The Destruction of the Jewish Community in Jedwabne, Poland*. Princeton, NJ: Princeton University Press, 2001.

Guha, Ranajit. *Elementary Aspects of Peasant Insurgency in Colonial India*. Durham, NC: Duke University Press, 1999.

Guilluy, Christophe. *Twilight of the Elites: Prosperity, the Periphery, and the Future of France.* Translated by Malcolm DeBevoise. New Haven, CT: Yale University Press, 2019.

Hagen, William W. *Anti-Jewish Violence in Poland, 1914–1920*. Cambridge: Cambridge University Press, 2018.

———. "The Moral Economy of Ethnic Violence: The Pogrom in Lwów, November 1918." *Geschichte und Gesellschaft* 31, no. 2 (2005):203–26.

Hajdu, Tibor. "Socialist Revolution in Central Europe, 1917–21." In *Revolution in History*, edited by Roy Porter and Mikuláš Teich, 101–20. Cambridge: Cambridge University Press, 1986.

Hammen, Oscar. "Marx and the Agrarian Question." *American Historical Review* 77, no. 3 (1972):679–704.

Hanák, Péter. "Die Volksmeinung des letzten Kriegsjahres in Österreich-Ungarn." In *Die Auflösung des Habsburgerreichs*, edited by Richard Georg Plaschka and Karlheinz Mack, 58–66. Vienna: Verlag für Geschichte und Politik, 1970.

Hanebrink, Paul. *A Specter Haunting Europe: The Myth of Judeo-Bolshevism*. Cambridge, MA: Harvard University Press, 2018.

Harre, Angela. "Demokratische Alternativen und autoritäre Verführungen: Der ostmitteleuropäische Agrarismus im Wechselspiel zwischen Ideologie und Politik." In *Bauerngesellschaften auf dem Weg in die Moderne: Agrarismus in Ostmitteleuropa 1880 bis 1960*, edited by Helga Schulz and Harre, 25–40. Wiesbaden, Germany: Harrassowitz Verlag, 2010.

Haynes, Rebecca A. "Reluctant Allies? Iuliu Maniu and Corneliu Zelea Codreanu against King Carol II of Romania." *Slavonic and East European Review* 85, no. 1 (2007):105–34.

Heiss, Hans. "Andere Fronten: Volksstimmung und Volkserfahrung in Tirol während des Ersten Weltkrieges." In *Tirol und der Erster Weltkrieg*, edited by Klaus Eisterer and Rolf Steininger, 139–77. Innsbruck, Austria: StudienVerlag, 2011.

Heka, Ladislav. "Posljedice Prvoga svjetskog rata: Samoproglašene 'države' na području Ugarske." *Godišnjak za znanstvena istraživanja* 6 (2014):113–70.

Henschel, Christhardt. "Front-Line Soldiers into Farmers: Military Colonization in Poland after the First and Second World Wars." In *Property in East Central Europe: Notions, Institutions and Practices of Landownership in the Twentieth Century*, edited by Hannes Siegrist and Dietmar Müller, 144–62. New York: Berghahn, 2015.

Heumos, Peter. "'Kartoffeln her oder es gibt eine Revolution': Hungerkrawalle, Streiks und Massenproteste in den böhmischen Ländern 1914–1918." In *Der Erste Weltkrieg und die Beziehungen zwischen Tschechen, Slowaken und Deutschen*, edited by Hans Mommsen, Dušan Kováč, Jiří Malíř, and Michaela Marek, 255–86. Essen, Germany: Klartext, 2001.

Himka, John-Paul. *Socialism in Galicia: The Emergence of Polish Social Democracy and Ukrainian Radicalism (1860–1890)*. Cambridge, MA: Harvard Ukrainian Research Institute, 1983.

Hitchins, Keith. "Hungary." In *The Formation of Labour Movements, 1870–1914: An International Perspective*. Vol. 1. Edited by Marcel van der Linden and Jürgen Rojahn, 347–66. Leiden: Brill, 1990.

———. *Rumania, 1866–1947*. Oxford: Clarendon, 1994.

Hoare, Marko Attila. *The Bosnian Muslims in the Second World War: A History*. London: Hurst, 2013.

———. "Yugoslavia and Its Successor States." In *The Oxford Handbook of Fascism*, edited by J. B. Bosworth, 414–33. Oxford: Oxford University Press, 2010.

Hobsbawm, Eric J. *The Age of Extremes: A History of the World, 1914–1991*. New York: Vintage, 1994.

———. *Bandits*. 4th revi. ed. London: Weidenfeld and Nicolson, 2000.

———. "Peasants and Politics." *Journal of Peasant Studies* 1, no. 1 (1973):3–22.

———. *Primitive Rebels: Studies in Archaic Forms of Social Movement in the 19th and 20th Centuries*. New York: Norton, 1959.

Holquist, Peter. "Violent Russia, Deadly Marxism? Russia in the Epoch of Violence, 1905–21." *Kritika: Explorations in Russian and Eurasian History* 4, no. 3 (2003):627–52.

Horváth, Sándor. "Ruralization, Urban Villagers and Perceptions of Migration in Hungary during 'De-Stalinization' (Budapest, Sztálinváros)." In *Mastery and Lost Illusions: Space and Time in the Modernization of Eastern and Central Europe*, edited by Włodzimierz Borodziej, Stanislav Holubec, and Joachim von Puttkamer, 159–81. Berlin: De Gruyter Oldenbourg, 2014.

Houlihan, Patrick. *Catholicism and the Great War: Religion and Everyday Life in Germany and Austria-Hungary, 1914–1922*. Cambridge: Cambridge University Press, 2015.

Hrabak, Bogumil. *Dezerterstvo, zeleni kadar i prevratna anarhija u jugoslavenskim zemljama 1914–1918*. Novi Sad, Yugoslavia: Filozofski fakultet u Novom Sadu, 1990.

Hronský, Marián. *Slovensko na rázcestí: Slovenské národné rady a gardy v roku 1918*. Košice, Czechoslovakia: Východoslovenské vydavateľstvo, 1976.

———. *The struggle for Slovakia and the Treaty of Trianon*. Translated by Martin Styan. Bratislava: Veda, 2001.

Indraszczyk, Arkadiusz. "Partie chłopskie w wybranych państwach Europy Środkowej i Wschodniej (Chorwacja, Czechy, Łotwa, Rumunia, Słowacja, Węgry)." In *Partie chłopskie i ludowe w Polsce oraz Europie Środkowo-Wschodniej (1989–2009)*, edited by Janusz Gmitruk, Indraszczyk, and Stanisław Stępka, 265–97. Warsaw: Muzeum Historii Polskiego Ruchu Ludowego, 2010.

———. *Zielona Międzynarodówka: Współpraca partii chłopskich z państw Europy Środkowej i Wschodniej*. Warsaw: Muzeum Historii Polskiego Ruchu Ludowego, 2008.

Ionescu, Ghiţa. "Eastern Europe." In *Populism: Its Meanings and National Characteristics*, edited by Ionescu and Ernest Gellner, 97–121. London: Weidenfeld and Nicolson, 1969.

Jackson, George G. *Comintern and Peasant in East Europe, 1919–1930*. New York: Columbia University Press, 1966.

———. "Peasant Political Movements in Eastern Europe." In *Rural Protest: Peasant Movements and Social Change*, edited by Henry A. Landsberger. Basingstoke, UK: Macmillan, 1974.

Jahić, Adnan. *Muslimanske formacije tuzlanskog kraja u drugom svjetskom ratu*. Tuzla, Bosnia and Herzegovina: Zmaj od Bosne, Preporod, 1995.

Jakovčev, Gojko. "Zeleni kadar Betine 1918. Godine." *Zadarska revija* 38, nos. 1–2 (1989):137–47.

Janos, Andrew C. "The Agrarian Opposition at the National Congress of Councils." In *Revolution in Perspective: Essays on the Hungarian Soviet Republic*, edited by Janos and William B. Slottman, 85–108. Berkeley: University of California Press, 1971.

Jarosz, Dariusz. "The Collectivization of Agriculture in Poland: Causes of Defeat." In *The Collectivization of Agriculture in Eastern Europe: Comparisons and Entanglements*, edited by Arnd Bauerkämper and Constantin Iordachi, 113–46. Budapest: Central European University Press, 2014.

Jelić, Ivan. *Hrvatska u ratu i revoluciji*. Zagreb: Školska knjiga, 1978.

Jeřábek, Rudolf. "The Eastern Front." In *The Last Years of Austria-Hungary: A Multi-national Experiment in Early Twentieth-Century Europe*, edited by Mark Cornwall, 149–65. Rev. ed. Exeter: University of Exeter Press, 2002.

Jessenne, Jean-Pierre. "Consensus or Conflict? Politics in Towns and Villages between the Seine and the North Sea, c. 1780–1830." In *Making Politics in the European Countryside, 1780s–1930s*, edited by Laurent Brassart, Corinne Marache, Juan Pan-Montojo, and Leen van Molle, 33–57. Turnhout, Belgium: Brepols, 2022.

Jones, Peter M. *The Peasantry in the French Revolution*. Cambridge: Cambridge University Press, 1988.

Jones, Stephen F. "Marxism and Peasant Revolt in the Russian Empire: The Case of the Gurian Republic." *Slavonic and East European Review* 67, no. 3 (1989):404–34.

Joyce, Patrick, ed. *Class*. Oxford: Oxford University Press, 1995.

Judson, Pieter. *Guardians of the Nation: Activists on the Language Frontiers of Imperial Austria*. Cambridge, MA: Harvard University Press, 2006.

Kaneff, Deema. "Work, Identity and Rural-Urban Relations." In *Post-Socialist Peasant? Rural and Urban Constructions of Identity in Eastern Europe, East Asia and the Former Soviet Union*, edited by Pamela Leonard and Deema Kaneff, 180–99. Basingstoke: Macmillan, 2002.

Karaula, Željko. *Mačekova vojska: Hrvatska seljačka zaštita v kraljevini Jugoslaviji*. Zagreb: Despot Infinitus, 2015.

Keep, John L. H. *The Russian Revolution: A Study in Mass Mobilization*. New York: W.W. Norton, 1976.

Keith, Jeanette. *Rich Man's War, Poor Man's Fight: Race, Class, and Power in the Rural South during the First World War*. Chapel Hill: University of North Carolina Press, 2004.

Kiraly, Bela. "Peasant Movements in the Twentieth Century." In *The Modernization of Agriculture: Rural Transformation in Hungary, 1848–1975*, edited by Joseph Held, 319–50. Boulder, CO: East European Monographs, 1980.

Kochanowicz, Jacek. "The Changing Landscape of Property: Landownership and Modernization in Poland in the Nineteenth and Twentieth Centuries." In *Property in East Central Europe: Notions, Institutions and Practices of Landownership in the Twentieth Century*, edited by Hannes Siegrist and Dietmar Müller, 29–47. New York: Berghahn, 2015.

Kocourek, Katya. "'In the Spirit of Brotherhood United We Remain!': Czechoslovak Legionaries and the Militarist State." In *Sacrifice and Rebirth: The Legacy of the Last Habsburg War*, edited by Mark Cornwall and John Paul Newman, 151–73. New York: Berghahn, 2016.

Korneć, Grażyna. "Udział Ludowego Związku Kobiet w walce o niepodległość 1942–1945." In *"Żywią i bronią": Wieś i chłopi w obronie ojczyzny*, edited by Janusz Gmitruk and Piotr Matusak, 187–94. Warsaw: Muzeum Historii Polskiego Ruchu Ludowego, 2009.

Košmrlj, Drago. "Društva kmetskih fantov in deklet: Nosilci naprednega mladinskega kmečkega gibanja." In *Pot kmečkega ljudstva v OF*, edited by Košmrlj and Janko Liška, 58–163. Ljubljana: Kmečki glas, 1986.

Koukal, Pavel. "Spisovatel a novinář Michal Mareš." In *Ze vzpomínek anarchisty, reportéra a válečného zločince*, by Michal Mareš, 9–23. Prague: Prostor, 1999.

Kovačević, Dražen. "Nemiri u Moslavini nakon osnivanja Države Slovenaca, Hrvata i Srba." *Zbornik Moslavine* 5–6, (2003):76–119.

Kranjc, Gregor. *To Walk with the Devil: Slovene Collaboration and Axis Occupation, 1941–1945*. Toronto: University of Toronto Press.

Kregar, Tone. *Med Tatrami in Triglavom: Primerjave narodnega razvoja Slovencev in Slovakov in njihovi kulturno-politični stiki 1848–1938*. Celje, Slovenia: Zgodovinsko društvo Celje, 2007.

Kržišnik-Bukić, Vera. *Cazinska buna 1950*. Sarajevo: Svjetlost, 1991.

———. *1950 Peasants' Revolt*. Translated by John Farebrother. N.p.: self-published, 2017.

Kubů, Eduard, and Jiří Šouša. "Sen o slovanské agrární spolupráci (Antonín Švehla—ideový a organizační tvůrce Mezinárodního agrárního bureau)." In *Agrární strany ve vládních a samospravních strukturách mezi světovými válkami*, edited by Blanka Rašticová, 35–41. Uherské Hradiště, Czech Republic: Slovácké muzeum, 2008.

———. "Z časů, kdy nebylo co jíst . . . : Český sedlák/rolník za Velké války." In *Venkov, rolník a válka v českých zemích a na Slovensku v moderné době*, edited by Jitka Balcarová, Kubů, and Šouša, 51–70. Prague: Národní zemědělské muzeum, 2017.

Kučera, Rudolf. "Exploiting Victory, Sinking into Defeat: Uniformed Violence in the Creation of the New Order in Czechoslovakia and Austria, 1918–1922." *Journal of Modern History* 88, no. 4 (2016):841–51.

———. *Rational Life: Science, Everyday Life, and Working-Class Politics in the Bohemian Lands, 1914–1918*. Translated by Caroline Kovtun. Oxford: Berghahn, 2019.

Kušan, Ivan. *Čaruga pamti: Dnevnik harambaše*. Zagreb: Mladinska knjiga, 1991.

Landis, Erik C. *Bandits and Partisans: The Antonov Movement in the Russian Civil War*. Pittsburg, PA: University of Pittsburg Press, 2008.

———. "Waiting for Makhno: Legitimacy and Context in a Russian Peasant War." *Past & Present* 183 (2004):199–236.

———. "Who Were the 'Greens'? Rumor and Collective Identity in the Russian Civil War." *Russian Review* 69, no. 1 (2010):30–46.

Leblang, Stanislawa. "Polnische Bauernparteien." In *Europäische Bauernparteien im 20. Jahrhundert*, edited by Heinz Gollwitzer, 271–322. Berlin: De Gruyter, 1977.

Lebow, Katherine. "Autobiography as Complaint: Polish Social Memoir between the World Wars." *Laboratorium: Russian Review of Social Research* 6, no. 3 (2014):13–26.

Lefebvre, George. *The Great Fear: Rural Panic in Revolutionary France*. Translated by Joan White. Princeton, NJ: Princeton University Press, 1973.

Leidinger, Hannes, and Verena Moritz. *Gefangenschaft—Revolution—Heimkehr: Die Bedeutung der Kriegsgefangenenproblematik für die Geschichte des Kommunismus in Mittel- und Osteuropa 1917–1920*. Vienna: Böhlau, 2003.

Lexa, Lukáš. "Skupinové násilí v letech 1918–1920 na moravsko-slovensko-rakouském pomezí se zaměřením na pachatele a jejich motivace k násilnému jednání." PhD dissertation, Masaryk University Brno, 2023.

———. "Slovácká brigáda a její důstojnický sbor v letech 1918 až 1919." *Jižní Morava* 52, no. 55 (2016):159–94.

———. "Vojáci Slovácké brigády očima historické statistiky." Master's thesis, Masaryk University Brno, 2018.

———. "Vojenská ochrana demarkačních linií na Mikulovsku a Valticku v letech 1918–1920." In *34. Mikulovská sympozia: Formování hranice na Moravě po roce 1918*, edited by Miroslav Svoboda, 61–96. Brno, Czech Republic: Moravský zemský archiv v Brně, 2020.

Lieven, Anatol. *The Baltic Revolution: Estonia, Latvia, Lithuania and the Path to Independence*. New Haven, CT: Yale University Press, 1993.

Lorman, Thomas. *The Making of the Slovak People's Party: Religion, Nationalism and the Culture War in Early 20th-Century Europe*. London: Bloomsbury, 2019.

Lovell, Julia. *Maoism: A Global History*. London: Vintage, 2019.

Luković, Jovica. "The Country Road to Revolution: Transforming Individual Peasant Property into Socialist Property in Yugoslavia, 1945–1953." In *Property in East Central Europe: Notions, Institutions and Practices of Landownership in the Twentieth Century*, edited by Hannes Siegrist and Dietmar Müller, 163–90. New York: Berghahn, 2015.

Lynch, Edouard. "Interwar France and the Rural Exodus: The National Myth in Peril." *Rural History* 21, no. 2 (2010):165–76.

Macartney, C. A. *The Habsburg Empire, 1790–1918*. London: Weidenfeld and Nicolson, 1968.

MacMillan, Margaret. *Peacemakers: Six Months That Changed the World*. London: John Murray, 2001.

Magocsi, Robert Paul. "The Ukrainian Question between Poland and Czechoslovakia: The Lemko Rusyn Republic (1918–1920) and Political Thought in Western Rus'-Ukraine." *Nationalities Papers* 21, no. 2 (1993):95–105.

———. *With Their Backs to the Mountains: A History of Carpathian Rus' and Carpatho-Rusyns*. Budapest: Central European University Press, 2015.

Manela, Erez. *The Wilsonian Moment: Self-Determination and the International Origins of Anticolonial Nationalism*. Oxford: Oxford University Press, 2007.

Margadant, Ted. *French Peasants in Revolt: The Insurrection of 1851*. Princeton, NJ: Princeton University Press, 1980.

Marin, Irina. "Rural Social Combustibility in Eastern Europe (1880–1914): A Cross-Border Perspective." *Rural History* 28, no. 1 (2017):93–113.

Maroslavac, Stjepan. *Donji Miholjac kroz stoljeća*. Donji Miholjac, Croatia: Župa sv. Mihaela arkanđela, 2007.

Martan, Željko. "Nemiri u Hrvatskoj od proglašenja Države Slovenaca, Hrvata i Srba do Prosinačkih žrtava." *Povijest u nastavi* 14, no. 27 (2016):1–30.

Mazower, Mark. *Dark Continent: Europe's Twentieth Century*. New York: Vintage, 1998.

———. *Inside Hitler's Greece: The Experience of Occupation, 1941–44*. New Haven, CT: Yale University Press, 1993.

———. *No Enchanted Palace: The End of Empire and the Ideological Origins of the United Nations*. Princeton, NJ: Princeton University Press, 2009.

Mazur, Zachary. "Mini-states and Micro-sovereignty: Local Democracies in East Central Europe, 1918–1923." *Contemporary European History*, 2023, 1–14. https://doi.org/10.1017/S0960777323000188.

McPhee, Peter. "Popular Culture, Symbolism, and Rural Radicalism in Nineteenth-Century France." *Journal of Peasant Studies* 5, no. 2 (1978):238–53.

Mikus, Joseph A. *Slovakia and the Slovaks*. Washington, DC: Three Continents, 1977.

Mikuž, Metod. *Pregled zgodovine Narodnoosvobodilne Borbe v Sloveniji*. Vol. 2. Ljubljana: Cankarjeva založba, 1961.

Miller, Daniel E. "Colonizing the Hungarian and German Border Areas during the Czechoslovak Land Reform, 1918–1938." *Austrian History Yearbook* 34 (2003):303–17.

———. *Forging Political Compromise: Antonín Švehla and the Czechoslovak Republican Party, 1918–1933*. Pittsburgh, PA: University of Pittsburgh Press, 1999.

Minamizuka, Shingo. *A Social Bandit in Nineteenth Century Hungary: Rósza Sándor*. Boulder, CO: East European Monographs, 2008.

Mitrany, David. *Marx against the Peasant: A Study in Social Dogmatism*. New York: Collier Books, 1961.

Moeller, Robert G. *German Peasants and Agrarian Politics, 1914–1924: The Rhineland and Westphalia*. Chapel Hill: University of North Carolina Press, 1986.

Moore, Barrington, Jr. *Social Origins of Dictatorship and Democracy*. Harmondsworth, UK: Penguin, 1977.

Morelon, Claire. "Sounds of Loss: Church Bells, Place, and Time in the Habsburg Empire during the First World War." *Past & Present* 244, no. 1 (2019):195–234.

Müller, Dietmar. "Colonization Projects and Agrarian Reforms in East-Central and Southeastern Europe, 1913–1950." Chapter 3 in *Governing the Rural in Interwar Europe*, edited by Liesbeth van de Grift and Amalia Ribi Forclaz. Abingdon, UK: Routledge, 2018.

———. "Property between Delimitation and Nationalization: The Notion, Institutions and Practices of Land Proprietorship in Romania, Yugoslavia and Poland, 1918–1948." In *Property in East Central Europe: Notions, Institutions and Practices of Landownership in the Twentieth Century*, edited by Hannes Siegrist and Müller, 117–43. New York: Berghahn, 2015.

Müller, Dietmar, and Angela Harre, eds. *Transforming Rural Societies: Agrarian Property and Agrarianism in East Central Europe in the Nineteenth and Twentieth Centuries*. Innsbruck, Austria: StudienVerlag, 2011.

Murgescu, Bogdan. "Agriculture and Landownership in the Economic History of Twentieth-Century Romania." In *Property in East Central Europe: Notions, Institutions and Practices of Landownership in the Twentieth Century*, edited by Hannes Siegrist and Dietmar Müller, 48–62. New York: Berghahn, 2015.

Nagy-Talavera, Nicholas M. *The Green Shirts and Others: A History of Fascism in Hungary and Rumania*. Stanford, CA: Hoover Institution, 1970.

Narkiewicz, Olga A. *The Green Flag: Polish Populist Politics, 1867–1970*. London: Croom Helm, 1976.

Nasakanda, Pero. *Klase, slojevi i revolucija: Radnička klasa, seljaštvo i srednji slojevi u NOB-u i socijalističkoj revoluciji Hrvatske*. Zagreb: Cekade, 1985.

Neel, Phil A. *Hinterland: America's New Landscape of Class and Conflict*. London: Reaktion, 2019.

Nekuda, Vladimír. *Břeclavsko*. Brno, Czechoslovakia: Musejní spolek, 1969.

Newman, John Paul. "A Croat Iliad? Miroslav Krleža and the Refractions of Victory and Defeat in Central Europe." In *The World at War, 1911–1949: Explorations in the Cultural History of War*, edited by Catriona Pennell and Filipe Ribeiro de Meneses, 243–59. Leiden: Brill, 2019.

———. *Yugoslavia in the Shadow of War: Veterans and the Limits of State Building, 1903–1945*. Cambridge: Cambridge University Press, 2015.

Nicholson, Paul, and Saturnino M. Borras Jr. "It Wasn't an Intellectual Construction: The Founding of La Vía Campesina, Achievements and Challenges—a Conversation." *Journal of Peasant Studies* 50, no. 2 (2023):610–26.

Nowak, Włodzimierz. "Udział chłopów w wojnie polsko-sowieckiej 1920 roku." In *"Żywią i bronią": Wieś i chłopi w obronie ojczyzny*, edited by Janusz Gmitruk and Piotr Matusak, 99–115. Warsaw: Muzeum Historii Polskiego Ruchu Ludowego, 2009.

Offer, Avner. *The First World War: An Agrarian Interpretation*. Oxford: Clarendon, 1989.

Okey, Robin. *The Habsburg Monarchy*. New York: St. Martin's, 2001.

Orzoff, Andrea. *Battle for the Castle: The Myth of Czechoslovakia in Europe, 1914–1948*. Oxford: Oxford University Press, 2009.

Pál, Ladislav. "K významu činnosti 'zeleného kádra"' na západním Slovensku koncom prvej svetovej vojny." In *Západné Slovensko: Vlastivedný zborník múzeí Západoslovenského kraja*, vol. 1, 9–21. Bratislava: Obzor, 1973.

Pan-Montojo, Juan, and Niccolò Mignemi. "International Organizations and Agriculture, 1905–1945: Introduction." *Agricultural History Review* 65, no. 2 (2017):237–53.

Pasiak-Wąsik, Dorota, and Janusz Gmitruk. *Młodzi idą! Polski ruch młodowiejski*. Warsaw: Muzeum Historii Polskiego Ruchu Ludowego, 2011.

Pavlowitch, Stevan K. *Hitler's New Disorder: The Second World War in Yugoslavia*. London: Hurst, 2008.

Paxton, Robert O. *French Peasant Fascism: Henri Dorgères's Greenshirts and the Crises of French Agriculture, 1929–1939*. Oxford: Oxford University Press, 1997.

Pedersen, Susan. *The Guardians: The League of Nations and the Crisis of Empire*. Oxford: Oxford University Press, 2015.

Petrungaro, Stefano. *Kamenje i puške: Društveni protest na hrvatskom selu krajem XIX. stoljeća*. Translated by Jana Rešić. Zagreb: Srednja Europa, 2011.

Pichlík, Karel. "Vzpoury navratilců z ruského zajeti na Slovensku v květnu a červnu 1918." *Historický Časopis* 4 (1963):580–98.

Plack, Noelle. "The Peasantry, Feudalism, and the Environment, 1789–1793." In *A Companion to the French Revolution*, edited by Peter McPhee, 212–28. New York: Wiley-Blackwell, 2012.

Plaschka, Richard, Horst Haselsteiner, and Arnold Suppan. *Innere Front: Militärassistenz, Widerstand und Umsturz in der Donaumonarchie 1918*. 2 Vols. Munich: Oldenbourg, 1974.

Pleterski, Janko. *Prva odločitev Slovencev za Jugoslavijo: Politika na domačih tleh med vojno 1914–1918*. Ljubljana: Slovenska matica, 1971.

Přikryl, Josef. *První partyzánská skupina: Zelený kádr*. Kroměříž, Czechoslovakia: Okresní výbor Československého svazu protifašistických bojovníků, 1985.

Prusin, Alexander V. "A 'Zone of Violence': The Anti-Jewish Pogroms in Eastern Galicia in 1914–1915 and 1941." In *Shatterzones of Empires: Coexistence and Violence in the German,*

Habsburg, Russian, and Ottoman Borderlands, edited by Omer Bartov and Eric D. Weitz, 362–77. Bloomington: Indiana University Press, 2013.

Przeniosło, Marek. "Republika Tarnobrzeska (1918–1919): Fakty i mity." In *Polska w XIX i XX wieku: Społeczeństwo i gospodarka*, edited by Wiesław Caban, 477–84. Kielce, Poland: Wydawnictwo Uniwersytetu Jana Kochanowskiego, 2013.

Przybysz, Kazimierz. *W konspiracji: Polski ruch ludowy 1939–1945*. Warsaw: Muzeum Historii Polskiego Ruchu Ludowego, 2010.

Purivatra, Atif. *Nacionalni i politički razvitak Muslimana (Rasprave i članci)*. Sarajevo: Svjetlost, 1969.

Rachamimov, Alon. *POWs and the Great War: Captivity on the Eastern Front*. Oxford: Berg, 2002.

Rahten, Andrej. *Slovenska ljudska stranka v dunajskem parlamentu: Slovenska parlamentarna politika v habsburški monarhiji 1897–1914*. Celje, Slovenia: Panevropa, 2001.

Ramet, Sabrina P. "Vladko Maček and the Croatian Peasant Defense in the Kingdom of Yugoslavia." *Contemporary European History* 16, no. 2 (2007):215–31.

Rašeta, Boris. *Čaruga: Legenda o Robinu Hoodu*. Zagreb: 24sata, 2019.

Rauchensteiner, Manfried. *The First World War and the End of the Habsburg Monarchy, 1914–1918*. Translated by Alex J. Kay and Anna Güttel-Bellert. Vienna: Böhlau, 2014.

Rausch, Josef. *Der Partisanenkampf in Kärnten im Zweiten Weltkrieg*. Vienna: Österreichischer Bundesverlag, 1979.

Řeháček, Karel. "Život venkovského obyvatelstva v okolí Plzně v době Velké války (1914–1918)." In *Venkov, rolník a válka v českých zemích a na Slovensku v moderné době*, edited by Jitka Balcarová, Eduard Kubů, and Jiří Šouša, 71–84. Prague: Národní zemědělské muzeum, 2017.

Řepa, Milan. "Between the Nation and Self-Interest: The Czech Peasantry in Moravia at the Daybreak of Civil Society, 1848–1914." In *Making Politics in the European Countryside, 1780s–1930s*, edited by Laurent Brassart, Corinne Marache, Juan Pan-Montojo, and Leen van Molle, 223–46. Turnhout, Belgium: Brepols, 2022.

Ress, Imre. "Das Königreich Ungarn im Ersten Weltkrieg." In *Die Habsburgermonarchie 1848–1918*, vol. 11, *Die Habsburgermonarchie und der Erste Weltkrieg*, pt. 1, *Der Kampf um die Neuordnung Europas*, edited by Helmut Rumpler, 1095–164. Vienna: Verlag der Österreichischen Akademie der Wissenschaften, 2016.

Retish, Aaron B. *Russia's Peasants in Revolution and Civil War: Citizenship, Identity, and the Creation of the Soviet State, 1914–1922*. Cambridge: Cambridge University Press, 2008.

Révész, Tamás. "Soldiers in the Revolution: Violence and Consolidation in 1918 in the Territory of the Disintegrating Kingdom of Hungary." *Hungarian Historical Review* 10, no. 4 (2021):740–51.

Richter, Klaus. *Antisemitismus in Litauen: Christen, Juden und die "Emanzipation" der Bauern (1889–1914)*. Berlin: Metropole, 2013.

———. "'An Orgy of License?' Democracy and Property Redistribution in Poland and the Baltics in Their International Context, 1918–1926." *Nationalities Papers* 46, no. 5 (2017):791–808.

Ristović, Milan. "Rural 'Anti-utopia' in the Ideology of Serbian Collaborationists in the Second World War." *European Review of History* 15, no. 2 (2008):179–92.

Roediger, David R. *The Wages of Whiteness: Race and the Making of the American Working Class*. London: Verso, 1991.

Romsics, Ignác. "The Great War and the 1918–19 Revolutions as Experienced and Remembered by the Hungarian Peasantry." *Region: Regional Studies of Russia, Eastern Europe, and Central Asia* 4, no. 2 (2015):173–94.

———. "War in the Puszta: The Great War and the Hungarian Peasantry." In *The Great War and Memory in Central and South-Eastern Europe*, edited by Oto Luthar, 38–54. Leiden: Brill, 2016.

Rosset, Peter. "Re-thinking Agrarian Reform, Land and Territory in La Via Campesina." *Journal of Peasant Studies* 40, no. 4 (2013):721–75.

Rothenberg, Gunther E. *The Army of Francis Joseph*. West Lafayette, IN: Purdue University Press, 1976.

Rothschild, Joseph. *East Central Europe between the Two World Wars*. Seattle: University of Washington Press, 1974.

Rumpler, Helmut, and Anatol Schmied-Kowarzik, eds. *Die Habsburgermonarchie 1848–1918*, vol. 11, *Die Habsburgermonarchie und der Erste Weltkrieg*, pt. 2, *Weltkriegsstatistik Österreich-Ungarn 1914–1918: Bevölkerungsbewegung, Kriegstote, Kriegswirtschaft*. Vienna: Verlag der Österreichischen Akademie der Wissenschaften, 2014.

Rychlík, Jan. "Collectivization in Czechoslovakia in Comparative Perspective, 1949–1960." In *The Collectivization of Agriculture in Eastern Europe: Comparisons and Entanglements*, edited by Arnd Bauerkämper and Constantin Iordachi, 181–210. Budapest: Central European University Press, 2014.

Saje, Franček. "Revolucionarno gibanje kmečkega ljudstva v Sloveniji 1917–1919." *Prispevki za novejšo zgodovino* 7, nos. 1–2 (1967):141–50.

Sandu, Traian. "A Model of Fascism in European Agrarian Peripheries: The Romanian Case." In *Transforming Rural Societies: Agrarian Property and Agrarianism in East Central Europe in the Nineteenth and Twentieth Centuries*, edited by Dietmar Müller and Angela Harre, 204–22. Innsbruck, Austria: StudienVerlag, 2011.

Šarenac, Danilo. "Serbia's Great War Veterans as Haiduks and Rebels: 1919–1924." *Der Donauraum* 49, nos. 1–2 (2009):109–15.

Scheer, Tamara. "Die Kriegswirtschaft am Übergang von der liberal-privaten zur staatlich-regulierten Arbeitswelt." In *Die Habsburgermonarchie 1848–1918*, vol. 11, *Die Habsburgermonarchie und der Erste Weltkrieg*, pt. 1, *Der Kampf um die Neuordnung Mitteleuropas*, edited by Helmut Rumpler and Anatol Schmied-Kowarzik, 437–84. Vienna: Verlag der Österreichischen Akademie der Wissenschaften, 2014.

Schneer, Matthew. "The Markovo Republic: A Peasant Community during Russia's First Revolution, 1905–1906." *Slavic Review* 53, no. 1 (1994):104–19.

Schnell, Felix. *Räume des Schreckens: Gewalträume und Gruppenmilitanz in der Ukraine, 1905–1933*. Hamburg: Hamburger Edition, 2012.

———. "'Tear Them Apart . . . and Be Done with It!' The Ataman-Leadership of Nestor Makhno as a Culture of Violence." *Ab Imperio* 3 (2008):195–221.

Schulz, Helga, and Angela Harre, eds. *Bauerngesellschaften auf dem Weg in die Moderne: Agrarismus in Ostmitteleuropa 1880 bis 1960*. Wiesbaden, Germany: Harrassowitz Verlag, 2010.

Scoones, Ian, Marc Edelman, Saturnino M. Borras Jr., Lyda Fernanda Forero, Ruth Hall, Wendy Wolford, and Ben White, eds. *Authoritarian Populism and the Rural World*. London: Routledge, 2021.

Scott, James C. *Domination and the Arts of Resistance: Hidden Transcripts*. New Haven, CT: Yale University Press, 1990.

———. "Hegemony and the Peasantry." *Politics and Society* 7, no. 3 (1977):267–96.

Scott, James C. *The Moral Economy of the Peasant: Rebellion and Subsistence in Southeast Asia*. New Haven, CT: Yale University Press, 1976.

———. "Peasants and Commissars." *Theory and Society* 7, no. 1/2 (1979):97–134.

———. *Seeing like a State: How Certain Schemes to Improve the Human Condition Have Failed*. New Haven, CT: Yale University Press, 1998.

———. *Weapons of the Weak: Everyday Forms of Peasant Resistance*. New Haven, CT: Yale University Press, 1985.

Scott, Joan W. "Gender: A Useful Category of Analysis." *American Historical Review* 91, no. 5 (1986):1053–75.

———. "On Language, Gender, and Working-Class History." In *Gender and the Politics of History*, edited by Scott, 53–90. New York: Columbia University Press, 1988.

Šedivý, Ivan. *Češi, České Země, a Velká Válka 1914–1918*. Prague: Nakladatelství Lidové noviný, 2001.

Seton-Watson, Hugh. *Eastern Europe between the Wars, 1918–1941*. New York: Harper and Row, 1967.

Shanin, Teodor. Introduction to *Peasants and Peasant Societies*, edited by Shanin. Harmondsworth, UK: Penguin, 1971.

———, ed. *Late Marx and the Russian Road: Marx and the Peripheries of Capitalism*. London: Verso, 2018.

———. "The Peasantry as a Political Factor." In *Peasants and Peasant Societies*, edited by Shanin, 238–63. Harmondsworth: Penguin, 1971.

———. *Russia, 1905–7: Revolution as a Moment of Truth*. London: Macmillan, 1986.

Siegrist, Hannes, and Dietmar Müller. Introduction to *Property in East Central Europe: Notions, Institutions and Practices of Landownership in the Twentieth Century*, edited by Siegrist and Müller, 1–26. New York: Berghahn, 2015.

Silber, Michael. "The Making of Habsburg Jewry in the Long Eighteenth Century." In *The Cambridge History of Judaism*, vol. 7, *The Early Modern World, 1500–1815*, edited by Jonathan Karp and Adam Sutcliffe, 763–97. Cambridge: Cambridge University Press, 2017.

Simpson, James, and Juan Carmona. *Why Democracy Failed: The Agrarian Origins of the Spanish Civil War*. Cambridge: Cambridge University Press, 2020.

Skocpol, Theda. "What Makes Peasants Revolutionary?" *Comparative Politics* 14, no. 3 (1982):351–75.

Slezák, Jaroslav. "Němčičští v první světové válce." *RegioM: sborník regionálního muzea v Mikulově* (2005):119–37.

Šmidrkal, Václav. "Abolish the Army? The Ideal of Democracy and the Transformation of the Czechoslovak Military after 1918 and 1989." *European Review of History* 23, no. 4 (2016):623–42.

Smiljanić, Vlatko. *Čaruga: Životopis slavonskoga razbojnika Jovana Stanisavljevića 1897.–1925*. Zagreb: Despot Infinitus, 2020.

———. "Zločin i kazna Jovana Stanisavljevića Čaruge." *Polemos* 20, nos. 1–2 (2017):29–52.

Snyder, Timothy. "The Causes of Ukrainian-Polish Ethnic Cleansing 1943." *Past & Present* 179 (2003):197–324.

———. *The Reconstruction of Nations: Poland, Ukraine, Lithuania, Belarus, 1569–1999*. New Haven, CT: Yale University Press, 2003

Šovagović, Đuro, and Josip Cvetković. *Valpovština u revoluciji (kronika revolucionarnih zbivanja 1918–1945)*. Valpovo, Yugoslavia: Općinski komitet saveza komunista Valpovo, 1970.

Šporin Šarh, Jelka. *Kronika družine Šarh*. Ruše, Slovenia: Sophiacall, 2017.

Sršan, Stjepa. *Povijest petrijevačke župe*. Osijek, Croatia: Državni arhiv u Osijeku, 2012.

Stankiewicz, Witold. *Konflikty społeczne na wsi polskiej 1918–1920*. Warsaw: Państwowe Wydawnictwo Naukowe, 1963.

Stauter-Halsted, Keely. *The Nation in the Village: The Genesis of Peasant National Identity in Austrian Poland, 1848–1914*. Ithaca, NY: Cornell University Press, 2001.

Stojar, Richard. "Venkov: Dějiště partyzánské války." In *Venkov, rolník a válka v českých zemích a na Slovensku v moderné době*, edited by Jitka Balcarová, Eduard Kubů, and Jiří Šouša, 39–47. Prague: Národní zemědělské muzeum, 2017.

Struve, Kai. "Tremors in the Shatterzone of Empires: Eastern Galicia in Summer 1941." In *Shatterzones of Empires: Coexistence and Violence in the German, Habsburg, Russian, and Ottoman Borderlands*, edited by Omer Bartov and Eric D. Weitz, 463–84. Bloomington: Indiana University Press, 2013.

Swain, Nigel. "East European Collectivization Campaigns Compared, 1945–1962." In *The Collectivization of Agriculture in Eastern Europe: Comparisons and Entanglements*, edited by Arnd Bauerkämper and Constantin Iordachi, 497–532. Budapest: Central European University Press, 2014.

Swanson, John C. *The Remnants of the Habsburg Monarchy: The Shaping of Modern Austria and Hungary, 1918–1922*. Boulder, CO: East European Monographs, 2001.

Szabó, Miloslav. "'Rabovačky' v závere prvej svetovej vojny a ich ohlas na medzivojnovom Slovensku." *Forum Historiae* 9, no. 2 (2015):45–55.

Szlanta, Piotr. "Unter dem sinkenden Stern der Habsburger: Die Osterfahrung polnischer k. u. k. Soldaten." In *Jenseits des Schützengrabens: Der Erste Weltkrieg im Osten: Erfahrung—Wahrnehmung—Kontext*, edited by Wolfram Dornik, 139–56. Graz, Austria: Studienverlag, 2013.

Ther, Philipp. *Europe since 1989: A History*. Princeton, NJ: Princeton University Press.

Thomas, William I., and Florian Znaniecki. *The Polish Peasant in Europe and America*. Vol. I. New York: Dover, 1958.

Thompson, Edward P. "Eighteenth-Century English Society: Class Struggle without Class?" *Social History* 3, no. 2 (1978):133–65.

———. *The Making of the English Working Class*. New York: Vintage, 1966.

———. "The Moral Economy of the English Crowd in the Eighteenth Century." *Past & Present* 50 (1971):76–136.

Titl, Julij. *Murska republika 1919*. Murska Sobota, Yugoslavia: Pomurska založba, 1970.

Tolkatsch, Dimitri. "Lokale Ordnungsentwürfe am Übergang vom Russischen Reich zur Sowjetmacht: Bauernaufstände und Dorfrepubliken in der Ukraine, 1917–1921." In *Akteure der Neuordnung: Ostmitteleuropa und das Erbe der Imperien, 1917–1924*, edited by Tim Buchen and Frank Grelka, 93–111. Frankfurt Oder: epubli, 2016.

Tomasevich, Jozo. *Peasants, Politics and Economic Change in Yugoslavia*. Stanford, CA: Stanford University Press, 1955.

———. *War and Revolution in Yugoslavia, 1941–1945: Occupation and Collaboration*. Stanford, CA: Stanford University Press, 2001.

Tombs, Robert. *France 1814–1914*. London: Longman, 1996.

Tönsmeyer, Tatjana. "Farming under Occupation: Rural Actors and the Social Dynamics of Occupation during World War II." In *Living with the Land: Rural and Agricultural Actors in Twentieth-Century Europe—A Handbook*, edited by Liesbeth van de Grift, Dietmar Müller, and Corrina R. Unger, 133–54. Berlin: De Gruyter Oldenbourg, 2022.

Tooze, Adam. *The Deluge: The Great War and the Remaking of Global Order*. London: Penguin, 2015.

———. *The Wages of Destruction: The Making and Breaking of the Nazi Economy*. New York: Penguin, 2006.

———. "The War of the Villages: The Interwar Agrarian Crisis and the Second World War." In *The Cambridge History of the Second World War*, vol. 3, *Total War: Economy, Society, and Culture*, edited by Michael Geyer and Tooze, 385–411. Cambridge: Cambridge University Press, 2015.

Toshkov, Alex. *Agrarianism as Modernity in 20th-Century Europe: The Golden Age of the Peasantry*. London: Bloomsbury, 2019.

Trapl, Miloš. "Zemědělská politika Československé strany lidové." In *Agrární strany ve vládních a samospravních strukturách mezi světovými válkami*, edited by Blanka Rašticová, 93–96. Uherské Hradiště, Czech Republic: Slovácké muzeum, 2008.

Trencsényi, Balász. "Thinking Dangerously: Political Thought in Twentieth-Century East Central Europe." Chapter 2 in *The Routledge History Handbook of Central and Eastern Europe in the Twentieth Century*, vol. 3, *Intellectual Horizons*, edited by Włodzimierz Borodziej, Ferenc Laczó, and Joachim von Puttkamer. Abingdon, UK: Routledge, 2020.

Trouillot, Michel-Rolph. *Silencing the Past: Power and the Production of History*. Boston, MA: Beacon, 1995.

Tunstall, Graydon A. *The Austro-Hungarian Army and the First World War*. Cambridge: Cambridge University Press, 2021.

———. "The Military Collapse of the Central Powers." *1914–1918 Online: International Encyclopedia of the First World War*, version 1.0, last updated April 30, 2015. https://encyclopedia.1914-1918-online.net/article/the_military_collapse_of_the_central_powers.

Turk, Janez. "Gorska vas v primežu vojne: Zgodba o koroških antifašistih; Zeleni kader od Karavank." *Mladika* 58, no. 9 (2014):18–23.

Überegger, Oswald. "Auf der Flucht vor dem Krieg: Trentiner und Tiroler Deserteure im Ersten Weltkrieg." *Militärgeschichtliche Zeitschrift* 62 (2003):355–93.

Užičanin, Salkan. "Agrarni nemiri u tuzlanskom okrugu poslije Prvog svjetskog rata." *Gračanski glasnik* 31, no. 16 (2011):36–49.

Van Boeschoten, Riki. *From Armatolik to People's Rule: Investigation into the Collective Memory of Rural Greece, 1750–1949*. Amsterdam: Adolf M. Hakkert, 1991.

———. "The Peasant and the Party: Peasant Options and 'Folk' Communism in a Greek Village." *Journal of Peasant Studies* 20, no. 4 (1993):612–39.

Van de Grift, Liesbeth, and Amalia Ribi Forclaz, eds. *Governing the Rural in Interwar Europe*. Abingdon, UK: Routledge, 2018.

Vanhaute, Eric. *Peasants in World History*. New York: Routledge, 2021.

Van Meurs, Wim. "The Red Peasant International." Chapter 12 in *Governing the Rural in Interwar Europe*, edited by Liesbeth van de Grift and Amalia Ribi Forclaz. Abingdon, UK: Routledge, 2018.

Van Molle, Leen. "Political Parties in the Countryside: Introduction," In *Making Politics in the European Countryside, 1780s–1930s*, edited by Laurent Brassart, Corinne Marache, Juan Pan-Montojo, and Van Molle, 215–222. Turnhout, Belgium: Brepols, 2022.

Veidlinger, Jeffrey. *In the Midst of Civilized Europe: The Pogroms of 1918–1921 and the Onset of the Holocaust*. New York: Metropolitan Books, 2021.

Vidovič Miklavčič, Anka. *Mladina med nacionalizmom in katolicizmom: Pregled razvoja in dejavnosti mladinskih organizacij, društev in gibanj v liberalno-unitarnem in katoliškem taboru v letih 1929–1941 v jugoslovanskem delu Slovenije*. Ljubljana: Študentska organizacija Univerze, 1994.

Volgyes, Ivan. Introduction to *The Peasantry of Eastern Europe*, vol. 1, *Roots of Rural Transformation*, edited by Volgyes. New York: Pergamon, 1979.

Volner, Hrvoje. *Od industrijalaca do kažnjenika: "Gutmann" i "Našička" u industrijalizacija Slavonije*. Zagreb: Srednja Europa, 2019.

Votruba, Adam. *Pravda u zbojníka: Zbojnictví a loupežnictví ve střední Evropě*. Prague: Scriptorium, 2010.

Vykoupil, Libor. *Český fašismus na Moravě*. Brno, Czech Republic: Matice moravská, 2012.

Wade, Rex A. *The Russian Revolution, 1917*. 3rd ed. Cambridge: Cambridge University Press, 2017.

Warriner, Doreen. "Changes in European Peasant Farming." *International Labour Review* 76, no. 5 (1957):446–66.

Watson, Alexander. *Ring of Steel: Germany and Austria-Hungary at War, 1914–1918*. London: Allen Lane, 2014.

Weiss, Jane. *Viniška republika: Pregled ob 90-letnici*. Vinica, Slovenia: Krajevna skupnost, 2009.

Weitz, Eric D. "Self-Determination: How a German Enlightenment Idea Became the Slogan of National Liberation and a Human Right." *American Historical Review* 120, no. 2 (2015):462–96.

Westad, Odd Arne. *The Global Cold War: Third World Interventions and the Making of Our Times*. Cambridge: Cambridge University Press, 2007.

Wingfield, Nancy M. "National Sacrifice and Regeneration: Commemorations of the Battle of Zborov in Multinational Czechoslovakia." In *Sacrifice and Rebirth: The Legacy of the Last Habsburg War*, edited by Mark Cornwall and John Paul Newman, 129–50. New York: Berghahn, 2016.

Wolf, Eric R. "On Peasant Rebellions." Chapter 5 in *Peasants and Peasant Societies*, edited by Teodor Shanin. Harmondsworth, UK: Penguin, 1971.

———. *Peasant Wars of the Twentieth Century*. London: Faber and Faber, 1971.

Wood, Ellen Meiksins. *Democracy against Capitalism: Renewing Historical Materialism*. Cambridge: Cambridge University Press, 1995.

Zahra, Tara. *Kidnapped Souls: National Indifference and the Battle for Children in the Bohemian Lands, 1900–1948*. Ithaca, NY: Cornell University Press, 2008.

Zaremba, Marcin. *Entangled in Fear: Everyday Terror in Poland, 1944–1947*. Translated by Maya Latynski. Bloomington: Indiana University Press, 2022.

Ziemann, Benjamin. *War Experiences in Rural Germany, 1914–1923*. Translated by Alan Skinner. New York: Berg, 2007.

Žižlavský, Bořek. "Chřibský Zelený kádr." *Malovaný kraj: Národopisný a vlastivědný časopis Slovácka* 33, no. 1 (1997):7.

Zorko, Tomislav. "Narodne straže Narodnog vijeća SHS-a na prostoru Banske Hrvatske." In *1918. u hrvatskoj povijesti*, edited by Željko Holjevac, 353–76. Zagreb: Matica hrvatska, 2012.

Zückert, Martin. "National Concepts of Freedom and Government Pacification Policies: The Case of Czechoslovakia in the Transitional Period after 1918." *Contemporary European History* 17, no. 3 (2008):325–44.

———. "Vojáci republiky? K národnostní politice československé armády." In *Armáda a společnost v českých zemích v 19. a první polovině 20. Století*, edited by Jiří Rak and Martin Veselý, 160–67. Ústí nad Labem, Czech Republic: Univerzita J. E. Purkyně, 2003.

Zupan, Gregor. "Dezerterstvo na Slovenskem v 18. in 19. stoletju ter 1. in 2. Svetovni vojni." *Vojnozdovovinski zbornik* 18 (2004):18–23.

Zurl, Marino. *Knjiga o Jovi Čarugi i Joci Udmaniću*. Zagreb: August Cesarec, 1977.

INDEX

Page numbers in *italics* refer to figures and tables.

A NOTE ON THE TYPE

This book has been composed in Arno, an Old-style serif typeface in the classic Venetian tradition, designed by Robert Slimbach at Adobe.